The economic ideas of ordinary people

The economic ideas of ordinary people

From preferences to trade

David M. Levy

London and New York

First published 1992
by Routledge
1 New Fetter Lane, London EC4P 4EE

Simultaneously published in the USA and Canada
by Routledge
a division of Routledge, Chapman and Hall, Inc.
29 West 35th Street, New York, NY 10001

© 1992 David M. Levy

Typeset by Columns Design and Production Services Ltd, Reading
Printed in Great Britain by MacKays of Chatham PLC, Kent

British Library Cataloguing in Publication Data
Levy, David M. 1944–
    The economic ideas of ordinary people: from preferences
    to trade.
    1. Economics. Theories
    I. Title
    330.1
ISBN 0–415–06770–7

Library of Congress Cataloging in Publication Data
Levy, David M.
    The economic ideas of ordinary people: from preferences to trade
    David M. Levy.
        p.   cm.
    Includes bibliographical references and index.
    ISBN 0–415–06770–7
    1. Decision-making. 2. Economics. I. Title.
    HD30.23.L48 1991
    330.1 – dc20   91–6976
                                                                      CIP

A REAL CONVERSATION

Jack.   David, I read your book. Who did you write it for? Who do you think will read it?

David.   (*Pause.*) Spinoza, Adam Smith?

Jack.   They buy a lot of books, do they?

David.   (*Long pause.*)

Contents

Part VI   Objections and applications

Illustrations

FIGURES

MATRIXES

TABLE

A preface to word-taking behavior

I have been asked to explain what this book is about in a statement which can be read in ten minutes.[1] What do I think I have done? Why have I included what I have included? And what paths have I not gone down?

Human action results from a compound of animal desires, brute constraints to these desires and the words we use to talk about desires and constraints. Economists over the last century have had wonderful thoughts about desires and constraints, but of late have not worried very much about the words we use to talk about them. The book is in large part about why we talk about desires and constraints and how this talk influences our action.

Much of the argument in the book takes the form of an extended commentary on the work of the eighteenth-century Scottish economists, David Hume, Adam Smith and their associates, on the interrelation between people's judgment about economic activity and the economic activity itself. In part, this book is an attempt to remember what economists once knew but have long forgotten. In this lost time economists were also philosophers, logicians, classicists and close students of poetry. If we seek to explain the relation between language and choice, none of these subject matters can be dismissed out of hand. Or so I shall argue as I traverse all these subjects. Because so many diverse research fields are crossed, I provide a glossary immediately after these prefatory notes.

One of the particular issues which the book considers is why people trade. This is an issue which modern economists have regarded as closed for over a century. Another particular issue which the book considers is why, in fact, people contribute small amounts to finance public goods. Their contribution will not be decisive and they surely have other uses for the money. This issue is so far from closed that it is the center of considerable research.

I shall argue that these two issues are, in fact, manifestations of the same deeper problem. To see their underlying unity, all we need do is to consider the basis for an economist's belief that the problem of trade has been solved by well-ordered preferences and the potential of mutual gains from trade. But this solution is not correct. Other species, such as rats and pigeons, have well-ordered preferences, but no other species trades outside a limited familial circle. Indeed, when one experiments with other species with the requisite preferences, one finds grabbing instead of trade. I shall explore the consequences of the fact that the same prisoner's dilemma, which ought to prevent people from voluntarily contributing to finance public goods, seems to block animals from trading. Thus preferences do not suffice to explain trade.

What is missing? The tack I shall take is to suppose that trade and voluntary contributions are in fact two aspects of the same problem. Often we can solve a problem by taking what we know from one of its manifestations and generalizing. Let us consider the reaction of an ordinary person to one well-known manifestation of the prisoner's dilemma. When a public choice economist explains to her neighbor why it is not rational to vote, the neighbor's reaction is often 'But it is my duty to vote'.

The usual reaction of an economist to such a conversation is to tell one's class why it is silly to talk to the neighbors about economic theory. I wish to argue against such an attitude. To be more precise, I shall argue that prisoner's dilemma issues can be at least partially overcome by language. Language is nothing if it is not a process by which people communicate. They communicate their true desires, make up stories, cast judgments and gossip about the neighbors. And they use words such as 'duty' on interesting occasions.

Language presents an interesting problem for social analysis, which seeks to start with an isolated, atomic individual and aggregate. One isolated, atomic individual would have no use for language. Of course, a society of n individuals would find language enormously helpful. Thus, when we take into account language, society cannot be one isolated individual times n. Indeed, one might even question whether a methodological individualist approach which does consider language is possible. Recent attempts to relate morality to social activity offer the dialogue as paradigm; it takes two to have a conversation.

But I do wish to remain within the context of the individualist tradition. To this end, I shall conceive of an atomic individual floating in an exogenous sea of language. Now, at this juncture I see two complementary approaches open. The more straightforward of the two stresses the possibility of a link between language and property rights. Add property to preferences and trade results. Because technological progress is surely based in language, one can approach the creation of the requisite property rights as a problem in technology. This approach would have many appealing properties, not the least of which is being able to take advantage of much recent thinking about technology. From this point of view language is purely a means.

But this is not how I wish to direct the argument. It might seem a minor matter that the problem of small donations is no more accessible on this line of attack than it was before. But this is, I believe, illustrative of the delicate problem of appealing to property rights as an ultimate explanation. This appeal raises the obvious question: why do we obey the law and respect property? Perhaps because it has received so little attention in two hundred years, the link between language and choice I shall stress is approbation. Inside a language community words matter for those who desire approbation. If an action I perform is judged 'right' or 'excellent' by standards I accept, I feel pleasure. 'Wrong' or 'shabby' action imposes pain on me. Adherence to or violation of the standards of some other community disturbs my tranquility with neither pleasure nor pain.

An individual in a language community, no longer isolated but still self-interested, takes these standards as determined independently of his choice. My fellow economists will get the point that I am describing 'word-taking' activity.[2] Obviously, the community as a whole can revise its standards, but this raises only questions of detail, which shall surprise no one.

And how is this supposed to relate to trade and to donations? Let us look at this as a problem of cooperation. An individual sensitive to disapprobation finds that going back on one's word is costly. If I know you will punish yourself for transgression, then it is more appealing for me to trade with you than with someone who won't. It is in this context that the Scots treat approbation as a component of the social order.

Does this mean that trade without approbation is not possible? Of course not. It just means I shall have to worry more about the enforcement costs. Moreover, since the use of language is the paradigm of creativity, it should be no surprise that when approbation cannot be depended upon, substitutes can be found. This is a particularly important consideration when trade extends beyond a community with shared standards. But my effort, again, is to look at what can be gained by locating exchange within this community of standards.

BY THE NUMBERS

Why have not economists for two hundred years considered what people say about their choice to be germane? I find two reasons in Chapter 1. First, what people say is inconsistent with what we know about the solution to optimization problems; second, economists can explain mute choice without reference to what people say. I point to a mathematical context in which neither claim is quite obvious; indeed, in this context both claims are probably false.

Then we look at rats' economics in some detail. Rats have preferences but they do not trade; therefore, preferences cannot suffice to explain trade. We encounter — not for the last time — the prisoner's dilemma. We find that Adam Smith was on to something; he traced trade to language because xiv A preface to word-taking behavior

he knew that animals did not trade. We discover here an old philosophical discussion about the relation of language and property.

The prisoner's dilemma is a stubborn problem, so, in Chapter 3, we consider the role of constraints carried by language – theories of conduct which issue judgments of 'right' and 'wrong' – for a single individual. Can constraints enhance an individual's utility? Certainly. When knowledge is really imperfect and people cannot effectively maximize by groping about them, talk about 'right' and 'wrong' can provide information to assist maximizing problems. We might even call this a natural morality. The bumper-sticker version of the imperative resulting from this morality is 'No pain, no gain'. The mathematical context of this possibility is one in which an individual, following the guidance provided by local information, does not find a global maximum. Multiple-person prisoner's dilemma problems have the same mathematical property: individuals each seeking their own interest will not naturally locate the global optimum. The mathematical property of non convexity is vital because here optimum solutions need not be unique. Non uniqueness opens the possibility that one solution is better than another.

Chapter 4 considers what kind of logical status our judgments of 'right' and 'wrong' may have if they are used to guide optimizing behavior and not revised in the process. We discover they are logic-like. In the process of this argument, we discover that 'true'/'false' can be viewed as assignments of approbation upon sentences and 'right'/'wrong' can be viewed as assignments of approbation upon actions. The operation of approbation itself results from a decision within a language community. The direction of approbation is a choice; it is not dictated imperiously by laws of logic. Indeed, the choice of approbation can create laws of logic.

Chapter 5 looks back at the position advanced by Thomas Hobbes which points out how judgments about 'right' and 'wrong' can be used to confuse people for the benefit of moralists. In the formulation of utility-enhancing moral constraints I advance, this is a real possibility. Hobbes also advances the challenging thesis that words without promises of pain and pleasure have no impact on choice. I find how this position was disputed by Smith and others. In Chapter 6 Susan Feigenbaum and I work through the details of Smith's argument that competition among moralists can solve the Hobbes problem.

Chapter 7 returns to the issue of the prisoner's dilemma in the context of the Lockean and the Humean theories of property. I find a sharp statement of the Scottish position that words of judgment are a basis of respect for property.

The discussion to this point has taken it for granted that theories can be created without self-conscious theorists. Is this possible? In Chapters 8 and 9 I work out in some detail how Homer does good applied economics without knowing how to write and Aristotle understands the properties of random representation without knowing mathematical statistics. Evolution can generate the ability to solve problems without being able to prove the solution correct. Inspired by such problem-solving ability, Chapter 10 returns, once again, to the prisoner's dilemma. The theories which ordinary people advance claim that public goods can be provided in response to approbation. Don't ordinary people, even today, say we vote because of duty? When mapped to canonical form, there is something to be said for this motive.

Modern economists, with the insulation provided by our mathematical devices, are cut off from much contact with the wider intellectual realm. Such remoteness was not always so. The classical Malthusian economists set an intellectual world on fire when they defended family limitation against Christian religious morality by making their case in terms of the natural morality we have already described. They did this by showing that Christian social policy created short-run gains at the expense of long-run disaster. The Malthusians stood for hard discipline and the long run against the flabby moralism of an established church. The Malthusians were the winning competitors to Christianity until some Christian churches changed their doctrine and saved their firm. This episode, described in Chapters 11 to 13, is included to illustrate Smith's thesis that under competition religion serves the interests of the people. But to do it correctly, we have to work out the details. The details, in this case, mean Ricardian distribution theory. The Malthusian story does not end where I leave it in this book; this is, however, where it starts.

The book concludes with a series of applications and extensions. Chapter 14 considers the Platonic principle that only when words carry promises of pleasure and pain can they motivate. This is the genesis of the supposition that atheists cannot be trusted to obey the laws. Chapter 15 considers the best known attack on Smith's principle of competition in the provision of morality and culture. It is included to illustrate the common temptation to confuse our words with God's thoughts. Chapters 16 and 17 provide a single counter-example to the two versions of the thesis that economists can ignore what ordinary people say about their choices. Chapter 18 considers how professional economists moralize about choice of institutions. Such moralizing turns out to have the same structure as the natural morality we encounter in Chapter 3.

One can read this book as a Kantian manifesto:

Kant wanted to prove in a way that would dumbfound the common man that the common man was right: that was the secret joke of this soul. He wrote against the scholars in favor of the popular prejudice, but for scholars and not popularity.[3]

A glossary

A defining characteristic of the philosophical position to which I adhere is that words take their meaning from the whole of the language. This being so, I am under an obligation to explain to the reader the interconnections among some key terms in my language. This glossary is found in the traditional location of an abstract because the interconnections among the terms will suggest to the reader how my argument is to be played out. The interconnections are made explicit because a term defined in the glossary is also emphasized when it is used to define other terms. The various grammatical forms of glossary entry are not listed separately, e.g. *approbation* has an entry, *approve* does not, but I have italicized such related parts in the definitions. Similarly, what I hope to be obvious compounds of entries, e.g. *religious factions*, are not given a separate entry.

Technical terms used in various research specialities are explained to provide information for the reader in other research specialities.

abundance. When choice is without *cost.*

agenda control. The results of a sequences of votes can depend upon the combination of alternatives and the order in which they are presented to the voters. This possibility allows those who set the agenda to gain from their position. See *rent-seeking activity.*

algorithm. A routine, perhaps a mechanical, procedure for solving problems.

analytic. In philosophy of logic, a statement which will be judged '*true*' or '*false*' regardless of observation.

approbation. The usual meaning is a favorable judgment passed upon a choice ('*right*'). I shall argue for the extension of meaning as a favorable judgment passed upon a sentence/belief/proposition/communication ('*true*'). See *pragmatic.*

'ατη. *Homeric* word for 'blind folly'. See *local information* and *nonconvexity.*

austere morality. *Rules* which *disapprove* of *optimizing* choice. See *liberal morality* and *Mandeville's Paradox.*

bimodal. A concept from mathematical statistics describing the condition when there are two *modes* in a data set some distance apart. The importance for our purpose is that in this context the *median* is not *robust*; consequently, a *bimodal* distribution of *preferences* in a political context implies that the *median voter* can be moved a great distance by a small number of violent acts. See *faction*.

Chicago school of economics. Those of us who accept the *maximizing postulate* and are willing to employ *unrealistic assumptions* in the matter of *price-taking behavior*. In many ways this is a revival of the research program of the *classical economists*.

classical economists. David Hume, Adam Smith, T. R. Malthus, David Ricardo, J. S. Mill and all the good people who traveled with them.

common. The unrestricted claim on some resource. See *property*.

communism. An economic system which proposes to separate one's consumption from what one produces. The importance for us is that the *Malthusian* controversy began with Robert Malthus's attack on William Godwin's proposed *communism*.

competitive religion. Separation of church and state.

convexity. The following mathematical property possessed by a set: if *a* and *b* are inside or on the boundary of a set then for $0 < \lambda < 1$, any $c = \lambda a + (1-\lambda)b$ is inside the set. This idea can appear in the context of a *relation*. An *indifference curve I* is *convex* if a line segment connecting any two points on *I* is completely above *I*; hence, any point on the line segment is given a higher mark than a point on the curve *I* itself. An example is provided in Figure 1. Some of these possible line segments are shown in gray; indeed, the gray area is completely above *I*. The

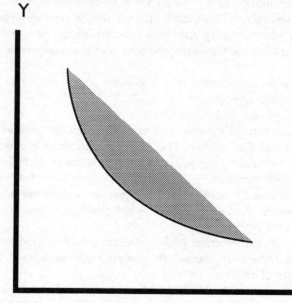

Figure 1   An example of convexity

importance of this property for us is that it allows *local information* to suffice for *optimizing* calculations. See *nonconvexity*.

cost. What one gives up to get something.

creative. A supra-*algorithmic* procedure for solving problems. See *language*.

dæmon. A being between human and God. See *Hermetism*.

disapprobation. The usual meaning is an unfavorable judgment passed upon a choice (*'wrong'*). I shall argue for the extension of its meaning as an unfavorable judgment passed upon a sentence/belief/proposition/ communication (*'false'*). See *pragmatic*.

economic theory. A description of choice in terms of goals and impediments to these goals. See *optimality* and *preferences*.

economic ideas of ordinary people. The *economic theory* in which *ordinary people* talk about their choice.

election by lot. The practice in classical antiquity of selecting political representatives by a random process. It was defended as a method for dealing with *factions*; none the less, ordinary Athenians and Socrates disagreed violently over its merits. See *economic ideas of ordinary people*.

endogenous. Influenced by one's choice.

established religion. State-owned and state-operated religious organization.

euphemistic. The school within Christianity holding that the pagan gods and goddesses are dead men and women remembered with *approbation* for providing *public goods*. Another school within Christianity holds that the pagan gods and goddesses are live *dæmons*. Great proponents of the respective positions are Lactantius and St Augustine. See *Hermetism*.

exogenous. Not influenced by one's choice; given from outside.

experimental economics. The research program which tests *economic theory* in a laboratory setting, using randomly selected human or animal subjects.

faction. The traditional term for those who vote as a group or as a party. See *bimodal*.

'false'. *Disapprobation* directed at a sentence.

fame. A dramatic type of *approbation*.

flow chart. A picture of an *algorithm*.

fuzzy. A mathematical context in which the 'equal to' *relation* is replaced with the 'similar to' *relation*. Thus, *fuzzy* mathematics is a natural setting in which to describe cases where perception is not perfect. The similarity *relation* is not *transitive*.

global. Concerning all *neighborhoods*, not just the immediate one. See *local*.

global information. Knowledge of all *neighborhoods*, not just the immediate one. See *local information*.

hard problem. A mathematical problem whose solution, at the current state of the *algorithmic* art, cannot be guaranteed even with a considerable expenditure of effort.

Hermetism. A type of *Neoplatonism* which makes the claim that the God within us can be used to control *dæmonic* forces. It is a presupposition of

S. T. Coleridge's criticism of the *classical economists*.

Hobbes's problem. How can society control the violence of *religious factions?*

Homer. The traditional name for the evolutionary process by which the *Iliad* and the *Odyssey* were created. See *economic ideas of ordinary people* and *oral poetics*.

Hume's theory of property. The thesis that, without *scarcity*, there is no reason to have *property*. See *Lockean proviso*.

indifference curve. A device employed in modern *economic theory* to specify the various combinations of commodities which satisfy equally well the desires of a consumer. Since *relations* are only '*true*' or '*false*', graphical representation of a *relation* takes the form of using a curve to split the combinations of commodities into those which are higher and those which are lower than the benchmark provided by the curve itself.

influence curve. A device employed in mathematical statistics to describe the impact of an additional observation upon an estimate. See *robust*.

infinitesimal. A mathematical concept of a number smaller in absolute value than any positive real number. See *neighborhood* and *local*.

interpretation. A *theory* of a text or texts.

isoquant. A device employed in modern *economic theory* to specify the various combinations of inputs which result in an equal amount of output. It is typically assumed to be *convex*. See *indifference curve*.

language. The *creative* form of communication.

language community. A group of people who agree upon the assignment of *approbation* and *disapprobation*. See *pragmatic*.

liberal morality. Rules which *approve* of an *optimizing* choice. See *austere morality*.

local. The immediate *neighborhood* of some point of interest. See *global*.

local information. Knowledge of the immediate *neighborhood* of some point of interest. See *global information*.

Lockean proviso. The requirement that when *common* resources become *property*, there is no reduction in the value of what remains in common. See *abundance* and *Hume's theory of property*.

Malthusianism. The doctrine that people ought not to marry until they can reasonably expect to support the resulting children. See '*vice*'.

Mandeville's Paradox. Our *optimizing* behavior does not follow our *rules*; none the less, our behavior, rather than our *rules*, bears the *disapprobation*.

maxims. The conclusions from *rules*.

maximum likelihood. An approach to mathematical statistics which employs explicit *optimization* methods.

maximizing postulate. All observed behavior is held to be the result of an *optimizing* consideration.

median. The middle observation in a data set which is sorted from lowest to highest. Thus, there are as many observations above as below the *median*.

median voter. A concept employed in the *economic theory* of the political process to describe that individual who splits the voters into two equal camps in the following sense. There are as many who want 'more' on some issue above the *median voter* as there are who want 'less' on that issue.

metatheory. An *algorithm* proposed to *approve* or *disapprove* of a theory. See *'true'* and *'false'*.

mode. The most frequently occurring observation in a data set.

Neomalthusianism. The doctrine that *Malthusianism* would be less onerous if a married couple had access to mechanical contraception to control the number of children they might reasonably expect to follow their marriage. It became an important political force in Britain following the 1877 trial of Charles Bradlaugh and Annie Besant for the crime of distributing 'obscene' birth-control material. See *'vice'*.

neighborhood. In mathematics the area within a positive *infinitesimal* of some specific point. See *local*.

Neoplatonism. The doctrine that ideas are to be discovered within the mind of God. From antiquity this doctrine has been associated with Plotinus' teaching.

nonconvexity. The failure of the *convexity* condition. An *indifference curve* is *nonconvex* if any line segment connecting two points on the *indifference curve* falls on or below the curve itself. The points on the line segment would then not be preferred to points on the *indifference curve* itself. Figure 2 gives three examples of failure of *convexity*. Curve *I* is complicated; none the less, it is not *convex* because the gray, dashed line segment indicated falls below *I*. In this context, *optimization* may be a *hard problem* because *local information* may not suffice. Hence, if *creativity* is important in human choice, here is where we should look.

optimality. The highest attainment of a goal which constraints permit. Characteristically, the solution to a technical optimization problem can be guaranteed to hold *locally* because the most powerful insight in optimality *theory* – that if we can still go up from where we are, we have not yet reached the top – only gives *local* guidance. To rule out other such *local* solutions, *convexity* is often assumed.

oral poetics. A description of the evolutionary process by which *Homeric* and other primary epic poetry is created. The resulting poems are characterized by rearrangement of a stock of formulaic expressions and narrative set pieces. This concept is associated with

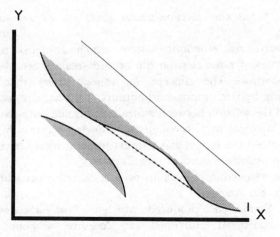

Figure 2   Three examples of nonconvexity

the work of Milman Parry and Albert Lord.

ordinary people. Those who have *rules* but no *metatheory.*

Platonism. The doctrine that ideas are discovered by people, not *created* by them. In modern times this is associated with the mathematical philosophy of Kurt Gödel.

positive time preference. To prefer to consume $1 today to $1 tomorrow. This choice is often held to violate widely held *rules.* Observation of people with positive time preference rarely suggests that these *rules* be judged *'false'* and abandoned. I shall argue that this *rule* is associated with issues of *optimization* under conditions of *nonconvexity.* See *Mandeville's Paradox.*

pragmatic. The philosophical tradition which takes into account the fact that people's desires influence the way they use the language. This is a position associated with the work of David Hume, William James, Frank Ramsey and W. V. Quine. See *approbation* and *disapprobation.*

preferences. The technical term which modern economists employ to describe an individual's goals/desires. So described, these goals are a *relation* with sufficient structure to make them suitable for the application of *optimization* techniques.

price-taking behavior. A description of individual and firm choice when prices are determined by *exogenous* market forces.

prisoner's dilemma. A mathematical representation of a game in which cooperation *optimizes* the combined interests of the players; nevertheless, individual *optimization* requires noncooperation. This is a particularly virulent manifestation of *nonconvexity.* Thomas Hobbes memorably argued that this game characterized the problem of society.

private cost. What the decision-maker gives up to get something. See *social cost*.

private property. An economic system which attempts to impose the consequences of a decision on the decision-maker. See *communism*.

production function. The concept in *economic theory* that specifies the relationship between inputs and outputs. Traditionally, economists have described the relation between a firm's inputs and outputs by a *production function*. More recently, economists, following the lead of Gary Becker, have described the inputs and outputs in nonmarket activity in terms of household *production functions*. See *isoquants*.

property. The restriction of a claim on a resource to particular individuals ('owners'). See *common*.

public goods. Goods, once produced, which are *locally abundant* in the sense that an additional individual can consume without *cost* to other individuals. See *Hume's theory of property*.

public-goods problem. Who must pay for the *public goods*? See *prisoner's dilemma*.

rational ignorance. If acquiring information costs me more than it is expected to benefit me, why should I acquire it? Usually applied to the political process, this concept is associated with the work of Anthony Downs and should be associated with the earlier work of Robert Filmer. See *prisoner's dilemma*.

rationality. In modern economics, the principle that the observed choice is a manifestation of *optimization*; in traditional philosophy, the principle of *theory-directed choice*. I shall argue for a link between these two meanings. See *nonconvexity*.

relation. The fundamental mathematical–logical concept which allows us to express how some individual or individuals stand in terms of some property. Inside a mathematical *theory*, '*true*' and '*false*' are determined by the details of the *relations*. Thus '3 is greater than 2' is '*true*' but '2 is greater than 3' is '*false*'. Modern economists formalize the idea of *preference* as a *relation* between alternatives.

religion. For our limited purposes, an organization which transmits *rules*.

rent-seeking activity. Expenditure of resources to transfer income from one person to another. This was introduced into the modern literature by Gordon Tullock. See *prisoner's dilemma*.

revealed preference. The line of research in modern economics which attempts to impute individuals' goals solely from their observed behavior. It is important for our purpose because at no time do those in the *revealed preference* research program need to ask individuals what they think about their choice. Paul Samuelson solved many technical problems to help economists think about choice in this way. The burden of my argument is to explain what *revealed preference* cannot accomplish.

'right'. A choice marked by *approbation*.

robust. A concept in mathematical statistics signifying that a small deviation from one's assumptions brings about only a small *cost*. *Robust* statistics have bounded *influence curves*; that is to say, no single observation can have an arbitrarily large impact upon the answer.

rules. The *theory* of what counts as '*right*' and '*wrong*' conduct.

scarcity. The absence of *abundance*: the situation in which one must sacrifice something to obtain another thing.

shame. A dramatic type of *disapprobation*.

single-peaked preference. Convex preferences on a political dimension.

social cost. What is given up by all people as a result of a decision-maker's action. See *private cost*.

synthetic. In philosophy of logic, a statement which will be '*true*' or '*false*' only after observation.

theory. A fragment of *language* sufficiently simple that its interrelations can be evaluated by an *algorithm* for *approbation* or *disapprobation*. See *metatheory*.

theory-directed choice. Choosing in accordance with one's *rules*. See *Mandeville's Paradox*.

trade. Voluntary exchange between two or more *optimizing* members of a species. Thus, men and women *trade* amongst themselves, but not with nature. My use here is narrower than is conventional, for reasons I hope to make clear.

transitive. A mathematical property of a *relation*, R, such that if a stands in relation R to b, and b stands in relation R to c, then a stands in relation R to c. If a, b, c are real numbers and the relation is 'greater than', then transitivity is obviously '*true*'. If a, b, c are people and the relation is 'father of', then transitivity is obviously '*false*'. If a, b, c are states of the world, and the relation is 'preferred to', the question of the transitivity of this relation is very important. The *revealed preference* approach to *economic theory* requires that an individual's *preferences* be transitive.

'*true*'. *Approbation* of a sentence/belief/proposition/communication. The correspondence *theory* of truth, in this framework, would then explain such a judgment as just that case when the sentence corresponds to an observed reality. The coherence *theory* of truth, in this framework, would insist upon the possibility that what we observe may depend upon our language and so our observation may be forced to correspond to the sentence in question.

unrealistic assumption. An aspect of *theory* which is obviously '*false*', but is not abandoned because that choice would *cost* too much. See *Chicago school of economics* and *Mandeville's Paradox*.

'*vice*'. The traditional Christian *disapprobation* concerning premarital sex, as well as sexual practices which prevent conception. The desire to avoid premarital sex served to motivate the traditional Christian recommendation to marry early. The controlling text is 1 Corinthians. See

Malthusianism and *Neomalthusianism*.

word-taking behavior. A recently coined term to describe individuals who accept *rules* which they employ to judge their behavior as *exogenously* determined. The term will resonate to those who know that economists have long described competitive markets as ones in which individual consumers and firms are *price takers*.

'wrong'. A choice marked by *disapprobation*.

Acknowledgments

The debts which I owe for particular ideas and devices are acknowledged in the text and notes. Here, I should like to acknowledge more general debts.

I am obligated to my teachers at Berkeley and Chicago for showing me the beauties of economic theory and for their vigorous encouragement to rigor. Chapters 11 and 12 began as thesis work for George Stigler. Lester Telser and the late Harry Johnson helped when difficulties arose.

About half of the book has appeared as articles in *Economics and Philosophy* (Chapters 3 and 16, Cambridge University Press), *History of Political Economy* (Chapters 11 and 12, Duke University Press), *Hume Studies, Interpretation, Journal of the History of Ideas, Journal of Legal Studies* and *Mill Newsletter*. Errors have been corrected, redundancy eliminated and blind alleys walled over.

The Center for Study of Public Choice under the leadership of James Buchanan, Robert Tollison and Gordon Tullock has provided an extraordinary environment to work on problems which have not been fashionable for two centuries. Where else could one engage in month-long arguments about why rats don't trade? Or do they? Through the Center I have been fortunate to talk about these issues with Buchanan, Tullock, Tollison, Susan Feigenbaum, Jennifer Roback, Roger Congleton, Charles Plott, Viktor Vanberg, Ronald Heiner, Tyler Cowen and the late Jack Wiseman.

W.W. Cooper and Abraham Charnes will recognize some of their teachings. Charles Griswold has read many drafts over the last two decades. Christine Holden corrected more errors than I can remember. Routledge's editorial staff saved me much embarrassment. Libby Masaitis helped with the typing, Carol Robert did most of the index and Gloria Yeager read the proofs.

My family has borne the real cost of this research. The benefits remain to be seen except for Nicholas who can take the book to 'show and tell'.

I regret not being able to tell Harry and Jack how much I miss them.

Part I

Introduction and background

Chapter 1

Why worry about the economic ideas of ordinary people?

Over the last century economists have industriously delved into the link between desires and deeds, but we have stopped attending to what ordinary people say about their desires or these deeds. Such a closing of our ears is a fairly recent event. Adam Smith, to give only the greatest name possible, listened to what people said about 'right' and 'wrong' and wrote a grand book about the judgments people make about actions. He asked such questions as: What is the basis on which we accept these judgments? What is the structure of these judgments? And, most importantly for economists, how could words of judgment have an impact on our choice? Where did this literature go?

Even if we have no interest in judgment *per se*, we who are so deeply involved with explanation of actions might wish at least to sketch a proof that what people say does not influence their action. If we cannot present such a proof, what is the basis for *our* judgment that the judgments of ordinary people do not influence their action? If we tried to come to grips with some of the questions Smith asked within the confines of neoclassical economics, how would we do it? What sort of machinery could we bring to bear on these topics? Would economic theory differ if we took into account what ordinary people say?

As I reconstruct the history of neoclassical economics, interest in the fact that people talk as well as choose did not just get mislaid accidentally, nor did it evaporate from *ennui*. Rather, I find two strong reasons why modern economists have found it desirable not to take into account what people say. To put the matter a bit brusquely, these reasons are, first, we cannot make sense of what ordinary people say and, second, even if we could, we can very well accomplish all we wish without the bother. Occam's razor then dispatches the topic.

What people say and what they do are all too often worlds apart. Here is George Stigler's pungent version of this consideration:

> The economist, and his brethren in the social sciences, have a second
> level of difficulty not shared by the physical sciences. Our main elements

of analysis are people, and people who are influenced by the practices and policies we analyze. Imagine the problems of a chemist if he had to deal with molecules of oxygen, each of which was somewhat interested in whether it was joined in chemical bond to hydrogen. Some would hurry him along; others would cry shrilly for a federal program to drill wells for water instead; and several would blandly assure him that they were molecules of argon.[1]

In this aspect of his work, Stigler has remained a faithful student of Frank Knight. Across the decades Knight emphasized over and over again the conflict between the choices we make in the market and the judgments which we make about these choices. No major religion or ethical system says what we do is 'right'.[2] A typical Knightian quip is:

Modern Christians and Jews are apparently saved from mental conflict by refusing to take their professed religious beliefs seriously in the conduct of political life.[3]

Knight understood the opportunity cost of ideas. If one holds A, one cannot consistently hold not A. Optimizing theory says A and articulated 'feeling facts' say not A.

Just so, too, logically speaking, we merely 'infer' consciousness in other human beings from the 'movements' of speech, facial expression, and the like, by which, as we say, they 'communicate' with us. There is no clear logical reason why we do not regard the behaviour of objects generally as communicative — at least until our attention is called to the problem and we have thought hard about it for a time — any more than there is a clear logical reason why we do interpret certain behaviour facts in human beings.[4]

Which will it be? If you cannot give up a precious thing in the face of necessity, you don't own it: it owns you. Knight had the courage to recognize that if we have to give up optimizing theory as the price of dealing with ordinary people's theorizing activity, then that's the answer. We walk away.

It [scientific economics] cannot deal with feeling facts, except as a mode of expressing behaviour facts, for two reasons. In the first place, the facts of desire and satisfaction cannot be accurately observed and measured, and scientific economics must dogmatically and rigorously identify them quantitatively with their objective expressions in measurable goods or services taken up or given off, just as the physicist identifies forces quantitatively with their expressions in movement. The second reason for the exclusion of feeling facts, as known through sources independent of their expression in action, is that this second kind of knowledge, in so far as it gives verifiable information, contradicts to a considerable extent that furnished by the first source. Therefore economics, in dealing with these data also, would be trying to ride two horses at the same time over courses too divergent for comfort. It is better to leave distinct sets of data to different sciences; and the facts of consciousness and their relation to the facts of behaviour form the province of the already well-established disciplines of psychology and ethics.[5]

The hope of the book is to put the evidence of these two worlds back together. I too must confront the question: what's it going to cost? Are demand curves still going to be downward sloping? Nothing is free, but my stubborn adherence to the neoclassical optimizing framework assures me that every principle I use has been bought and paid for long ago. There is an old optimizing principle that if you are going to be hanged for stealing a lamb, you might as well drive off with the whole flock in the back of the pickup.

Since we shall encounter the problem of the mixed messages from mute choice and talk about choice so often, it deserves a name. It is hard to find a sharper statement of the paradoxical issues involved than that provided by Bernard Mandeville in 1720:

> Another Proof, that Men generally are persuaded of the Truth of the Gospel, is, that the Duties and Severities of the Christian Religion seem so reasonable to them, that they would abominate any one who would preach up loose Morals; and there is hardly a Drunkard, a Whoremaster, or any loose Jilt in Town, if ever they go to any Publick Worship, but what would be ready to throw Stones at a Minister, who should tell them, that their Actions were commendable, and God approv'd of the Life they led.[6]

So, 'Mandeville's Paradox' it will be. Is there any doubt that Mandeville has a point?[7] Just what do we make of all this?

The second reason for the lack of interest in talk is more technical. Paul Samuelson and others demonstrated that it is possible, under certain mathematical conditions, to reconstruct everything we want to know about people's desires from their mute choice.[8] If what is known as the 'revealed preference' approach goes through, it obviates the need for economists to pay attention to talk. Don't listen, look. It is fitting that, to explain what the revealed preference approach really means, Stigler introduces students to Mandeville:

> I don't call things Pleasures which Men say are best, but such as they seem to be most pleased with; . . . John never cuts any Pudding, but just enough that you can't say he took none; this little Bit, after much chomping and chewing you see goes down with him like chopp'd Hay; after that he falls upon the Beef with a voracious Appetite, and crames himself up to his Throat. Is it not provoking to hear John cry every Day

that Pudding is all his delight, and that he don't value the Beef of a Farthing?[9]

In another context, economists know all about ignoring most of the world to get on with the work at hand. If, for instance, we are vitally interested in the market for eggs, we probably should pay attention to the market for bacon. But, unless we ignore such 'distant' markets as that for pig iron, we are unlikely to proceed very far.[10] Such partial equilibrium analysis buys explanatory power by taking risks. 'What we don't study won't matter' is the fundamental lemma of the strong law of wishful thinking.[11] The case I shall attempt to make is that even if we are not very interested in the fact that ordinary people talk about their choices, simply wishing this chatter would go away jeopardizes our understanding of such 'straightforward' problems as how people trade. More delicately, by not paying attention to what ordinary people say, we misunderstand the logical basis of a controversial class of theorems in welfare economics. What we, *qua* ordinary person, believe can influence what we, *qua* professional economist, prove. Thus, I shall argue on several fronts that what we do not study can influence what we do study.

The peril of treating ordinary people as if they were mute is then twofold. We misunderstand the world and we misunderstand what it is we prove. None the less, this is what I propose to prove about our theorems. The economist reader may find this enterprise even odder than Mandeville's Paradox.

WHAT IS TO BE PROVEN?

Because this book is written by a working econometrician with no aspirations to heterodoxy, it should come as no surprise that the argument will be centered around three basic organizing metaphors:[12]

- What good would it do an ordinary person to have ideas? What is the demand for these ideas?
- Who produces these ideas? What is the supply?
- Is there competition in the market for these ideas? Would monopoly make any difference?

'Demand' and 'supply' will be employed in this context with deplorable looseness. I am not attempting to counterfeit theorem with metaphor.

To forge a link between words and deeds, I shall posit that people desire approbation and shun disapprobation. Although approbation can be conveyed by inarticulate smiles or gestures, it can also be carried in language by words of praise and blame. In particular, my argument will suppose that the ideas of ordinary people which carry this approbation can be represented as having much in common with technical economic theory.

In this sense I shall talk of the economic ideas of ordinary people.

Approbation has the wonderfully interesting property that we need only consider a single individual accepting the standards of his language community. Approbation can then be treated as flowing mechanically from a comparison between variable choice and fixed standards. Is the choice 'right'? Is the performance 'shabby'? Of course, standards change and evolve, but our individual can treat them as fixed with respect to the particulars of the choice which confronts him. We can ask about the conditions required for word-taking equilibrium.

Variable action and fixed standards avoid the indeterminacy of free-floating conversation within the dialogue which is offered by non-economists as a template for an analysis of society.[13] Those who would have us think this way are aware of the indeterminacy problem and so propose the dialogue be hedged by constraints. The participants must tell the truth about their beliefs, constrain themselves with a universality principle and constrain themselves to be consistent. If we seek to explain the role of moral constraints in society, it seems somewhat odd to this economist to assume at the outset that everyone *wants* to be constrained and that we honor a moral code to tell the truth.[14] The constrained dialogue seems to me to assume far too much which must be proven. Even so, the dialogue metaphor emphasizes the possibility that one participant can change the opinion of the other. If we are attempting to link words and deeds – the weak link in the dialogue approach – then if my action changes the words of judgment emanating from community standards, I would despair of deducing equilibrium conditions.[15]

My fellow economists, who would no more think that dialogue is a sensible paradigm for social analysis than they would of calling a talk-radio show to respond to an accusation that Jewish bankers rule the world, grow impatient to ask me a question. In what sense, I hear it objected by those who share my worldview, do ordinary people have an economic idea or an economic theory unless it is in the trivial sense that they know some economics? There is a refined sense in which I mean that ordinary people have economic ideas. I conceive that the economic theory of ordinary people shares abstract structure with neoclassical economics. That is to say, it specifies an actor's goals, the constraints to these goals and the rule that 'rational choice' is to be found at the maximization of these goals subject to these constraints. There is also a crude sense in which I mean the term. Ordinary people will need to know something about average behavior if they are to say, 'How surprising! How wonderful!' I suppose they can get this average by sampling their neighbors with some inexpensive procedure. In these senses, the economic theory of ordinary people has the same structure as the common sort of technical economic theories. Some of our technical theories are reduced to microfoundations, some are not. We cannot demand more of ordinary people as theorists than we demand of ourselves.

Why do I ignore the infinite multicolored riches of language to focus on such gray, impoverished aspects? The answer is very easy and rather sad. I too must leave a sacrifice on the altar of the goddess of tractability. Word-taking behavior I can model.[16]

Having stated the issue this way, a seemingly fatal objection can be launched. Taking Mandeville's Paradox seriously, even if only for the sake of clearing up my confusion, it says that ordinary people have a theory of conduct which says, 'You maximize at point A', when, in fact, they maximize at some point other than A. A curt judgment about the proposition 'You maximize at A' is 'false'. How could maximizers have systematically 'false' theory? Why don't they drop this dead weight and get on with their lives? To tip my hand as to how I shall come to grips with this objection, do professional economists always drop 'false' theory? What are 'unrealistic' premises but 'false' theory that some economist finds useful?

THE DEMAND FOR 'FALSE' THEORY

Long ago, economists bet their chance for scientific immortality upon the hypothesis that individual behavior can be well described by the mathematics of optimization. One chooses a in lieu of b because there is more of what one desires at a than b. For reasons suggested above, I firmly refuse to leave this tradition. My proposed reform consists mainly of filling in the mundane details of just how we propose this optimization is accomplished. When we fill in this gap, it appears to me that modern economists – unlike the classical economists – have settled upon a class of easy optimizing problems.[17] The devices appropriate to these easy problems beg as many questions as they answer.

Easy optimization problems begin early in economic education. Students of economics first see consumers optimizing when preferences are assumed to be convex and assumed to be fully known. For our purposes, all that matters about convexity is that it is a convenient way of assuring that an optimal solution determined from local information be unique. A good consumer theory class will demonstrate what happens when the assumptions of convexity or full information are separately relaxed.

The favorite chalkboard illustration of nonconvexity is addictive commodities. Here the principle of diminishing marginal utility, which underlies the more formal notion of convexity, does not seem to apply. And it is a remarkable fact that dropping either the assumption of full information or that of convexity, but not both, results in a theory which is very close to the paradigm case. In particular, individuals maximizing with local information feel their way rather than fly to equilibrium. Nonconvexity gives discontinuous demand curves at an individual level and a bimodal distribution of consumption at an aggregate level. Neither of these results requires a drastic change in one's intuition formed with convex preferences and full information. Thus assured that one's intuition is sound when the assumptions are relaxed, economists continue to employ full information and convexity as training ground. To persuade our students that these are important cases, we must first believe them to be so.

Students seem absolutely taken aback when a teacher works through the consumer model, showing how it handles apples and opium with equal aplomb. In this book I shall try to work out why my students have a good right to be startled. (Fortunately, it is too late for them to apply for a refund.) The problem is simply that when nonconvexity and local information are conjoined to frame the paradigm case, one's intuition, built on textbook optimizing examples, fails dramatically. Textbook intuition says that constraints to optimization are necessarily a bad thing. In the case of nonconvexity and local information, this is just not so. With this seemingly trivial modification of some technical details, we can attack the Mandeville Paradox from within standard neoclassical economic optimization theory.

To state the paradox in the least intuitive form possible: how can a theory which is obviously 'false' when added as a side constraint to a maximization problem increase the value of that which is to be maximized? To make the case easy to judge one way or another, let us temporarily restrict our attention to numerical optimization problems of the sort encountered in nonlinear maximum likelihood estimation. Figure 1.1 presents what I take to form the paradigm case.

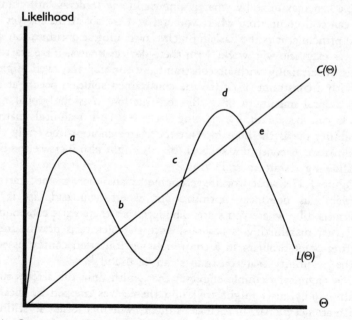

Figure 1.1 Constraints and optimal solutions

Let us first consider the textbook case where we suppose the likelihood surface is single-peaked. So, for the moment, ignore all but the peak nearest the origin in Figure 1.1. The problem is to maximize the likelihood with respect to some parameter θ, thus $L(\theta)$. The maximum clearly is at a. However, when a side constraint, $CC(\theta)$, is added to the maximizing problem, the new maximum is b. (This side constraint will be taken to represent a portion of the content of ordinary people's talk about consumption problems.) Only in the case when a and b exactly agree will the constraint not decrease the computed $L(\theta)$.[18] And, such agreement has been precluded by the assumption that the constraint is 'false'.

In this formal framework constraints function as impediments to maximization. By extension to our worry over what people say, this result is equivalent to the claim that this talk is a barrier to happiness. Inside this optimization framework, there is good reason to follow Knight and walk away from any concern with ordinary people's theorizing. It makes no sense whatsoever in this framework. But this surface does not comprise the world of possible optimization problems.

Now let us open our eyes to the second peak in $L(\theta)$. Here, we must pay something for our results by giving some details of the optimizing procedure. Suppose ordinary people maximize, as is traditional in technical nonlinear optimization, by looking for a point where the first derivative of the objective function with respect to the parameter is zero. Thus, my radical simplification – the price I pay for tractability – is to suppose that people can maximize by what is known in the trade as 'hill-climbing'. If you can still go up from where you are, you are not at the top yet. That's a good principle; it is the basis for a class of nonlinear optimization methods. But, as everyone who works with these devices knows, if we start from the origin maximizing without constraints, we might very well alight at a.

With a constraint of $CC(\theta)$ the constrained solution occurs at e, higher than a local maximum of a. By construction, d is the global maximum which can be found by starting from e. This technical mathematical possibility opens the door for barriers to free choice to be freely chosen by maximizers. A constraint such as $CC'(\theta)$ might also increase the likelihood by allowing restarting from f.

Figure 1.1 is what working econometricians know as the 'starting-point problem' in nonlinear optimization: where you end up is partially determined by where you start. The fact that there exist constraints which can assist maximizing is obvious, once the picture is drawn. Indeed, the starting-point problem in a continuous optimization context is equivalent to the possibility that constraints can be useful.[19]

The technical example suggests that, with only the ability to perceive locally, individuals might well find themselves trapped by local maxima which are not global. In such cases theory which is 'false' can still be useful; it can give individuals the ability to find parts of consumption space which are hidden from their immediate view. Hence, constraints can be more than an impediment to maximization; they can provide information which cannot be extracted from the local surface. Of course, this mapping to ethical imperatives from the starting-point problem in nonlinear optimization theory supposes that individuals can have rules which they do not exactly follow. This is surely the case if a judgment which points to f as the 'best' is to be of assistance to a maximizer. But that's what the Mandeville Paradox is all about, isn't it?

The picture is drawn to represent a single decision-maker in a situation with multiple maxima. There can be local maxima which are not the global maximum. Not only is such nonconvexity of interest in the case of a single individual, it is precisely in the context of nonconvexities that we can expect to find prisoner's dilemma problems. We know this by taking three steps. First, there is an intimate relation between nonconvexity and indivisibility.[20] Second, there is an intimate link between indivisibility and public goods production.[21] Third, prisoner's dilemma problems and the production of public goods cohabit.

The argument pressed below is that ordinary people have good reason to hold normative theory with $CC(\theta)$ or $CC'(\theta)$ as imperatives. It tells them how they ought to consume. This raises an interestingly complicated problem: how could an outside observer tell if someone had such a theory? We have agreed that $CC(\theta)$ and $CC'(\theta)$ are judged 'false'. The theory tells them that a maximum occurs at e or f, but clearly it doesn't. To detect theory-directed choice, we cannot just look at mute choice; we must also consider what is said about choice. In my account, we must learn to look and listen at the same time.

When we listen we discover something truly disconcerting: $CC(\theta)$ functions as if it were a law of logic even though it does not have 'logical form'. As I shall make the case, from the point of view of the ordinary person, if $CC(\theta)$ is not observed in the world, so much the worse for the world. The controversial methodological position that 'unrealistic' assumptions are useful will turn out be quite germane to this aspect of the argument.[22] This result will help in the decoding of some old debates where the participants were in complete agreement over the implications of the theory and the state of the real world. The question one might well ask: what's left to debate? My answer: practically everything.

At various places I consider the arguments which have been advanced against the positions I defend. Just why is talk supposed orthogonal to choice? As far as I can see, economists have been led to this position by assuming that ordinary people have much more information than I am willing to assume. How these informational assumptions are made will be described below.

THE SUPPLY FOR THEORY

Once one gets the hang of taking optimization with such limited information as the analytical benchmark, a series of questions immediately hurl themselves forward. Where do these constraints come from? What guarantees that they work? We certainly cannot assume an informed consumer in the market for moral guidance, can we? It is well to recall that all these problems can be raised in the context of the seventeenth- and eighteenth-century discussions of the relationship between moral instruc-tion and religion. Indeed, the context in which Mandeville's Paradox was historically important was as a way station for Adam Smith's defense of the free market in religion and morality. Citizens of the United States know this result first-hand if only because we live with a very sharp separation of church and state. It is not a joke to state that this separation is an article of faith (the only one?) of American civic religion. The rest of the world finds this as bizarre as the religious seriousness of Americans.[23] It would be a refutation of Smith's principle of rational ignorance if most Americans actually knew we are living out the predictions of a Smithian conjecture.

COMPETITIVE EQUILIBRIUM

If we take seriously the idea that ordinary people would value a certain type of economic advice as to how to solve optimizing problems of the dreadful complexity sketched above, there is an immediate difficulty. Even if there is competition on the supply side to keep away rent-seeking activity, where does this constraining information come from? In the long millennia across which ordinary people have been talking about choice, systematic economic theorizing can be observed for only a few hundred years. Surely, I don't propose to argue that ordinary people can create complicated economic theory; else, they would be extraordinary economists!

Here is the heart of one of my problems. I wish to argue that, yes, such economic ideas can evolve by a trial-and-error procedure and, furthermore, as is characteristic of evolutionary or tacit knowledge, ordinary people are not conscious of their status as economic theorists. Milton Friedman's expert billiard player who makes his shots as if he were a mathematician could not, in fact, write down the equations of motion of the balls. It so happens that students of oral poetry know a good deal which I find germane to my project. For the past sixty years, oral poetics has been the most rigorous test ground for the study of the evolution of ideas.[24] When a problem is solved by a trial-and-error procedure, it may very well be solved correctly, but there is no reason to believe that the problem solver can either prove that the solution is correct, or present a method by which other such problems can be solved. Our theory can be better than our metatheory would suggest. This may not be an accident but may arise from the nature of theory and metatheory.[25]

Oral poetics here includes the Homeric epics, the *Iliad* and the *Odyssey*, the fountainhead of all civilizations which claim affinity to the Greeks. When we read this literature, which we know now to be composed by a trial-and-error evolutionary process, we encounter the gods. Economists, who do not often encounter the gods in their daily work, may require an introduction. For this, we call upon a great poet, a faithful servant to both men and gods, to tell us about their ways. One of Virgil's heroes, worn by past killing and the need to harden himself against his own death in the mist just beyond the present, slackens his shield arm and is pierced by thought:

> is it
> the gods who put this fire in our minds
> or is it that each man's relentless longing
> becomes a god to him?[26]

The gods shall be taken to embody much of the economic ideas of ordinary people we seek.

What do we know about these gods? An older poet, whom some think even greater, can speak to this:

> To die is evil.
> The gods think so,
> Else they would die.[27]

Sappho, who tells the truth about the fires of passion from inside the storm, gives us our answer. The gods are what we would be in a better world.[28]

If the gods are the considered reflection of ordinary people's desires, then can we read back from the stories about the gods the content of ordinary people's theory of conduct? The case of Greek and Hebrew literature is enormously promising because the only way ideas survived from generation to generation was by the expenditure of resources on copying and preservation. What survive, on average, are the texts of the median believer. If a text does not survive, it forms no one's canon.[29] The survival of the texts of believers far from the center of a distribution is much more problematical.[30]

To these texts we shall ask the questions: What is it the gods want? What do the gods fear? By answering these questions, we find what ordinary people think to be the structure of their own desires. What we find in every direction we read is the desire for approbation. Approbation is what we have to give to the gods; approbation is what they give back.

Of course, it is not just ordinary people who have thought about the gods. Extraordinary people (Plato's name suffices) have also thought long and hard about the gods and they have declared ordinary people's ideas contemptible. A modern expression of this contempt is:

That God could be tempted is perhaps the most absurd of all the many absurd assertations which belief has set in the world.[31]

This is a dramatic statement of such Platonism from *inside* a religion which names its scriptures after a contract of mutuality between God and Abraham, a covenant, and not a one-sided gift, a testament.

This book is not a polemic against Platonism. It would not be consistent of me to make such an argument; Plato's books survived because generations of ordinary people thought enough of his work to copy these texts industriously. So many copies survived that only yesterday one heard the complaint that the text of Plato's *Republic* was more reliable than A. N. Whitehead's *Process and Reality*. This suggests to me only that we must attend to both the harmony and the discord. One of the things that Plato points out is that ordinary people have 'false' ideas about the gods. But we are now back where we began. That 'false' ideas can be systematically useful is the thesis I will argue for.

A SHORT DEFENSE OF THE PAST

Where did Knight's insight fail? Knight had the raw materials and the technical insight to do everything I propose to do. That this is true will be obvious after the next chapter. Knight implicitly recognized that constraints can be good things when he defended the *moderate* consumption of opiates.[32] But because Knight thought that all the important economic insight from the past had been absorbed in the present textbooks,[33] and the profession confronted only easy optimization problems, he did not try to put this insight into an optimization framework.[34] Since I shall argue that Knight was premature in walking away from a full theoretical confrontation with talk, it is entirely appropriate that we should find, in very old books, the analytical avenue which provides a way to make sense of Mandeville's Paradox.

A great student of the Greek classics once compared reading the books of long dead men and women to Odysseus' visit to the underworld; the ghosts will speak for the price of blood. I have found this to be true.

Part II

The demand for ideas

The best way to appreciate the importance of language is to take it away. We first consider some of the results from the economic theory experiments with animal consumers. Remarkably enough, rats and pigeons at a suitable level of abstraction – the level at which economic theorists prefer to operate – look very much like us. What does language do for us? What can we do that rats and pigeons cannot? Perhaps, language helps us trade. We encounter the fact that language gives humans an additional method by which to carry approbation.

Restricting our attention to that sort of approbation carried by the words 'right' and 'wrong', we then ask about the context in which we might expect to see such approbation. We fall into very hard optimization problems and discover, perhaps to our surprise, that Greek poets and philosophers of antiquity have been here before, pointing out the way. We just have not understood what they were saying, I believe, because of our fixation on problems we can solve easily.

The third chapter in this section considers whether we can really make sense of the idea that language carries approbation. Aren't sentences in which we ought to be interested just 'true' or 'false'? It turns out that Adam Smith was here before us and is widely thought to have fallen into an intellectual bog. I think that he did not; rather, he walked on a path available in his time only to friends of David Hume. We who can walk in the steps of Frank Ramsey and Alfred Tarski see both the bog and the path.

Chapter 2

Adam Smith and the
Texas A&M rats

Modern experimental economics reports that there is not much at a utility-theoretical level to distinguish humans from rats, since the utility theory developed to explain human behavior seems equally able to explain the behavior of other animals.[1] It seems not to have been widely noticed that this presents a considerable problem for the neoclassical theorem which reduces trade to utility gains: animals do not trade even though there would be utility gains for them too. It is worthy of note that Adam Smith knew something about this when he traced trade to language.[2]

In the trading situation we consider, when there is the potential gain from trade there is also the potential gain from grabbing. What allows people to trade very frequently, but keeps animals from ever trading outside rather odd and dramatic cases? If preferences do not distinguish people from animals, what does? In the sections to follow, I propose how we might explain the origin of trade by appealing to the possibility of creative, theory-directed choice.

When we inquire into what separates human consumers from animal consumers – we have language and property, which they do not – we confront the problem of human creativity.[3] There are two senses in which it is said that human choice is 'creative'. The first is that choice is 'unpredictable' or 'non-deterministic'. That choice is creative is the opinion of a very small minority of the economics profession.[4] Roger Penrose's recent book encourages statement of the 'creativity' thesis this way: human behavior cannot be described by a tractable algorithm, that is to say, an algorithm which can be solved in polynomial time. Unpredictability enters because, absent a polynomial time algorithm, we have no good reason to believe that an attempt to optimize will succeed. These sorts of problems are usually considered to be too 'hard' to guarantee solution.[5]

The possibility of unpredictability resulting from optimization problems is usually blocked by assumption. When textbook models of choice deduce, without further ado, optimal conditions from first and second derivatives, it is simply *assumed* that the local solution turned up is unique. It is an unpleasant truth, known all too well to those who support a family by solving numerical optimization problems, that the answers which this local information provides depend upon where one starts looking for the solution.[6] In an important class of optimization problems – those in which there is such a starting-point problem – exact formal solution techniques are not thought to be polynomial time algorithms even in the best case.[7] Thus, if a global optimum solution in this class of optimization is to be found, one cannot depend upon mechanical, algorithmic procedures. If our algorithms do not work reliably, perhaps we can do better by using nonalgorithmic procedures. Call this nonalgorithmic procedure 'creativity'.

The second sense in which an activity is said to be creative is in case it is theory-directed.[8] The creation of economic theory is itself widely thought creative. More controversially, our will is said to be 'free' because our choice can be influenced by our ideas.[9]

Suppose the two senses of creativity are related. What might this theory-directed activity look like? And what has this to do with hard optimization problems? I wish to argue for a quite simple relationship: inside the confines of continuous optimization problems, one can prove whenever we have a starting-point problem that there exist constraints which can *improve* upon what is being optimized.[10] If these constraints can be found to be carried by words of judgment, then we have evidence of the importance of creative choice in both senses of the word. First, people could employ nonalgorithmic procedures in optimization problems; second, these procedures are somehow related to their own theory of conduct. Or at least that is how I shall argue.

Let me pause to consider a possibly fatal objection to my whole enterprise. Isn't it blatantly contradictory to give a mechanical account of creative choice? Perhaps. But surely, if we posit that human choice is creative, we can then ask what good this creativity does. It is not self-contradictory to posit that human choice can solve a problem creatively even though we cannot prove that such a problem can be solved. Logicians have cleared this up long ago.[11] Supposing this creativity is feasible, then what good would it do? If creativity means theory-directed choice, what sort of theory would a theory-accepting agent accept? Perhaps we can give a mechanical answer for this. To motivate this possibility from another angle, we can repeat Penrose's wonderful question: why would evolution turn up something like self-consciousness?[12] If what we count as evidence of self-consciousness is theorizing activity, then the short answer I propose is that theorists can trade. And, in hard cases, only theorists can trade.[13]

SMITH'S COUNTER-EXAMPLE AND CONJECTURE

There are many parts of the *Wealth of Nations* which inspire less than reverence from modern economists. Surely, the second of these occurs in Chapter II of Book I where Adam Smith traces the beginning of trade to an instinct:

This division of labour, from which so many advantages are derived, is not originally the effect of any human wisdom, which foresees and intends that general opulence to which it gives occasion. It is the necessary, though very slow and gradual consequence of a certain propensity in human nature which has in view no such extensive utility; the propensity to truck, barter, and exchange one thing for another.[14]

Smith hints that this instinct is not itself a primitive instinct but rather something which can be explained by speech:

Whether this propensity be one of those original principles in human nature, of which no further account can be given; or whether, as seems more probable, it be the necessary consequence of the faculties of reason and speech, it belongs not to our present subject to enquire. It is common to all men, and to be found in no other race of animals, which seem to know neither this nor any other species of contracts.[15]

This proposed link between trade and language I shall call 'Smith's conjecture'.[16]

Smith's reason for tracing trade to speech and not desire is reasonably clear: animals do not trade.[17] As he describes the process, trade requires some sort of communication of the notion of fairness. Here is what Smith says:

Nobody ever saw a dog make a fair and deliberate exchange of one bone for another with another dog. Nobody ever saw one animal by its gestures and natural cries signify to another, this is mine, that yours; I am willing to give this for that.[18]

This appeal to animal evidence to block the move from preferences to trade I shall call 'Smith's counter-example'.

Although this seems to have been his last word on the subject, it was not his first, and in this instance his first words are rather interesting because in *Lectures on Jurisprudence* it is clear that speech's persuasive function is critical to Smith's account. In this, as in so many other aspects of his work, Smith is a faithful servant of his Greek masters.[19]

If we should enquire into the principle in the human mind on which this disposition of trucking is founded, it is clearly the naturall inclination every one has to persuade. The offering of a shilling, which to us appears to have so plain and simple a meaning, is in reality offering an argument to persuade one to do so and so as it is for his interest. Men always endeavour to persuade others to be of their opinion even when the matter is of no consequence to them. . . . And in this manner every one is practising oratory on others thro the whole of his life. – You are uneasy whenever one differs from you, and you endeavour to persuade [?him] to be of your mind.[20]

Historians of economics tend to quarrel with Smith over this argument. If Smith had command over neoclassical economics, we tell our classes, he would have been able to dispense with the bartering instinct. Utility functions, in this account, are sufficient to generate an explanation for trade. Construct indifference curves, put two individuals in an Edgeworth box; *voilà*, trade. Preferences can force trade; neither trading instincts nor speech are required.

We shall call this the neoclassical theorem NCT.[21] Letting ⇒ stand for implication, we have

Preferences ⇒ Trade

Let us reflect upon the Texas A&M animal consumers. Have not their preferences been shown to satisfy what neoclassical economics requires of the rational consumer? Their static preferences are isomorphic to ours.[22] In a sense we might wish to think of rats and pigeons as if they were utility-maximizing machines. They are perfectly capable of groping their way to a solution to a conventional maximizing problem. Rats and pigeons do indeed seem to maximize by hill climbing.

None the less, rats and pigeons do not trade. When put in an experimental setting which allows trade, one of the animals simply grabs. Indeed, there have been experiments which have 'failed' to demonstrate that animals can trade. Perhaps because 'failures' are often not deemed worthy of publication, the experiments have not been much discussed in public.[23] Does not this show that 'Smith's counter-example' holds? Utility functions are not sufficient to motivate trade. The objection that trade is risky, so we need to have preferences over risky outcomes, may be correct. However, animals seem to satisfy the demands of expected utility theory just as well as we do.[24]

Let us audit the basis of the neoclassical theorem. Consider an Edgeworth box in one moment in time where Agents 1 and 2 have convex preferences over apples and nuts. (Figure 2.1) Without loss of generality we suppose that trade begins from corner α. The endowment of Agent 1 is nuts and that of Agent 2 is apples. In the textbook account trading from α to β puts both 1 and 2 in a preferred position; hence, trade is a sensible result.

What is proven in the Edgeworth box is that there is the potential for gains from trade. What has not been proven, in general, is that there is not the potential for gain from some other kind of action. Potential gains from trade will manifest themselves as actual gains from trade if we make the seemingly innocuous technical assumption that exchange takes place simultaneously. This may be a case where the assumption that time is discrete is at fault. The assumption of continuous time would make it entirely implausible that any trade started randomly would be exactly simultaneous. Save for an infinitesimal probability, one individual or

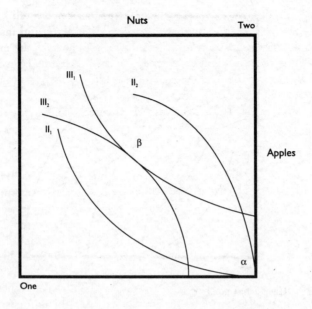

Nuts

Two

III₁

III₂

II₂

II₁

β

Apples

α

One

Figure 2.1   Gains from trade

another would always be first.

Consider the result of dropping the simultaneity assumption to require that one individual goes first. Suppose Agent 1 must give up his nuts before Agent 2 gives up his apples. Then we must redraw the Edgeworth box to emphasize Agent 1's vulnerability. (Figure 2.2) Trade proceeds from α to γ to β. Now, the hole in the proof is transparent. Why cannot Agent 2 simply pick up the nuts and leave? In terms of maximizing problems, there is more than one *local* maximum in what is obviously a prisoner's dilemma problem.

TRADE AND PROPERTY

The line of argument I wish to spell out is that we must look for the explanation of trade in something which people have and animals do not. Smith said as much. Moreover, we should consider the cases when animals do trade. What makes these cases special? At one level, the answer to why animals do not trade is simple enough. They don't have property rights. Property rights would block the grabbing possibility and make trade sensible. This explanation is correct, I believe, because when the experimentalists impose what we might call 'property rights' on the animals' allocation, they will trade. The experimental design when animals

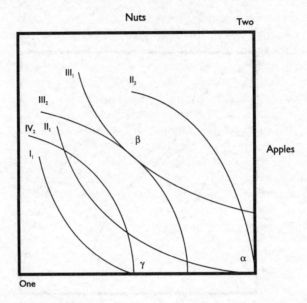

Figure 2.2 Gains from grabbing

trade with animals through vending machines prevents one animal from simply grabbing everything.[25] We trade because we have preferences and property rights; they don't trade because they have only preferences. If this is satisfactory then the corrected neoclassical theorem (CNCT) is:

Preferences + Property ⇒ Trade

To establish the equivalence of NCT and CNCT we need something like a neoclassical patch:

Preferences ⇒ Property

Then, we would have a clear, albeit indirect, inference from preferences to trade. The failure to mention property rights in the classroom is an easily mended fault. We would have the result:

Preferences ⇒ Property ⇒ Trade

Suppose that enforceable property rights are something that any species with well-defined preferences could evolve. If this is so, then there would be no reason to look beyond preferences to explain trade, no reason to consider language or an instinct to truck and barter. But the fact that rats and pigeons have not evolved such a system of property in the millions of years which they have had to get the hang of it – even though they do have the requisite preferences and for the last million years they have had us to study – suggests strongly that property cannot be explained just by preferences.[26]

So, this patch doesn't work. If preferences were sufficient to generate property, why don't animals have property? We are back to the experiments again. Our four-legged or two-winged friends have the same structured preferences as we do. They don't trade and they don't have property. Nobody, to vary Adam Smith's phrase, saw a police rat take a robber rat to jail for stealing. It is simply not clear whether animals without language can have property. Thus, appealing to lack of property to explain lack of trade may simply be appealing to a lack of language.

The failure of the neoclassical patch has a remarkable logical consequence. If we can derive some activity, such as territorial instinct or vocalization, from mere utility-maximizing considerations, then we know immediately that this activity cannot explain property. Consider some activity, A. If preferences sufficed to obtain A and A sufficed to obtain property, then by the transitivity of deduction we would know that preferences sufficed to generate property. This train of inference, albeit long and scenic, is equivalent to the neoclassical patch. But we know that it fails and so too do all such patches.

The CNCT precludes grabbing by appeal to the external constraint of an enforced system of property rights. But surely there is more than one way to repair a theorem. Another patch to the NCT, ACNCT for short, is discussed below, when we consider the possibility of self-restraint. The ACNCT precludes grabbing by appeal to an internal constraint. Desire for approbation fits neatly into the context of the ACNCT, or so I shall argue at length below.

Working with the CNCT or the ACNCT instead of the NCT is rather more complicated for reasons which I shall need this book to work out. The CNCT is also much less informative than the NCT. Ignoring the details, we can look at the converse of the NCT as the revealed preference position; from trade we attempt to impute preferences. Obviously, however, the converse of the CNCT is false. People can figure out how to trade even in some circumstances where property does not exist. For instance, in very hostile surroundings, one can sometimes create an environment where the exchange in fact is simultaneous.

The additional complexity of the CNCT is this. To explain individual trade — a project which distinguishes economists from the rest of the world — we must simultaneously explain the institution of property. To illustrate the complications, I shall consider a case where there is no economic rationale for *private* property. Of course, when I say this, I presume we have a theory of the economic rationale of property. Part of the problem is that there are at least two different theories of property in use. I shall employ the property theory advanced by David Hume in the 1730s, used by Adam Smith in the 1770s and generally forgotten thereafter until its modern, modest revival.[27] Hume argued in the 1730s that when either of two conditions hold: (1) there is sufficient affection between people or (2) there is no scarcity, private property will not exist. When these two conditions hold, supposing only that the resource is something desired, there will be common property. Everyone will have a 'right' to use the resource.

Is there any reason to prefer Hume's theory over some alternative? To determine this, we need a more general theory inside which we can work out a theory of property. I propose to ask the question this way: do we obtain the 'no scarcity, no private property' implication from Winston Bush's economic theory of anarchy? Bush's theory supposes a two-person economy where each individual can spend time producing income by creating new products (production) or by attempting to steal from the other individual (predation).[28] Because nothing in the model precludes predatory behavior at the outset, this seems an appropriate test-bed for those conditions under which we expect no predation even without enforced property rights.

In terms of the Bush model, we can consider Hume's conclusion established if we can prove that free goods require that the optimum expenditure of effort in predation be zero. It is unfortunately true that after hundreds of years of study there are still terrible pitfalls in the analysis of free goods.[29] We can have several distinct cases in mind when we consider 'free' goods. (1) The good, like air, can come independent of individual effort. I cannot take your air from you so I shall not try; therefore, Hume's result easily flows from anarchic equilibrium. This definition will not work for land or water, even in the most idyllic setting, so we resort to a more contrived definition of free goods. Let us suppose that some good, x, is free when (2) the marginal product of effort in the production of x is always greater than the marginal product of predation in the extraction of x. This definition is completely nonobvious, so let me give an example. If a stream runs by both our cabins and a bucket of water can be obtained for the cost of bending over and lifting, then, as long as I cannot obtain the water more cheaply by knocking you over the head, I shall expend no effort on predation. Symmetry gives the same result for your time use. Thus, Hume's result – no scarcity, no private property – is a theorem in Bush's anarchic equilibrium. Of course, if the marginal product of effort in the production of x fell below that in predation, then it would cease to be rational to invest nothing in predation.

The Humean case of sufficient affection can be also be described within Bush's model. If I am sufficiently concerned about your welfare – your loss is my loss and your gain is my gain – then it obviously makes no sense to invest time in predation. Commonality rules again.

In the Humean cases of abundance and affection, the (common) property relation follows mere preferences themselves. Thus, the neoclassical patch adheres. The property which follows from preferences is common, not private property, but this matters not. Whenever something blocks predation so that property follows from preferences, the CNCT collapses to the NCT. This collapse of the CNCT to the NCT in the two Humean cases has the interesting implication that we would expect, that in just these cases trade will occur whenever there are preferences. The implication can be tested by considering the cases in which animals exchange or cooperate.

HUME'S THEORY OF PROPERTY AND ANIMAL EXCHANGE

Let us test the argument by considering where private property has no rationale, when there is either no scarcity or no affection between traders. Lack of scarcity is an odd, but dramatic, case. Affection or animal altruism is surely more important if only because failure of scarcity is not something one would anticipate widely occurring.

Consider the case in the wild where predators and prey will peacefully drink out of the same water hole. Isn't this trade, or at least cooperation?[30] If the lions have eaten recently, they may be willing to let zebras share a water hole in such times as there is enough water for all that wish to drink. Predation is blocked by sufficiency.

Let me point out a potential weak spot in this argument. I shall maintain below that, while animals do have territory, this is not the same thing as property. Now, if it were the case that territory was respected by animals only when there was enough for them to eat on their own territory, then respect for territory would be a condition of lack of scarcity. Respect for territory would occur for the same reasons which lead to peace at the water hole. This would, of course, fit quite neatly into my argument. Moreover, if animals started to fight over the territory when there was not enough for all, this too would be consistent with the argument.[31] However, if animals respected territory even when it meant they went hungry, then this aspect of my argument would be seriously compromised.

Let us turn to the second condition under which Hume's theory finds no rationale for property and consider animal cooperation. Chimpanzees provide the most interesting example of team production and sharing.[32] Suppose that the Humean condition of sufficient affection is satisfied by genetic similarity. Then, when biologists find the basis of animal cooperation or altruism in genetic similarity,[33] they may be reporting a condition which obviates the need for private property. Jane Goodall's report of chimpanzee cooperation stresses the importance of family relationships because chimpanzees are more likely to cooperate with members of their family than members of the group with whom they are not related.[34] She also reports that chimpanzees spend a vast amount of time touching each other in the activity called 'grooming'. This is very suggestive of one line of attack on our problem.

It will have escaped no one that the identification of genetic similarity and the Humean condition of sufficient affection is established by assumption. I believe this is only an illustration of the unpleasant fact that it is more difficult to work with the CNCT than the NCT. In the CNCT we require a theory of property; in the NCT we do not. Theories of property have opportunity cost; they cannot be established from 'A is A'.

'RIGHT' AND TRADE

It is obvious that property and preferences are, at best, sufficient conditions for trade. Are there other sufficient conditions? Next, we turn to consider the possibility that Smith is correct, that language is sufficient to add to preferences to give trade.[35] What is there about language that might make a difference? What convinces people to trade and not grab? What about self-restraint?

We can now define another correction to the NCT, the ACNCT mentioned above as:[36]

Preferences + Self-restraint ⇒ Trade

This approach might be useful to model exchanges among social insects because the self-restraint condition seems to be forced by genetic evolution. Consider the hard case in which an animal must sacrifice herself for the good of the nest. In specialists' accounts a soldier ant encountering a threat to the nest does not hesitate; she does not reflect upon the benefits of deserting to an ant equivalent of Sweden. She just attacks. Don't think, do.[37] If your hard wiring restrains you, then that is the answer.

In a human context the ANCNT would be useful to model exchanges where there are no formal property rights. Drug deals are conducted without explicit property rights, but, to judge by the surely authoritative accounts on *Miami Vice*, in a setting where it is to the interest of neither party to try to grab. It is obvious that both the CNCT and the ANCNT are at best sufficient conditions. Unless we can demonstrate that property and self-restraint are equivalent, then necessary conditions for trade are going to be hard to come by.

I will conjecture that, among humans, language, property and self-restraint are indeed interrelated. When I say to you that I'll give you this for that, my words acknowledge that there is some aspect of the material world which is not mine. If trade is partly seduction – as Smith insists in his lectures – then soft words offering 'mine' for 'thine' may be a vital aspect of the process. Property rights need not be defined in any objective sense, but the offer of trade *acknowledges* your rightful claim on some part of the material world.[38] If I were to grant this 'right' and then seize it when you were vulnerable, then my own words would say this would be 'wrong'.

Why would 'right' and 'wrong' possibly matter? The short answer is that these are words which carry approbation or disapprobation. Of course, there are many other carriers of approbation – a touch, a gesture, a sigh. Such inarticulate forms of approbation are obviously limited in distance and duration. It is important, again, to note how much time chimpanzees spend touching each other.[39] Perhaps the range of inarticulate approbation circumscribes a family or a pack. When carried by language, however, approbation is unlimited in time and space. When we read Aristotle or Adam Smith, we think to ourselves, 'What a pretty argument, how nice'. Our reaction would have been easily foreseen by thinkers of such ability. Relative to other species which desire approbation, language gives human beings an enormous advantage; the approbation carried by language can transcend touch or gesture. I shall play out the argument by focusing on approbation as the link between talk and choice.

This explanation might seem only to push the problem back one step. Can such judgments of 'right' and 'wrong' serve as constraints to my preferences? This is what my account would require to get trade started. The next chapter demonstrates as a mathematical possibility in hard optimizing problems that real-world judgments of 'right' and 'wrong' can constrain choice and make us better off at the same time. In the introductory chapter I illustrated the possibility of such constraints by a picture of $CC(\theta)$. Can one really point to judgments out there which would have this effect? Once trade starts, then it is all learning by doing. 'Right' and 'wrong' disappear into the background of our consciousness. Once trade has started then we can take language and judgment as much for granted as we who live in the pleasant part of the twentieth century can take for granted writing, the concept of zero and the failure of planned economies. Everyone knows these things and we forget that once upon a time we did not.

The idea that self-constraints are related to a desire for approbation, and approbation is in part carried by language, is consistent with some otherwise puzzling results from experimental economics concerning contributions to finance public goods. Experimental conditions can allow people to talk about donating or they can enforce silence. The experimental evidence suggests that talking about contributions to finance public goods makes a large difference. If the subjects of the experiment can talk, contributions soar.[40] This evidence is terrifically important if only because it allows us to make sense of such activities as 'pledge week' on noncommercial radio and television.

What is obviously missing from the naive Edgeworth box is some constraint upon grabbing. To the extent that words of judgment, 'right' and 'wrong', can serve as internal constraints, this might repair the gap in the neoclassical movement from preferences to trade. Is there something about language which constrains us?

In this context let us think about language as a constraint.[41] Is it not the first system of constraint that we as human beings learn? If we wish to obtain something from someone other than our parents, we are required to ask in a common language and say 'please'. We have to use the same words

as everyone else in our language community in a syntax imposed by the
demands of a grammar.

Philosophers have long known about the relation between language
acquisition and preferences. Ludwig Wittgenstein's *Philosophical Investigations* starts with a quotation from St Augustine's *Confessions*:

> Thus, as I heard words repeatedly used in their proper places in various
> sentences, I gradually learnt to understand what objects they signified;
> and after I had trained my mouth to form these signs, I used them to
> express my own desires.[42]

In our public language we learn quickly that some words give pain and
some words give pleasure. If language is an instrument for dispensing pain
and pleasure to those sensitive to disapprobation and approbation then talk
cannot be orthogonal to trade. Other things being equal, someone who is
sensitive to approbation would rather deal with those who provide it than
with those who do not. There is an old joke that the trouble with murder is
that it leads to robbery and from thence to incivility and social collapse.
There may be a point here.

HOW TO TEST SMITH'S ACCOUNT

Animals make all manner of sounds and they engage in all manner of
cooperation. Is it not possible that animals really do have something like
the ability to talk? Specialists agree that there is a 'creativity' to human
speech which animal communication simply lacks.[43] This is not to say that
animal communication has no creative aspect.[44] Indeed, if there were none
it would be hard for us to explain where human creativity came from. This,
in turn, is related to the question of whether other primates have the
potential for language.[45]

Suppose that a group of chimpanzees were introduced to sign language
and given enough time to get good at signing.[46] One rather direct test of
Smith's thesis is to compare the willingness to trade of chimpanzees who
can sign with that of chimpanzees who cannot. It is clear that chimpanzees
will share food in the wild inside an extended family.[47] The question which
could be tested is whether an enhanced ability to communicate with other
chimpanzees would increase this willingness to cooperate. In fact, an
experiment involving two signing chimpanzees where they had to take
alternate turns to ask one another for food generated considerable food
sharing and cooperation.[48] This looks terrifically promising. However, a
true test would be to compare signing chimpanzees with those who could
not sign.

Smith pointed to language as possibly the key; is the issue really
intelligence?[49] Here we confront an enormously important problem of
simultaneity. While language requires intelligence, language also develops

intelligence. Everyone knows that muscles and exercise are interrelated. Specialists tell us that language and brain development seem to be mutually determining.[50] If this is so, perhaps, there is something to be said for the claim that humans differ from apes *because* we stumbled upon language.[51] It is remarkable that something akin to this position was held by an 'eccentric' contemporary of Smith, Lord Monboddo.[52]

Smith's conjecture would further suggest why language would be such a valuable characteristic to evolve. If one could trade as easily without language as with language, then what do we gain by having language? Of course, we can talk about our coming death and the activities of the gods. Perhaps it is only because I am an economist that I do not find these conversational topics as offering enormous advantages. 'Let's make a deal' and 'I love you' sound more like it. Thus, Smith points out a route by which we might find an answer good enough for Penrose's question.

LANGUAGE AND PROPERTY RIGHTS

Let us think about the creativity of language in relation to property rights. If language used by humans is unpredictable, and property requires language, might not we expect property rights to be unpredictable? In fact, philosophers have long made an interesting analogy between language and money, one aspect of property. In an illuminating comparison between language and money, Wittgenstein points to how little sense private money would make:

> Why can't my right hand give my left hand money? – My right hand can put it into my left hand. My right hand can write a deed of gift and my left hand a receipt. – But the further practical consequences would not be those of a gift. When the left hand has taken the money from the right, etc., we shall ask: 'Well, and what of it?' And the same could be asked if a person had given himself a private definition of a word; I mean, if he has said the word to himself and at the same time has directed his attention to a sensation.[53]

It is delightful how philosophers from George Berkeley through Smith and then Wittgenstein have made the analogy between money and language.[54] While Berkeley and Smith have a semiotic theory of money, Wittgenstein has a monetary theory of language!

The monetary metaphor is not much in evidence in Saul Kripke's exposition of Wittgenstein's private language argument. There is, however, a stunning footnote which ties together the notion of private language and private prices: one might be sensible if the other is sensible. Of course, public prices and a monetary economy are two aspects of the same process. Prices are just exchange rates in a public medium:

I might mention that, in addition to the Humean analogy emphasized in this essay, it has struck me that there is perhaps a certain analogy between Wittgenstein's private language argument and Ludwig von Mises's celebrated argument concerning economic calculation under socialism. . . . According to Mises, a rational economic calculator (say, the manager of an industrial plant) who wishes to choose the most efficient means to achieve given ends must compare alternative courses of action for cost effectiveness. To do this, he needs an array of prices (e.g. of raw materials, or machinery) set by *others*. If *one* agency set *all* prices, it could have no rational basis to choose between alternative courses of action. (Whatever seemed to it to be right would be right, so one cannot talk about right.) I do not know whether the fact bodes at all ill for the private language argument, but my impression is that although it is usually acknowledged that Mises's argument points to a real difficulty for centrally planned economies, it is now almost universally rejected as a theoretical proposition.[55]

Kripke was misinformed about the outcome of the central planning debate. The socialists 'won' the debate by giving up central planning, in the private prices sense, and going back to a market system and declaring victory. Prices became public again in the sense required for Kripke's argument.[56]

In what sense do not animals have property? It is clear that if animals are forced to treat themselves as vending machines – to vary a nice phrase from Immanuel Kant – then they will exchange. In the field – where experimentalists do not impose strict property rights – what do we observe? Of course, animals have a well-defined territorial sense. Territorial limits are not the same as property rights. To see this it is sufficient to note that, even if an animal had no competition, it would still restrict itself to feeding in a limited space. This is a simple application of the theory of marginal productivity.[57] Respect for territory can evolve by a mechanical procedure.[58] An animal learns that when it crosses a scented 'marker' it will be attacked. An animal which does not defend its territory will be driven out and have difficulty feeding itself. But, by avoiding picking a fight by crossing territorial markers, it lives longer and has more offspring. Hence, respect of territory can come into being by a trial-and-error evolutionary process.

It is a remarkable testimony to Bush's theory of economic anarchy that his simple model can rationalize much that is reported by students of animal territory. In Bush's model the amount of time spent in predation or production depends, in part, on the value of the alternative time uses. This seems consistent with specialists' reports.[59] This fact is important because Bush's natural equilibrium only requires constrained maximizing behavior. If preferences give us territory then territory cannot give us property because we know the neoclassical patch fails.

Similarly, in the field, we observe animals giving all sorts of vocal signals to one another. Noam Chomsky argues that these vocalizations can be explained mechanically; that is, there is a one-to-one correspondence between these sounds and stimulation. This mechanism allows, one would think, an easy evolutionary explanation for the origin of animal sounds.

Characteristically, when specialists explain animal behavior, we are in the mechanical world because animal behavior can be described by an algorithm. This is, of course, why Chomsky's great book is called *Cartesian Linguistics*: he revives Descartes's claim that animals are machines. We cannot construct such a flow-chart for human behavior, at least not in the same *successful* sense. Language, human vocalization, cannot be described by a flow-chart as a reaction to external stimuli. Because of the neoclassical patch failure, property rights cannot be described by this flow-chart either.

Let me give an example of this creativity of property rights. Property rights change in all sorts of interesting ways. For example, the great central planning debacle gave property rights to price setters. Rent control gives property rights to tenants. Many economists – myself included – think these are foolish property rights, but that reaction, as we shall see, provides evidence that these sorts of rights are not in our flow-chart explanation. Central planning had its defenders but is there now any dispute about the staggering human cost of socialism? Is this not evidence that property rights do not flow from preferences in a nice maximizing fashion?

I am taking it for granted that animal territory and animal sounds can be described by a mechanical model of maximizing response: a flow-chart will suffice. However, the flow-chart will not suffice to explain either human property or human language. In particular, animals seem not to be able to make the leap in imagination from territory – which they have – to property rights, which they don't have.

We have contrasted the mechanical flow-chart explanation of behavior with theory-directed, creative choice. Can this distinction be made precise? Supposing that the trading agents have a theory, what sort of a theory might it be? This is considered in the next chapter.

A SERIES OF OBJECTIONS AND IMPROVEMENTS

There have been all sorts of interesting objections, as well as sharpenings of the argument, which have been launched by my friends, or reported by my friends. From the trail of acknowledgments, it should be obvious that much of my argument has evolved to deal with these objections.

1. Animals do something which looks a lot like trade and animals do something which has a lot of language-like features, and animals do have something which looks a lot like property. If trade, language and property are fuzzy concepts, what evidence is there for Smith's conjecture? Indeed,

are we even sure that Smith's counter-example holds?

There is no more difficulty establishing Smith's counter-example in animal experiments than there is in finding animal preferences. Given known preferences, compute Pareto-optimal trading outcomes. These do not occur unless the experiments preclude the possibility of grabbing. In the wild we need a theory of property to be able to test the CNCT. With Hume's theory, the CNCT seems consistent with the crude outlines of animal behavior. Whether it is consistent with fine details I'm not sufficiently informed even to speculate.

Moreover, as I have argued above, if human intervention can give chimpanzees more linguistic ability than they have in the wild, then we have the possibility of a direct test of Smith's thesis. Does language assist trade? Even better, we could test Lord Monboddo's proposition that dæmonic forces could jump-start an evolutionary process. From an ape's point of view, humans satisfy Monboddo's definition of dæmonic.[60] Could we teach them language and bring human-type civilization about?

2. Is the difference between people and rats simply that of perceptive-cognitive abilities, or just plain intelligence? As a nonspecialist I can afford the luxury of a difficult position that intelligence and language are two aspects of the same process. I'm very impressed by John Eccles's position that brain mass and language are self-determining. Perhaps, once brains get big enough, we get flexible responses.[61] I wouldn't be surprised if, when we started out on the road to humanity, we came with a sense of territory and a repertory of warning sounds. Because of our intelligence, we would be able to try out a new idea. What I don't know, in the sense that I don't even know how to propose a test, is which came first, trade or language; nor do I believe it matters much.

3. Isn't the problem really time preference? Look at the Edgeworth box again. Breaking trade into two successive segments – α to γ and then γ to β – is really nothing more than introducing a prisoner's dilemma problem into the foundation of trade. It is to the interest of the members of society to trade α to β. By construction, it is to the interest of the agent who goes last to remain at γ. This is so even though γ is inefficient. Surely the agent who goes first knows this. Will the agent be constrained from grabbing by the possibility of repeat trades? This is another way of raising the issue of time preference. If my time preference is high enough, I shall not care about the possibility of repeat trades.[62] Thus, isn't the difference between people and rats that people have sufficiently lower time preference than rats? If so, we need not appeal to human language to explain the difference between people and animals. Can we obtain the following result?

Preferences + Low time preference $\Rightarrow$ Trade

This might escape Smith, but it would not save the NCT. Even so, this escape route has also been blocked by very recent results in animal

economics. In this research Kagel and associates have shown that rats have
the same structure to their time preference as people do.[63] That is to say,
an animal will exchange over time with a vending machine on much the
same basis we would expect human consumers to exchange. The animal
will simply not trade with another animal. If the problem were just 'high'
time preference, then we would expect to observe interanimal trade when the
gains from a one-shot trade were sufficient to overcome high time preference.

The issue of time preferences is worth raising because the proposition
that high time preference is 'wrong' is an implication of a moral theory
which it makes sense for maximizers to possess. Thus, discomfort with the
'rationality' of grabbing might manifest itself in the hope that low time
preference might be the way out. This possibility is a very long story which
is considered below.

4. Is all this really necessary?[64] Suppose we look at the problem as the
formulation of expectations by two different procedures. First, I can form
expectations of your future behavior by studying your past behavior.
Second, I can form expectations of your future behavior by you telling me
what your conduct will be. In the first case one must both form and test a
theory; in the second, one need just test a theory. The latter is
characteristically a much easier statistical procedure requiring far fewer data
than the former.[65]

WHAT NOW?

Let me be clear about what I think I have established. We cannot explain
trade, in the general case, by simple appeal to preferences. At a minimum
we require some theory of property or self-restraint to explain what it is
that constrains grabbing. Moreover, these theories of property or self-
restraint will need to draw upon something more than mere preferences. I
think these points are clear. I am less certain that Smith's conjecture, trade
requires language, is correct. It certainly is not obvious. If language is a
substitute for touching, then there may be a way to connect language with
a solution to the prisoner's dilemma problem. Hence, much of the
remainder of the book will be concerned with the issue of how aspects of
language might function as a constraint upon grabbing. The questions to
be addressed are manifold. Is self-constraint associated with language? Is
the enforcement of property associated with language? It is plausible that
either property or self-constraint conjoined to preferences will generate
trade, so it is only natural that these avenues be explored. In back of all
this is the question: how might theory direct choice? The link I find is
approbation; language can serve where touching fails.

For those who cannot wait to get to the good parts, in Chapter 4 we
consider the relation among theory, ethics and approbation. In Chapters 7
and 10, we connect up approbation and the provision of public goods.

Chapter 3

Utility-enhancing consumption constraints

INTRODUCTION

The Greek poets and philosophers are united in a belief that men and women perceive the world around them very poorly, describing as they do much of human behavior as fumbling for happiness in the dark. By contrast perception failure is anathema to the modern tradition; even the most innocent sort plays havoc with modern preference axioms.[1]

This chapter contains a modern reconstruction of the classical discussion of choice and perception failure. The benefits purported to flow from the analysis are (1) an explanation of some of the roles of words of praise and blame in choice and (2) a suggestion of the curvature properties of consumption space likely to be associated with these words. One offshoot of the exercise is to construct the content of what might be considered an equilibrium moral code over consumption space. There are costs because economic modeling becomes a good deal more complicated: the revealed preference approach fails because what is chosen need not be on a higher indifference curve.[2]

To preclude misunderstanding, let me emphasize the very limited range of morality which I even purport to model. Some of the limitations are blatant, e.g., there is only one agent in my account. This severs my construction from those modern discussions which find moral issues only in a social context. A less obvious limitation is my attempt to rationalize a class of moral facts; that is, the maxims which people in fact employ to talk about their conduct. On the contrary, many philosophers attempt to construct moral systems inside which various maxims hold. I am unsure whether the sorts of maxims I explain are sufficient to define any one of the traditional moral systems. I would suppose, however, that they best fit into a prudential system.

A MODEL OF SYSTEMATIC PERCEPTION FAILURE

The troubles which befall men and women who fail to mediate their passions with reflection are a commonplace in the classical Greek tradition. In particular in the Homeric epics it is claimed that there is a link between perception failure and failure to choose sensibly. The Homeric word 'ατη which Liddell and Scott translate as 'bewilderment, infatuation, caused by blindness or delusion sent by the gods . . .' seems at the center of the claim.[3] An instance which has attracted much recent scholarship is Agamemnon's apology in the nineteenth book of the *Iliad*. Here is Richmond Lattimore's translation:[4]

> I am not responsible
> but Zeus is, and Destiny, and Erinys the mist-walking
> who in assembly caught my heart in the savage delusion ['ατη]
> on that day I myself stripped from him the prize of Achilleus.
> Yet what could I do? It is the god who accomplishes all things.
> Delusion ['Ατη] is the elder daughter of Zeus, the accursed
> who deludes all . . .
> She has entangled others before me.
> Yes, for once Zeus even was deluded.[5]

What can be done? Some advice is offered in the *Odyssey*: 'Always moderation is better' (7.310) and 'In all things balance is better' (15.71).[6]

Is there really such a link between perception failure and moral difficulties? Skepticism here may be in order. Perception failure is simply a version of incomplete information, and what has incomplete information to do with morality? In an attempt to resolve this issue, a model of systematic perception failure is constructed next.

A model of perception failure is easy to build within Gary Becker's model of consumer behavior.[7] In this framework it is straightforward to distinguish between the subjective ends of consumers and the decisions which they make in the material world to attain these ends. Individuals in a Beckerian model may have perfect knowledge of their utility function even though they have only imperfect information about how these ends can be attained in the objective world. In the standard model of consumer choice, where objective goods are the only arguments in the utility function, an individual who knows his subjective utility function would also know how to realize his goals in the objective world. In economic models where material goods are the only arguments of utility function, there is no natural method to represent someone who knows his ends but not how to attain them. In Becker's model such a possibility can be formulated with very little difficulty.

Following Becker's terminology, we assume the existence of a vector of unobservable arguments of a utility function, denoted Z goods, k in number, common to all individuals across time and space.[8] These Z goods are functionally related to the vector of n observable goods located at specific addresses in time and space, X goods, by means of household production functions. The Z goods are supposed objective. For instance, health, something which might well satisfy competing conceptions of a basic good, responds in some complicated, but objective, fashion to cigarette consumption.

So formulated, the consumer's problem is to maximize $U(Z)$ subject to various constraints, i.e. time is fixed by the length of life, income to purchase market goods is scarce and knowledge of the various household production functions is costly. A household production function, here for one of the basic goods, is written as:

$$z = f(x_1, x_2, \ldots, x_n; \text{ time}; M)$$

M denotes the stock of information which the individual possesses about the production of z.

There is no novel difficulty specifying a household production function when the consumer has perfect information, we simply mimic the usual textbook production function for a firm – pausing only to note that a household will have a budget constraint. Unlike a firm with access to a capital market in which to borrow on future earnings, an individual cannot borrow using future labor as collateral. In Figure 3.1 we draw isoquants for the basic good z as a function of two observable goods x_1 and x_2. The subscripts specify the amount of z: $z_j > z_i$ if and only if $j > i$. The isoquants drawn in solid lines are convex, a fact of considerable importance in what is to follow. These isoquants are the true isoquants: the locus of all pairs of x_1 and x_2 which will generate an equal quantity of z. The budget constraint is tangent to the z_6 isoquant at a; thus, a is the least-cost method of producing z_6.

Our problem occurs when the consumer does not know what his household production function is, at least not in the detail usually supposed in neoclassical discussions of production. Start our individual at some point j interior to the budget constraint. Perhaps his income has increased and he is in the process of looking for the new equilibrium. The isoquants which he perceives are indicated by the dotted curves. The perceived z is denoted $\tilde{z}$. The convention that higher subscripts indicate larger amounts of z is also honored even when isoquants exist only in the mind.

If the individual thinks his perceptions correct and if he can perceive the budget constraints, he thinks producing at b would generate $\tilde{z}_7$, more than the $\tilde{z}_5$ which he perceives to be produced at a. Moving to b, as is allowed by the construction of his budget constraint, he discovers his mistake: with the combination at b of x_1 and x_2 he produces only z_4, less than the z_7 which he had expected.

Consider how the individual chooses when he knows that his perceptions

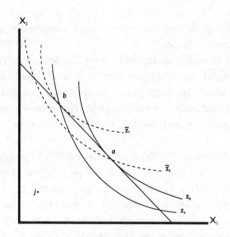

Figure 3.1 Household production of z: imperfect information

are likely to be incorrect. We allow the individual two sorts of correct perceptions. First, he perceives without error all the true household production at an infinitesimal distance of his current location and, second, he knows both that more is preferred to less and what constraints he confronts. Thus, the movement from j to b is justified even for an individual who is aware of his failings. Even though the outcome of the move will be a surprise, he will still improve his position.[9]

There are implications about choice from these limited abilities which are worthwhile noting. The most obvious is that, since zero is an infinitesimal, the individual knows his true household production at his current location. The slightly less obvious inference is that the individual can always correctly observe the slope of the household production function at his current location: the slope of the function is simply the ratio of two infinitesimals.[10]

Finally, we suppose that an individual will not move from a point in X space which he perceives correctly to a point which he neither perceives nor about which he has theoretical knowledge. This supposes an individual will not leap in the dark, but will only move between points in space where his preferences are known. Such a supposition weakens the revealed preference approach, which stipulates that an individual will not knowingly choose to move to a lower indifference curve.[11] Here, it is only assumed that an individual will not move from a to b without knowing how to compare a and b.

Some suppositions about movement in time are necessary to preclude the possibility that an individual can move over the entire space in an instant. Such speed would completely gut the limited perception assumptions of substance. Fortunately, all that is necessary is to assume that z is a continuous function of X and movement in X must take at least a positive infinitesimal amount of time.[12]

The conjunction of our assumptions with the specification that isoquants are convex gives us a very simple but important implication: whatever mistake the individual makes, there is always sufficient information to decide whether adjustments are to be made (the relative marginal products differ from relative prices) and in what direction to make these adjustments.

In terms of the literature of maximizing models, the construction above is maximizing by hill-climbing. The choosing agent does not get to an equilibrium with one jump; rather, he gropes toward one. It is pleasing to report that groping to equilibrium is something which is invariably observed in experimental studies of exchange, at least until the participants have sufficient experience to solve the puzzle quickly.[13]

If the household production functions are convex, then the local information we allow is sufficient to direct an individual toward a global cost minimum. This is the critical property of convexity in minimization problems.[14]

Under convexity of household production isoquants, the individual making mistakes will move toward the same equilibrium he would without mistakes. Moreover, the revealed preference approach holds because at each point in time the individual increases his production of z.[15] Even with convexity, mistakes are costly because the time spent at lower isoquants guarantees production forgone.

INTO MORAL DIFFICULTIES

Have we not now justified the initial skepticism about a link between perception failure and moral difficulties? In the model constructed above the perception failures do not raise moral difficulties. Indeed, there are no difficulties of any novel sort, since there is never a doubt about what is a sensible method of adjusting to error. The evidence of one's senses, local information, always tells the individual how to proceed.

This lacuna can be easily mended by simply dropping the assumption of convexity. Consider the nonconvex isoquants in Figure 3.2. Again, the individual starts at j and moves to c. This move is justified by the stipulation that more is known to be preferred to less. Once at c, the individual perceives that the efficient level of production occurs in the direction of b. This, of course, is not true, as we who see all of Figure 3.2 know, because efficient production occurs at a. However, unless the individual is guided by something other than his limited perceptions, he will move toward the local cost minimum b and not make his way to global cost minimum a.

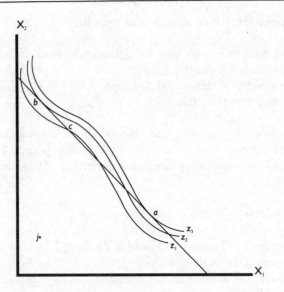

Figure 3.2 Household production of z: imperfect information and nonconvexity

Now a difficulty has been generated: with only local information, nonconvex production surfaces will not generally allow individuals to approach a global minimum. An individual with limited perceptions, who will not leap in the dark, is constrained to move continuously along the budget constraint. With these limited perceptions, how is the individual going to obtain knowledge about the existence of a? What can overcome his blindness to his own ends? Clearly, it is to the interest of an individual to find out about the existence of a, at least as long as this information does not cost much.

GREEK ADVICE

If the Greeks recognized the problem of perception failure, perhaps they found a way out of these difficulties. Indeed, it is easy to demonstrate that a problem which shares structure with the one described in Figure 3.2 was reported in very early Greek literature. The Pandora story is particularly interesting.[16] Hesiod in *Works and Days* worries about desire; indeed, he tells us that it functions as an agency for divine punishment:

'As the price of fire I will give them an evil,
   and all men shall fondle
this, their evil, close to their hearts,
   and take delight in it.'

> So spoke the father of gods and mortals;
> . . .
>
> while Aphrodite was to mist her [Pandora's] head
>   in golden endearment
> and the cruelty of desire and longings
>   that wear out the body. (57–9, 65–7)[17]

If we can overlook his misogyny, Hesiod draws a remarkable moral from the Pandora story. This is advice which makes perfect sense when one thinks about nonconvex optimization problems of the type pictured in Figure 3.2:

> Look, badness is easy to have, you can take it
>   by handfuls
> without effort. The road that way is smooth
>   and starts here beside you.
> But between us and virtue the immortals have put
>   what will make us
> sweat. The road to virtue is long
>   and goes steep up hill,
> hard climbing at first, but the last of it,
>   when you get to the summit
> (if you get there) is easy going after the hard part. (286–93)

What are we to do? Like the advice on moderation quoted above from the *Odyssey*, the oldest, pre-Socratic philosophy offers constraining rules of conduct which, unfortunately, come shorn from a context. Such imperatives as 'Know thyself' and 'Nothing too much' seem to respond constructively to the poetic distrust of unchecked desire.[18] Unfortunately, the first celebrated systematic thinker, Heraclitus (ca. 500 BCE) was also celebrated for his oracular pronouncements. However, one of the fragments is quite to the point: 'It is not better for men to obtain all that they wish' (¶110). Such fragments are so sparse that they underidentify any interpretation.[19]

Happily, there are enough fragments which survive from Democritus' writing (ca. 420 BCE) to make clear that he defends constraints in a frankly consequentialist system. 'Pleasure and absence of pleasure are the criteria of what is profitable and what is not' (¶4).[20] More than this, what we might call Democritus' utility theory is person-specific: 'For all men, good and true are the same; but pleasant differs for different men' (¶69). Perhaps this view results from his attempt to explain all sensation by the battering of a changing body by a swirling physical universe.[21]

Moderation is defended upon such consequentialist grounds as 'Moderation multiplies pleasures, and increases pleasure' (¶211). And again, 'If one oversteps the due measure, the most pleasurable things become most unpleasant' (¶233).

It is not torturing the texts to read these fragments as offering an instrumental defense of moderation; moderation is good as a means to something else; presumably, happiness or pleasure. Thus, in typical fragments, Democritus claims, 'Well-ordered behavior consists in obedience to the law, the ruler, and the man wiser [than oneself]' (¶47) and 'Medicine heals diseases of the body, wisdom frees the soul from passions' (¶31) can be read as prudential advice within a goal-directed system, possibly not all that different from modern economics.[22]

Aristotle's surviving lecture notes provide a coherent system in which constraints are defended in the context of a maximizing system. Like modern economists, Aristotle employs a goal to account for human nature. This goal is happiness and, while Aristotle distinguishes pleasure and happiness,[23] this is of no essential matter. As long as happiness is a universal goal – everyone wants to be happy – and there are impediments to happiness which activity overcomes, the structure of the argument holds.[24]

Happiness for Aristotle is clearly a function of more general considerations than the arguments in the standard economic utility function, e.g., apples, oranges, Ritz crackers and the like. While individuals in standard consumer theory have utility functions with such observable goods, Aristotle's happiness is built out of more subtle matters: honor, pleasure, intelligence and excellence.

> Now happiness above all else appears to be absolutely final in this sense, since we always choose it for its own sake and never as a means to something else; whereas honour, pleasure, intelligence, and excellence in its various forms, we choose indeed for their own sakes (since we should be glad to have each of them although no extraneous advantage resulted from it), but we also choose them for the sake of happiness, in the belief that they will be a means to our securing it.[25]

It is important to recognize that Aristotle uses the word which is translated as 'choice'[26] to mean something more than revealed preference:

> Choice is manifestly a voluntary act. But the two terms are not synonymous, the latter being the wider. Children and the lower animals as well as men are capable of voluntary action, but not of choice.[27]

Choice is distinct from unrestrained desire. An example of unrestrained desire which Aristotle cites is one of the famous cases in the *Iliad* when Zeus clouds a man's mind to make him take the worse for the better.[28] Unrestrained action is not what Aristotle means by choice:

> Also a man of defective self-restraint acts from desire but not from choice; and on the contrary a self-restrained man acts from choice and not from desire.[29]

Aristotle's definition of 'choice' is 'voluntary action preceded by deliberation', a definition he defends this way: 'choice involves reasoning and some process of thought'.[30] From this definition several results are deduced:

> Pursuit and avoidance in the sphere of Desire correspond to affirmation and denial in the sphere of the Intellect. Hence inasmuch as moral virtue is a disposition of the mind in regard to choice, and choice is deliberate desire, it follows that, if the choice is to be good, both the principle must be true and the desire right, and that desire must pursue the same things as principle affirms. We are here speaking of practical thinking, and of the attainment of truth in regard to action . . .
>
> Now the cause of action (the efficient, not the final cause) is choice, and the cause of choice is desire and reasoning directed to some end. Hence choice necessarily involves both intellect or thought and a certain disposition of character.[31]

Aristotle's analysis of pleasure is especially instructive because Aristotelian pleasure can be represented as a Beckerian basic good. That is, pleasure is an end, but it is not the end for which all other ends are instrumental. Aristotle attacks the anti-pleasure views:

> men choose what is pleasant and avoid what is painful.
>
> It would therefore seem by no means proper to omit so important a subject, especially as there is much difference of opinion about it. Some people maintain that pleasure is the Good. Others on the contrary say that it is altogether bad: some of them perhaps from a conviction that it is really so, but others because they think it to be in the interests of morality to make out that pleasure is bad.
>
> Possibly however this view is mistaken. In matters of emotion and of action, words are less convincing than deeds; when therefore our theories are at variance with palpable facts, they provoke contempt, and involve the truth in their own discredit.[32]

Stating Eudoxus' claim that pleasure is the Good, he shows that the argument only proves that pleasure is a good:

> He also said that the addition of pleasure to any good – for instance, just or temperate conduct – makes that good more desirable; but only the good can enhance the good.
>
> Now as for the last argument, it seems only to prove that pleasure is *a* good, and not that it is in any way better than any other good.[33]

Aristotle gives his own opinion:

It seems therefore that pleasure is not the Good, and that not every pleasure is desirable, but also that there are certain pleasures, superior in respect of their specific quality or their source, that are desirable in themselves.[34]

Aristotle and Democritus have indicated their acceptance of the Homeric concern about unreflective impulses. Aristotle, moreover, gives some mathematical structure to the tradition with his claim that the good is a mean between two bads: '[Virtue] is a mean state between two vices, one of excess and one of defect'.[35] This is in turn linked to his argument that the proportions of approved behavior are correct:

Virtue, therefore, is a mean state in the sense that it is able to hit the mean. Again, error is multiform (for evil is a form of the unlimited, as in the old Pythagorean imagery, and good of the limited), whereas success is possible in one way only (which is why it is easy to fail and difficult to succeed — easy to miss the target and difficult to hit it); so this is another reason why excess and deficiency are a mark of vice, and observance of the mean a mark of virtue.[36]

In summary, at least part of the Greek philosophical tradition emphasizes the difficulty of choice when desires press upon decisions.

It is hard to fight against impulse; whatever it wishes, it buys at the expense of the soul.[37]

It is hard to fight desire; but to control it is the sign of a reasonable man.[38]

Finally, Aristotle's discussion explicitly defends the traditional view that moral choice is difficult against Socrates' paradox (*Protagoras* 352) that knowledge is self-enforcing.[39] Socrates' position will be considered below.

MORAL CONSTRAINTS

Can moral information help the optimizing problem in Figure 3.2? As documented above, traditional Greek morality has the imperatives 'the good is limited' and 'nothing in excess'. Since Aristotle himself attributes this teaching to the Pythagorean school, we honor this tradition by imposing on Figure 3.3 both the details of Figure 3.2 and a 'Pythagorean cone' (P-cone) which specifies the 'moderate' combinations. Inside the cone is 'moderate'; outside is 'excess'.

This moral teaching provides what we might call a 'soft' constraint; there is no *physical* barrier to consumption outside the cone. The P-cone is provided by words carried by a theory of conduct: inside the cone is 'right' conduct; outside is 'wickedness'. The only barrier provided by this

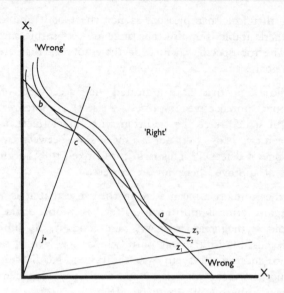

Figure 3.3 Household production of z: imperfect information and moral constraints

constraint is that of moral consciousness.[40] The moral teaching imbedded in the P-cone tells the choosing agent that the good life is to be found in obedience to this constraint.

In terms of Figure 3.3, the individual who honors the P-cone would start search at c, at the edge of what is morally permissible. Will he do better than c? For an individual with the limited perceptions allowed in the model, c appears to be the best which can be attained subject to the moral constraint. Suppose, however, the moral teaching is more than just a constraint upon choice; rather, it informs the agent that utility maximization – the good life, if you will – is found within the constraint. If the teaching is accepted as true, then c cannot be accepted as an equilibrium: it is evidently at a lower level of utility than points outside the constraint in the neighborhood of c.[41] Thus the individual who both accepts this morality and wishes to maximize utility will search for the global maximum which is hidden from his imperfect perceptions. Instead of proceeding to the local maximum at b, he will turn the other way and search in the direction of a. This is one utility-enhancing aspect of such a theory of morality: without moral information the individual has nothing with which to overcome local information.[42]

It is noteworthy that a goal-artifact with the mathematical structure of a P-cone has been proposed by Abraham Charnes and W. W. Cooper for social evaluation, quite independently of the classical discussions.[43] Like the Greek classical discussion, the Charnes–Cooper goal-artifact is not related to utility functions; indeed, it is offered as a computable substitute in cases where there is no reason to believe a utility function can be specified. The robustness of the construct will be apparent from the fact that such a goal-artifact can function when the revealed preference approach fails.

Let me consider a serious objection which can be lodged against the construction above. Have not I simply exchanged an assumption of perfect perception in the domain of household production for an assumption of a moral code which gives perfectly sharp guidance; that is, a code which splits space into two mutually exclusive areas, the 'right' and the 'wrong'? What if the code only offers vague guidance, such as 'be moderate'? Fortunately, the mathematics of vague, fuzzy objects is now tractable.[44] Suppose that our moral code gives us fuzzy guidance, that some parts of space are clearly moderate and 'right' and other parts of space are clearly immoderate and 'wrong'. However, between these regions of white and black there is a gray area. Some of the grays shade off into white, others of the grays shade off into black.

Regardless of the fuzzy areas, suppose that we must judge whether a subset of commodity space is 'right' or 'wrong'. It is a remarkable mathematical fact that, for any arbitrary fuzzy subset, it is always possible to find a nearest ordinary (i.e. sharp) subset.[45] This means that even for the fuzzy, morally ambiguous, parts of space it is always possible for an individual to make a decision whether space is closer to the 'right' or to the 'wrong'. Of course, different individuals will make different judgments about whether a particularly gray area is really white or black. Thus, moral constraints can function even in the presence of ambiguity. How well, in fact, these moral constraints function in moral ambiguity, or indeed how well, in fact, they function without ambiguity is a question which the present machinery does not treat.

HOW WE TALK ABOUT INTERTEMPORAL OPTIMIZATION

The argument above has been made in terms of objective, basic goods. Can we generalize the discussion to one which makes sense in terms of subjective, possibly changing, utility functions? Suppose, now, that utility at some point in time is a positive monotonic function of z. In terms of the encapsulated argument in Figure 3.3, the utility function, $U(\ )$, has the following order: $U(a) > U(b) > U(c)$.

The link between the machinery above and traditional moral discussion can be clarified if we explicitly draw out the intertemporal consequences of the maximizing problem in Figure 3.3, using the utility-theoretic language. We start at point c and consider moving to either point a or b. The capabilities which we grant choosing agents allow them only to tap out infinitesimal steps along the budget constraint. The trajectory with b as

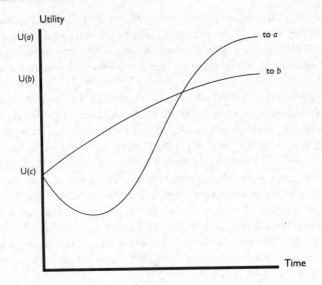

Figure 3.4   Movement in time

endpoint is self-justifying, the production of z, and thus utility, increasing monotonically with movement toward b. This self-justification is missing in the trajectory to a. The production of z, and thus utility, must fall before it can rise. The choosing agent must disregard the evidence of the senses; rather, he must trust in 'the evidence of things hoped for'. These trajectories are pictured in Figure 3.4.

The traditional discussions of the difference between the long run and the short run are now in place. Looking out from c, with a 'high' enough time preference the individual may prefer the move to b. An individual may know the 'good' but choose the pleasant. Thus, the trajectory which follows from limited perceptions and nonconvex production surfaces generates 'weakness of will' problems when interpreted in utility terms.

Our discussion of 'weakness of the will' does not start with a *normative* specification of time preference and describe as 'weak' choice which is contrary to this assumption. (Just out of curiosity, how do we know that Odysseus should not have yielded to the sirens? Or, why should Ahab not have been allowed to die of gangrene and thus been spared the pain of amputation?) Rather, we start with a description of limited perceptions and nonconvexity and generate a description of what might well be described as 'weakness of the will' for individuals with positive time preference. Hence, 'weakness of will' problems, in the limited perception approach, would seem to be restricted to nonconvex curvature. This implication might well be one which allows a limited perception model to be tested *vis-à-vis* competing explanations.[46]

A conjecture which I think to be true, but for which I cannot offer good evidence, is that the moral difficulties which come in addiction problems ultimately result from a nonconvexity in the structure of the consumption space. My friends are always 'giving up' smoking, an odd thing to do with convex isoquants. Addiction problems are central to the discussion of self-control in Thomas Schelling's work.[47]

The picture in Figure 3.4 shows that the reconstructed classical model is not generally consistent with the revealed preference approach. The individual who chooses the trajectory to *a* will *knowingly* reduce his production of *z* for a time to pursue his 'long-run' interests. Of course, one could define the revealed preference approach as holding only for trajectories, but this would trivialize it. Moreover, such a trivialization would not suffice: revealed preference would have to be defined over subjective trajectories.

The revealed preference approach restricts the consumer to movements which increase well-being. In the nonconvex case with imperfect information, this precludes the individual from seeking a global maximum which conflicts with a local maximum. The importance of global maximizing which bypasses local maxima has been stressed by Jon Elster.[48]

Suppose the moral cone is shared by the members of the community who wish to persuade one another that 'right' action ought to be done. Further suppose that this community shares a utility-maximizing theory of conduct and agrees that this utility-maximizing model can be employed for moral issues. What this requires is that a choice with a higher utility level is said to be 'rational'.[49] How would the moral conversation justify the trajectory to *a* in lieu of that to *b*? Here we work backwards from the 'result' to the justification. We know which one of these trajectories is within the 'right' part of space, so the only difficulty is finding parameters which force the 'right' answer. None the less, the rationalization for taking the trajectory toward *a* is quite another problem because all that is known is what is in Figure 3.4. Nothing is known about how far 'down' the individual must fall before going back up, nor is anything known about how far $U(a)$ exceeds $U(b)$. This rationalization would seem to be a tall order.

Necessary conditions would require the details of utility functions; however, it is easy to state two conditions which when conjoined would suffice to find the trajectory to *a* 'rational'. First, it is assumed that there is an infinite time remaining after *b* is exceeded and, second, it is assumed that there is no time discounting. These two conditions suffice to prove that, regardless of the details of the trajectories to *a* and *b*, the one to *a* is given a higher mark in utility space.[50]

The classical example of such a conversation is presented in Plato's *Protagoras* 356a–b:

And what other way is there for pleasure not to be worth pain, except that one should be more and the other less? And that is a matter of being larger and smaller, or more and fewer, or more and less intense. For if someone said, 'But, Socrates, there is a great difference between immediate pleasure and pleasure and pain at a later time,' I should say, 'Surely not in any other respect than in simply pleasure and pain; there isn't any other way they could differ.' . . . And if you weigh pleasant against painful, if the painful are outweighed by the pleasant, no matter which are nearer and more distant, you have to do whatever brings the pleasant about, and if the pleasant are outweighed by the painful, you have to avoid doing it.[51]

Socrates' argument requires that rational time preference is zero. The argument that no one knowingly acts contrary to 'interest' assumes that anyone who 'knows' that time preference is zero, and has an infinite horizon over which to maximize, will choose the trajectory to a. Hence, no one will 'rationally' choose the trajectory to b. What appears to be 'weakness of will' is simply evidence that people do not really believe in these conditions.

Historically, the importance of a belief in the 'rationality' of zero time preference and an infinite horizon has been manifest in the Platonic claim (*Laws* 885b) that only atheists are criminals. Those who 'truly' believe in the moral conversation will decline the short-term gains from criminal conduct for fear of the long-term consequences. This literature is discussed below in Chapter 14.

The need to use a utility-maximizing framework to justify choice within the 'right' cone generates what I propose to be natural morality. Natural morality is simply the long view of things. If the identification of the long view with morality came as a surprise to many readers I would suppose the model falsified. It is pleasant to know, however, that simple optimization principles suffice to generate the results.

CONCLUSION

The construction has offered an explanation of such devices as rules of 'right' conduct which Ron Heiner has stressed.[52] Unlike his argument, we stay within a standard (Beckerian variant) utility-maximizing theory of consumption; consequently, we are able to use this well-known theory to develop some interesting implications. Our novel result is an ability to identify traditional moral problems with curvature properties of consumption space. This equivalence allows a sharp implication about what commodities and situations are likely to present moral difficulties. We demonstrate why common morality will disapprove of 'short-run' considerations.

The construction gives reason to believe that moral discourse will have a constant core. While it is important to acknowledge real differences among different moral philosophers,[53] there is reason to believe that a class of consumption problems will draw a unique moral reaction. This, in turn, raises an interesting problem for normative economics: do we base our evaluations on what people do or on what they say they ought to do? Welfare economics gives reason to take people's revealed choices as data. Welfare economists, however, often find reason to employ zero time preference as a benchmark from which to evaluate choice. If the argument above is correct, this is simply common morality invading technical economics.

Chapter 4

Ethics and the basis of logic

Adam Smith's 'Fallacy'

It will not have escaped the attentive reader that an eccentric claim advanced in the introduction – the assertion that 'false' theory can assist maximizing problems – was not defended in the opening chapters. In the description of utility-enhancing consumption constraints, it was explicitly supposed that the global-maximizing solution is encompassed by the moral constraints. Hence, this ethical theory is a 'true' description of what is to be maximized. Even if a 'false' theory of conduct were turned up, how do ordinary people come to accept it? If we are willing to waive the considerations of risk or uncertainty, doesn't acceptance of a theory require a belief that the theory is 'true'?

In fact, I shall argue that, in the case we consider, not only is it not the case that acceptance requires 'truth', but an important type of 'truth' can be *defined* by acceptance. In keeping with the antiquity of my enterprise, it is well to consider a very early attempt to explain our judgments by appeal to a sharing of experience. It was Adam Smith who said this:

> To approve of another man's opinions is to adopt those opinions, and to adopt them is to approve of them. If the same arguments which convince you convince me likewise, I necessarily approve of your conviction; and if they do not, I necessarily disapprove of it; neither can I possibly conceive that I should do the one without the other. To approve or disapprove, therefore, of the opinions of others is acknowledged, by every body, to mean no more than to observe their agreement or disagreement with our own. But this is equally the case with regard to our approbation or disapprobation of the sentiments or passions of others. . . .
>
> Every faculty in one man is the measure by which he judges of the like faculty in another. I judge of your sight by my sight, of your ear by my ear, of your reason by my reason, of your resentment by my resentment, of your love by my love. I neither have, nor can have, any other way of judging about them.[1]

Smith used this principle in his memorial for David Hume. Here is Smith's evaluation of future evaluations of Hume:

> Thus died our most excellent, and never to be forgotten friend; concerning whose philosophical opinions men will, no doubt, judge variously, every one approving or condemning them, according as they happen to coincide or disagree with his own; but concerning whose character and conduct there can scarce be a difference of opinion.[2]

Smith's approach received a crushing blow from Arthur Prior, who wrote in 1949 (the date is worthy of note) that acceptance of matters of fact is surely based in the supposition of truth:

> Plainly, many would say, because to make an opinion 'our own' is to regard it as true, i.e. as a perception or representation of a fact beyond the opinion itself; and it is because of the supposed accordance of another man's opinion with this fact, rather than because of its known accordance with our own opinion, that we approve of it, i.e. consider it true.[3]

From this it is an easy inference that Smith is confused. His principle of acceptance cannot be correct because matters of fact differ from matters of ethics:

> We can always envisage the possibility that although we consider the other man's opinion to be true, it may not be so in fact, because our own may not be so either. The coincidence of another man's opinion with ours we take to be a sign of its truth, but we do not identify this coincidence with its truth. On the other hand, Smith does identify the 'propriety' of another man's feeling with its coincidence with our own. The supposed analogy between propriety and the truth of an opinion therefore disappears.[4]

Prior does not think that Smith is ultimately to blame, for the root fallacy is in a 'ridiculous theory' propounded by Hume:

> A belief or opinion, i.e. a judgement, is simply a conception or idea which happens to have greater 'force and vivacity' than fictitious ones; and a completely certain belief, e.g., the belief that I am having a certain feeling, would on this view be identical with what Hume calls an 'impression,' in this case with the feeling that I am having. No doubt Hume's formal adherence to this ridiculous theory accounts for his indifference to the distinction between the feeling of approval and the judgement that we have a feeling . . .[5]

But perhaps there is a way out. Indeed, a difficulty with Prior's criticism is hinted at by Hao Wang, who prefaces his discussion of Kurt Gödel's philosophy with this evaluation of evaluations:

There are two different questions: (1) What are Gödel's philosophical views? (2) To what extent are these views 'true'? For any person A, an answer to these questions of course depends very much on the data available to A and on A's own views. In practice, (2) is likely to be weakened to (2') To what extent does A agree with G?[6]

Even though Hume and Gödel have roughly equivalent status as logicians (akin in my opinion to Lord Monboddo's dæmons), the resemblance of Smith's metaevaluation of Hume and Wang's metaevaluation of Gödel is almost too close to be accidental. How could this be? What has happened, I shall argue next, is that the mid-twentieth century marked an explosion in research on the foundations of mathematical logic matching in importance Hume's demolition of the pretensions of inductive logic. We who have inherited these results are now able to free ourselves from a premature intellectual straitjacket and look back at the freewheeling Scottish discussion with a more open mind about logic and ethics. To this we now turn.

THE CHOICE OF LOGIC

We bring back Mandeville's Paradox to the fore. How is it possible that admittedly 'false' theories can be relevant? Does not the demonstration that theory is nondescriptive simultaneously show it to be irrelevant? Here is how the question shall be posed. When the rational choice 'prediction' inside a goal-constraint model is compared with the observed action, what conclusion is drawn?

We allow two possible conclusions to be drawn from a match of prediction and reality. If the prediction matches the observation, is the choice said to be 'right', or is the theory said to be 'true'? If the prediction diverges from the observation, is the choice said to be 'wrong', or is the theory said to be 'false'? What determines which direction the assignment of praise or blame takes?

By opening the possibility of this valuational ambiguity, we encounter a nest of controversies which have occupied many philosophers in the middle third of this century. We confront, in a very real sense, the possibility that the distinction between matters of fact and matters of logic is determined by the usage of a language community.[7] On first glance, this possibility seems simply absurd. In my logic courses at Berkeley a claim by Ludwig Wittgenstein still echoed:

It is the peculiar mark of logical propositions that one can recognize that they are true from the symbol alone, and this fact contains in itself the whole philosophy of logic. And so too it is a very important fact that the truth or falsity of non-logical propositions *cannot* be recognized from the propositions alone.[8]

This proposition became one mark of spiritual membership in the Vienna Circle, for it served, to pick one example of many, to refute Immanuel Kant's claim that some sentences of synthetic form could be known true by *a priori* considerations.[9] Hence, Wittgenstein's popularization of the method of truth-tables as a mechanical method for distinguishing between logical and factual statements takes on considerable importance.

But does Wittgenstein's method really solve the problem of how people actually use language? Let us follow up a 'pragmatic'[10] suggestion from C. I. Lewis that the distinction between fact and logic depends upon how the speakers of a language use the language:

> The dividing line between the *a priori* and the *a posteriori* is that between principles and definite concepts which *can* be maintained in the face of all experience and those genuinely empirical generalizations which *might* be proven flatly false.[11]

Let us take the sentence 'All swans are white' as a test case. Even when the number of things in the world is finite, so we could seemingly test the swan sentence by exhaustive enumeration, it is obvious that this sentence cannot be proven 'true' by the usual logical devices; hence, on the Wittgenstein test, it is empirical. On the older test – is it possible to conceive of a non-white swan? – it is also plausible that this sentence is empirical. Not only is it possible to conceive of a world with off-white swans, the National Zoo, five miles from where I write this, features black birds which are remarkably swanlike.[12]

None the less, just how do we prevent the people who admit seeing a black 'swan-like' bird from concluding that it is an 'elongated raven'? Ravens, we all know, are black. Unless we are ready to assume the existence of an infinitely capable swan police, we cannot force people to see things 'our' way.[13] It seems now to be agreed by all sides that 'black swans' could be transformed into 'elongated ravens' and so the sentence 'All swans are white' can become logically true, from a pragmatic point of view of logic, in some language community.[14]

The modern philosophical literature generally attributes an aspect of this pragmatic thesis to Pierre Duhem for his argument that, by choosing what parts of a theoretical system to give up when confronted with experimental failure, pieces of a theoretical system could be saved from falsification.[15] The full-dress thesis that the distinction between matters of fact and logic are relative to a language, or, in our terms, the 'laws of logic' are endogenous, is made in W. V. Quine's 'Two Dogmas of Empiricism', to which the philosophical literature usually assigns priority.[16]

However, to put the issues in a semblance of historical context, before Quine's decisive objections were launched, some associated with the Vienna Circle attempted to defend Wittgenstein's position against Alfred Tarski's skepticism about the possibility of distinguishing sharply between matters of fact and matters of logic. Here is Tarski's conjecture:

> Underlying our whole construction is the division of all terms of the language discussed into logical and extra-logical. This division is certainly not quite arbitrary. . . . On the other hand, no objective grounds are known to me which permit us to draw a sharp boundary between the two groups of terms. It seems to be possible to include among logical terms some which are usually regarded by logicians as extra-logical without running into consequences which stand in sharp contrast with ordinary usage. . . .
>
> In order to see the importance of this problem for certain general philosophical views it suffices to note that the division of terms into logical and extra-logical also plays an essential part in clarifying the concept 'analytical'. But according to many logicians this last concept is to be regarded as the exact formal correlate of the concept of *tautology* (i.e. of a statement which 'says nothing about reality'), a concept which to me personally seems rather vague, but which has been of fundamental importance for the philosophical discussions of L. Wittgenstein and the whole Vienna Circle.
>
> Further research will doubtless greatly clarify the problem which interests us. Perhaps it will be possible to find important objective arguments which will enable us to justify the traditional boundary between logical and extra-logical expressions. But I also consider it to be quite possible that investigations will bring no positive results in this direction, so that we shall be compelled to regard such concepts as 'logical consequence', 'analytical statement', and 'tautology' as relative concepts which must, on each occasion, be related to a definite, although in greater or less degree arbitrary, division of terms into logical and extra-logical. [17]

Even earlier, Frank Ramsey reached pragmatic conclusions in his arguments with Wittgenstein. [18]

It will be noted that the names associated with the pragmatic position include many of the century's greatest logicians: Lewis, Ramsey, Tarski and Quine. This economist did not catch the point until more colorful versions of the pragmatic position were offered by Thomas Kuhn and Imre Lakatos. The sentences which are empirical on the Wittgenstein test, but are employed as matters of logic, are called 'paradigms' by Kuhn and 'hard core' by Lakatos. The relation of obligation between the later versions of the pragmatic point of view and the earlier ones is very confusing. [20]

The pragmatic thesis holds that we cannot, *a priori*, split theoretical systems into two mutually exclusive boxes, one labelled 'logic employed' and one labelled 'facts stipulated', on the basis of the *form* of the sentence. Rather, to make this distinction, it is absolutely necessary to consider the means by which theoretical language was employed to tackle the problems of the day.

The glorious aspect of the Wittgenstein thesis, that there is a *mechanical* method for proving whether or not a sentence is a matter of logic or fact, seems lost in the pragmatic view. What can be offered as evidence for the claim that a sentence is used as a matter of logic?

Let us consider the fact/logic problem as a matter of decision. Making the choice of logic an aspect of the logic of choice is the hard core of the pragmatic thesis. To make the choice mechanical, we suppose that a flow-chart can be constructed to specify the decision rules. Start with our sentence, 'All swans are white', and evidence which may or may not bear upon it. In particular, a black 'swan' is reported. The decision which must be made is whether or not the reported 'swan' is the sort of thing about which the sentence speaks. By this choice, the sentence can be either logically 'true' or empirically 'false'. When we know this decision, we know where the blame falls. If 'All swans are white' is logically true, then the black 'swan' is defective. Perhaps the reporter cannot tell swans from ravens. If the black 'swan' is really a swan then the sentence 'All swans are white' is defective. It is 'false'.

In Figure 4.1 we draw a picture to mechanize the logic of decision by which sentences may become matters of logic. The diamond decision box in the traditional flow-chart has been replaced by something gray and elliptical. To put it in a crystalline form would be to deny the ambiguity inherent in a situation with real opportunity cost.

Where there is choice, there are economic considerations. Which path will be taken? This pragmatic test, I believe, illustrates the status of the maximizing postulate in much of modern economics. It is easy to move the utility-maximizing hypothesis from the 'fact' to the 'logic' box. After we predict that people with ends we think to be A and means we think to be B will choose C, but we observe not C, then we may very well reject our description of ends A or means B, but many of us still continue to accept the postulate that individuals maximize.[21] Therefore, the maximizing postulate may not be hostage to the state of the world; it may be safe in a logic box. We may presuppose the maximizing principle; we need not discover it in the world.

This is, I believe, the appropriate context in which to view Milton Friedman's willingness to work with 'unrealistic' assumptions. Relative to the Chicago language community, these assumptions are *de facto* matters of logic. Fortunately, I need not belabor this reading of Friedman's work; a better defense for it than I can muster is now available.[22]

ETHICAL IMPERATIVES ARE *DE FACTO* LOGICAL

To demonstrate the pragmatic equivalence of matters of logic and moral guidance, all we need show is that normative theories pass the pragmatic test proposed above for matters of logic. Consider the imperative 'Murder is

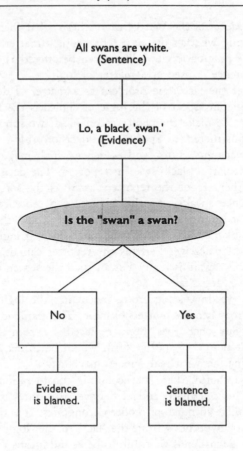

Figure 4.1   A pragmatic test for logical truth

irrational'. We observe murder; what conclusion do we draw? If we hold fast to the theory, it is a norm; otherwise, it is empirical. Do we blame the theory (it is said to be 'false') or do we blame the reality (the murderer is said to be 'irrational')? See Figure 4.2.

Thus, the simple pragmatic test which distinguishes matters of logic and fact also distinguishes normative sentences from empirical sentences.[23] It does not matter whether we use old fashioned words like 'wicked', or words with less emotional content like 'rational'. The question is, where is the blame laid? Is the sentence at fault or is the murderer at fault? The logic of the enterprise is invariant to labels.

We have one decision operation: approbation. We can approve of theory – it is said to be 'true'. We can approve of behavior – it is said to be 'right'. Approbation is the link between language and choice which I find

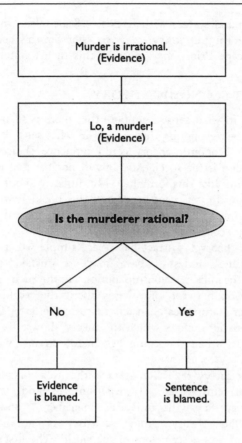

Figure 4.2   The logical structure of norms

central to this project. We shall ask below whether it is a link strong enough to hold the social world together.

SMITH AND PRIOR'S ANALYTICS

If ethical imperatives have the same algorithmic structure as pragmatic laws of logic then it is easy for Smith to escape Prior's criticism. With an ethical imperative there is no doubt about its 'truth'. Regardless of what the world turns up, we will hold fast to it. We consider ethical imperatives *de facto* logical, so they hold in all states of the world. Thus, in Prior's reformulation of Smith there is no difference between acceptance of facts and imperatives of this absolutist variety.

This is a formal justification for my previous impressionistic identification of Smith's moral system with Kant's.[24] Kant takes ethical imperatives as synthetic in form but known *a priori*. For Smith's account of theory acceptance to escape Prior, they must be this in his system too.

AN ABSTRACT ECONOMIC THEORY

Now, I consider in what sense I suppose that there is such a mathematical entity as an abstract economic theory, and in what sense I suppose that an ordinary person's economic theory could influence choice without being 'true'. This exercise is for specialists. It will not be used elsewhere in the book with anything like this formality. My thinking about the operation of approbation surely directs many aspects of this book; I would like to play this particular game with all my cards face up. The most direct explicit use of the machinery occurs in Chapter 18.

The economic theory I abstract has a very simple structure. Indeed, the only novel features, unless I have made a mistake somewhere, are employment of the nice relationship notion employed in model theory,[25] and the distinction between our words about the world and the world itself. The former feature neatens the structure; the latter feature allows us to describe various judgments which the theory allows. By this abstraction we can keep tabs, when the going gets hard, on just what it is we are proving.

Our economic theory takes for granted the usual first-order logic. The symbols we shall employ are $\neg$ (negation), & (and), $\Rightarrow$ (implication) and the two quantifiers, the universal quantifier $\forall$ and the existential quantifier $\exists$. The theory proper consists of an ordered pair of primitive relations and descriptions of the world. The first of the primitive relationships is a two-place utility relation $U(\ ,\ )$; the second is a one-place feasibility relation $F(\ )$. A one-place relation has one blank to fill; a two-place relation has two blanks, separated by a comma, to fill. The informal details of the economic theory will manifest themselves when the possible states of the world, $a, b, c, \ldots, x, y \ldots$, fill in the blanks in the relation symbols.

These symbols are the words in our formal language which we use to talk about the world, they are not the world itself. $F(x)$ holds (or is true) in the case that state of the world x is feasible. (Obviously, one can move between $F(\ )$ as a relation and F as a set because $F(x)$ holds just in case $x \in F$.) $U(x, y)$ holds in the case that, in terms of some order, x is given a higher mark than y. We call an ordered pair $\langle U, F \rangle$ an economic theory E.

To bring approbation into the account we must distinguish very sharply the world from sentences about the world. This is an old, difficult problem:

In order to apply the theory to real phenomena, we need some rules for establishing the correspondence between the idealized objects of the theory and those of the real world. These rules will always be somewhat vague and can never form a part of the theory itself.[26]

The world itself is marked by a star; thus, a^*, b^*, c^*, . . . , x^*, y^* . . . are the objective correlatives of a, b, c, . . . x, y. All we can do with the world is to affirm or deny, but that is enough. If x^* then x is the case. Similarly, if not x^* then x is not the case.

In many cases which we consider, we do not suppose that there is anything in the world which corresponds with our relation symbols; they are only in our books and on our chalkboards. We only observe states of the world, not states of mind. But, if objective correlatives to $U(\ ,\ )$ or $F(\ )$ need not exist, how do we compare the words or pictures on chalkboards with the world? If the objective correlatives *did* exist it would be straightforward to test the maximizing hypothesis.[27] However, as we cannot count on this evidence, we might use a maximizing postulate to make sense of the world.

The maximizing postulate, which we abbreviate as $E \rightarrow x$, forces E to point to x in the following sense:

$$E \rightarrow x \text{ iff } \exists(x)\ (F(x)\ \&\ \forall(y)\ (U(y,x) \Rightarrow \neg\ F(y)))$$

Our ability to distinguish the world and our words about the world let us state what we require for a true theorem in E in which we have $E \rightarrow x$

E is true iff x^*
E is false iff not x^*

In this positive context, we might say that E predicts x. In this formulation, we judge an economic theory as a whole by its encounter with a piece of the world. Thus, we can imbed our theory of choice within a Quinean metatheory of scientific discourse.[28]

'True' and 'false' are words which we use to judge our theory in the light of reality. This is one use of the approbation operator. Here, we approve or disapprove of the theories by the standard of the world. But they are not the only judgment possible. We can judge the world by the shadows cast by our theory. By treating an economic theory as a collection of symbols employed to talk about the world, we can easily conceive of another use of these words.

x^* is right iff E
x^* is wrong iff not E

In this account 'right' and 'wrong' are words we use to judge reality in the light of theory. The operation of approbation now judges our reality in the light of theory.

In Chapter 18 we shall ask an impertinent question. What results from a decision process which rejects all theories as 'false' that do not correspond to reality? The short answer, I would think, is one gets a 'science'. What then happens when one wishes to employ that 'scientific' theory to judge reality? Haven't we, by ruling out all noncorresponding theory, forced reality to be 'right'? On one reading of his doctrine, it would be fair to call this Spinoza's Paradox. The thesis of Chapter 18 is that what you do not study can very well make a difference. If we have not attended to the malleability of approbation, we may well not understand what it is we prove. We also may fail to understand why 'false' theory might be useful.

One goal of the economic approach to ideas is to determine the context in which ordinary people will judge a consumption activity to be 'wrong'. The argument above has been to look for this judgment in the case of nonconvexity of consumption space.

Now, we can see what is required for trade to be influenced by language. Our theory of choice must modify either our goals or what we take to be feasible. Suppose we, observing economists, have a theory E concerning some agent who may or may not possess a theory. The theory of the choosing agent is denoted E^*. To make theory-directed choice interesting, E^* must make a difference. Thus, E, applied in such a case when E^* is accepted ($E|E^*$ for short), differs from E when this E^* is not accepted.

The linkage between theory and choice I wish to argue for is that people's goals include a desire for approbation. Since some forms of approbation are carried by language — at least the argument above demonstrates how one can get approbation out of language — then the exercise becomes a matter of details.

Notice the consequence. If approbation is carried by language or theory, then we really cannot test an account of theory-directed choice without knowing what the theory is. What counts is the theory of the agent, not the theory which some outside observer thinks the agent should have. The latter, perhaps not surprisingly, often turns out to be the same theory as the outside observer accepts. Smith's principle of acceptance surely explains this comfortable confusion!

It is vital to my account that it does not matter in the least whether E^* corresponds to what the agent does. What matters is the question: does the acceptance of the theory change the agent's choice? This position, as we shall see, is rather controversial.

For example, if an agent has a theory of choice which says that it is 'wrong' to grab, and we have constrained ourselves, now and again, to obviate the cost of 'wrongful' action, then a theory of choice which predicts that trade will occur is 'true'. Trade does occur. But, in this account, it would not occur unless the agent thought it to be 'right'. If our normative theory can modify reality, then our normative theory can switch the truth values of positive theory.

Let us now consider the issue of trade and property within this notation. Property rights decompose $F(x)$, that which is technically feasible. If individual i 'owns' x then we can say that $F_i(x)$ holds. Thus, individual i can truly say that 'x is mine'. If i does not 'own' x then $F_i(x)$ does not hold. We allow each individual to say 'x is mine' in the case of common property.

Let x be the whole of the world over which individuals 1 and 2 have ownership rights. 1 owns x_1 and 2 owns x_2 such that x is exhausted. We write down the exhaustion condition – everything feasible is 'owned' – as the union of individual rights:

$$F_1(x) \cup F_2(x) = F(x)$$

We assume that this is a requirement for all theories of property. There are two interesting cases in the Humean theory of property which we can write down immediately. The first is the case of pure private property where what is mine is not yours. This gives us a mutually exclusive claim to characterize private property:

$$F_1(x) \cap F_2(x) = \varnothing$$

The second case is that of pure common ownership:

$$F_1(x) \cap F_2(x) = F(x)$$

What is mine is also yours.

Let us start the trading problem with individual 1 owning x_1 and individual 2 owning x_2. These pieces are supposed to exhaustively decompose x so $x = x_1 \cup x_2$ and $x_1 \cap x_2 = \varnothing$. Thus, we know that $F_1(x_1)$ and $F_2(x_2)$ hold prior to exchange. To satisfy the maximizing postulate for both individuals, we must know (first) that $U_1(x_2,x_1)$ and $U_2(x_1,x_2)$ hold and (second) that the exchanged commodity bundles are not infeasible. Thus, $F_1(x_2)$ and $F_2(x_1)$ must hold after exchange. If we cannot slice the physical universe into spheres of 'right' then we cannot apply the maximizing principle in the case of trade precisely because we have not precluded $F_i(x)$ for either $i = 1, 2$. With one individual such a slicing is trivial; it gets more interesting when there is more than one individual.

What happens when ordinary people desire approbation from their own theories? Can the words from theory make a difference to behavior? Can approbation from a theory of conduct preclude $F_i(x)$? This is what has to be argued for below.

Part III

The supply of ideas

If we are to seek the role of economic ideas in the life of ordinary people in such hard optimizing contexts as we have argued for above, then it is obvious that people cannot obtain ideas fully informed about the consequence of these ideas. This limited information opens the door to exploitation by the providers of such ideas. What constrains those who provide moral information to do so for the benefit of ordinary people and not solely for their own?

As a matter of historical record, Thomas Hobbes argued that one could trace the origin of the English civil war to the ability of priests to cloud the minds of men, to hide their true interests from them by vain promises of Heaven or Hell. Hobbes also argued that men were not influenced by words, *per se*, only by those words which are tokens for the threat of pleasure or pain.

It is in this context I believe that one should read the Scottish discussion of the linkage among individual morality, property and social behavior. The Scots were persuaded that words like 'right' and 'wrong' mattered for choice even when they were unconnected to promises of pleasure and pain. Words themselves carry pleasure and pain. It should be apparent that I write in this tradition. They debated amongst themselves about the merits of competition in the market for the provision of moral information. David Hume took Hobbes's side against competition in morality whereas Adam Smith defended a competitive market in religion.

The first chapter provides a general overview of the debate, pointing to several issues and solving none. The next two chapters discuss the special issues of competition in religion and the origin and stability of property. We discover how often the Scots discussed prisoner's dilemma issues. No, the Scots did not think that words suffice; they understood something about institutions and material incentives. They did come to believe that words of judgment are necessary inputs into the social order.

Chapter 5

Adam Smith's 'natural law' and contractual society

INTRODUCTION

The problem to which I address myself is reconstructing Adam Smith's argument that a free and pleasant society might be feasible.[1] This requires that we pay attention to the British criticisms of Thomas Hobbes's claim that a free society is, of necessity, a state of war.[2] In particular, it is necessary to read with some care David Hume's *Treatise of Human Nature*, in which the theologically encrusted concept of natural law was reformulated to mean the content of the ethical imperatives which would be observed in social equilibrium.[3] We must consider both Adam Smith's *Theory of Moral Sentiments* and *Wealth of Nations* because, as I read Smith's result, the maintenance of a free and pleasant society requires a subtle redirection of self-interested choice by ethical judgment.

I accept as the central challenge to any study of the interaction of judgment and choice Frank Knight's position that, unless moral judgment changes the preferences of individuals, ethics cannot be considered as a guide to action. That is to say, if preferences are given with respect to any problem, all that remains is a maximization of utility subject to the constraint of resources and knowledge, i.e., prudence.[4] Therefore, I consider Smith's position, in both the *Theory of Moral Sentiments* and the *Wealth of Nations*, that the formation of individuals' characters as expressed through their choice and judgment must be explained in a discussion of social evolution.[5]

HOBBES'S CHALLENGE

In a 'state of nature', in Hobbes's argument, it is to each individual's interest, when there is no possible retaliation, to rob or take advantage of his neighbors; therefore, in a 'state of nature' in which all are limited only by their own strength and cunning:

> every man is Enemy to every man . . . men live without other security,

than what their own strength, and their own invention shall furnish them withall. In such condition, there is no place for Industry; because the fruit thereof is uncertain: and consequently no Culture of the Earth; no Navigation . . . no Arts; no Letters; no Society; and which is worst of all, continuall feare, and danger of violent death; And the life of man, solitary, poore, nasty, brutish, and short.[6]

Hobbes is exploiting what has come to be known in game theory as the 'prisoner's dilemma', that state of affairs in which an individual's maximizing of his own utility does not seem to lead to maximizing results for the group. Part of what makes Hobbes's challenge so intriguing is that he fully realized that the imperatives entailed by the law of nature obligated men not to try to rob their neighbors:[7] 'This is [also] that Law of the Gospell; *Whatsoever you require that others should do to you, that do ye to them.*'[8]

Indeed, if individuals maximized utility on the expectation that their actions would be replicated by their neighbors, the society would not be troubled by the prisoner's dilemma, since individuals maximizing their utility would lead to an efficient decision for the group. Hobbes's claim that moral judgment, of the sort codified in the law of nature, has no effect upon our action is at the heart of his argument:

The finall Cause, End, or Designe of men, (who naturally love Liberty, and Dominion over other,) in the introduction of that restraint upon themselves, (in which wee see them live in Common-wealths,) is the foresight of their own preservation, and of a more contented life thereby; that is to say, of getting themselves out from that miserable condition of Warre, which is necessarily consequent . . . to the naturall Passions of men, when there is no visible Power to keep them in awe, and tye them by feare of punishment to the performance of their Covenants, and observation of those Lawes of Nature . . .

For the Lawes of Nature (as *Justice, Equity, Modesty, Mercy,* and (in summe) *doing to others, as wee would be done to,*) of themselves, without the terrour of some Power, to cause them to be observed, are contrary to our naturall Passions. . . . And Covenants, without the Sword, are but Words, and of no strength to secure a man at all.[9]

The laws of nature are in Hobbes's argument outside the social order; they are foundations of the ethics which individuals ought to have. The ethics they do actually follow are generally a reflection of their passions: men call things they desire 'good' and what they fear 'evil'.[10]

Although the laws of nature, 'words without swords', have no impact upon the actions of men, religion, which is in origin a fear of invisible powers, has an effect upon the actions of men.[11] Men may fear Hell more than they fear the state; consequently, Hobbes (who is quite conscious in

Leviathan that he is writing civil theology)[12] takes it upon himself to prove that there is no threat from God in the afterlife.[13] Indeed, he proves to his own satisfaction that a soul does not exist separately from the body:

> But to what purpose (may some man say) is such subtility in a work of this nature, . . . It is to this purpose, that men may no longer suffer themselves to be abused, by them . . . [that] would fright them from Obeying the Laws of their Countrey, with empty names; . . . Or who will not obey a Priest, that can make God, rather than his Soveraign; nay than God himselfe? . . . And this shall suffice for an example of the Errors, which are brought into the Church, from the *Entities*, and *Essences* of Aristotle . . .[14]

Hence it is that Hobbes finds the source of civil war in the doctrines of religion: priests fool the multitude into thinking they possess the power over men's future happiness.[15] Originally religion was the handmaiden of the state; now it is corrupt, i.e., free from the state, and it darkens the understanding of men to take away their knowledge of their true interests.[16]

It is, I think, a serious misreading of Hobbes to see in his argument simply an objection to anarchism. The argument that men are not ruled by words but only by swords culminates in Hobbes's rejection of the concept of the rule of law. Hobbes claims that government does not exist by law alone, since the enforcement of the law in all political states must be done by men. No man believes that the written law *per se* can hurt him; hence, when he must obey the law, it is out of a fear of punishment by men.[17] It was and is the doctrine of those like Adam Smith who defend the rule of law that men obey positive law partly because it reflects their commonly accepted morality.[18]

RESPONSE TO HOBBES

Hobbes's attempt to explain the behavior of men by the drive of their passions[19] is at best hard to reconcile with his assertion that religions manipulate men by lies.[20] There is no difficulty in explaining why certain individuals would lie; the difficulty is to explain why others so often accept the lies. This flaw in Hobbes's argument was detected by Bernard Mandeville, who contended that even though designing priests and other impostors invented lies and fables for their own advantage, no one would have accepted them if these fables did not remedy some want of understanding. Mandeville's program attempts to locate the origin of institutions in their social benefit to frail human nature:

> When I have a Mind to dive into the Origin of any Maxim or political Invention, for the Use of Society in general, . . . I go directly to the

Fountain Head, human Nature itself, and look for the Frailty or Defect in Man, that is remedy'd or supply'd by that Invention.[21]

Mandeville follows Hobbes in distinguishing between moralities originating inside and outside the social order. Mandeville accepts the truth of Christian revelation, if only for the sake of the argument; he reads the revelation as the promise that, if men renounce their passions, they will attain infinite bliss.[22] Our Christianity influences only the words we use in moral judgment, of ourselves as well as of others; it does not influence our actions.[23] The religions of the world preach a morality adapted to the world, a morality which serves to channel the passions of men into socially beneficial conduct. By praise men are induced to trade their natural passions for socially approved passions.[24]

Mandeville concludes that an evolved ethical code is a convention which evolved to mend defects in human nature, that is, to channel our anti-social passions into harmonious social conduct. A moral code which is not a channeling of passions but a renunciation of passions, even when true and enforced by God, may be safely ignored when we wish to explain human action.[25]

Mandeville's analysis was not able to trace the evolution of particular ethical imperatives from particular social conditions. It is one thing to say that moral codes evolve for socially beneficial purposes, it is another to say what imperatives the codes will or will not contain.

This defect was to a large extent remedied in David Hume's argument that justice, narrowly defined, is sufficient and, for nonbenevolent men outside the case of abundance, necessary to the existence of a stable social order.[26] Hume accepts Hobbes's statement of the problem:

'tis certain, that self-love, when it acts at its liberty, instead of engaging us to honest actions, is the source of all injustice and violence; nor can a man ever correct those vices, without correcting and restraining the *natural* movements of that appetite.[27]

Hume also denies that general benevolence influences our actions;[28] however, what may influence our actions is the notion of justice, which Hume considers a non-arbitrary law of human nature:

Tho' the rules of justice be *artificial* they are not *arbitrary*. Nor is the expression improper to call them *Laws of Nature*; if by natural we understand what is common to any species, or even if we confine it to mean what is inseparable from the species.[29]

To act justly is to honor contracts and to respect the property of others.[30] Justice is a social convention which Hume sees as a relatively complicated calculation which must be learned:[31] the individual learns that it is to his own interest to respect the property of another, provided that this respect is reciprocated.[32] Once learned, justice is done because each individual finds it to his interest:

> And even every individual person must find himself a gainer, on ballancing the account; since, without justice, society must immediately dissolve, and every one must fall into that savage and solitary condition, which is infinitely worse than the worst situation that can possibly be suppos'd in society.[33]

It is clear that Hume has extended the Mandevillian program by constructing the content of an ethical system endogenous to human society. He accepted as fact that politicians cannot alter at will the fundamental passions of human nature; they can only redirect to more socially desired directions the means chosen to effect these ends.[34]

Hume's leap from self-interest to conventional justice is patently questionable. Even if we grant Hume that an individual's act of injustice may lead to the eventual destruction of society, and even if we add to Hume's premise the supposition that the individual who is unjust will live forever in a wretched state of affairs, it does not follow that an individual who is being unjust will act against his own interests.[35] If the individual prefers a 'smaller' immediate gratification to a 'larger' future gratification, then the individual's gains from injustice may well exceed the costs to him resulting from the destruction of society.[36] Hume did not succeed in integrating religion into his scheme of social evolution: religion as a demonstrable doctrine fell short of conviction,[37] and as a social force it was productive of social unrest.[38]

Hume does make what is perhaps the decisive criticism of Mandeville's argument that men are influenced only by their passions and the redirection of them by politicians. If the artifice of politicians were the sole basis of distinction between virtue and vice, why do statesmen use words like 'honor' and 'dishonor'? Without some natural sentiments to which such words correspond, their meaning would be perfectly unintelligible.[39] Consequently, Hume treats the moral sense as independent of the passions at the foundation of his discussion. And this was, I believe, the state of the art when Smith wrote.

SMITH'S CONTRIBUTION

Smith argues that the moral sense was formed by Providence, just as it had created the instincts of sex, self-preservation and the propensity to truck and barter.[40] It is, I think, useful simply to follow the argument, assuming the moral sense as independent of the passions.

The separation of moral sentiment from utility allows Smith to state the problem of the impact of moral judgment on choice in stark relief. Individuals in Smith's analysis do not much worry over the fate of others.

His famous account of the effect of an earthquake in China on a 'man of humanity' in Europe is sufficient supportive evidence.[41] Regardless of this unconcern, no one would decline to trade a little finger to save all of China:

> To prevent, therefore, this paultry misfortune to himself would a man of humanity be willing to sacrifice the lives of a hundred millions of his brethren, provided he had never seen them? Human nature startles with horror at the thought, and the world, in its greatest depravity and corruption, never produced such a villain . . . But what makes this difference? When our passive feelings are almost always so sordid and so selfish, how comes it that our active principles should often be so generous . . .[42]

Smith's sympathetic principle is a remarkably supple device which is used to explain how we come to judge the fortunes and actions of others. In Smith's account, we neither exchange passions, nor enter the mind of others. Rather, we exchange situations preserving our present passions; thus, sympathy makes eccentric judgments. For example, we can feel remorse for the dead and compassion for the insane even though we have no reason to believe that they are unhappy.[43] The sympathetic principle leads to grossly anti-social behavior in the presence of individuals of rank, since we are led to misestimate their worth and submit to them when we should resist them.[44] While it has been asserted that Smith's treatment contains no testable implications,[45] none the less, the operation of the sympathetic principle predicts that the political process will be paternalistic in such cases as self-induced madness.[46] We do not judge others on a revealed preference basis.

Smith's main construction is the account of the process by which respect for justice – the negative virtue of not doing to others the things which we would not wish to be done to us[47] – enters our passions. It is important to note that Smith accepts Hume's argument that social utility is sufficient to explain our respect for justice. The preservation of society requires the tolerable observation of the laws of justice; indeed, we frequently reinforce our natural approval of punishment by reflecting on the necessity for preserving society.[48] However, Smith claims that utility is not necessary in order to explain this approbation of justice.[49] He argues that the approval of justice predated the recognition of the utility of justice, and that our hatred of injustice is something which manifests itself in forms which do not seem to relate to social utility:

> Our sense of its ill desert pursues it, if I may say so, even beyond the grave, though the example of its punishment there cannot serve to deter the rest of mankind, who see it not, who know it not, from being guilty of the like practices here . . . In every religion, and in every superstition that the world has ever beheld, accordingly, there has been a Tartarus as

well as an Elysium; a place provided for the punishment of the wicked, as well as one for the reward of the just.[50]

Smith does not believe that the fear of Hell deters men from injustice.[51] Thus there is a sentiment which does not seem reducible to social utility. Smith accounts for the acceptance of the general rule of duty, i.e., only performing just acts, as an inductive process resulting from our sympathetic judgment of resentment of injustice in individual cases. We are led to formulate a general rule that justice ought to be done.[52] The concept of duty is critical for Smith's account, since it is the only effective check on our passions:

> There is scarce any man, however, who by discipline, education, and example, may not be so impressed with a regard to general rules, as to act upon almost every occasion with tolerable decency, and through the whole of his life avoid any considerable degree of blame. Without this sacred regard to general rules, there is no man whose conduct can be much depended upon.[53]

This inductive process leads to the acceptance of general rules before the utility of these rules is understood. Specifically, the rules of morality become the demands of the gods:

> the gods were universally represented and believed to be the rewarders of humanity and mercy, and the avengers of perfidy and injustice. And thus religion, even in its rudest form, gave a sanction to the rules of morality, long before the age of artificial reasoning and philosophy. That the terrors of religion should thus enforce the natural sense of duty, was of too much importance to the happiness of mankind, for nature to leave it dependent upon the slowness and uncertainty of philosophical researches.[54]

The end of this process of turning natural man, one without regard to others, into a social man is the acceptance of duty, and the desirability of behaving in a praiseworthy manner. Smith points out that men have often sacrificed their lives for a renown which they could never experience. There is no profound difference between this act and that of giving their lives for a renown which would be due if society knew of their choice.[55] Thus, in Smith's account, duty constrains choosing; its imperatives prohibit nonpraiseworthy action. Smith declines to dispute with Mandeville whether this means that duty is simply self-love.[56]

It is important to notice the fact that Smith traces the diffusion of duty through society by means of religious instruction. Duty is taught as a command from the gods, not as a Humean theorem.[57] This fact leads men to pass favorable judgment on those with religious sentiments,[58] a judgment which may or may not be warranted.[59] Smith is worried about the corruption of religion in so far as religious doctrine is a carrier of morality:

False notions of religion are almost the only causes which can occasion
any very gross perversion of our natural sentiments in this way; and that
principle which gives the greatest authority to the rules of duty, is alone
capable of distorting our ideas of them in any considerable degree.[60]

Under what conditions will the true notions of religion be produced? The
question is not posed in the *Theory of Moral Sentiments*; it is, however,
considered at length in the *Wealth of Nations* when Smith examines in detail
David Hume's position that religions are responsible for civil unrest. Smith
rejects this because Hume has confused religion *per se* with religion that has
access to state power. It is Smith's contention that, with competition
among religious sects, the zeal of religious teachers would lead to no harm;
their ability to attain temporal power vanishes.

The teachers of each little sect, finding themselves almost alone, would
be obliged to respect those of almost every other sect, and the
concessions which they would mutually find it both convenient and
agreeable to make to one another, might in time probably reduce the
doctrine of the greater part of them to that pure and rational religion,
free from every mixture of absurdity, imposture, or fanaticism, such as
wise men have in all ages of the world wished to see established.[61]

Hence, it is under conditions of competition that Smith expects the
production of pure, rational religion. It is also under conditions of
competition that religious doctrine will make its greatest contribution to
action, since the teachers of religion will find it to their interest to associate
with the poor and to lead lives of rectitude.[62]

Smith's account of the process by which selfish individuals acquire regard
for their fellows sufficiently to form a stable and free society does not, I
think, conflict with his account of other economic processes. It is to be
remembered that Smith does not assume that individuals start with
information sufficient to plot efficient means to their own ends.
Individuals, in Smith's account, must have an incentive to perform a
difficult task.[63] Merchants can ravage the rest of the community because
they, and only they, have sufficient incentive to calculate efficient means to
their ends.[64] However, education, when supplied under competitive
conditions, can be counted upon to counteract individuals' natural
inclination to sloth.[65] Indeed, the well-known corrupting process
engendered by the division of labor, i.e., the systematic withdrawal of
incentives to diligence outside a narrow speciality,[66] is not sufficiently
strong to counteract a good education. Hence, the educational process by
which the importance of duty is inculcated is simply one of many other
processes by which individuals acquire knowledge of how their ends can be
effected.

Thus, Smith has considerably improved upon a lacuna in Hume's view:

he has avoided jumping from individual self-interest to duty. He has constructed a testable theory of the interrelation between religions and the stability of society. A competitive religion industry will result in a more stable society than one where religion is either monopolistic or oligopolistic. Finally, under competitive conditions in the religion industry, the ethical imperative acted upon by a sufficient number of individuals to produce social peace in a contractual society will be that law of nature which Hobbes thought was irrelevant to the choices of men.

Chapter 6

Who monitors the monitors?

Susan Feigenbaum, co-author,
shares praise and blame for this chapter

RENT-SEEKING AND MORAL INSTRUCTION

Thomas Hobbes's position that civil war resulted from the ability of priests to cloud the minds of men is an open possibility where people accept moral instruction without full information. In fact, we must put the question this way: what blocks the possibility that this moral instruction is provided for rent-seeking motives for the good of the seller but not of the buyer?[1]

Hobbes's position, that civil peace could not be assured until church and state spoke with one voice, was reformulated by Adam Smith's great friend David Hume. Hume contends that the ignorance of religious adherents leads competing religious leaders to promote superstition and violent factionalism. We cite Smith's quotation of Hume's statement:

> It may naturally be thought, at first sight, that the ecclesiasticks belong to the first class, and that their encouragement, as well as that of lawyers and physicians, may safely be entrusted to the liberality of individuals, who are attached to their doctrines, and who find benefit or consolation from their spiritual ministry and assistance. Their industry and vigilance will, no doubt, be whetted by such an additional motive; and their skill in the profession, as well as their address in governing the minds of the people, must receive daily increase, from their increasing practice, study, and attention.
>
> But if we consider the matter more closely, we shall find, that this interested diligence of the clergy is what every wise legislator will study to prevent; because, in every religion except the true, it is highly pernicious, and it has even a natural tendency to pervert the true, by infusing into it a strong mixture of superstition, folly, and delusion. Each ghostly practitioner, in order to render himself more precious and sacred in the eyes of his retainers, will inspire them with the most violent abhorrence of all other sects . . . No regard will be paid to truth, morals, or decency in the doctrines inculcated. Every tenet will be adopted that best suits the disorderly affections of the human frame.[2]

The modern literature knows this as the celebrated problem of asymmetric information.[3]

Smith does not dispute the history. This we see from his discussion of the results of competition for the position of religious monopoly:

> As long as the people of each parish preserved the right of electing their own pastors, they acted almost always under the influence of the clergy, and generally of the most factious and fanatical of the order. The clergy, in order to preserve their influence in those popular elections, became, or affected to become, many of them, fanatics themselves, encouraged fanaticism among the people, and gave the preference almost always to the most fanatical candidate. . . . When the parish happened to be situated in a great city, *it divided all the inhabitants into two parties*.[4]

Here and elsewhere, Smith is deeply concerned with a bimodal distribution of beliefs, contending fanatics damning each other across a vacant plain of moderation. 'Faction' is a word often used by Smith to describe this situation. We shall see in Chapter 9 the genesis of Smith's concern with bimodality and violence. Supposing majority rule, policy made by the median believer will be very fragile. The median can be moved a considerable distance by violence directed at the extremes.

None the less, he disputes Hume's policy result. He claims that under conditions of religious competition, augmented by a policy one might call 'informational antitrust', toleration of religious diversity will emerge and produce religious moderation. How is this supposed to constrain the factions? One part of the answer is competition. However, as is characteristic with asymmetric information problems, the requisite information is not automatically provided as the number of competing fanatics goes up. His summary argument, quoted next, contains two points to which we believe particular attention should be paid:

> But if politicks had never called in the aid of religion, had the conquering party never adopted the tenets of one sect more than those of another, when it had gained the victory, it would probably have dealt equally and impartially with all the different sects, and have allowed every man to chuse his own priest and his own religion as he thought proper. There would in this case, no doubt, have been a great multitude of religious sects. *Almost every different congregation might probably have made a little sect by itself, or have entertained some peculiar tenets of its own*. [1] . . . The teachers of each sect, seeing themselves surrounded on all sides with more adversaries than friends, would be obliged to learn that candour and moderation which is so seldom to be found among the teachers of those great sects, whose tenets, being supported by the civil magistrate, are held in veneration by almost all the inhabitants of extensive kingdoms and empires, and who therefore see nothing round them but

followers, disciples, and humble admirers. The teachers of each little sect, finding themselves almost alone, would be obliged to respect those of almost every other sect, and the concessions which they would mutually find it both convenient and agreeable to make to one another, *might in time probably reduce the doctrine of the greater part of them to that pure and rational religion, free from every mixture of absurdity, imposture, or fanaticism, such as wise men have in all ages of the world wished to see established*; [2] but such as positive law has perhaps never yet established.[5]

Our objective is to identify the conditions under which Smith's moderation through competition theorem, passage 2, is true. Unlike some previous contributions on the subject, we emphasize that this competitive outcome arises *only* when randomization of doctrine also exists the condition described by passage 1 holds.[6] In this context we should read how much of Smith's hopes for checking fanaticism rest upon the diffusion of science and philosophy:

The first of those remedies is the study of science and philosophy, which the state might render almost universal among all people of middling or more than middling rank and fortune; not by giving salaries to teachers to make them negligent and idle, but by instituting some sort of probation, even in the higher and more difficult sciences, to be undergone by every person before he was permitted to exercise any liberal profession . . . Science is the great antidote to the poison of enthusiasm and superstition; and where all the superior ranks of people were secured from it, the inferior ranks could not be much exposed to it.[7]

There is a second requirement to check fanaticism:

The second of those remedies is the frequency and gaiety of publick diversions. The state, by encouraging, that is by giving entire liberty to all those who for their own interest would attempt, without scandal or indecency, to amuse and divert the people by painting, poetry, musick, dancing; by all sorts of dramatic representations and exhibitions, would easily dissipate, in the greater part of them, that melancholy and gloomy humour which is almost always the nurse of popular superstition and enthusiasm. Publick diversions have always been the object of dread and hatred, to all the fanatical promoters of those popular frenzies.[8]

To appreciate how Smith's argument proceeds, it is important to focus on conditions in which ordinary people would find moral information valuable. To this we now turn.

ERROR IS SYSTEMATIC

In an important essay, George Stigler documented the case that Smith regarded people as very poorly informed in political matters.[9] Stigler took it for granted that Smith did not have such a view of people in their market activity. This willingness to bifurcate Smith's work into a piece which holds some position to be true and another piece which holds the same position to be false seems to be a methodological legacy of some important reactions to 'Das Adam-Smith-Problem'.[10] The problem of reconciling *Theory of Moral Sentiments* and *Wealth of Nations* started when German scholars recognized that there is much in *Theory of Moral Sentiments* to remind one of Immanuel Kant's theory of morality. We have seen that, in fact, Smith's theory-acceptance model passes muster if and only if morals are absolute in the sense which Kant intended. Since the larger purpose of the book is to argue that acceptance of such absolutist ethical imperatives is consistent with utility-maximizing behavior, perhaps the interpretator's failure to resolve this paradox has been seen as Smith's fault.

We shall argue that Smith's theory of conduct has perception failure front and center. The modern fashion is to treat individual error as unsystematic; what is most remarkable to our eyes is that Smith believes that perception failure is predictable. In this line of argument, Smith expands upon Bishop Berkeley's celebrated account of systematic physical perception failure to give an account of individuals' failure to perceive their own interests. In *Theory of Moral Sentiments* Smith makes clear how his moral construction ties in with Berkeley's theory of vision. The emphasized passage tells us how this error will be corrected:

As to the eye of the body, objects appear great or small, not so much according to their real dimensions, as according to the nearness or distance of their situation; so do they likewise to what may be called the natural eye of the mind: and we remedy the defects of both these organs pretty much in the same manner. In my present situation an immense landscape of lawns, and woods, and distant mountains, seems to do no more than cover the little window which I write by, and to be out of all proportion less than the chamber in which I am sitting. I can form a just comparison between those great objects and little objects around me, in no other way, than by transporting myself, at least in fancy, to a different station, from whence I can survey both at nearly equal distances, and thereby form some judgement of their real proportions. . . .

In the same manner, to the selfish and original passions of human nature, the loss or gain of a very small interest of our own, appears to be of vastly more importance, excites a much more passionate joy or sorrow . . . than the greatest concern of another with whom we have no particular connexion. . . . *how little we should be affected by whatever relates to him, if the sense of propriety and justice did not correct the otherwise natural inequality of our sentiments.*[11]

Berkeley's theory of vision introduces reason to believe that perception failures will be systematic, empirical regularities. Smith ties in systematic perception failure with the activities of moralists:

The over-weening conceit which the greater part of men have of their own abilities, is an antient evil remarked by the philosophers and moralists of all ages.[12]

It has been widely noted, for instance, that Smith believes that individuals systematically misperceive the probability of gambles. Smith offers this as his contribution to an understanding of the mechanics of perception failure:

Their absurd presumption in their own good fortune, has been less taken notice of. It is, however, if possible, still more universal. There is no man living who, when in tolerable health and spirits, has not some share of it. The chance of gain is by every man more or less over-valued, and the chance of loss is by most men under-valued . . .[13]

During the utilitarian hegemony, Smith's spectator theory was kept in popular memory mainly by Robert Burns's poetry. Here is the prosaic version of verses too well known to need recall, where the emphasis on 'light' is both metaphorical and tribute to Berkeley's vision:

This self-deceit, this fatal weakness of mankind, is the source of half the disorders of human life. If we saw ourselves in the light in which others see us, or in which they would see us if they knew all, a reformation would generally be unavoidable. We could not otherwise endure the sight.[14]

The role of moral rules is, in Smith's account, to correct our mis-perceptions. Society hangs together on the basis of the moral rules which flow out of these error-correction activities:

Without this sacred regard to general rules, there is no man whose conduct can be much depended upon. It is this which constitutes the most essential difference between a man of principle and honour and a worthless fellow. The one adheres, on all occasions, steadily and resolutely to his maxims,[15]

By now, Smith's Kantianism should come as no surprise. But unlike Kant, Smith found moral motivation in the desire for approbation revealed in common judgment:

Our continual observations upon the conduct of others, insensibly lead us to form to ourselves certain general rules concerning what is fit and proper either to be done or to be avoided. Some of their actions shock all our natural sentiments. We hear every body about us express the like detestation against them. This still further confirms, and even exasperates, our natural sense of their deformity. It satisfies us that we view them in the proper light, when we see other people view them in the same light. We resolve never to be guilty of the like, nor even, upon any account, to render ourselves in this manner the objects of universal disapprobation. . . . Other actions, on the contrary, call forth our approbation, and we hear every body around us express the same favourable opinion concerning them. Every body is eager to honour and reward them. They excite all those sentiments for which we have by nature the strongest desire: the love, the gratitude, the admiration of mankind. We become ambitious of performing the like; and thus naturally lay down to ourselves a rule of another kind, that every opportunity of acting in this manner is carefully to be sought after.[16]

Unfortunately, the cases in which moral rules can provide guidance are also cases in which there is the possibility of rent-seeking by moralists. Smith's praise of the clergy – in the same sentence which recalls a history of their corruption, frivolity, violence, perfidy and fraud – employs a serpentine prose style which may recall that of the great English poet whom the Scots most praised:

It is in this manner that religion enforces the natural sense of duty: and hence it is, that mankind are generally disposed to place great confidence in the probity of those who seem deeply impressed with religious sentiments. . . . And wherever the natural principles of religion are not corrupted by the factious and party zeal of some worthless cabal; wherever the first duty which it requires, is to fulfil all the obligations of morality; wherever men are not taught to regard frivolous observances, as more immediate duties of religion, than acts of justice and beneficence; and to imagine, that by sacrifices, and ceremonies, and vain supplications, they can bargain with the Deity for fraud, and perfidy, and violence, the world undoubtedly judges right in this respect . . .[17]

Once again, we find Smith worried about faction:

False notions of religion are almost the only causes which can occasion any very gross perversion of our natural sentiments in this way; and that principle which gives the greatest authority to the rules of duty, is alone capable of distorting our ideas of them in any considerable degree.[18]

Hume's *History of England* is a mother-lode for those mining for nuggets of fraud, perfidy and violence. Although moral guidance is an input into public order, governments and religions can oft-times serve their own interest by fostering the ignorance and superstition of the public. By keeping individuals in the dark, the government can increase its revenue at the expense of its subjects.[19] Ignorance may loosen the control which citizens have over their government; consequently, an intellectual monopoly may allow the ignorance which maximizes government wealth to persist.[20] Hume's discussion is not unrelated to the claim in the *Wealth of Nations* that ignorance can be exploited in the political process, e.g., Smith explains the ability of merchants to use the political process by their superior knowledge of their *own* interests.[21]

DEMAND FOR AUSTERE MORALITY

It is in the context of systematic perception failure that Smith puts forward an account of moral rules. Smith notes that there are actually two sets of moralities, a liberal and an austere version:

> In every civilized society, in every society where the distinction of ranks has once been completely established, there have been always two different schemes or systems of morality current at the same time; of which the one may be called the strict or austere; the other the liberal, or, if you will, the loose system. The former is generally admired and revered by the common people: the latter is commonly more esteemed and adopted by what are called people of fashion. The degree of disapprobation with which we ought to mark the vices of levity, the vices which are apt to arise from great prosperity, and from the excess of gaiety and good humour, seems to constitute the principal distinction between those two opposite schemes or systems.[22]

Smith asks how these rules become disseminated. It is as disseminator of morality that Smith insists upon the importance of religion. Before philosophy there were the gods. Smith reads the doings of the pagan gods as accounts of ordinary people written upon the heavens. From these accounts we learn both good and evil:

> This reverence is still further enhanced by an opinion which is first impressed by nature, and afterwards confirmed by reasoning and philosophy, that those important rules of morality are the commands and laws of the Deity, who will finally reward the obedient, and punish the transgressors of their duty.
>
> During the ignorance and darkness of pagan superstition, mankind seem to have formed the ideas of their divinities with so little delicacy, that they ascribed to them, indiscriminately, all the passions of human nature, those not excepted which do the least honour to our species, such as lust, hunger, avarice, envy, revenge. They could not fail, therefore, to ascribe to those beings, for the excellence of whose nature they still conceived the highest admiration, those sentiments and qualities which

are the great ornaments of humanity, and which seem to raise it to a resemblance of divine perfection, the love of virtue and beneficence, and the abhorrence of vice and injustice. . . . religion, even in its rudest form, gave a sanction to the rules of morality, long before the age of artificial reasoning and philosophy.[23]

Smith notes the incidence of austere morality in religions adhered to by the common people:

Almost all religious sects have begun among the common people, from whom they have generally drawn their earliest, as well as their most numerous proselytes. The austere system of morality has, accordingly, been adopted by those sects almost constantly, or with very few exceptions; for there have been some. It was the system by which they could best recommend themselves to that order of people to whom they first proposed their plan of reformation upon what had been before established. Many of them, perhaps the greater part of them, have even endeavoured to gain credit by refining upon this austere system, and by carrying it to some degree of folly and extravagance; and this excessive rigour has frequently recommended them more than any thing else to the respect and veneration of the common people.[24]

An austere theory of morality gives simple rules of conduct, thereby providing a clear distinction between 'right' and 'wrong'. If we take the liberal system Smith describes to correspond to that system of moral constraints spelled out in Chapter 3, liberal morality requires reflection. One must think about what one is doing. Poor people, in Smith's account, have little experience dealing with ideas:

The employments too in which people of some rank or fortune spend the greater part of their lives are not, like those of the common people, simple and uniform. They are almost all of them extremely complicated, and such as exercise the head more than the hands. The understandings of those who are engaged in such employments can seldom grow torpid for want of exercise. . . .

It is otherwise with the common people. They have little time to spare for education. Their parents can scarce afford to maintain them even in infancy. As soon as they are able to work, they must apply to some trade by which they can earn their subsistence. That trade too is generally so simple and uniform as to give little exercise to the understanding; while, at the same time, their labour is both so constant and so severe, that it leaves them little leisure and less inclination to apply to, or even to think of any thing else.[25]

Liberal morality can be self-monitoring. In fact, there were no moral monitors in ancient Greek religions; the position of a monitoring bishop was an important Christian innovation.[26]

In small villages, austere morality can be enforced by automatic mutual monitoring. However, when country boys move to the city, they are hidden from view. Smith's solution is to rely on the division of labor to provide a religious sect:

> A man of low condition, on the contrary, is far from being a distinguished member of any great society. While he remains in a country village his conduct may be attended to, and he may be obliged to attend to it himself. In this situation, and in this situation only, he may have what is called a character to lose. But as soon as he comes into a great city, he is sunk in obscurity and darkness. His conduct is observed and attended to by nobody, and he is therefore very likely to neglect it himself, and to abandon himself to every sort of low profligacy and vice. He never emerges so effectually from this obscurity, his conduct never excites so much the attention of any respectable society, as by his becoming the member of a small religious sect.[27]

Smith is very clear why the rigors of austerity are attractive to poor people. There is so little margin for error in their lives that they cannot afford to take the chance of misapplying moral rules:

> The vices of levity are always ruinous to the common people, and a single week's thoughtlessness and dissipation is often sufficient to undo a poor workman for ever, and to drive him through despair upon committing the most enormous crimes. The wiser and better sort of the common people, therefore, have always the utmost abhorrence and detestation of such excesses, which their experience tells them are so immediately fatal to people of their condition. The disorder and extravagance of several years, on the contrary, will not always ruin a man of fashion, and people of that rank are very apt to consider the power of indulging in some degree of excess as one of the advantages of their fortune, and the liberty of doing so without censure or reproach, as one of the privileges which belong to their station.[28]

Next, we sketch a model of austere morality in which our understanding of Smith's requirements can be expressed. Inside this model, does Smith's conclusion hold upon the premises we suppose him depending upon?

A PICTURE OF AUSTERITY

We are now in a position to reclaim our promise to present a moral code which is demonstrably 'false' as a theory of conduct but none the less something which is sensible to accept.

Once again, to allow morality a utility-enhancing role, we require preferences to be nonconvex and information to be local. In Figure 6.1 we

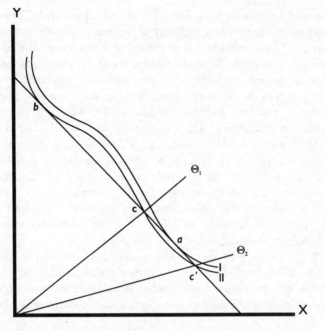

Figure 6.1   Two austere moralities

consider two different austere moral doctrines which teach that moral conduct permits those choices that lie on and only on constraint θ_1 or θ_2, respectively. Both θ_1 and θ_2 are theories of conduct with the role of changing choice, not understanding it. Austere morality reserves approbation for the rays in Figure 6.1. Only the straight and narrow path is rightful. Living in accord with constraint θ_1 at point c would be no worse than the local maximum b, into which the individual might stumble without moral guidance. Moral constraint θ_2 would enhance well-being at point c' relative to b. However, the best outcome – in terms of preferences for the two commodities pictured in Figure 6.1 – occurs when the individual moves to a. Hence, austere morality can also enhance utility to the extent that it provides a starting point for interaction toward a global optimum.

Unlike the liberal system (pictured in Chapter 3) which is self-justifying – one can live in accord with one's morals and maximize at the same time – maximizing behavior requires that one violate austere morals. A liberal moral code requires reflection and information; an austere moral code simply requires obedience. This suggests that once someone departs from the moral constraint, the issue is not 'how close' the code is to the global optimum, but the curvature properties of the space between the code and the optimum. Once one releases from the constraint, can maximizing by hill-climbing suffice to find the global optimum? This argues for an external monitor when morality is austere: someone who can say in this particular instance whether a particular violation of the morality is small enough to neglect. With an austere morality which can only be followed with an external monitor, what is to keep individuals from collapsing into a situation of no morality? There is no reason to believe that a person who wishes to maximize can monitor his own behavior. This is precisely because he cannot maximize without constraint and be moral at the same time.

The danger of austere moralities is obvious from the construction above. For morality to contribute to the optimization problem, one must sometimes distrust one's initial instincts about the direction of a global maximum. Consider someone who finds himself at the local maximum b and is told that the global maximum is really at a. If an individual will not, or cannot, jump direct from a to b, the individual must suffer a utility loss before eventually enhancing his position.

What keeps this moral information correct, i.e., a utility-enhancing guide of conduct? What is to prevent the disseminators of morality from exploiting the situation of limited, local information simply to generate rents? Smith admires, but not uncritically, austere religions:

> In little religious sects, accordingly, the morals of the common people have been almost always remarkably regular and orderly; generally much more so than in the established church. The morals of those little sects, indeed, have frequently been rather disagreeably rigorous and unsocial.[29]

It is precisely to curb these excesses, as we have seen, that Smith recommends twin remedies of philosophy and gaiety. To these we turn now.

PHILOSOPHY AND SCIENCE FROM LIBERAL MORALITY

It is important to realize that, in Smith's view, remedies to the excesses to austerity cannot come from within an austere morality. A multitude of austere sects will create neither gaiety nor philosophy. Gaiety, for instance, is most unlikely:

> We cannot expect the same sensibility to the gay pleasures and amusements of life in a clergyman, which we lay our account with in an officer. The man whose peculiar occupation it is to keep the world in mind of that awful futurity which awaits them, who is to announce what may be the fatal consequences of every deviation from the rule of duty, and who is himself to set the example of the most exact conformity, seems to be the messenger of tidings, which cannot, in propriety, be delivered either with levity or indifference.[30]

The fate of science and philosophy within Christian universities gives good evidence of what Smith thought would happen to science and philosophy in an intellectual world dominated by austere moralists:

> The proper subject of experiment and observation, a subject in which a careful attention is capable of making so many useful discoveries, was almost entirely neglected. The subject in which, after a few very simple and almost obvious truths, the most careful attention can discover nothing but obscurity and uncertainty, and can consequently produce nothing but subtleties and sophisms, was greatly cultivated.

> But if subtleties and sophisms composed the greater part of the Metaphysicks or Pneumaticks of the schools, they composed the whole of this cobweb science of Ontology, which was likewise sometimes called Metaphysicks.[31]

In an extremely revealing passage in *Wealth of Nations*, Smith locates himself firmly in the liberal tradition of ancient moralists. Morality is an instrument to happiness in this world; let the devil take the next:[32]

> Wherein consisted the happiness and perfection of a man, considered not only as an individual, but as the member of a family, of a state, and of the great society of mankind, was the object which the ancient moral philosophy proposed to investigate. In that philosophy the duties of human life were treated of as subservient to the happiness and perfection of human life. But when moral, as well as natural philosophy, came to be taught only as subservient to theology, the duties of human life were treated of as chiefly subservient to the happiness of the life to come. In the antient philosophy the perfection of virtue was represented as necessarily productive, to the person who possessed it, of the most perfect happiness in this life. In the modern philosophy it was frequently represented as generally, or rather as almost always inconsistent with any degree of happiness in this life; and heaven was to be earned only by penance and mortification, by the austerities and abasement of a monk; not by the liberal, generous, and spirited conduct of a man. Casuistry and an ascetic morality made up, in most cases, the greater part of moral philosophy of the schools. By far the most important of all the different branches of philosophy, became in this manner by far the most corrupted.[33]

In addition to his merits as an economist, Smith was a considerable historian of philosophy. In his history of the ancient moral philosophy, he finds that it grew up as a critique of religion:

> In every age and country of the world men must have attended to the characters, designs, and actions of one another, and many reputable rules and maxims for the conduct of human life, must have been laid down

and approved of by common consent. As soon as writing came into fashion, wise men, or those who fancied themselves such, would naturally endeavour to increase the number of those established and respected maxims . . . sometimes in the more artificial forms of apologues, like what are called the fables of Aesop; and sometimes in the more simple ones of apophthegms, or wise sayings, like the Proverbs of Solomon, the verses of Theognis and Phocyllides, and some part of the works of Hesiod.

(The motivation of 'wise men' will be addressed in Chapter 10.) Perhaps modern readers miss the point, but Smith's neighbors would note that his list has a book of the Hebrew Bible nestled between pagan writers. We start with religion, but then something remarkable happens:

They might continue in this manner for a long time merely to multiply the number of those maxims of prudence and morality, without even attempting to arrange them in any very distinct or methodical order, much less to connect them together by one or more general principles, from which they were all deducible, like effects from their natural causes. The beauty of a systematical arrangement of different observations connected by a few common principles, was first seen in the rude essays of those antient times towards a system of natural philosophy. Something of the same kind was afterwards attempted in morals. The maxims of common life were arranged in some methodical order, and connected together by a few common principles, in the same manner as they had attempted to arrange and connect the phenomena of nature. The science which pretends to investigate and explain those connecting principles, is what is properly called moral philosophy.[34]

The competition of philosophers brings about the creation of logic as a discipline.[35] Consistent with his unified treatment of the acceptance of moral rules and scientific theory, Smith treats the evolution of moral rules in tandem with the evolution of scientific information.

Philosophy is, in Smith's opinion, a challenge to the claims of religion; gaiety is a challenge to the 'whining and melancholy' moralists with which religions are both blessed and afflicted. The question is how the common judgment could agree that it is 'right' for such liberality to exist? What keeps the upper classes from being as fanatical as the lower? It is from the upper classes one expects science:

Science is the great antidote to the poison of enthusiasm and superstition; and where all the superior ranks of people were secured from it, the inferior ranks could not be much exposed to it.[36]

A MULTITUDE OF AUSTERITIES

We have seen that in Smith's account there is a natural tendency for the rich to be attracted to liberal morality. They are more experienced in dealing with the idea than poor people. Moreover, they do not have as much to lose with loose morals as poor people; genteel dissolution can take years to run its course. None the less, these are not the only incentives the upper class face; they confront the court of a public opinion formed by austere morality:

> A man of rank and fortune is by his station the distinguished member of a great society, who attend to every part of his conduct, and who thereby oblige him to attend to every part of it himself. His authority and consideration depend very much upon the respect which this society bears to him. He dare not do any thing which would disgrace or discredit him in it, and he is obliged to a very strict observation of that species of morals, whether liberal or austere, which the general consent of this society prescribes to persons of his rank and fortune.[37]

We know that Smith found theory acceptance in agreement. What the poor all judge to be 'wrong' is the intersection of all the austere moralities hold to be 'wrong'. You say θ_1 is 'right' and I say θ_2 is 'right'. Upon what can you and I agree? We can agree that everything except θ_1 and θ_2 would be 'wrong'.[38] Increase the number of sects and suppose that every position between θ_1 and θ_2 is occupied. Then the common locus of 'wrong' shrinks to only those positions outside θ_1 and θ_2! *Voilà*, moderation of judgment!

SMITH'S THEOREM

The problem Smith faces is that there is more than one position of equilibrium in his model of austere morality. The pleasant equilibrium of moderation is not the only one. If the poor in society are polarized into moral extremes, then we can expect nothing else from the rich. Civil war is a perpetual threat in such a fragile context:

> The animosity of hostile factions, whether civil or ecclesiastical, is often still more furious than that of hostile nations; and their conduct towards one another is often still more atrocious. What may be called the laws of faction have often been laid down by grave authors with still less regard to the rules of justice than what are called the laws of nations.[39]

What would prevent this bimodality?

Suppose that θ_1 and θ_2 are only two of ι elements of a set of utility-enhancing theories of conduct Θ. How do these two particular theories come to be selected? We suppose that theorists know no more than ordinary people. This is a very weak version of rational expectations.[40]

What a theorist is able to do is to propose a theory θ_i and to try to live according to it. He can then report to others about his experience. Of course, there is no guarantee that he will tell the truth and thus no guarantee that he will be believed.

Let us first state a well-known version of the issue. How do we know where to eat on an interstate far from home and guidebook? Looking for a restaurant with a full parking lot or remembering where one got a decent meal in the past are two popular solutions. It is obvious that the conjunction of these will generate a dependence over time in the sequence of customers. Many customers in the past will argue for many customers in the future even if the meals have changed in the meantime.

As we have seen previously, we can reclaim Smith's principle of theory acceptance if we can give an account of what persuades people to accept morals as laws of logic. In our context, we do not shop for meals, but for morals. We think to ourselves, if someone tries out θ_i and prefers it to the alternatives, there must be something to be said for θ_i. At least this would suggest that, in a production function for persuasion, one might offer one's life as demonstration.

Hume gives many examples of how people judge the merit of moral ideas by the personal behavior of the proponents.[41] Ideological entrepreneurs who succeed live lives of stern rectitude; reformers who believe that they are exempt from their own pronouncements are less likely to be successful. If they are caught, their cause suffers. The puritan in the brothel discredits puritanism itself.[42]

We shall pose the problem of religious competition as one of the distribution of the random selection of doctrine. It makes no sense to choose moral theory fully informed of its consequences. If one could, there would be, in our account, no need for morality. The numbers of people who live their lives according to θ_i provide a signal of its efficacy. Alternatively, one can choose to create one's own theory, to find another θ_i which leads to an acceptable life. If there is one path there are probably many others.

We are now in a position to address Smith's moderation theorem in terms of our model of austere morality. What is necessary to block the possibility that all society will be divided between θ_1 and θ_2? As we have seen above, this is the case about which Smith was persistently worried.

To see the issue, we begin a competitive process which can generate the bimodal result. Start with two theories θ_1 and θ_2 which have evolved by some trial-and-error procedure. We allow the individual to have two options: (1) accept one of the two theories which has been offered by others or (2) find another theory by which to live. We suppose that those who do not wish to theorize will simply select one of those θ_i in existence by some randomization procedure. Presumably, if one judges the efficacy of θ_i by the number of adherents, there is no reason to suppose that the choice of doctrine is independent of the numbers of those adhering. Surely, the more adherents of θ_i relative to θ_j the more the reasonable believer would be likely to pick θ_i. The simple possibility of dependence in choice of θ_i on the number of those previously choosing θ_i offers an easy explanation for the conditions under which religious monopoly or oligopoly tends to persist.

By our weak rational expectations principle, the new theorist is faced with exactly the same problem as the new believer as long as one can only judge theory by the number accepting and not by arguments. The numbers accepting at time t provide evidence for theory at t which induces numbers accepting at $t + 1$. The alternative to an existing theory is to try living in accord with a new theory. Thus, the new theorist has to redo the evolutionary process by which the old θ_i came to be. Why would this experience persuade anyone else? Thus, free entry in religious theory may not do more than preserve the existing religious divisions. This is the old problem that numbers of entrants are no guarantee of competitive equilibrium without sufficient information in the market.

Now, let us introduce something new into the economy of belief, philosophy. Philosophy, by giving some insight into why θ_1 and θ_2 help the consumer, allows theorists to propose alternatives to either θ_1 or θ_2. Of course, the philosophy need not be true. Smith had no more naive a view of philosophy than of any other aspect of life. Listen to a great historian of philosophy tell the story:

> Speculative systems have in all ages of the world been adopted for reasons too frivolous to have determined the judgment of any man of common sense, in a matter of the smallest pecuniary interest. Gross sophistry has scarce ever had any influence upon the opinions of mankind, except in matters of philosophy and speculation; and in these it has frequently had the greatest.[43]

No matter, for bad arguments generate good ones:

> The patrons of each system of natural and moral philosophy naturally endeavoured to expose the weakness of the arguments adduced to support the systems which were opposite to their own. In examining those arguments, they were necessarily led to consider the difference between a probable and a demonstrative argument, between a fallacious and a conclusive one; and Logick, or the science of the general principles of good and bad reasoning, necessarily arose out of the observations which a scrutiny of this kind gave occasion to.[44]

Philosophy breaks the dependence between number of believers at t and theory at t, and thus believers at $t + 1$. Philosophy allows someone to think that if both θ_i and θ_j work, then something between them should work. Even if he has no interest in setting up a religion, his life offers a demonstration that it can be done. One can live according to one's own light, freed from the traditional imperatives.

Reflecting upon Smith's moral absolutism, one might ask: what could someone do to give evidence that he takes his own morality seriously? The absolute respects death. The executioner's axe, shearing flesh apart, welds choice and words into an undying unity:

> Had the enemies of Socrates suffered him to die quietly in his bed, the glory of even that great philosopher might possibly never have acquired that dazzling splendour in which it has been beheld in all succeeding ages. In the English history, when we look over the illustrious heads which have been engraven by Vertue and Howbraken, there is scarce any body, I imagine, who does not feel that the axe, the emblem of having been beheaded, which is engraved under some of the most illustrious of them; under those of the Sir Thomas Mores, of the Rhaleighs, the Russels, the Sydneys, etc. sheds a real dignity and interestingness over the characters to which it is affixed, much superior to what they can derive from all the futile ornaments of heraldry, with which they are sometimes accompanied.
>
> Nor does this magnanimity give lustre only to the characters of innocent and virtuous men. It draws some degree of favourable regard even upon those of the greatest criminals; and when a robber or highwayman is brought to the scaffold, and behaves there with decency and firmness, though we perfectly approve of his punishment, we often cannot help regretting that a man who possessed such great and noble powers should have been capable of such mean enormities.[45]

Millennia have passed and still we think that, since Socrates was willing to die for his beliefs, there must be something to them.

In Chapter 10 we shall ask what might prompt individuals to act so heroically. Let it be noted that, until we do give such an explanation, we are in some danger of explaining the existence of new moral codes by the desire to be moral.

Thus, philosophy is a technological shock to the economy of belief which reduces the cost of theory-creation. With a fall in the cost of theory-creation, one would expect more theory. With some independence of theory from the number of believers comes random, independent generation of theory. With this new generation comes dispersion and the applicability of limit theorems.[46] With such application, we have reason to believe that the distribution of belief will be symmetrical and unimodal. Under this condition, the median attains its position of maximal robust estimator.[47] Thus, the median believer is little changed by violence directed at the extremes. Hence, there would be little reason to engage in such violence.

Hence, Smith's odd-looking provision that a scientific education might be a reasonable state requirement for a liberal profession, e.g., to be a clergyman, makes sense as an antitrust provision. Philosophy maintains competition among religions; philosophers compete amongst themselves.

CONCLUSION

With a large number of austere sects in a community, with sufficient philosophical-scientific information comes a widening of the range of approved ways of living. This does not make the austere moralities any less austere:

> But though this equality of treatment should not be productive of this good temper and moderation in all, or even in the greater part of the religious sects of a particular country; yet provided those sects were sufficiently numerous, and each of them consequently too small to disturb the publick tranquillity, the excessive zeal of each for its particular tenets could not well be productive of any very hurtful effects, but, on the contrary, of several good ones: and if the government was perfectly decided both to let them all alone, and to oblige them all to let alone one another, there is little danger that they would not of their own accord subdivide themselves fast enough, so as soon to become sufficiently numerous.[48]

The importance of information to a competitive process is well known because a monopoly position of suppliers can be maintained by restricting information to consumers. In Smith's account, religious competition, in conjunction with a minimal amount of philosophical knowledge, offers a means by which the claims of religion can be tamed and toleration attained.

> The interested and active zeal of religious teachers can be dangerous and troublesome only where there is, either but one sect tolerated in the society, or where the whole of a large society is divided into two or three great sects; the teachers of each acting by concert, and under a regular discipline and subordination. But that zeal must be altogether innocent where the society is divided into two or three hundred, or perhaps into as many thousand small sects, of which no one could be considerable enough to disturb the publick tranquillity.[49]

Living under the United States Constitution, we catch Smith's point.

Chapter 7

Property, justice and judgment

INTRODUCTION

We have seen how the experiments with animal consumers have blocked any hope of constructing a theory of private property directly from mute preferences. This raises a puzzle because it is sometimes claimed that John Locke was able to construct successfully a theory of property on just such an attractive basis. More than this, even when it is recognized that there are problems with the specific details of Locke's own theory, one aspect of his argument, the 'Lockean proviso', has been actively advocated as an important requirement for *any* theory of the just appropriation of property.[1] As we shall determine when we audit the Lockean argument, this Lockean proviso assumes away scarcity, so it is at the heart of the failure.

This brings us back to Adam Smith's conjecture that the persuasive power of language allows us to trade. This conjecture is intimately related to the contemporary Scottish discussion of how words carrying abstract concepts such as duty help us evade prisoner's dilemma traps. The simple fact is that David Hume pointed out precisely why Locke's theory of property failed. And as far as I can see in the historical record, the only ones who paid any attention to Hume's argument were his intellectual peers in the Scottish Enlightenment. Why Hume was ignored outside his circle mystifies me.[2]

To appreciate how systematically the Scots confront the prisoner's dilemma, it is vital to see how Hume begins his theory of property on the blasted ruins of Locke's theory. Of course, if one does not believe that there is anything defective with Locke's theory of property then there isn't much point to Hume's. There are, in fact, several instances in Locke's work which attempt to evade the prisoner's dilemma. The most successful evasion is an argument which isn't there. This I consider next.

LOCKE AND RATIONAL IGNORANCE

One of the founding classics in the field of inquiry now known as public choice is Anthony Down's *An Economic Theory of Democracy*. Perhaps the result which most startled Down's readers is now called the theory of rational ignorance:[3]

> We therefore conclude that (1) information is relatively useless to those citizens who care which party wins and (2) those citizens for whom information is most useful do not care who wins. In short, nobody has a very high incentive to acquire political information.[4]

The surprise with which this result was greeted provides evidence about how carefully even classics can be read; the principle was explained in simple declarative sentences some three hundred years earlier by the most vilified Robert Filmer:[5]

> On the contrary, in a popular state every man knows that the public good doth not depend wholly on his care, but the Commonwealth may be well enough governed by others though he tend only his private benefit. He never takes the public to be his own business. Thus, as in a family, where one office is to be done by many servants, one looks upon another, and every one leaves the business for his fellow until it is quite neglected by all. Nor are they much to be blamed for their negligence, since it is an even wager their ignorance is as great. For the magistrates among the people, being for the most part annual, do always lay down their office before they understand it, so that a Prince of a duller understanding, by use and experience, must needs excel them.[6]

I know of no commentator on Locke or Filmer, post-Downs, who has caught the import of Filmer's argument.[7]

The point, however, was not lost upon Filmer's most scrupulous opponent, Algernon Sidney. Sidney, whose learning was legendary, gives Filmer backhanded credit for breathtaking orginality at this precise juncture:

> Our Author delighting in strange things, dos in the next place, with an admirable sagacity, discover two faults in Popular Governments that were never found by any man before him; and these are no less than Ignorance and Negligence. Speaking of the Care of Princes to preserve their Subjects, he adds . . .

After quoting the appropriate passage, Sidney continues:

> This is bravely determin'd, and the world is beholden to *Filmer* for the discovery of the Errors that have hitherto bin Epidemical. Most men had believed, that such as live in Free States, are usually pleas'd with their condition, desire to maintain it; and every man finding his own good

comprehended in the Publick, as those that sail in the same Ship, employs the Talent he has in endeavouring to preserve it, knowing that he must perish if that miscarry.[8]

As if to emphasize the importance of this argument, Sidney sketches a way out for popular government by forming institutions which, by one method or another, privatize the common good:

All men follow that which seems advantagious to themselves. Such as are bred under a good discipline, and see that all benefits procured to their Country by virtuous Actions, redound to the honour and advantage of themselves, their Children, Friends, and Relations, contract from their infancy a love to the Publick, and look upon the common Concernments as their own.[9]

This thought is developed at some length in his chapter. Sidney's argument turns on the role of honor as a motive, a favorite topic of the classical republicans. We shall have occasion in Chapter 10 to consider whether Sidney's way out of the prisoner's dilemma passes muster.

Unlike Sidney, who quotes Filmer accurately and says why he thinks the argument to be incorrect, Locke has no response whatsoever to this claim. The fact of this silence might actually help resolve an old textual puzzle about Locke's compositional order.[10] Recognizing that Sidney speaks to an issue which Locke ignores might help free Sidney from Locke's shadow.[11]

LOCKE ON PROPERTY

Again, we begin with Filmer. Filmer does not present Locke with the challenge of justifying existing property holdings; rather, Filmer argues against the proposition that the world was given by God to mankind in common.[12] Filmer's argument can be summarized in four steps:[13]

1 If private property were originally common, then private property is rightful if and only if mankind consented.
2 Assume private property is rightful.
3 We know mankind did not in fact consent.
4 Therefore private property was not common originally.

Not bad, for someone with Filmer's press notices.

Locke's strategy is to challenge Filmer by changing the debate from one over the fact of consent to a debate over the rationality of consent. With this reformulation from actual to tacit consent Locke then attempts to establish that there is no inconsistency between rightful property at present and rightful commons at the beginning.

Locke takes three propositions as true by revelation:

R1 All individuals are God's property, so that no one has the right to harm himself or anyone else.[14]

R2 God gave the world in common to men.[15]

R3 God gave man reason.[16]

With these three revelations and a critical empirical specification to be examined later, Locke argues that property could have arisen rightfully because mankind had reason to consent.

The first step in Locke's argument is very elegant, it turns the strongest part of Filmer's argument back on him. In a common state does an individual require consent before he consumes? Since universal consent is impossible, *pace* Filmer, no one would be able to consume. Waiting for universal consent is quite literally suicidal. But we know that suicide conflicts with R1. Therefore, universal consent for consumption conflicts with revelation.[17] Locke assumes, *explicitly*, that there is plenty left for all; hence, the survival of individuals is not in conflict.[18] This assumption is the Lockean proviso.

The justification of appropriation of a stock of land is more complicated than the justification of appropriation of commodities for consumption.[19] To justify appropriation of land Locke supplements R1 with R3. A characteristic of reason, Locke argues, is to exchange voluntarily the worse for the better.[20] To make his case on these revelations, Locke must show that property could arise in such a way that no one is made the worse.

Locke's justification of a private appropriation from a common stock of land assumes away any condition of scarcity. If there is plenty left after appropriation[21] – or if appropriation itself increases the amount afterwards available[22] – then property harms no one.[23] This Lockean proviso is critical, since as long as someone is made the worse by a transaction, he would not give his rightful consent. Indeed, the seriousness of the proviso can be judged by Locke's assertion that waste is an invasion of rights.[24] Thus, the unanimity of rational consent is established only in the case of a unanimity of benefit. The relation of this argument to Paretian welfare economics is too obvious to belabor.

HUME'S COUNTER-EXAMPLES

Although serious scholars have asserted otherwise, Hume has no quarrel with the use of a 'state of nature' assumption in the modeling procedure:

'tis utterly impossible for men to remain any considerable time in that savage condition, which precedes society . . . . This, however, hinders not, but that philosophers may, if they please, extend their reasoning to the suppos'd *state of nature*; provided they allow it to be a mere philosophical fiction, which never had, and never cou'd have any reality. Human nature being compos'd of two principal parts, which are requisite in all its actions, the affections and understanding; 'tis certain, that the blind motions of the former, without the direction of the latter, incapacitate men for society: And it may be allow'd us to consider separately the effects, that result from the separate operations of these two component parts of the mind. The same liberty may be permitted to moral, which is allow'd to natural philosophers; and 'tis very usual with the latter to consider any motion as compounded and consisting of two parts separate from each other, tho' at the same time they acknowledge it to be in itself uncompounded and inseparable.

This *state of nature*, therefore, is to be regarded as a mere fiction, not unlike that of the *golden age*, which poets have invented.[25]

In particular, Hume looks at a Golden Age modeling procedure as a proving ground for his theory of social institutions:

This, no doubt, is to be regarded as an idle fiction; but yet deserves our attention, because nothing can more evidently shew the origin of those virtues, which are the subjects of our present enquiry. I have already observ'd, that justice takes its rise from human conventions; and that these are intended as a remedy to some inconveniences, which proceed from the concurrence of certain *qualities* of the human mind with the *situation* of external objects. The qualities of the mind are *selfishness* and *limited generosity*: and the situation of external objects is their *easy change*, join'd to their *scarcity* in comparison of the wants and desires of men.[26]

Recall the Lockean proviso. Property can be made out of commons if and only if 'there is enough, and as good left in common for others'. This is, of course, nothing more than the absence of scarcity. I can take all I wish without reducing what is available for your wants. Hume tells us what lack of scarcity entails:

if every man had a tender regard for another, or if nature supplied abundantly all our wants and desires . . . the jealousy of interest, which justice supposes, could no longer have place; nor would there be any occasion for those distinctions and limits of property and possession, which at present are in use among mankind.[27]

We know from observation that without scarcity there is neither property nor moral codes to constrain grabbing:

when there is such a plenty of any thing as satisfies all the desires of men: In which case the distinction of property is entirely lost, and every thing remains in common. This we may observe with regard to air and water, tho' the most valuable of all external objects; and may easily conclude, that if men were supplied with every thing in the same abundance, or if *every one* had the same affection and tender regard for *every one* as for himself; justice and injustice would be equally unknown among mankind.[28]

As we have seen above in Chapter 2, Hume's result – no scarcity, no property – flows from Winston Bush's theory of anarchy.

Can Locke evade Hume's counter-example by an appeal to economic growth which private property surely engenders? By working through this argument we can see the same large number prisoner's dilemma problem which Filmer raised in his claim of rational ignorance. Economic growth is simply a public-good aspect of private property. The problem is always: who is going to pay for the public good?

Consider two people A and B at time 0. A seizes common resources, which, by the hypothesis of scarcity, makes B worse off; B has been stripped of a valuable claim. Somewhat later, time 1, the superior productivity engendered by private property asserts itself so that both individuals are richer at time 1 than they were at time 0. Giving Locke's argument the benefit of the doubt, let us assume that both A and B know this: would B give consent for the seizure?

So stated, the argument is ludicrous. Why would not B propose to A 'Look, I'll seize the commons and by and by you will be better off.' Showing that everyone will be eventually better off with property does not settle the question whether a rightful claimant to the common stock will give up such a claim voluntarily.

CONSTRAINED BY ABSTRACTIONS

If Locke's model is not satisfactory, how does private property come into being? In Hume's account in the *Treatise*, property starts when hostilities cease, when those who have are allowed to hold.[29] 'Justice' is a word which is inapplicable to the time before the stability of property. Moral codes, *per se*, will not suffice; therefore, government arises to mend the 'defect' in human nature of preferring the present to the future. People cannot change their natures, but they can change the incentives they confront.[30] The brutality of the initial appropriation in this Humean theory of the origin of property is very much in evidence in Adam Smith's account. Although Smith is second to none in the sustained defense he mounts for the importance of property and economic growth for the material well-being of the working class, he claims that property originates as spoil at the expense of the working class.[31]

We encounter the prisoner's dilemma again. What keeps this Humean truce? It is with this background, I believe, that one should read the Scottish moralists. We shall see that Smith's tentative thesis that trade is founded in persuasion is not unrelated to the larger moral discussions of the period. The answer the Scots provided was to look for the power of words – duty, honor and the like – to constrain our desires. We should also take seriously the ideas Smith put forward about the dissemination of such morality by religion if only to ask just how this might work.

One common reaction to prisoner's dilemma problems is to appeal to benevolence. Careful reading of Hume's passages above would suggest why Hume would not find this an attractive option. Too often discussions of the Scottish tradition will rightly emphasize Francis Hutcheson's early identification of benevolence and morality,[32] but ignore the reason why the Scottish school, Hutcheson included, came to deny the importance of benevolence towards strangers as a motive for choice. The main Scottish result which will concern us here is that benevolence is too weak a motive to hold society together, whereas rules of conduct constraining individuals to act justly are of sufficient strength. Of course, the Scots had the realistic opinion that the public hangman's hemp was an effective teacher for those who might be tempted to loosen themselves from a more delicate web of obligation.

Thomas Hobbes forced the issue of the prisoner's dilemma to be central to the matter of social order. The first Scottish response to Thomas Hobbes, that of Hutcheson, employed the idea that benevolence could obviate the prisoner's dilemma. In 1725 Hutcheson pointed out how conduct conducive to social advantage is so often judged good:

> It is true indeed, that the Actions we approve in others, are generally imagin'd to tend to the *natural Good* of *Mankind*, or that of some *Parts* of it. But whence this *secret Chain* between each *Person* and *Mankind*? How is my *Interest* connected with the most distant *Parts* of it?[33]

Verbally and mathematically, he defines benevolence and [self] interest as mutually exclusive terms.[34] The 'perfection of virtue' occurs when interest is zero.[35]

As an intelligent reader of Bernard Mandeville, Hutcheson would hardly claim that men are paradigms of the virtue they profess. But he does insist that both benevolent and selfish motives influence human conduct;[36] indeed, he recognizes that a statistical procedure may be required to identify the independent influence of the two. Hutcheson, in fact, makes relatively modest claims about human nature:

> Our *passionate* Actions, as we shew'd above, are not generally *Self-interested*; . . . And I see no harm in supposing, that Men are *naturally* dispos'd to *Virtue*, . . .[37]

The modesty of the claim results from his recognition that such a 'natural disposition' is frequently sidetracked:

> The ordinary Springs of *Vice* among Men, must then be suppos'd to be a *mistaken Self-love*, made too violent, so as to overcome *Benevolence*; or *Affections* arising from *false* and *rashly form'd Opinions* of *Mankind*, which we run into thro the weakness of our *Benevolence*.[38]

In 1728 Hutcheson modifies his position in a subtle but far-reaching manner. Defining virtue as conduct approved by our moral sense[39] means that the relation between benevolence and virtue is not definitional but factual:

> *Benevolence* may denote only 'the Desire of another's *Happiness*'; . . . abstractly from any Approbation or Condemnation by our *Moral Sense*.[40]

This shift has no substantial impact on his immediate argument. He still claims that our benevolence may nearly balance our selfishness:

> Were we to strike a *Medium* of the several Passions and Affections . . . we should perhaps find the *Medium* of the publick Affections not very far from a sufficient *Counter-ballance* to the *Medium* of the Selfish;[41]

Thus, benevolence in Hutcheson's work prior to Hume's *Treatise of Human Nature* is taken very seriously as a motive to conduct. However, in Hume's *Treatise* two important results are established which shatter a complacent identification of virtue and benevolence. As we have read, if there were either general benevolence or absence of scarcity there would be no property. Second, strict justice, i.e., respect for the property of others, in the absence of either plenty or general benevolence can hold society together. Hence, the existence of general benevolence is contrary to an equivalent of common observation. Needless to say, this makes alternative explanations of property and justice more attractive.

Lord Kames uses Hume's results specifically to criticize Hutcheson's *Beauty and Virtue*. First, he claims Hutcheson neglects the importance of justice and thus the role of duty:

> [he] founds the morality of actions on a certain quality of actions, which procures approbation and love to the agent. But this account of morality is imperfect, because it excludes justice, and every thing which may be strictly called Duty. The man who, confining himself to strict duty, is true to his word, and avoids harming others, is a just and moral man;[42]

Second, Hutcheson fails to attend to the consequence of a scarcity theory of property when general benevolence does not prevail:

> The surface of this globe does scarce yield spontaneously food for the greatest savages; . . . that man should labour for himself and his family . . . before he thinks of serving others.[43]

Kames suggests that, even if benevolence towards strangers is not observed, abstract concepts are effective restraints on choice:

> Arriving at that point, where benevolence would vanish by the distance of the object, nature has an admirable artifice for reviving its force; by directing it on the abstract idea of a Public and a Whole.[44]

Hutcheson's posthumous *System of Moral Philosophy* fully incorporates

Hume's and Kames's criticism, as we observe in the discussion of Plato's and More's communism. Benevolence, Hutcheson concludes, is too weak a motive to replace the incentives provided by a system of private property:

> Tho' men are naturally active, yet their activity would rather turn toward the lighter and pleasanter exercises, than the slow, constant, and intense labours requisite to procure the necessaries and conveniences of life, unless strong motives are presented to engage them to these severe labours.[45]

> If they are not thus secured, one has no other motive to labour than the general affection to his kind, which is commonly much weaker than the narrower affections to our friends and relations, not to mention the opposition which in this case would be given by most of the selfish ones.
> Nay the most extensive affections could scarce engage a wise man to industry, if no property ensued upon it. He must see that universal diligence is necessary. Diligence will never be universal, unless men's own necessities, and the love of families and friends, excite them. Such as are capable of labour, and yet decline it, should find no support in the labours of others. If the goods procured, or improved by the industrious lye in common for the use of all, the worst of men have the generous and industrious for their slaves. The most benevolent temper must decline supporting the slothful in idleness.[46]

Hutcheson extends Hume's 'no scarcity, no property' theory of property formation by demonstrating the rationale for government-financed public goods:

> The origin of property above explained, shews the reason why such things as are inexhaustible and answer the purposes of all, and need no labour to make them useful, should remain in common to all, as the air, the water of rivers, and the ocean . . . Where the use is inexhaustible, but some expense is required to secure it, this may be a just reason for obliging all who share in it to contribute in an equitable manner to the necessary expence, such as that of light-houses, or ships of force to secure the sea from pyrates.[47]

Although Hutcheson accepts that benevolence is a weak motive, he abandons neither sympathy nor disinterestedness as the basis of morality. Indeed, he extends the sympathetic principles to the problem of cruelty to animals.[48] The sympathetic principle, with no fixed class to operate upon, may very well cross species lines.

The constructive conclusion of the Scottish tradition is that men and women are bound, in part, by abstractions. People who act with regard to others need not themselves be benevolent. We are capable of acting out of respect for duty even though the well-being of others plays an inconsequential role in our concerns. This, of course, is Smith's answer:

> It is not the soft power of humanity, it is not that feeble spark of benevolence which Nature has lighted up in the human heart, that is thus capable of counteracting the strongest impulses of self-love. It is a stronger power, a more forcible motive, which exerts itself upon such occasions. It is reason, principle, conscience . . . It is not the love of our neighbour, it is not the love of mankind, which upon many occasions prompts us to the practice of those divine virtues. It is a stronger love, a more powerful affection . . . the love of what is honourable and noble, of the grandeur, and dignity, and superiority of our own characters.[49]

Smith tells us the content of duty:

> As every man doth, so shall it be done to him, and retaliation seems to be the great law which is dictated to us by nature.[50]

Rules of justice are unique in Smith's system because they are *exact*. If I owe you £10, then it is not £10 ± 1d that I owe:

> There is, however, one virtue of which the general rules determine with the greatest exactness every external action which it requires. This virtue is justice. The rules of justice are accurate in the highest degree, and admit of no exceptions or modifications, but such as may be ascertained as accurately as the rules themselves . . . If I owe a man ten pounds, justice requires that I should precisely pay him ten pounds, either at the time agreed upon, or when he demands it. . . . Though it may be awkward and pedantic, therefore, to affect too strict an adherence to the common rules of prudence or generosity, there is no pedantry in sticking fast by the rules of justice. On the contrary, the most sacred regard is due to them;[51]

The precision of moral rules is, of course, a characteristic one would hope for in an account of how moral information helps to overcome perception failure.

SOCIAL COOPERATION, MORALS AND MONITORS

It is important to distinguish two theses: (1) Words suffice for civil order. This is surely not true. (2) Words are necessary for civil order. If self-restraint is based on words carrying rules, then, perhaps, these words are also one basis of the respect for property. Supposing that talk about duty and justice is an input into social order, how might it be employed? What is the productive or entrepreneurial context in which words of duty are inputs? Just as we have seen utility-enhancing constraints carried by judgments of 'right' and 'wrong' in the context of an individual's choice, we now attempt to repeat this at the social level.

Of all the Scots we consider, Smith seems to put the most emphasis on the positive role of (competitive) religion. Can we extend his ideas of the type of morals which poor people might find attractive, the austere morality which requires an external monitor, to consider the provision of public goods? We know that Smith thinks highly of the performance of the clergy who live by voluntary alms. Just how might this work in the context of the prisoner's dilemma?

Consider a society of two individuals 1 and 2 who have preferences over two commodities, a private good and a public good. We write the individual's bundle as [α, β] for $\$\alpha$ private goods and β public goods. The public good is financed by voluntary contributions, so we can define the traditional prisoner's dilemma matrix. The numerical example supposes that each individual with an endowment of $10 considers contributing $1 of private good to financing the public good. All the money collected will be spent on the public good (Matrix 7.1). Individual 1 prefers [9, 2] to [10, 0] and [10, 1] to [9, 2]. Thus, he would like some public goods, but he would rather have fewer public goods if he can escape paying for any. In such a case, Nash equilibrium is the [10, 0], [10, 0] cell and public goods are not financed. This is so even though [9, 2], [9, 2] is preferred to [10, 0], [10, 0] by both individuals.

Individual 1

Does not contribute   Contributes

Does not contribute	[10, 0], [10, 0]	[9, 1], [10, 1]
Contributes	[10, 1], [9, 1]	[9, 2], [9, 2]

Individual 2

Matrix 7.1   Contributions to finance public goods

Traditional morality has a reciprocity imperative. 'Do unto others as you would be done by' is the Christian version of a much older imperative. This is Smith's reading of the 'great law' of nature. Let us look at the game matrix in terms of approbation. What is 'right' and what is 'wrong'? If you contribute, I will contribute. If you do not contribute, then I will not contribute. This defines a game which these days is called 'tit for tat' (Matrix 7.2).

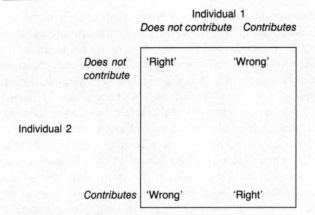

Matrix 7.2   Judgment about the prisoner's dilemma

We have added a new dimension to the optimization problem. What would happen if individuals were sufficiently sensitive to disapprobation that they acted only in a rightful manner? This constraining ethic – if it were to be followed – shuts down the possibility of free-riding. The game matrix becomes modified because only the diagonal elements – both contribute or both do not contribute – are 'rightful'. This is shown in matrix 7.3. Trivially, this ethic – if followed – would result in the optimum amount of public goods. Both individuals by assumption prefer [9, 2] to [10, 0].

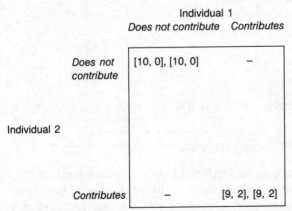

Matrix 7.3   Contributions to finance public goods (constrained)

As we have noted above, when experimentalists compare the voluntary production of public goods with and without talk, talk matters considerably. Donations go up quite significantly when participants in the experiment are allowed to discuss the amount of their contributions.[52]

Suppose that something like a desire for approbation links talk to choice. Words of praise and blame can matter in prisoner's dilemma problems. It is important to take this as an insight and not the answer. Approbation ought to be seen as an input to the solution, not the solution itself. Approbation *per se* seems able to generate some public goods. To hold that approbation is itself all that is required is to deny the efficacy of the division of labor. Inside the prisoner's dilemma context, wouldn't there be a strong incentive for someone to learn how to turn off the appeals of conscience?

Let us consider why organized religion might be important. Consider a variation on matrix 7.4 where a third person, whom we call 'bishop', takes 10 percent of the donations as a commission for persuading people to contribute the public goods.[53] Thus, if $1 is donated the bishop receives $0.1 and $0.90 goes to provide the public goods themselves. For this argument we assume that persuasion is the only instrument at the bishop's disposal. The bishop also benefits from the public good provided and we suppose that the bishop's play does not enter the calculations of the other two. Writing the bishop's income below the line, the three-person game becomes as in matrix 4. We suppose that public goods are valuable enough so that the individual prefers [9, 1.8] to [10, 0]. If he prefers [10, 0] to [9, 1], he will surely prefer [10, 0] to [9, 0.9].

Individual 1

	Does not contribute	Contributes
Does not contribute	[10, 0], [10, 0] [0, 0]	[9, 0.9], [10, 0.9] [0.1, 0.9]
Contributes	[10, 0.9], [9, 0.9] [0.1, 0.9]	[9, 1.8], [9, 1.8] [0.2, 1.8]

(Individual 2 labels the rows)

Matrix 7.4 Contributions to finance public goods with a bishop

Let the position of bishop be auctioned.[54] It is an ironic comment on our ability to forget ideologically inconvenient history that one of Christianity's great contributions to the organization of religion was precisely that of selling the office of bishop.[55] The condition of rationality we impose is that a person is willing to pay at most the private equivalent of his expectation of the vector of his share of private contributions and public goods produced. It is trivial to find a relation between contributions and the amount an individual would pay to become the bishop. To wit: if a rational individual is willing to pay to become the bishop, he must expect the voluntary production of public goods to be positive. Also: the more a rational individual is willing to pay to become the bishop, the more voluntary public goods he must expect to be produced. If expectations are realized then voluntary public goods must be produced.

We cannot prove, of course, that the optimum amount of public goods will be provided. This is so, in part, because it is not at all clear what 'optimum' means with transactions costs.[56] None the less, if the problem is to finance *some* amount of public goods, the case is made. Obviously, it is very much in the spirit of Hume's and Smith's work to give someone an incentive to provide public goods.

What makes the individual keep the constraint when he knows full well that he can gain financially by violating it? But, we can ask the question another way: how does the bishop persuade? Presumably, the bishop's persuasion takes the form of augmenting the link between talk and approbation. Perhaps when he drops by the talk is of the difference between [10, 0], [10, 0] and [9, 1.8], [9, 1.8]. The rational, rule-constrained individual who makes the decision on what seems to work – dollar in and public goods out – will have nothing to complain about. As long as the individual judges his contribution as worthwhile, the bishop will prosper. Or perhaps the talk is about the difference between 'right' and 'wrong'.

To see how this works, recall that each individual prefers [9, 1.2] to [10, 0] but prefers [10, 0] to [9, 0.9]. If he is the only person financing the public good, he will consider the bishop a waste and stop contributing. Thus, as long as the bishop's position is valuable, the rational rule-constrained individual has judged it sensible to contribute. Since the bishop is the guide in matters of personal morality, there will be no conflict between local evidence and the claims of morality. In the model of moral behavior developed above in Chapters 3 and 6, moral information gives an individual reason to question the evidence of local information. Of course, if the individual decided to experiment by not contributing, and discovered that the world did not actually collapse to [10, 0], then the voice of moral information would tell him that this was just a 'short-run' gain. It is to the interest of the bishop not to encourage such experiments.

CONCLUSION

The fact that social organizations do not collapse when confronted by the prisoner's dilemma ought to be extremely interesting to economists. A. K. Sen has been particularly pointed in reminding us of this.[57] The social gains for avoiding the prisoner's dilemma are surely considerable. If this is so, then this offers a reason why a society might well afford to hire monitors or to invest in some substitute process.

I have only touched on the micro-foundations of public goods provision. This will be the problem I address in Chapter 10. Just how are words supposed to be transformed into deeds? Just how do we link the desire for approbation to language? And what has this to do with the prisoner's dilemma?

Part IV

Equilibrium ideas

Enough abstraction, now we get down to details. Can ordinary people really evolve systematic economic ideas without knowing it? Not only can they do this, but they can also talk sensibly about the properties of random representation two millennia before probability theorists are on the scene. This is the content of the first two chapters of the secion. Here we cannot separate demand from supply, but we can observe systems of ideas which were stable over a long time. In the Homeric chapter we attend in very great detail to the seemingly absurd question of what the gods want.

The third chapter looks into the possibility that ordinary people's ideas about the gods tell us about their own utility functions. We have found that the gods desire a competitive form of approbation; let us suppose that we do too. Here is where we take ordinary people's economic theory seriously enough to write down the resulting specification of a utility function and constraints. Let us consider a very special case of competitive approbation, that of fame. This is a competitive form of approbation because we cannot all be famous. Indeed, one might think of the competition for fame as a negative sum game: if we stopped the competition, we could all be better-off. Perhaps this is so. But it is also the case that one prisoner's dilemma can trap another.

Chapter 8

Rational choice in the Homeric epics

INTRODUCTION

One continuing philosophical controversy has been between adherents of some classical Greek schools of political and moral philosophy, and the tradition now articulated in modern economic choice theory. High-level controversy is hidden these days, in part, because of the enormous complexity of modern economics. Modern economists mainly write for each other. The controversy was public − 'spectacular' might be a better term − in the early eighteenth century when Bernard Mandeville attacked not only the classical Greek doctrines themselves but the Platonic Christianity explicit in such eminent philosophers as Blaise Pascal and John Locke. Bishop Berkeley joined the dispute, attacking and being attacked by Mandeville. The debate flowed into new channels when David Hume, Samuel Johnson, Adam Smith and later S. T. Coleridge joined the fray.[1]

This raises a puzzle. How is it that the Greek tradition knew enough about human behavior to be worth arguing against? High authority informs us that there is nothing in surviving Greek writings which demonstrates even a meager command over economic analysis.[2] This report is not conclusive, and does not help escape our present quandary, because historians of ideas have constrained their search for economic insight to those accounts which strive for self-conscious universality.[3]

In reaction, perhaps, to unfulfilled promises of modern scientific economics, which would make a sharp distinction between theorems and stories, there is an ironic undertone in some of the modern economics literature which would understand economic theory itself as a story-telling activity.[4] Without entering this debate, I shall attempt to establish that there is substantive economic content in real stories by demonstrating that the Homeric epics display a staggering ability to apply rational choice principles. Through them, indeed, a Greek philosopher could learn enough about rational choice principles to dislike them because the Homeric gods are the best exemplars of rational choosers. In their relations with men, and with other immortals, the gods take what they can and buy and sell practically anything else, e.g., the enforcement of moral law, in accord with standard economic principles.

What is ultimately at issue between the Homeric and the Platonic conception of divinity is whether or not divinity can be constrained by men. Rational choice considerations are trivialized in a world without constraints; hence, the question of whether the gods are rational economic agents in their dealings with men is the same as the question of whether we can influence the actions of the gods.

Let me confront the seeming absurdity of my enterprise. Am I not claiming that there is something akin to twentieth-century concepts in poetry from a preliterate culture three millennia ago? How could Homer, or a gaggle of Homers, have known devices which would take another thirty centuries to work out? In short, how could there be philosophy without philosophers or economics without economists?

Here, we must entertain the possibility of knowledge without metaknowledge. Homer did not 'know' rational choice concepts in the sense that Euclid knew geometry. If asked why the sum of the interior angles of a triangle is 180°, Euclid can give a proof. Homer nowhere exhibits such ability. None the less, inside the Homeric epics, we can find solutions to rational choice problems which are correct. Why did Zeus do α and not β? There is an answer in the poetry which is not hard to find; scholars before me have found almost all of the answers, and the answer is invariably that the net benefit to Zeus of α is greater than the net benefit of β. In a rough-and-ready sense, we can apply to the Homeric epics something like an applied economics examination. Does the explanation for the decisions solve a series of rational choice problems?

Here, we pile head-on into the issue of evolutionary, nonabstract knowledge. The line of attack made by Plato on the nonabstract knowledge, claimed by these poetic sources, is to require those who claim to know to prove they know by articulation. This is to deny the very possibility of inarticulate knowledge, since a proof is an articulation. Philosophers have become accustomed to the notion of inarticulate knowledge in many areas, but poetry? How could a poet know enough to solve complicated problems without being able to give a proof? Or, if not a proof, a reason for the solution? Inarticulate knowledge we might expect from expert billiard players (to use Milton Friedman's famous example) or businesswomen going about their daily life. But how could there be *inarticulate* knowledge in the fountainhead of Western language and literature?

ECONOMIC IMMORTALS?

The narrative style, which an oral tradition encourages, requires that such economic 'analysis', or cost/benefit explanations of choice, as there is will be found only as a plausible motivation for a particular agent's action. Why did Achilleus do this? Why did Zeus accept that sacrifice?[5] While narrative style does not much resemble that typified by 'All real income-compensated demand curves are negatively sloped', we know, from the importance economists attach to successful predictions of individual actions, that one crucial role of economics is precisely to explain particular choices.

No, Homer does not present explanations of choice in the form 'A performed an act because of benefits B and costs C where B > C.' However, if we read carefully, we can find evidence of just such benefits and costs which will allow a rational reconstruction of the motivation for the action.[6] Some of the cost/benefit analysis is surprisingly nontrivial; in particular, what is the economic rational for Zeus allowing himself to be 'fooled' by Prometheus in the division of sacrifice?

The reality behind the Homeric gods, and their relationship with mortals, has been debated for millennia. The approach taken here is occasionally at variance with two alternative views of this matter. The first alternative thesis is that the gods are simply *façons de parler*, words which we can translate, either to subjective states or physical processes, without loss of information. 'A gift of Aphrodite' is the best singers, ignorant of the distinction between objective and subjective states, can do to express 'lust'. Ingenious scholars find it possible even to translate such statements as 'Athene returns Achilleus' spear'.[7] Possibly 'Zeus accepts this sacrifice and not that one' can be translated to 'This will happen but not that'. Doubtless, it is possible to find an acceptable translation for 'Dionysos gave Thetis a vase for Achilleus' ashes which Hephaistos made'. While such translations do not lose information, they seem not to gain much, either.

Why does translating an arbitrary sentence from 'god language' to 'subjective state language' tell us why, or even if, things happen? It certainly will help in instances when we have more secure knowledge of our subjective states than the gods' motivations. Such secure knowledge does not seem to help answer how Achilleus' ashes came to rest in such a lovely vase. Perhaps more troubling, it is easy enough to translate such statements as 'Zeus gave Achilleus immortality' from 'god language' even though the statement does not occur in the canonical text. If our translation scheme is not inhibited by the awkward fact that the sentence to be translated is not in the text, what can this translation tell us about the text? A good translation scheme would refuse to parse passages not in the source language.

The second alternative thesis is the claim that the gods, as well as other facets of the epics, embody and articulate background myth and ritual from society outside.[8] The second approach certainly offers the possibility of gaining very precise information in that case when we have secure knowledge of the myth and ritual. If, for example, we know that Dionysos is really a χ-spirit and that, generally speaking, χ-spirits give divinely crafted vases to the goddess mothers of recently slain heroes, then we have explained the transaction. We know why it happens. There are considerable difficulties with this approach. First, there is a general problem: when is the particular story close enough to the general pattern to count as an instance of it? When competing patterns are proposed, how closely they fit the particular story is vital. Which pattern is closer? Second, there is a problem specific to the Homeric epics: how does this thesis help shed light on the unique plot twists? It is well known that rather important aspects of the poems are unknown from other sources. Why is one myth or ritual selected and another disregarded?

Excepting for some terminology, the reading offered here is both old and simple. The gods are what men would be if men had more power and lived forever young.[9] Men die because they must; gods do not because they need not. Sappho told us this a long time ago.[10] The burden of the argument is twofold. First, even scholars, deeply sympathetic to such a point of view, object that men and gods are incomparable because gods are immortal.[11] This phase of the argument requires a demonstration that gods and mortals have the same objectives, and their behavior differs only because the constraints they face differ. Such a demonstration provides evidence for the economic content in the poems.[12] To answer the obvious 'So what?' there must be a second part, a demonstration that insight into the poems is to be gained with this approach. Just why did Dionysos give Thetis the vase? It is easy to establish that Dionysos had an obligation to Thetis, and that the other such obligations in the poems were paid with favors for Achilleus. Achilleus had just died and a funeral vase was one of a few appropriate gifts.

WHAT DO THE GODS WANT?

Stated sharply, the gods can be represented as rational agents who maximize their utility subject to constraints. The interest of an individual god is (first) to continue to exist and (second) to acquire income in the form of food, status and recreation. The question to be attacked is well known: 'How and why do the gods need men, and for what reason, in turn, do men have need of the gods?'[13] The approach taken is a natural one for an economist: the gods can obtain income from humans.[14] The linchpin for the interpretation is that a god's divine status can be increased by human sacrifices and decreased by human competition. Here is testimony from Poseidon on the link between human activity and divine well-being:

'Father Zeus, no longer among the gods immortal
shall I be honored, when there are mortals who do me no honor.'[15]

The gods in the Greek tradition compete for status;[16] consequently, humans can, under some circumstances, gain by helping a god obtain higher status. We who live now are blasé about rich men paying to have universities named after them. The Greek tradition we study thought it perfectly reasonable that their gods would pay to have cities named after them. So it is that Athens acquires its name. In an amazing auction Athene provides more valuable services to the Athenians than Poseidon. Status is a complicated concept to analyze in matters of exchange; trade can never be simply between two parties. That is, when Athene deals with the Athenians, and her status is improved, Poseidon's is necessarily decreased. When the gods compete for mortals' favors, mortals can expect both costs and benefits to flow to them.[17] The Trojan war owes its genesis to another auction, one which improved the status of Aphrodite *vis-à-vis* Hera and Athene.[18] If a human's sacrifice augments the status of a god, it is easy to appreciate that it could backfire. For instance, if a sacrifice moved many gods up one rank, at the expense of one god who moved down many ranks, the sum of the benefits to those gods who gained might be less than the cost to the god who lost. Or at least it would appear so from the human's point of view.[19]

Status is a matter of rank order, and from the logic of rank order, only 50 percent of the gods can rank above the median. Other constraints are less subtle: a god can be at only one place at one time, and any act takes a noninfinitesimal amount of time. The wonderfully important text where Poseidon worries about how *human* activities bear on his *divine* status has been quoted above. There is a text which demonstrates a concern about the real time of activity. Here, Hermes complains to Kalypso about the time it has taken him to run an errand for Zeus; time running errands is sacrifice forgone:

'It was Zeus who told me to come here. I did not wish to.
Who would willingly make the run across this endless
salt water? And there is no city of men nearby, nor people
who offer choice hecatombs to the gods, and perform sacrifice.'[20]

These constraints even bind Zeus. If he could be in two places in one time, he might simultaneously rape and establish an alibi against Hera's wrath. But he cannot do this. It seems that even Zeus can only be at one place at a time, to rape one person at a time, and this rape requires real time. Consequently, even for Zeus, there are limits to the amount of effort which can be expended to obtain goods and services.[21] As long as output is a real valued function of input – that is, finite input results in finite output – gods with infinite desires cannot be satiated.

If gods who prefer present pleasure to future pleasure have constraints at a point in time, then an infinite life does not result in a life without constraint.[22] Infinite-lived beings so constrained who prefer present pleasures to otherwise identical future pleasures will behave as if they confront a finite horizon.

CONSTRAINED DIVINITY

A characteristic of rational choice is that behavior changes to follow the constraints upon desire. A god can do two sorts of things to obtain goods and services from mortals: he can trade or he can take. Gods desire both recreation and status. One form of recreation is sex. For the sake of simplification, I ignore gender differences in attitudes toward sex. This simplification shows in treating sex as a contributor to recreation but not status. This simplification seems plausible for male immortals' activities – Zeus' conquests do not bother Poseidon – but there are serious difficulties representing female immortals this way. Three of these difficulties are as follows. (1) Hera's status is doubtless degraded every time Zeus reveals his preference for some human of either sex, hence her anger at such activity. (2) Kalypso alleges that there is a systematic Olympian double standard at work, *Odyssey*. 5.118–200: 'You are hard-hearted, you gods, and jealous beyond all creatures/besides, when you are resentful toward the goddesses for sleeping/openly with such men as each has made her true husband.' Examples are given at *Odyssey* 5.121–8. (3) Some goddesses are virgins by choice. Since a god is much more powerful than a human, interbeing sex seems mainly a matter of taking. Status is different because, if a god takes a status-enhancing sacrifice from a human, he is also taking something from other gods. Thus, from the god's point of view, grabbing status is more costly than grabbing sex. Next, we consider a series of activities which illustrate rational choice principles.

Gods trading with gods

One transaction recalled in the *Iliad* provides decisive evidence of the constraints upon divinity: that is the division of the world *by lot* amongst Zeus, Poseidon and Hades (*Iliad* 15.187–92). If Zeus is unconstrained, why does he not take all he wants?[23] This transaction seems to provide the template for Athenian democratic theory and practice.[24]

A god trading with another god is perfectly straightforward in the case where one god cannot simply overpower the other. One example illustrates how very easy this is to explain. In the *Iliad* Hera wants Zeus out of action, and Sleep is the only god with such power. Moreover, Hera does not have the power to coerce Sleep and so must trade for his service. Hera offers Sleep a golden throne and a footstool.[25] The deal does not go through. As Sleep points out, the last time he distracted Zeus (as a previous favor to Hera) his existence was almost terminated (*Iliad* 14.245–59). Hera has an instructive reaction. First, she points out that in the previous adventure Zeus' own son Herakles was involved (*Iliad* 14.264–6). This time Hera claims, untruthfully to be sure, that she is interested in ordinary mortals; consequently, Sleep will not have to bear such risks. Second, she raises the offer: one of the younger Graces is now part of the bargain, the very one after whom Sleep has been lusting (*Iliad* 14.267–9). The deal is done, after the appropriate oaths (*Iliad* 14.271–80).

This exchange is hardly unique.[26] What is remarkable is how simple all this is. Hera and Sleep haggling over the price of a service differ in no interesting respect from a camera-laden tourist talking down the price of a rug. We can tell the dancers apart but the dance itself is as it always is.

Gods exchanging with men

The analysis is considerably more interesting when gods trade with men because gods characteristically have the ability to take things from men without saying 'please'. Consider a constrained divinity facing two possible time uses: (1) trading with mortals and (2) grabbing from mortals. Trades between gods and mortals are commonplace in the *Iliad*, if we know what to look for. Gods perform services for mortals who have performed services for them. Thirty-five lines into Book 1 we read:

> Over and over the old man prayed as he walked in solitude
> to King Apollo . . . 'Hear me,
> lord of the silver bow . . .
> . . . if ever it pleased your heart that I built your temple,
> if ever it pleased you that I burned all the rich thigh pieces
> of bulls, of goats, then bring to pass this wish I pray for:
> let your arrows make the Danaans pay for my tears shed.'[27]

Apollo promptly proceeds to waste the Greek forces, dogs, mules and men.[28]

There are two sorts of seizures which are frequently reported in the *Iliad*. The first is sex. Sex between immortals and mortals is surely a one-sided affair when gods can rape invisibly.[29] The second is fame. The gods systematically destroy mortals who challenge their claim to superiority. Fame confers the shadow, if not the substance, of immortality. And the gods are sometimes afraid of what lurks in such shadows.[30] Humans with great technical skill or great beauty are in some peril.[31] Below, we consider how the gods punish those who would cheat death.

There are changes in constraints upon the gods in the *Iliad* (first) over poetic history and (second) in combat. What changes the constraints on the gods is a change in the power of men. First, in poetic history there was a precipitous decline in men's ability even within the memory of Nestor.[32] Within the memory of the gods, men could, with impunity, bully the great gods themselves. Poseidon built the wall of Troy for a mortal's wages and was cheated by his employer.[33]

Before the Trojan war, when men were stronger, or perhaps the gods were weaker, there was reason for the gods to trade more frequently with men.[34] The gods could not get what they wanted by simple grabbing, but conditions had changed by the time of the war. At Troy the Homeric gods had three staggering powers over humans: (1) they could put uncontrolled desires into the mind of men; (2) they could shift their shape[35] and (3) if wounded, they could be patched up as good as new.

These are all technical advantages. If by chance a mortal can overcome the shape-shifting advantage, some gods are in considerable difficulty. This we see in the initial charge to the wall of Troy in Book 5 of the *Iliad*. Diomedes is given the temporary power to see the gods in their true being, and is assured that he is operating under divine protection.[36] First, he stabs Aphrodite, who promptly whines off to Olympos to get an ichor transfusion. Although Aphrodite is not a war goddess, she certainly has the ability to send desires, but a man can fight desire. Then Diomedes gets a little excited and encourages Apollo to leave the battle, and, with help from Athene, wounds Ares.

At Troy, even with all these advantages, gods still act in response to sacrifices. These sacrifices are unambiguously described as trades between men and gods. Since there are trades in the epics, it does not seem appropriate to read the relation between gods and men in a simple hierarchical fashion of the 'Whatever God wants, God gets' sort. If we can trade with the gods, they can be bound by their desires. If one god does not honor sacrifices by doing favors, but another does, the rational mortal will shift his offering. Competition among the gods is the great constraint upon divinity. When so bound, the gods lose their mysteriousness. E. R. Dodds has found something remarkable in the spirit of the *Iliad*, a world less god-haunted than the Greek worlds to come. Homeric gods are like government:

> Homer's princes bestride their world boldly; they fear the gods only as they fear their human overlords; nor are they oppressed by the future even when, like Achilles, they know that it holds an approaching doom.
>
> So far, what we meet in the Archaic Age is not a different belief but a different emotional reaction to the old belief. . . . The doctrine of man's helpless dependence on an arbitrary Power is not new; but there is a new accent of despair, a new and bitter emphasis on the futility of human purposes. We are nearer to the world of the *Oedipus Rex* than to the world of the *Iliad*.[37]

Divine IOUs

The interpretative principle 'What God wants, God gets' certainly applies to a Platonic monotheism. None the less, in Homer Zeus is not coeval with divinity, as Poseidon reminds Iris, citing as evidence the division of the world by lot:

Therefore
I am no part of the mind of Zeus. Let him in tranquillity
and powerful as he is stay satisfied with his third share.[38]

Homeric religion can take on the guise of monotheism if we think in terms
of collectives, groups of men and groups of gods. Gods as a group cannot
be constrained by men as a group. But such holism asks the wrong
question. 'What does Achilleus have that Zeus wants?' may have a very
different answer from 'What do men have which the gods want?'[39] Such
holism abstracts from the possibility that the gods compete amongst
themselves and, by this competition, are constrained. An important series
of exchanges in the *Iliad* is precisely a result of divine competition being
used by mortals.

A very old question is: what does Achilleus have to offer Zeus to enlist
divinity in his cause?[40] While he has nothing directly to trade, this is of no
matter because he has an immensely valuable asset in his mother's affection.
And his mother, as the *Iliad* makes clear, has accumulated divine
obligations of staggering worth which she is willing to transfer to
Achilleus. Even the high gods cannot take such obligations by force. The
penalty for such repudiation of debts is presumably the same on Olympos
as it is here on earth: one can never borrow on the same terms again.
Whether it is to the interests of the blessed immortals as a group to allow
such obligations to be transferred to mortals is not clear; nevertheless, only
a very brave immortal will be the first one to go back on his debt. These
gods did not get to where they are by taking needless risks.

Three great gods owe Thetis their existence. When she transfers the
outstanding obligations to her son, each of these gods is obliged to pay off
the debt by a favor for Achilleus. While two of the favors are simple gifts
of material, the first favor suspends the laws of justice.

Debt 1: Zeus' debt to Thetis. The *Iliad*'s plot depends upon Zeus
nodding to Thetis' supplication. Achilleus suggests a reason why he might
do so:

I have heard you
making claims, when you said you only among the immortals
beat aside shameful destruction from Kronos' son the dark-misted,
the time when all the other Olympians sought to bind him,
Hera and Poseidon and Pallas Athene. Then you,
goddess, went and set him free from his shackles, . . .
Sit beside him and take his knees and remind him of these things.[41]

How does Zeus pay off this debt? Among other things, he does not enforce
the oath to end the war with a single combat between Paris and
Menelaos.[42]

'Zeus, exalted and mightiest, and you other immortals,

let those, whichever side they may be, who do wrong to the oaths sworn
first, let their brains be spilled on the ground as this wine is spilled now,
theirs and their sons', and let their wives be the spoil of others.'
They spoke, but none of this would the son of Kronos accomplish.[43]

This episode suffices to show that even Zeus has many objectives and that
even he cannot have all that he wants. Here, Zeus' interest in the
maintenance of justice among men is overwhelmed by his interest in self-
preservation.

Debt 2: Hephaistos' debt to Thetis. The obligation to discharge a debt
upon demand is most explicit in this passage:

'Then there is a goddess we honour and respect in our house.
She saved me when I suffered much at the time of my great fall
through the will of my own brazen-faced mother, who wanted
to hide me, for being lame. Then my soul would have taken much
    suffering
had not Eurynome and Thetis caught me and held me, . . .
Now she has come into our house; so I must by all means
do everything to give recompense to lovely-haired Thetis
for my life.'[44]

As a consequence, Achilleus obtains his grand new armor.

Debt 3: Dionysos' debt to Thetis. This seems to be an odd debt out
because, while the obligation is clear, it is not expunged in the *Iliad*:[45]

    Lykourgos the powerful, did not
live long; he who tried to fight with the gods of the bright sky,
who once drove the fosterers of rapturous Dionysos
headlong down the sacred Nyseian hill, and all of them
shed and scattered their wands on the ground, stricken with an ox-goad
by murderous Lykourgos, while Dionysos in terror
dived into the salt surf, and Thetis took him to her bosom,
frightened, with the strong shivers upon him at the man's blustering.[46]

No matter, the debt is paid, as we discover in the *Odyssey*:

    Your mother gave you
a golden jar with handles. She said that it was a present
from Dionysos, and was the work of renowned Hephaistos.
In this your white bones are laid away, O shining Achilleus.[47]

Possibly it is worthy of note that although Book 24 of the *Odyssey* has been
long considered a dubious addition to the poem,[48] it is one of the places
where loose ends are tied up.[49]

The wrath of Poseidon

The exchanges between man and gods in the *Odyssey* studied next are very much more complicated than those in the *Iliad*. The texts are harder to interpret partly because Odysseus himself tells much of his story and, unlike the muse, he has no insight into the doings of the gods.[50] While his statements about the gods are informed, they are not necessarily decisive. In particular, Odysseus' compensation to Poseidon for blinding the Cyclops Polyphemos is not the result of face-to-face negotiations. Rather, it seems to be an arbitrated compensation scheme. The question addressed is why it Odysseus who is punished, not Polyphemos.

One seemingly crushing objection is that Odysseus is not punished. Indeed, Odysseus says exactly the contrary: Polyphemos' blinding is punishment for his actions.[51] Not only does Odysseus say this, he surely must believe it to be so: else why would he give his real name? Odysseus clearly has convinced many commentators who find Zeus morally improved from the *Iliad*.[52] And, it must be frankly acknowledged, Odysseus has two good pieces of evidence which led him to his conclusion that his action would receive divine sanction. The first is that a great god 'breathed courage into us' (*Odyssey* 9.381). The second is that Polyphemos *systematically* blasphemes the moral order. Polyphemos knows the right and chooses the evil. By asking the formulaic question given seafarers in even the most friendly houses, he locates himself within the shared moral discourse of the poem:

> 'Strangers, who are you? From where do you come sailing over the watery
> ways? Is it on some business, or are you recklessly roving
> as pirates do, when they sail on the salt sea and venture
> their lives as they wander, bringing evil to alien people?'[53]

He publicly scorns the power of Zeus and the other gods (*Odyssey* 9.273–9). Having accepted Odysseus' wine, he violates the obligations due to guests, offering Odysseus the guest-present of being eaten last (*Odyssey* 9.369–70).

Odysseus has no insight into the calculations of the divine, so his opinions on the matter are not conclusive. Normally, Odysseus' evidence would suffice.[54] None the less, he erred frightfully in ignoring the fact (*Odyssey* 9.412) that Poseidon is Polyphemos' father, and Poseidon's affection must be assumed as real as Thetis'. We must read Polyphemos' prayer with care. Its tricky conditional form' – 'I would like A, but if A is not feasible, please do B' – has been overlooked.[55] The A part is that Odysseus 'may never reach that home' (*Odyssey* 9.531); the B part (*Odyssey* 9.534–5) is:

> 'let him come late, in bad case, with the loss of all his companions
> in someone else's ship, and find troubles in his household.'

The prayer is answered (*Odyssey* 1.68–75). The problem facing Odysseus' Olympian allies, Zeus (*Odyssey* 1.65–75) and Athene (*Odyssey* 1.47–50), is to have Poseidon accept the lesser punishment in lieu of the greater.

Zeus decides that the lesser punishment will suffice, a decision which Poseidon does not contest (*Odyssey* 13.132–4). But what could compensate Poseidon for honor lost from forgoing the greater? If he cannot punish a mortal as he desires, will men still fear him? If they do not, will not he lose honor on Olympos? (*Odyssey* 13.128–38). Zeus, as a minor compensation, allows Poseidon to turn the Phaiakians' ship into a rock for their temerity in assisting Odysseus (*Odyssey* 13.154–8).

It is in this context that I would read the controversial Teiresias encounter in Hades.[56] As I read Teiresias' instructions, Odysseus is required to perform missionary work for Poseidon. He is to seek out people ignorant of the sea and, as an obvious consequence, ignorant of the lord of the sea, to bring them the cult of Poseidon.[57] Here is how he tells Penelope of his obligation:

> he told me to go among many cities
> of men, taking my well-shaped oar in my hands and bearing it,
> until I come where there are men living who know nothing
> of the sea . . .
> . . .
> then I must plant my well-shaped oar in the ground, and render
> ceremonious sacrifice to the lord Poseidon[58]

Constrained to enforce only the lesser option in his son's curse, Poseidon loses honor and status. Odysseus compensates Poseidon by bringing knowledge of him to new lands. By this missionary work, up goes Poseidon's fame and with it his divine status. Honor gained compensates for honor lost.

If, out of selfless concern for the moral order, the *Odyssey*'s Zeus were enforcing justice on earth, one would expect the compensation scheme to be from Poseidon to Odysseus. In a self-interested model, our expectation runs in another direction.

Walter Burkert has proposed a wonderfully instructive explanation for Odysseus' difficulties. Burkert starts with the same problem: there is no *moral* reason for Odysseus to be punished. Is there a ritual behind inversion of the moral order?[59] The ritual Burkert finds is based on a werewolf story where, to return to human company, the werewolf must abstain from human flesh and stay away for eight years.[60] Odysseus fits part of the pattern, Burkert claims, because Odysseus' maternal grandfather had werewolf attributes. Burkert's proposal illustrates the difficulties which bedevil pattern recognition algorithms. In what sense is such a pattern close to the actual story? We are one year shy in the time away from home, but even so this is only one of the punishments upon Odysseus. The werewolf does not (2) lose companions nor (3) come home on an alien ship nor (4) find his home in chaos nor (5) is he required to carry an oar seeking out people who have never heard of the sea. 'Almost one' of five attributes is hard to defend as 'close'.

Moreover, the werewolf pattern is not the only one put forward to illuminate the *Odyssey*. Forty years ago, Rhys Carpenter presented an elaborate identification of Odysseus with a family of traditional tales, the 'bearson'. Carpenter too makes use of creative genealogy, supposing that Odysseus is actually the illegitimate son of Sisyphos.[61] It is doubtful whether both Burkert's and Carpenter's proposed patterns can be true, but no evidence has been offered to distinguish between the two.

GODS WHO SEE WELL AND MEN WHO DO NOT

One important distinction between men and gods in the epics is that gods see consequences better than men. Humans are all too often under the influence of 'ατη, and 'ατη, translated by 'disaster' or 'blindness', has been central to the study of Homeric psychology in recent years.[62] One important version of this general thesis is that men who do not perceive correctly will sometimes act contrary to their objective interests. Again the link between 'ατη as disaster and 'ατη as blindness is central. Thus, cost/benefit considerations do not completely determine the action of men. Gods, on the other hand, see better than men and perform cost/benefit calculations correctly.

Of the many possible examples, consider one which has been discussed in both the ancient and the modern commentary. Glaukos trades gold armour for bronze (*Iliad* 6.234) after Zeus has taken away his wits.[64] Only when they can perceive the consequences of their actions do individuals systematically act in accord with cost/benefit calculations.

Consider one divine choice, also much discussed, Zeus' decision to allow Sarpedon to die on Patroklos' spear. Hera points out (*Iliad* 16.440–9) that, if he saves Sarpedon, other gods will doubtless intervene to save their children, plunging Olympos into who knows what chaos. Zeus' bloody tears acknowledge the soundness of her calculation, and he acts accordingly. This passage crystallizes many aspects of the poem. Zeus fears the consequences of unchecked desires, and so calculates what modern economists know as an optimizing strategy. Contrast this with Agamemnon, who is also told (*Iliad* 254–84) what the consequences of his actions will be, but does not check his desire with calculation. As he will later explain (*Iliad* 19.88), 'ατη is to blame. He simply did not work out the consequences correctly.

It is demonstrated above that a certain class of moral codes can be explained as instruments to economic efficiency.[65] For individuals with perception failings, moral imperatives can provide useful information for utility-maximizing problems. Such moral codes will contain such imperatives as 'Nothing in excess' and the like.[66] Moral codes are essential, on this account, if humans in Homer are to behave sensibly. The formal result that moral codes can be of assistance to utility-maximizing under conditions of perception failing, combined with the omnipresence of mortals' perception failure in Homer, gives a justification for men's moral codes. But since gods do their cost/benefit analysis correctly, they have no need for the same moral codes as humans. Their actions will automatically take into account the consequences of their choice.

PUNISHMENT IN HADES

As an example of the problems which can be illuminated by cost/benefit considerations, we address the notorious question of what motivates the fate of Tityos, Tantalos, Sisyphos and Teiresias in Hades. Given the fact that Odysseus sees the unpunished shade of 'Eriphyle the hateful,/who accepted precious gold for the life of her own dear husband' (*Odyssey* 11.326–7), there is no reason to believe that Hades has any function in righting the wrongs of mortals.[67] What maximizing policy would select this group for reward and punishment? Teiresias is easy. He is an accidental victim of divine policy to whom the gods make compensation.[68]

What seems to connect Sisyphos and Tantalos is their threat to the gods' monopoly on immortality.[69] The gods' status would take a terrible beating if men became immortal.[70]

Think about punishing someone who tricks death. Simply killing him will not deter others from trying. Re-killing someone, as sole punishment for escaping death, has the same illogic as 'punishing' a bank robber by making him give back the money. Foreknowledge of capture would still make robbery the cheapest way to borrow. To punish someone for tricking death, one must do something more than kill him. Torture after death seems a perfectly reasonable punishment. These old gods are not stupid; their elegance pierces this economist's heart.

This explanation has nothing to say to the punishment of Tityos. It does, however, speak to the fate of Sisyphos, whose punishment has long disturbed commentators.[71] Again, the episode in Hades demonstrates how important it is to ask the question: what connection does the activity of the gods have to do with the maintenance of their status?

A SIMPLE MODEL OF A HOMERIC ECONOMY

Texts have been collected above which seem consistent with the hypothesis that the objectives of the Homeric gods have much in common with men's. It is now necessary to write down the details of the exchange economy to demonstrate the underlying rationale of trade. To minimize inessential details, the economy will be made as simple as possible. Thus, the gender distinction noted above is not taken into account. In technical terms the goal of the exercise is to solve for the optimal tax which the gods levy upon humans. Why is it that the great gods of Olympos, whose fame shall indeed last as long as the daylight is scattered, work for dog food?

There are two sorts of agents in the model: mortals and gods. We consider a representative from each group as contemplating trade on one twenty-four-hour market day. Each agent has one resource: twenty-four hours of time. Since human time is not the same as divine time, we have the possibility of exchange. Suppose that man and god exchange: the mortal would obtain divine time in exchange for human time. From the fact of exchange we cannot conclude that both parties gain. A god has the power to compel. A rape serves as the only needed example.

We suppose that mortals and immortals share a common utility function with three arguments: food, status and recreation. Sex, listening to poetry, playing with children, are the sorts of activities which this model lumps together as recreation. Thus:

Utility $= U$ (Food, Status, Recreation)

It is further assumed that the marginal utility of all arguments is defined and everywhere non-negative. What distinguishes men and gods is their productive capabilities, which we write in Table 8.1. To simplify, we allow there to be a fixed amount of time for each agent during this day. So we ignore the possibility that a man can, by risking his life in battle, obtain more food and higher status (*Iliad* 12.310–28). This possibility is real, but it is deferred until the next section. Successful war can also increase status among the gods, but this too is risky: the Homeric epics are littered with dead gods who have attempted to grab more status and failed.

Table 8.1 The production of well-being

Gods	Mortals
Food $=$ FD(Time$_{df}$)	Food $=$ FH(Time$_{df}$, Time$_{hf}$)
Recreation $=$ XD(Time$_{dx}$, Time$_{hx}$)	Recreation $=$ XH(Time$_{dx}$, Time$_{hx}$)
Status $=$ SD(Time$_{hs}$)	Status $=$ SH(Time$_{ds}$)
$24 = \Sigma_i$Time$_{di}$	$24 = \Sigma_i$Time$_{hi}$

The notation we employ is that Time$_d$ is divine time and Time$_h$ is human time. Time$_i$ is divine time spent on activity i, where i can take on values food, status or recreation. Corresponding notation is used for human time. All of the arguments to the production functions are supposed to have a positive impact. The production functions for the two groups differ, since the gods are obviously more powerful. The 'cross-species' production is vital. Consider the case of recreation: the more time the gods spend on sex, the more sex mortals will experience, because gods seduce humans. (Recall that this specification simplifies a complicated matter by treating sex as recreation and not as status-seeking.) The more time mortals spend on making themselves attractive, doubtless a vital consideration to obtaining more sex, the more the gods will be interested in them. The gods do not eat human food, and humans cannot collect what the gods do eat; consequently, the divine production of food is not influenced by human time. The gods change the weather, so they influence humans' food production.

The most interesting production functions are those for status. We suppose that, at the beginning of the day, status is given; thus, the production relation can be interpreted as a change in status. As specified in Table 8.1, status is given to humans by the gods and by humans to the gods. The texts above have demonstrated the importance of humans for divine competition for status. Human reliance upon the gods is obvious. To give the most far-reaching instance, Agamemnon acquired his status, which even Achilleus must respect (*Iliad* 16.54), by divine gift (*Iliad* 1.277–81).[72] Of course, humans can spend time to increase their status by raising cattle to sacrifice to the gods and the gods can increase their status by running errands for humans to pay for all the sacrifices. Obtaining such time motivates trade in the model.

Table 8.1 gives the productive capabilities agents in the economy. The subscripts f, x and s denote food, recreation and status. In the aggregate time constraint, the subscript i ranges over f, x and s.

One implication of the Homeric exchange economy is that if humans did not exist, the gods' status would be undefined. The best evidence for this interpretation is in the Homeric *Hymn to Demeter*. Demeter certainly cannot contend with Hades for her daughter by strength of arms. No matter, she can wipe out mankind:

> And she would have destroyed the whole race of mortal men
> with painful famine and would have deprived
> the Olympians of the glorious honor of gifts and sacrifices.[73]

Needless to say, her doomsday threat is dramatically effective.

In conjunction with the utility function above, this productive system gives a reason for gods to trade with mortals: gods and humans can increase their status by trade. Indeed, since the model abstracts from the risks of war, and war allows beings to gain status by risking life, trade is the only way in which beings of either sort can increase their status rank. Both gods and mortals can make use of that which the other has: both can use either human or divine time for productive use. However, there is no reason to believe that exchange is mutually beneficial; gods have power to take. Moreover, if a mortal trades with one god, another god may punish the mortal. This is a very uninformative result: we cannot even prove that trading with a god puts a mortal on a higher indifference curve. However, this failing is redressed next when we confront the most famous oddity noted in the commentary on Homeric religion.

There are two odd facts about Homeric sacrifices. First, sacrifices are characteristically things which the gods do not 'use'.[74] Second, the gods receive things which even men do not use, the inedible parts of animals.[75] The Prometheus story in Hesiod's *Theogony* seems to provide an explanation which flies in the face of the gods' rationality; in fact, Hesiod did not claim that Prometheus fools Zeus.[76] The question we must ask is: if the gods were really utility maximizers, would they allow themselves to receive this inconsequential sacrifice?[77]

We return to the question of productive capability. It is important to note that gods and men differ considerably in what serves to nourish them. Gods eat nectar and ambrosia, which is available in unlimited amounts; consequently, food to the gods costs only the time required to eat it. This has an important implication: the gods' food input will not be increased if they are given cattle to eat. However, the gods acquire status by receiving cattle as offerings. Men acquire status by spending time raising cattle for sacrifices, so sacrifices increase the status of both the giver and the receiver. Here we make a critical technical assumption: we assume that from the gods' point of view sacrifices are a *counter* to obtaining status.[78] What matters for the status of a god, we shall suppose, is the share of the total offering. Call this fraction P. If a sacrifice is a counter, it would make no difference to the utility of an individual god were he to receive P of a bull or P of the bones of a bull, just so long as his share is unchanged.

In the production equations above, we specify that human time spent in recreation contributes to the amount of recreation which gods enjoy. The idea is straightforward: the gods get less pleasure seducing someone of either gender who has spent the last month shoveling cow manure, skinning carcasses and on other food-producing activities than someone who has taken time out for an occasional sexuality-enhancing bath. Similarly, gods, who appreciate spectator sports, but not animal husbandry, would like to induce farm boys to turn their pitchforks into swords and ride away to an early death.

In Figure 8.1 we use indifference curves to represent mortal equilibrium. We assume the absence of 'ατη so the consumer is fully informed. The utility level of a mortal increases if both food and recreation increase. We represent the time spent in sacrifice-producing activity as a tax in time such that two levels of taxation are considered: $\tau_\alpha < \tau_\beta$. The outer constraint is attained when the tax in time required to produce cattle for sacrifices is at the low tax, τ_α, and the inner constraint is attained when the tax in time is the high tax, τ_β. For simplicity, we assume linearity of production. Supposing that both recreation and food are normal goods, mortals will consume more of both under the lower tax regime than under the higher.

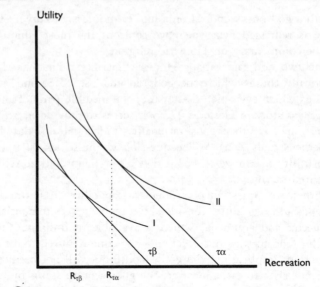

Figure 8.1   Consumption and divine taxation

Thus, recreation at τ_α exceeds recreation at τ_β because less time is spent in sacrifice-producing activity.

Now the rationality of a sacrifice policy can be asked in the following form: what tax makes a god best off? We demonstrate that the only stable equilibrium will have the gods receiving a positive infinitesimal amount of cattle (and hence time) for sacrifices.[79]

We consider only cases of non-negative sacrifices.[80] (1) The amount has to be positive. Assume the contrary. If the total sacrificed were zero, the status of gods is not well defined, since the undefined 0/0 would enter the production function for status. We have seen the danger which Demeter posed to the *gods* when she threatened to wipe out mankind. As modeled, a state with no sacrifices would be disastrous for the immortal economy. Thus, sacrifices cannot be zero. (2) Suppose, contrary to what is to be proven, that the gods receive some nonzero real (i.e., noninfinitesimal) amount of sacrifice. We prove this is not in the interest of a god. Figure 8.1 demonstrates that a decrease in the amount of human time for sacrifices increases the amount mortals will spend producing both food and recreation. An individual god will not suffer a status reduction from a lower time tax as long as the portions of the sacrifice are not changed. P of the bones is as good as P of the whole bull. Moreover, the god will benefit from a smaller tax because mortals spend more time making themselves attractive or heroic. Thus, it will be to the god's interest to favor a reduction in the amount of time which humans spend raising cattle for him. This shows that the optimal sacrifice exceeds zero but is smaller than any positive real number. Thus, it is positive infinitesimal.

Modern economists know a variation on this argument which 'proves' that a society can profit by replacing metallic money with paper money. The costs of production of paper money are inconsequential *vis-à-vis* the costs of metallic money. But money is just a counter; one paper dollar, as long as it is accepted for transactions, serves just as well as one gold dollar. If a commodity is really just a counter, the social utility maximizing amount of resources devoted to the commodity is infinitesimal. The benefits to society are from a monetary economy and this can be implemented more cheaply with paper money than with metallic money. Or so the argument runs.

An alternative solution to this problem was offered by Martin Nilsson. It is as follows:

> The sacrifice is a meal common to the god and his worshippers, linking them together in a close unity. The god is invited by prayer to come to the meal. He receives his portion, and the men, who are the greater number, feast on their portions. This is the reason why only a small portion of the flesh is offered on the altar of the god, a custom which had already struck Hesiod as so peculiar that he invented a mythical explanation of it.[81]

Nilsson's explanation does not, I think, come to grips with the fact that the gods receive inedible portions of the animal. A human who came a long way for dinner, expecting to share a meal, would surely be unpleasantly surprised to receive a thigh bone to gnaw upon. Would not the god?[82]

We find that a policy of infinitesimal taxation results in the highest utility for the gods. The skeptical, but polite, reader may well ask whether this whole exercise is not itself as odd as the practice studied. Who among the Greek writers wrote about optimal sacrifice policy? In fact, the line of argument that sacrifices result from a divine optimizing appears in both Hesiod's *Works and Days* and Plato's *Symposium*.

We have assumed that some forms of mortals' activity benefit the gods, and so gods have an incentive to direct human time use into these activities, and away from others about which they are indifferent. What if mortals could threaten the gods? We learn from Hesiod and Plato that the divine answer is to get new mortals. The gods in Hesiod's account are very crude: they seem only to exterminate and create with inexactitude. No matter, their desire for sacrifices is presented to motivate their acts:

> they live for only a poor short time; by their own foolishness
> they had troubles, for they were not able to keep away from
> reckless crime against each other, nor would they worship
> the gods, nor do sacrifice on the sacred altars of the blessed ones,
> which is the right thing among the customs of men, and therefore
> Zeus, son of Kronos, in anger engulfed them, for they paid no due
> honors to the blessed gods who live on Olympos.[83]

Plato's reaction to Homer is too complicated to discuss in any but the briefest fashion. None the less, in the *Symposium*, Plato has 'Aristophanes' improve upon Hesiod by giving an elegant account of an optimizing sacrifice policy in which the gods make modifications in their human creation. Men and women, it seems, were initially united, and could threaten the gods. By surgery the gods were able to maximize their income from sacrifice. This policy is described explicitly:

> 'Now, they were of surprising strength and vigour, and so lofty in their notions that they even conspired against the gods; and the same story is told of them as Homer relates of Ephialtes and Otus, that scheming to assault the gods in fight they essayed to mount high heaven.
>
> 'Thereat Zeus and the other gods debated what they should do, and were perplexed: for they felt they could not slay them like the Giants, whom they had abolished root and branch with strokes of thunder – it would be only abolishing the honours and observances they had from men; nor yet could they endure such sinful rioting. Thus Zeus putting his wits together . . . "I propose now to slice every one of them in two, so that while making them weaker we shall find them more useful by reason of their multiplication" ';[84]

It deserves to be remarked that, in Hesiod's and Plato's account, Zeus and associates do not do anything in return for particular sacrifices. In Homer the gods seem to check the sacrifice balance of a human before deciding to act upon a request to enforce justice. Thus, from a human's point of view, sacrifice is a purely private good. This is because (as seen above) gods compete for status. Homer's account agrees with neither Hesiod's nor Plato's; rather, Hesiod's and Plato's explain sacrifices as expenditures to finance what economists would call pure public goods. In *Works and Days*, Zeus has an interest in enforcing justice among men; but Zeus cannot be bribed by an individual's sacrifices:

> Straighten your decisions
> you eaters of bribes. Banish from your minds
> the twisting of justice.[85]

Plato can play with the idea of gods making optimizing decisions about human nature because this does not threaten his conception of divinity. For Plato, a god does not confront constraints and so will attain a maximum in all dimensions of quality of being. For example, Plato gives a 'proof' that a god would never disguise his true being. This proof actually goes through if and only if gods are unconstrained:

> 'Then does he change himself for the better and to something fairer, or for the worse and to something uglier than himself?' 'It must necessarily,' said he, 'be for the worse if he is changed. For we surely will

not say that God is deficient in either beauty or excellence.' 'Most rightly spoken,' said I. 'And if that were his condition, do you think, Adeimantus, that any one god or man would of his own will worsen himself in any way?' 'Impossible,' he replied. 'It is impossible then,' said I, 'even for a god to wish to alter himself . . .'[86]

If there were ever a reason for a god to disguise himself – for example, to sneak up behind someone – then the argument would fail. In such a case the loss in beauty must be balanced against gains in other dimensions. Since Homer's gods face constraints, and must trade for what they wish, they cannot be counted on to enforce justice and to fulfill the other tasks which philosophy sets for them.

If the above interpretation of Homer's immortals is correct, one of Plato's objections is obvious: they can be bribed.[87] As we have seen, Zeus will suspend the enforcement of justice if the price is right. Belief in these sorts of gods is, for Plato, the third type of atheism. Greek philosophical religion as it developed stripped the gods of their desires. And, ultimately, of their interest in man.[88] Avoiding Plato's third class of atheism may result in his second class. If the gods cannot trade with humans, why would they be interested in us?[89]

FAME AND DIVINE RECREATION: THE SUPPLY SIDE

There is no doubt that the immortals obtain pleasure from watching humans in bloody combat.[90] From the divine point of view, is it possible to increase the amount of time humans spend providing recreation? In the previous section we explored the rationale of a taxing policy which encouraged humans not to spend too much time raising cattle. One key step is the supposition that the gods acquire no utility from human food production which cannot be obtained in a cheaper fashion by sacrificing counters. This provides a partial answer. In this section we consider the incentives of humans to engage in combat, risking their lives, and so providing pleasure for the gods. Since humans acquire no utility from the gods' pleasure, this fact itself will not be an inducement. The gods will have to trade something which men value to get them to endure pleasing risk.

The exchange we now encounter has the most delicate mechanics of any we have yet considered. By the time of the war, it has been embodied in divine law, and its function is more presupposed than noted. While other exchanges are often called exchanges by the poet, or by a character, the payment for heroics is presupposed. The poem itself is the payment.

Why is it that men will even knowingly give up their life? Achilleus is absolutely clear: for fame (*Iliad* 9.410–16). Fame is the best that mortal man can do to rival the status of the immortals. Fame is a pale imitation of life; consequently, if men could live forever, fame would not be worth the risk of life (*Iliad* 12.322–8).

What guarantees that fame will be paid for services rendered? The mechanics of fame seem to be automatic, embodied into supernatural law. There seem to be two guarantors of fame: the goddess who inspires true poets to sing of heroic deeds[91] and human memorials.

Of the divine policy which sets in motion heroic epics, it is unnecessary to speak further. The poems are their own evidence.[92] Human memorials are rather more complicated because it seems that a more or less intact body is important for the fame-embodying memorial.[93] It is in the context of an exchange of fame for divine recreation that I would read the concern of the gods for Hektor's *corpse*.[94] There is no difficulty to explain why Aphrodite and Apollo are concerned about the state of his remains (*Iliad* 23.184–91). It is straightforward to explain why Hera, Poseidon and Athene share Achilleus' fury (*Iliad* 24.25–30). The puzzle is: why are nonpartisan gods concerned? Gods who sneer at the transitory existence fated to humans, who amuse themselves at the blood sports which turned Hektor into a corpse, ought really to have few scruples about what happens to the remains of a dead hero. One answer is that the gods are changed by the war, more concerned in Book 24 with human suffering than they were before.[95]

A god's motivation, like nature, surely does not leap. And, divine concern over a corpse is found much earlier in the poem than Book 24. We will treat concern over Hektor's corpse as simply one instance of what is called in the poem the 'privilege of the perished'. The hero cares about the state of his remains.[96] With his body intact, and a proper memorial erected, a hero can anticipate more fame than without the body.[97] If the hero cares, then utility-maximizing gods out to obtain more recreation will also care. Consider divine policy about corpse return. The question for debate is: will a hero who considers risking his life for fame be more likely to take the risk with or without a divinely enforced policy of corpse return? There seems to be no doubt that such a divine policy exists. Hera, certainly no friend to Sarpedon, says this to Zeus:

> then send
> Death to carry him away, and Sleep, who is painless,
> until they have come with him to the countryside of broad Lykia
> where his brothers and countrymen shall give him due burial
> with tomb and gravestone. Such is the privilege of those who have
>   perished.[98]

There are two interesting possibilities to consider. In case one, without a body some fame disappears from the world. If I kill you and destroy your body, your fame lessens and mine increases, although my gain is less than your loss. This is not the only conceivable case. Consider case two: what if fame is merely transferred? Suppose I kill you and destroy your body, and I absorb your memory and fame. The total fame is not changed, only its distribution.

In case one, it is clearly to the interest of the gods to adopt a return of the body policy. There will be more net fame available to heroes and, hence, more heroics. Even in case two, the corpse return policy makes sense as a method to attenuate the gambles a hero takes: he can only lose his life, not his fame. Moreover, the perfect transfer case seems a little precious and in conflict with the texts. How can the rational hero boast of killing helpless people? The little obituary notices posted throughout the epics acknowledge some ability, some reason to believe that under another sky the battle might have gone the other way. Why would we remember one who kills those without the ability to defend themselves? Who remembers executioners even in good causes? Achilleus will be famous because he killed his peer, the great Hektor, in a fair fight.

The remainder of the argument is straightforward. Achilleus told us all we need to know about the relationship between the supply of heroics and the amount of fame: the supply of heroics increases as the price paid to heroes increases (*Iliad* 9.315–420).[99] Hence, Zeus' anger at Achilleus' failure to allow Hektor's corpse to be ransomed (*Iliad* 24.111–16) makes sense as a policy of maintaining the desired supply of heroics. As long as heroes are willing to provide more interesting sport when their fame payments are guaranteed, such a fame insurance policy makes excellence sense for rational divinity.

THE PARRY HYPOTHESIS

Having given some evidence that the Homeric gods are engaging in making choices which seems consistent with what we know about rational economic behavior, it is important to describe a mechanism through which the Homeric poems could incorporate such modern machinery. The Parry hypothesis tells us that the composition of the Homeric epics was the result of an efficient adaptive, evolutionary process. As Milman Parry describes this process, a poem evolved which exceeded the ability of any single poet, or small group of poets at some time, to create.[100] The epics developed incrementally as individual singers over generations accepted the successes, and rejected the failures, of their predecessors as the foundation upon which to rest their own contributions.[101]

What deserves to be noticed is that Parry's description of the evolutionary process through which the Homeric epics developed is strikingly similar to Adam Smith's description of other evolutionary systems. Problems are confronted by individuals, one individual's successful solution or failure is employed or avoided by those who follow. While Smith's discussion of changes in the conditions of material production resulting from widening the division of labor is most famous, Smith himself employed the evolutionary machinery to give a conjectural history of formal logic.[102] Such evolutionary systems employ vast amounts of information.[103] Parry himself exploited this information utilization property to explain why the Homeric poetry is so grand. For our purposes, if the epics were composed by a single poet, or stitched together out of fragments composed by single poets, there would be no plausible basis to find such advanced concepts in the poems. However, if the poems were constructed as the Parry hypothesis suggests, then there is reason to believe that the singers could *narrate* an account of rational choice without being able to give a generalized account of the choice. In an interesting sense the singers may know how to solve an economic problem – to explain some behavior – without being able to prove to (persuade?) a skeptic that the solution is correct. Hence, as Eric Havelock emphasizes, the importance of the Platonic device of the dialogue form in the attack on Homer: a speaker is asked to explain what he means, to convince a skeptical audience of the truth of his account.[104] Knowing how to solve a problem is not quite the same as knowing how to persuade someone else that the solution is correct. As a consequence, there are famous instances in the history of science where a problem was solved correctly long before the machinery was developed by which to prove that the solution was correct.[105] Problems can be solved in an evolutionary process without conveying to the solver the ability to convince others that the solution is either correct or generalizable.[106] The song can be far better than the singers know.

The cost/benefit model of divine activity sketched above has an interesting similarity with the epithet formula system which Parry identified. The cost/benefit calculation approach gives a uniform, and exceedingly simple, explanation for choices. The activity of all informed agents, divine and mortal, can be explained on the simple, unified basis.[107] The singer does not have to find a different explanation for each act; on the contrary, for an informed agent, what to do is determined once the costs and benefits are spelled out. This unifies the poems on a motivational level.

WHY NO MIRACLES?

There is another useful way of looking at the evolutionary explanation. Parry's explanation of the evolutionary creation of the poetry emphasizes the feedback from audience to performer. Expressed bluntly, Parry forces us to think of Homer the way television critics tell us to think of profit-maximizing programming. What is produced is what sells. And what sells appeals to the 'lowest common denominator'.[108] If the audience approves of a phrase, the performer, sensitive to the audience's mood, will retain it and, perhaps, find another use for it elsewhere in the poem. This explanation gives the audience members veto power over the poetry. All the audience does not have to approve, but a large number of members must. This means that explanations for activities must be made in common terms. Ordinary people get to vote on the poetry. And, in equilibrium, the poems will embody something like a popular consensus.[109]

Suppose this voting holds true for the explanations of choice as well as the phrasing. Let us think of the sinews of the plot, the motivation behind the choices which are made. What is going to appeal to a large number of the audience? Because we must focus on the common understanding, not the refined understanding of a few, it seems plausible that an explanation for choice which rings true in terms of the everyday experience of the audience will be preferred to an explanation which is foreign to their routine. Or, if one prefers Platonic terminology, ordinary people's opinion will be preferred to experts' knowledge.[110] An audience which understands buying and selling from personal experience will be more likely to accept explanations for transactions which are motivated by concepts of buying and selling than by any concept which is foreign to their experience.

If we could rummage through the evolutionary failures, the verses which were tried but failed to meet with audience approval, could there be a different motivation for choices? Achilleus might go to Troy to die for the pleasure of the gods. In practice, where are such scraps? What if we suppose that the fragments of the cycle which survive are precisely such evolutionary failures? Could a test be conducted on this body of data? Fortunately, we can take advantage of Jasper Griffin's recent study of the differences between the canonical books and the fragments from the cycle.[111]

Griffin's report highlights important differences between the Homeric epics and the cycle. In the latter (1) talismans and magical properties abound; (2) immortality for heroes is very common;[112] (3) great heroes do not freely choose to go to Troy, they are dragged kicking and screaming.[113]

Clearly, the facts which Griffin reports are inconsistent with the exchange model developed above. These facts are also blatantly inconsistent with the canon. The immortality of men is particularly jarring. In terms of the exchange model above, a gift of immortality would raise the status of men to rival that of the gods. A god who grants immortality reduces the status of his kin. And, as we have seen, they do not take kindly to such reduction; hence, in the *Iliad* Zeus will not even rescue Sarpedon for fear of stirring up Olympos. Other points are less obviously inconsistent. Perhaps they only seem so because the context of the cycle poems has been lost. But as matters stand, there are other difficulties with the motivation of agents in the cycle. If Achilleus did not want to leave home for Troy in the first place, why did he stay, risking his life and his friends? Achilleus' choice in the *Iliad* is motivated by exchanges: life is given freely for fame. Finally, the existence of talismans raises the question: why did the gods give away such wonderful weapons and magical abilities? In the *Iliad*, as we have seen, Achilleus obtains material favors from the gods by his mother's transferred obligations. Why do the gods give away in the cycle what they offer in trade in the *Iliad*?

Evolutionary accounts have often been criticized as being untestable. However, in the case of Greek poetry we are fortunate to have evidence of failures, poems which did not survive. And these failures, from the fragmentary evidence available, offer a very different picture of the motivation of gods and men. From the fragmentary evidence available, motivation in the failed verses is a good deal less lifelike, more fairy-tale, than what is found in the poems which survived.[114]

CONCLUSION

I have argued that the Olympian gods act in their self-interest. Most dramatically, Zeus places concerns of his self-preservation and divine status over the demands of the moral law. There is evidence that the Olympians' behavior toward mortals is a simple function of a maximizing calculation: if it is efficient to grab desired goods and services, they will; if not, they will trade for them. These are interesting gods; perhaps, they are gods only an economist could admire. And, gods who have their own interests to pursue cannot be trusted to run errands for philosophers. The reaction of such philosophers as Plato seems to be to hire new gods. Be this as it may, the stories in the Homeric epics do demonstrate a remarkable ability to motivate a complex series of transactions by appeal to some basic principles of rational choice.

From the above reading of the mechanism of divinity in the Homeric epics, it follows that the quarrel between economic explanations and the Platonic–Christian tradition is indeed an old one. And, this quarrel cannot be described as one between 'ancients' and 'moderns' without taking into account the fact that the most ancient is also most modern.

Ultimately, the reading of Homer I argue for is a defense of Plato's reading of Homer. Is our conception of divinity a matter for popular vote or a matter for experts? As Plato writes, if Homer is right, there is no need for expert knowledge; popular opinion will suffice. While Plato certainly has convinced experts of their own importance, it is less clear that he has convinced ordinary people. The reader who thinks that the gods cannot be bribed has never watched television religion nor a mass to speed the progress of souls through purgatory. The reaction that these are not real gods is to assume Platonism. Ion, in Plato's account, answers Socrates' questions very poorly; perhaps, we who know more about the informational properties of evolutionary systems can find better answers.

Chapter 9

The statistical basis of Athenian and American constitutional theory

INTRODUCTION

How do we know what the 'public interest' is? The modern approach to the subject is to assume that all individuals in society act on their preferences and through some collective choice procedure, such as majority rule, construct an outcome that we can call the public interest. This approach has the attractive feature of fitting neatly with a methodological individualism which finds in the individual the conceptual unit from which larger social groups can be constructed. Unfortunately, the seminal work of Kenneth Arrow[1] and others has shown how little this modern approach allows us to say about the public interest. Even when the constituent individuals in society are assumed to have stable, non-cyclical preferences, aggregation remains a formidable task. There is no obvious linkage between individual and social choices, and the proper definition of the latter is only weakly constrained by the former.

There is another approach to the subject of the public interest, one found in ancient Greek constitutional theory, equally consistent (I shall argue) with methodological individualism. My reconstruction of this ancient approach presumes that the public interest is the center of private interests. Accordingly, it views the political process as a method by which this center can be estimated or discovered. I propose to explore some of the properties of this ancient approach, in particular the feature which allows political participation to be a random variable.

One unanticipated dividend of this approach is that it provides us with ancient examples that confirm the power of modern social choice theories. Thus it is possible to show how ancient Athenian institutions, known to us today with considerable particularity, were well adapted to estimating the public interest by statistical procedures. There can be no claim that the Athenians consciously used modern theories to fashion their own public institutions. But the weaker claim, that these institutions flourished in practice because they helped identify the political center, is consistent with the available evidence and attractive in its own right.

To see how this case can be made, start with two claims about Athenian democracy widely reported in classical scholarship. First, the ordinary Athenian citizen thought highly of it. Second, it was the best known example of pure, direct democracy considered by the classical political theorists. The texts at our disposal tell us who was for Athenian democracy, and who against. None the less, any serious attempt to come to grips with the Athenian intellectual defense of democracy, to go beyond who was for and who was against, by asking what sort of properties were claimed for this political institution, runs headlong into the fact that no pro-democratic text has survived.[2] Not only this, but the randomization process central to the Athenian democracy, election by lot, received no contemporary philosophical defense:

> The Athenians also attached great importance to the equality of all citizens in formulating and deciding public policy. This was secured by the right of every citizen to speak and vote in the assembly, and by the composition of the Council of Five Hundred, *which prepared the agenda of the assembly*; this body was annually chosen by lot from all the demes of Attica. . . . It is a proof of the poverty of our information on democratic theory that no reasoned defence of this cardinal institution, the lot, has survived.[3]

It is wonderfully ironic that the best known feature of the lot today is that Socrates had to face charges because of his determined opposition to its use in the random selection of public officials. As Xenophon writes:

> he taught his companions to despise the established laws by insisting on the folly of appointing public officials by lot.[4]

In this chapter I argue for a model of Greek constitutional theory where politics is viewed as a method of estimating the public good. Within this metaphor, the use of randomization procedures to select voters is explicable. The model has contemporary power. First, I develop the conditions under which democracy has ideal properties and, second, the conditions under which democracy has terrible properties. The model can be easily extended from a policy level to a constitutional level. And, at the constitutional level it is easy to give a rent-seeking explanation of why some types of individuals would be entirely hostile to this random decision-making procedure.

The interpretative problem I confront is very straightforward when I attempt to apply this reconstruction to ancient arguments. Statistics, as a recognizable discipline, did not evolve until modern times. Moreover, mathematical ability, of which there was a considerable amount in Plato's academy, does not necessarily translate to anything like the intuition required for statistical analysis.[5] The problem is how to interpret the opinions of those who wrote without the benefit of a statistical language to describe the solution to a statistical problem. I propose that we look in the texts to check (first) to see what problems were posed. To the extent that these problems can be expressed in a naive language, e.g., 'Will democracy get closer to the 'best' than monarchy?', then (second) to test our statistical solution with the results in the texts, e.g., 'Yes'. If our solution matches the solution in the text, then at least we have a useful model of the texts in question.

It is a fact that most of our knowledge of the Athenian lot comes from various works of Aristotle. Indeed, Aristotle argues at many places that the lot is an entirely appropriate device for a democracy. Moreover, one exceedingly interesting passage in the traditional Aristotelian corpus asserts some properties of the lot, when it should be used and why:

> In democratic states legislation ought to provide for appointment by lot to the less important and the majority of the offices (for thus faction will be avoided), while the most important magistrates should be elected by the votes of the multitude.[6]

The reconstruction which follows will be tested against these forty-one words. They shall be called 'Aristotle's conjecture'. One goal of the chapter is to convert the conjecture to a theorem.

In fact, the link between the model and the texts is especially strong in the case of the democratic failures because we encounter the 'problem of factions'. Factions, in which voters decide to vote in groups, allow a rather sharp test of the interpretation of the metaphor of votes as estimation. Aristotle initiates a discussion that reaches its constitutional culmination only in *Federalist* 10.

The Athenian randomization procedure, as well as that of the Venetian polity, has been discussed before. Jean-Jacques Rousseau's *Social Contract* is probably the most famous instance of this literature.[7] However, there seems to be no systematic attempt to construct a model inside which voting and drawing lots are complementary methods for discovering the public interest, and by which Aristotle's conjecture can be evaluated.[8] Such a model is offered below.

LOTS AND RELIGION

The author of the first full-length treatment of the Athenian election by lots starts by acknowledging the greatest barrier to scholarly appreciation:

> There is no institution of ancient history which is so difficult of comprehension as that of electing officials by the lot. We have ourselves no experience of the working of such a system; any proposal to introduce it now would appear so ludicrous that it requires some effort for us to believe that it ever did prevail in a civilised community. There can be

few people who, when they first hear that it existed at Athens and in other Greek states, do not receive the information with incredulity. The first impulse is to doubt the fact and to suppose there is some misunderstanding.[9]

A second barrier to an appreciation of the lot may result from the conjecture advanced by scholars that election by lot had a religious origin.[10] Presumably, when religion enters, rationality exits.

There are at least two senses in which one can look for the religious aspect in casting lots. The most straightforward is to look to the practice of religions. Here, the religious aspect of casting lots is so obvious that there is a word for the procedure, 'sorcery'. As the *Oxford Dictionary of English Etymology* testifies, the root of 'sorcery' is 'sort', Latin for 'lot'. Thus, in terms of its Latin basis, 'sorcery' is a technical term for 'divination by lot', a usage long forgotten.[11] Consistent with Aristotle's conjecture, the lot was used for minor, routine matters of religion.[12]

But, there is another way of viewing the religious aspect of the lot, to take the texts seriously and ask what in these religious texts made lots so special. In Greek religion, the lot was very special indeed because it allowed a peaceful division of the world among contending gods. The early history of Greek gods is so incredibly bloody that any peaceful method of resolving disputes is worthy of note:

> But Earth, grieved at the destruction of her children, who had been cast into Tartarus, persuaded the Titans to attack their father and gave Cronus an adamantine sickle. All they, all but Ocean, attacked him, and Cronus cut off his father's genitals . . . And, having dethroned their father, they brought up their brethren who had been hurled down to Tartarus, and committed the sovereignty to Cronus.
>
> But he again bound and shut them up in Tartarus . . . since both Earth and Sky foretold him that he would be dethroned by his own son, he used to swallow his offspring at birth. . . .
>
> But when Zeus was full-grown, he took Metis . . . to help him, and she gave Cronus a drug to swallow, which forced him to disgorge first the stone and then the children whom he had swallowed, and with their aid Zeus waged the war against Cronus and the Titans. They fought for ten years . . . the gods overcame the Titans, shut them up in Tartarus . . . but they themselves cast lots for the sovereignty, and to Zeus was allotted the dominion of the sky, to Poseidon the dominion of the sea, and to Pluto the dominion in Hades.[13]

WHY MAJORITY RULE?

The argument will presume, and this presumption is sufficiently odd to be stated explicitly, that majority rule is valued as an instrument to reach a desirable position. We presuppose that majority rule is in force because society, in some sense, finds something desirable about having the result on each issue, separately, decided by the median voter.[14] The median voter applied to a sequence of single issues can be viewed as a strategy which reduces the maximum loss for all individuals in the community relative to that which might come about through agenda control or vote trading.[15] The idea is simple enough. Through vote trading or agenda control, each individual must consider the possibility that the political process can reach an arbitrarily dreadful output. The median voter position can put limits on the amount of the loss. Hence, at a constitutional level within the framework which John Rawls has made famous,[16] there is something to be said for this as a desired goal.

Immediately we confront a problem which is at the center of research in mathematical voting theory: how can this median voter result be attained? A generation of research has shown that, when there are multiple issues to consider, rational voters will trade their votes on one issue for votes on other issues,[17] or be led by agenda setters to vote for something other than median voters' preferences.[18] Only when the Plott conditions hold does it seem that the median voter will prevail.[19] The Plott conditions require that voters' preferences over all issues are symmetrical around a grand median, so a motion in any direction from any single issue median will lose more votes than it gains. The Plott conditions do not seem very likely, so we can have no confidence that the median voter will prevail.

These results, however, force us to look at the constitutional framework inside which majority rule operates. Sometimes we can find some institutional structure that can induce the median voter outcome.[20] This will lead to us to the question of why an agenda setter might be chosen at random.

THE MODEL

The Greek poets and philosophers championed a view of choice which stresses the imperfection of human perception.[21] Where individuals perceive poorly, their perceptions cannot be transitive,[22] so it is unlikely that their preferences would be transitive either. Thus, with this simple objection we can immediately rule out any routine possibility of representing their view with such modern devices as indifference curves and the like. Rather, it is possible to write down a model which allows us to deduce many hard aspects of Greek choice theory, e.g., 'weakness of will', as a problem of producing well-being guided by local information supplemented by the knowledge that more is better than less.[23]

Suppose that the discussion can be formulated in the following paradigm problem. Consider the question of national defense, where society agrees that it wishes to produce an amount of national defense D^*. The society

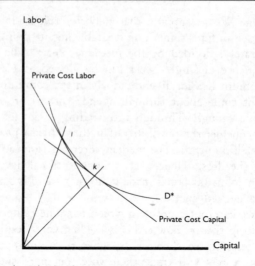

Figure 9.1   Desired methods of production (1)

possesses a production function for national defense which depends upon labor and capital, thus: $D(L,K)$. What makes the problem difficult is that there are many ways of producing D^*. The locus of all possible combinations of labor and capital which can produce D^* is what economists like to call an isoquant. Much capital and little labor will suffice, as will much labor and little capital or more nearly equal amounts of both. Each individual in a democracy under a system of private property will face private interests to favor a particular method of producing D^*. People who own only labor will favor a labor-intensive method of production – call it l – because the increase in the demand for labor will cause their wages to increase so their share of taxes will be lower than under a capital-intensive defense. The argument goes through, with the obvious modifications, for owners of capital who prefer a capital-intensive method, k.

We can draw a picture in Figure 9.1 of the isoquant for D^*. The different private costs of defense, taking into account the rent received by different factors, cause different factor owners to favor different methods of production. Indeed, each factor owner will, in general, have a different desired expansion path. As the desired amount of defense changes, an expansion path specifies the amount of labor and capital which an individual would prefer to have employed.[24] What makes this easy exercise of rent-seeking in defense economics relevant is that this very result was known in the Athenian discussion. Aristophanes has a good laugh at the poor people of Athens who go to the assembly to vote more money for the navy and higher wages for themselves.[25]

Suppose, again, that we can simplify the general Greek discussion into a dispute over which of these expansion paths is desirable (Figure 9.2). Over

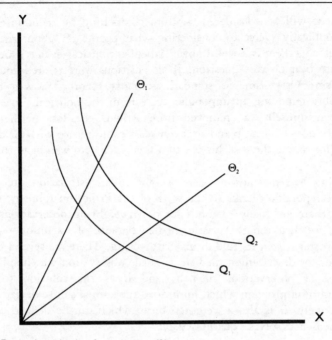

Figure 9.2   Desired methods of production (2)

arbitrary commodities X and Y, the question is whether one goes up path θ_1 as preferred by citizen 1 or up path θ_2 as preferred by citizen 2.[26] The machinery develops only a partial order of space, but as long as movement is confined to a ray it can be described with the plausible axiom 'More is preferred to less'. Of course, the desired expansion path would be changed by shifts in factor prices and technology.

What we have done is construct the machinery, surreptitiously to be sure, for treating policy as a random variable. If individual i were allowed to select the policy, θ_i would occur. If K individuals were selected without replacement at random, and policy decided by majority rule, then the median voter, med[1. . .K], would select the policy, thus $\theta_{med[1. . .K]}$. Of course, this outcome results from our ignoring the possibility of log-rolling or other multiple-issue considerations.

If we suppose that the socially optimum policy occurs at some weighted average of the individual proposed policies then many of our nontechnical problems are settled. Is it reasonable to believe that the Greeks believed that every opinion was equally entitled to representation in the political process, no matter how far from center this position? If this is so, then the mean of the voters' desired policies would be appropriate. There are two reasons to think not. The first is the general distrust for extremes found explicitly in Homer and more obviously in later philosophical texts.[27] This argument will be considered far from compelling by economists who are philosophically averse to considering what people say about their choice. Fortunately, there is a well-known Athenian political device which one can bring to bear on this question. If all positions were treated equally, why ostracism? Ostracism, as standard accounts report,[28] was a device for honorably removing an unpopular voice from the political process. While the man himself was removed from Athens, he lost neither material property nor citizenship and after ten years could return without disgrace or disability. None the less, his position was given zero weight in the political process.

Giving extremes low or zero weight in an estimation procedure has become reputable thanks to the work of the Princeton robustness study.[29] While there are many methods for downweighting observations far from center, we focus on the classic median because of its unique status as a location statistic in its role in majority voting. There are several equivalent methods for describing a median: it is the observation which splits an odd number of observations in half, and it is the solution to a linear programming problem which minimizes the sum absolute deviations. Most instructively, it is also a weighted mean which can be defined as follows. The median θ solves equation (9.1):[30]

$$\sum_{i=1}^{n} w_i(\theta_i - \text{median } \theta) = 0 \tag{9.1}$$

where $w_i = 1/(|\theta_i - \text{median } \theta|)$ iff $\theta_i - \text{median } \theta \neq 0$
$ = 1$ iff $\theta_i - \text{median } \theta = 0$

In this formulation of a median, it is immediately apparent (not the case in the 'sorting' formulation) that the further an observation is from center, the lower weight it will receive. Hence, the policy of ostracism may be a sensible method of weighting someone's vote even less than does a median. Even today, some released felons who have 'paid their debt' lose their right to vote, although not their rights to own property or make contracts. Looking at votes as estimators makes sense of this procedure.

Let us abbreviate the median of θ_i, $i = 1...N$ as $M(\theta)$. Without recourse to organic political philosophy we may also speak of $M(\theta)$ as the 'general will' of the existing citizens. We could make the argument more difficult by asking Platonic–Rawlsian questions about an infinity of possible people, N of whom are realized in this particular state of the world. Moreover, and here is where our construction touches bases with much post-Athenian political theory, we could start with $M(\theta)$ as a primitive and define individual interests in terms of deviation from $M(\theta)$. While this approach would fit most comfortably within a Platonic metaphysical system, where we have more secure knowledge of the universal than we do of the particulars, as we shall see below one cannot escape such conceptions even in that most anti-Platonic document, *Federalist* 10.

Now, the whole range of statistical inference can be brought to bear on the problem of interpreting Greek political theory. Suppose we know the optimum, $M(\theta)$, and observe the actual policy, $\theta_{med[1. . .K]}$: we can define the statistical loss, $SL(\ )$ as some appropriate distance between $M(\theta)$ and $\theta_{med[1. . .K]}$.[31] A large statistical loss for housekeeping details would surely have a different economic consequence than the same statistical loss for the invasion plans for Syracuse. Even considering some fixed issue, we can ask many interesting questions about this loss. For instance, what happens to the divergence between actual and optimum as K changes? Since elections by lot are made without replacement of voters, it is trivial that as K approaches N the actual policy approaches the optimum, so the loss vanishes.

Consider the text of Aristotle's remarkable defense of something like mass democracy. Here we encounter an important example of the difference between knowing the solution to a problem and being able to prove that the solution is correct:

> For the many, of whom each individual is not a good man, when they meet together may be better than the few good, if regarded not individually but collectively, just as a feast to which many contribute is better than a dinner provided out of a single purse. For each individual among the many has a share of excellence and practical wisdom, and when they meet together, just as they become in a manner one man, who has many feet, and hands, and senses, so too with regard to their character and thought. Hence the many are better judges than a single man of music and poetry; for some understand one part, and some another, and among them they understand the whole.[32]

Aristotle's argument, such as it is, is not terribly impressive.[33] But, Aristotle is absolutely correct that there is something powerful about averaging errors. If Aristotle had known how to *prove* how errors cancel out when averages are taken, modern statistical research would have had a two-millennia head start.

When did the Athenians employ the lot? Except for the matter of agenda setting, we are told by recent scholarship that the answer is clear: for routine matters. For more important issues, direct elections were held:

> The Athenian democracy is sometimes described as a form of government in which every citizen could rule and be ruled in turn and in which tenure of office was largely determined by the lot. But this is at best a half-truth, since only those magistrates were chosen by lot who had routine duties to perform; the important offices that required special political and diplomatic skills were filled by direct election.[34]

The import of this is clear. There are two sorts of losses in the problem; one is the loss in terms of nonoptimum social policy described above. But there is also the loss in terms of the time it takes to make decisions. Put crudely, we can fight the Persians by manning the ships or we can talk about how to fight the Persians efficiently.

The fact that there are two sorts of losses means that we can write the production function for economic loss as a function of the statistical loss, the issue, here J, and the amount of time to make a decision. We represent the latter as a function of the share of the citizens making the decisions, hence, K/N.

$$\text{Loss} = \text{L}(J, SL(M(\theta), \theta_{\text{med}[1 \ldots K]}), K/N).$$

Thus for any issue J loss comes either from an imprecise decision rule or from increasing the manpower to get a better decision rule. Making the usual curvature assumptions, we can describe this trade-off in Figure 9.3 in terms of the aversion of loss. We are producing less of a negative thing so the isoquants seem to have the 'wrong' direction, $\text{Loss}_0 < \text{Loss}_1$.

Of course, one can repeat the argument above about private optimum expansion paths, only now at the constitutional level. To solve this out, we ask: what is the rent-adjusted private optimum expansion path over this particular space? Let us call this path ϕ with the appropriate subscripts. Obviously, someone whose time has very low value in alternative employment would favor a labor-intensive procedure whereas someone whose time was very valuable in alternative employment would favor less participation. This traces out the rays ϕ_1 and ϕ_2 respectively.

Akira Yokoyama raises the good question which sharpens the point at issue. Why are officials selected at random? If you stipulate you wish to have decisions made by K individuals as a labor-saving device, why not elect them by vote?

We can try out our model by asking the question: which of the two devices, random selection or direct election, will be less likely to be biased? Suppose that it were known that only routine matters would be voted upon today, would participation be uniform across individual interests? Of course not. Those whose time was most valuable would be loath to come to vote on such minor matters. Consequently, one could expect direct election of minor officials to be a biased method of making decisions. On the contrary, the sample median has optimum properties as a method for minimizing bias in a wide range of circumstances.[35]

Who might one expect to have lots of leisure time to debate and deliberate? What figure was well known for hanging around the Agora associating with youth of dubious morals? Here is what he is reported to have said about the lot:

it was silly that the rulers of the city should be appointed by lot, when

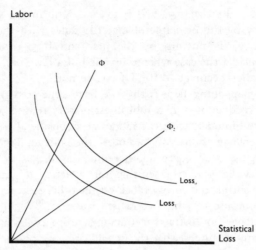

Figure 9.3   Debate at a constitutional level

no one would be willing to employ a pilot or a carpenter or a flautist chosen by lot.[36]

Only someone whose time was absolutely worthless, or who positively enjoyed disputing, could reasonably defend a decision-making policy always to minimize the statistical loss. On the contrary, ordinary people with farms to worry over and pots to throw could well decide that a positive amount of statistical error is optimal. Of course, philosophers with lectures to give, constitutions to collect and fish to study might well welcome time off from political discussion. Needless to say, the systematic weighting of costs and benefits from policy error is evidence of an extremely sophisticated political system.[37]

We have now established one of Aristotle's claims, that the lot makes best sense for minor officials. Now, we turn to the issue of factions and violence, where the ancient texts insist on the importance of the lot.[38]

WHEN THE MEDIAN IS NON-ROBUST, OR, DO YOU REALLY WANT TO DECIDE?

To employ the model to analyze factional politics we need only drop the assumption that the votes were cast at random, i.e., independent. We have assumed that my vote was not influenced by yours.

Let us suppose there are two factions in society, each with ($0.5N$) members. The members of each faction agree to vote as a block, with the policy proposed by each faction decided in a faction caucus. Voting is open, so contracts can be enforced. Suppose that citizens 1 . . . ($0.5N$) form the first faction and citizens $(0.5N + 1) \ldots N$ form the second. The caucus forms policy by the principle of majority rule, with the result that policy $\theta_{med[1 \ldots (0.5N)]}$ is put up by the first and $\theta_{med[(0.5N + 1) \ldots N]}$ by the second. Consider the case when everyone but a few vote, so K almost equals N. Will policy occur at $M(\theta)$? Of course not.

What is happening here is that we have generated the best-known case where the median is a non-robust estimator; that is, when the random variables are bimodal, with the modes at a considerable distance from each other.[39] A change of one vote can move the policy a large distance from one mode at $\theta_{med[1 \ldots (0.5N)]}$ to another mode at $\theta_{med[(0.5N + 1) \ldots N]}$. In this case, it may be perfectly sensible for violence to erupt as one faction attempts to shrink the voting block on the other side. In fact, this seems to have been one use to which ostracism was put.[40]

This violence- or ostracism-inducing property of a nonrobust voting procedure might suggest that the benefit of being politically decisive has an associated cost. If my voice moves the election result a large distance, my participation benefits me. But, simultaneously, my participation costs other people quite a bit. If they are sufficiently annoyed, perhaps they will find a method to bring my participation to a halt.

The technical device we have employed to generate a nonrobust voting procedure is a bimodal distribution of voters, two extreme parties confronting each other from their modes. In fact, this precise situation is employed by Aristotle to explain revolution and the rise of tyranny:

> Thus it is manifest that the best political community is formed by citizens of the middle class, and that those states are likely to be well administered in which the middle class is large, and stronger if possible than both the other classes, or at any rate than either singly; for the addition of the middle class turns the scale, and prevents either of the extremes from being dominant. Great then is the good fortune of a state in which the citizens have a moderate and sufficient property; for where some possess much, and the others nothing, there may arise an extreme democracy, or a pure oligarchy; or a tyranny may grow out of either extreme – either out of the most rampant democracy, or out of an oligarchy; but it is not so likely to arise out of the middle constitutions and those akin to them.[41]

The best state, to paraphrase Aristotle, is a unimodal distribution of interests.[42]

There is nothing easier to document than the opposition to factions or parties by traditional political theorists. The nice properties of the sample median, in particular its convergence to the general will with the expenditure of labor resources, depend upon factions not being terribly strong. With factionalism, the actual results will swing wildly. This large influence of a single vote is a remarkably promising method of explaining political violence.[43]

Now, we can come to grips with the lot as a partial remedy for violence. Suppose instead of a direct election with factions exactly balanced, policy is decided by a random draw. While killing one opponent without generating retribution when a vote is to be taken will insure that one's side will be decisive, this incentive is reduced considerably if (say) policy is decided by selecting one official at random. The change in probability is easy to compute. With equal-sized factions, the probability of winning is:

$$P_{win} = 0.5N/(0.5N + 0.5N) = 0.5$$

whereas with one fewer opponent the probability only changes slightly to

$$\lim (N \rightarrow \infty) \ P_{win} = 0.5N/(0.5N + (0.5N)-1) = 0.5$$

Hence, the incentive to violence falls considerably as N rises.

Unfortunately, as long as votes are taken on the important issues, it is not clear that a lot will suffice. All offices would have to be filled at random for such a procedure to inspire great confidence. In this context, consider the Platonic communistic response. Plato's proposals, taken seriously, propose that the decision-makers be freed from private economic interest.[44] Instead of voting on their interest, they will vote directly for their perception of $M(\theta)$. Presumably a good education helps one to appreciate the common good; under communism one would have no private interest to act otherwise.[45] The independence of the Platonic rulers from interest and faction lives today in the new welfare economic proposals to guide policy by a consideration of social costs and benefits. James Buchanan is correct that there is an equivalence between new welfare economics and applied Platonism: if one can identify social costs and benefits by technical means (as the new welfare economists presume) then one can identify the $M(\theta)$. The rest is just implementation.

JAMES MADISON GETS IT RIGHT

Adam Smith and James Madison consider two manifestations of the same problem of factions. Smith worries about how religions find it to their interest to inculcate natural religion; Madison worries about how factional politics can serve the public interest. Their tack is to suppose that factions are inevitable; interest is codetermined by life itself. Hence, the Platonic move is blocked by human nature. In terms of the model, what would it take to have factional politics or religion attain the same process as independent politics? The answer is: many small factions. Instead of having armies at two modes staring across a vacant plane of moderation, K modes spread across the distribution return us to something approximating a unimodal distribution where a sample median is most robust.

As the number of factions increase, the amount of independence in the system increases, so what is exactly true for the independent case becomes approximately true for the factional case. The incentives to violence decrease because the reduction, whether by murder or by intimidation, of the number of citizens in the other factions would change the vote only slightly. The median is robust once again.

All this we read in *Federalist* 10. First, Madison defines a faction in terms which presuppose the public interest can be identified as easily as actual people's interests:

> By a faction I understand a number of citizens, whether amounting to a majority or minority of the whole, who are united and actuated by some common impulse of passion, or of interest, adverse to the rights of other citizens, or to the permanent and aggregate interests of the community.
>
> There are two methods of curing the mischiefs of faction: the one, by removing its cause; the other, by controlling its effects.
>
> There are again two methods of removing the causes of faction: the one by destroying the liberty which is essential to its existence; the other, by giving to every citizen the same opinions, the same passions, and same interests.
>
> It could never be more truly said than of the first remedy, that it is worse than the disease.[46]

Large numbers of factions solve the problem:

> The influence of factious leaders may kindle a flame within their particular States, but will be unable to spread a general conflagration through the other States: a religious sect may degenerate into a political faction in a part of the Confederacy: but the variety of sects dispersed over the entire face of it, must secure the national Councils against any danger from that source . . .[47]

The fact that Madison's first example of the competition of factions is the competition of sects proves that Madison and Smith were drawing upon the same evidence.[48]

CYCLICAL MAJORITIES AND TRADING VOTES

The problems considered above are an odd lot. Why were the Athenians, other than some philosophers, so attached to their random selection procedure? What is the 'trouble' with factions? These are historical problems; and economists have a remarkable habit of forgetting problems which their current technical machinery cannot handle. The 'problem' of factions is a wonderful instance because factions pose no problem whatsoever in the post-Arrow literature. In canonical form the modern issue is to determine what can be said about social decisions, given the preferences of N individuals in society. The 'violence of factions' raises the issue of under what conditions there are incentives to reduce by violence the population to $N - 1$. This factional issue drops out of concern when N is taken as a fixed number. Moreover, in the modern literature, individual preferences are taken as determined outside the analysis, so it matters not whether votes are statistically independent or dependent. If the problem does not even make sense within the technical confines, why bother?

So the question should be confronted: what does the machinery above, such as it is, say about cyclical majorities and other central issues of post-Arrow mathematical politics? Trivially, when the decision is made with some $K > N$ then the possibility of cycling is always present. For any process with a random component the possibility of intransitivity is obvious. Sports competitions, for example, are invariably intransitive. Consequently, we restrict the argument to issues where all N citizens participate.

The argument is in two stages. First, we restrict the voting to a single issue such as the appropriate factor intensity method of defense. We generate reason to believe that voting preferences will be single-peaked over this dimension. Second, we open the argument to multiple-issue considerations. Then the randomization of the office of agenda setter becomes central.

Two figures are drawn in Figure 9.4; one is another version of Figure 9.1, where the convex isoquant for defense, D^*, is drawn with two private shadow prices, one for a labor owner and one for a capital owner. The second, immediately below the first, is a picture of the labor intensity of D^*, moving from maximum labor intensity to maximum capital intensity.

Points l and k present private minimum cost method of producing D^* for two individuals, each with the same twenty-four hours of time to labor, but one with less capital than the other. The convexity of the isoquant tells us that there is a unique local minimum which is also the global minimum. Hence, the further one gets from this private optimum, measured along the D^* isoquant in terms of factor intensity, the more private costs must be borne to produce D^*. A unique cost minimum, with lower costs as one approaches the minimum from either side, gives a single-peaked cost avoidance method of producing D^*. Suppose that votes follow economic interest so in all pairwise cases the individuals will vote in favor of the lower private cost method of production. The convexity of the isoquant requires, as a simple mathematical fact, that the voting preferences for factor intensity will be single-peaked. Mapping from cost avoidance to votes, we get voters with single-peaked preferences over factor intensity. And, the Arrow–Black theorem tells us, majority rule when voting preferences are single-peaked, and the vote is taken over a single issue, does not cycle.[49]

The argument has assumed, implicitly, that each voter perceived the

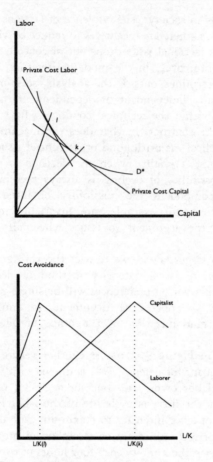

Figure 9.4   Desired factor intensity

same isoquant. Of course, this is not really at issue. As long as the voter perceives a convex isoquant, the cost avoidance method of production is single-peaked. When voting on a single dimension issue, single-peaked voting preferences of any sort generate stable majority rule.

This approach does not escape Arrow because all we need do is find, in the midst of convex isoquants, an appropriate number of nonconvex isoquants. Nonconvexity of isoquants will generate multiple local cost minima which in turn will generate multiple peaks in voting preferences. However, it is to be noted that we have 'reduced' the Arrow problem over a single issue to a problem of nonconvexity in production. Nonconvexities raise hard problems, e.g., one can generate cases where a maximizing agent can choose to make herself worse off. These sorts of hard problems characterize much of what we can recover from the classical Greek discussions of the matter.[50]

But, the objection must be made: what restricts the votes to a single issue? Here we recall the literature summary with which we began: the Athenians used a random selection process for the agenda setters.[51] In fact, there is a lengthy discussion in Aristotle's *Constitution of Athens* which describes the contemporary procedure for selecting the Council of Five Hundred:

> The Council of Five Hundred is elected by lot, fifty from each tribe. Each tribe holds the office of Prytanes in turn, the order being determined by lot; the first four serve for *thirty-six days* each, the last six for *thirty-five*, since the reckoning is by lunar years. The Prytanes for the time being, in the first place, mess together . . . It is also their duty to draw up the programme of the particular day, and where the sitting is to be held. They also draw up the programme for the meetings in the Assembly.[52]

Let us formulate the problem of multiple-issues as a sequential voting problem over $1 \ldots S \ldots$ issues. The median vote on issue J is denoted $M(J)$. The issue is: will the sequence $M(1) \ldots M(S) \ldots$ result from a majority rule procedure? We have agreed that this sequence is the desirable outcome. The answer, from either James Buchanan's and Gordon Tullock's log-rolling perspective or Richard McKelvey's agenda-setting perspective, is almost surely not.[53] Looking at the issue in terms of log-rolling, the voters can trade their vote on issue 1 for some issue later in the sequence. Looking at the issue in terms of agenda setting, the voters are given a conditional sequence of agenda where they reveal a preference for something other than the position of the median voter on each issue considered separately. The difference between the Buchanan–Tullock and the McKelvey results is one of distribution of rent. In the Buchanan–Tullock framework the vote traders gain whereas in the McKelvey set-up the agenda setter gains. Only when the Plott conditions hold can such trades not be found.[54]

First, consider vote trading. Since the traders do not have control of the agenda – indeed, the agenda setters are changed every month – it is risky to engage in log-rolling. If I trade my vote on issue 1 for a vote on issue 2, what guarantee do I have that issue 2 will actually come up?

The possibility of only short sequences in office will also complicate the life of the McKelvey agenda setter, for there will be fewer sequential combinations which can be offered the voter.[55] In the McKelvey framework the combination of randomization and very short terms makes it less likely that an agenda setter will invest as much in obtaining knowledge about the voters' preferences as he would when the position of agenda setter could be anticipated or held for a long term. Hence, the agenda setter would be less likely to force the results to fit his preferences than he would in the absence of the Athenian precautions.

Let us reconsider the argument. Have we not done something illicit in considering 1 . . . S . . . issues sequentially? Certainly, when faced with a fixed term of office, it is to the interest of the agenda setters to put forward a multiple-issue bundle.[56] They have one lunar month to make and seal all deals. This raises some technical difficulties which suggest we consider what we know about the production of knowledge. Suppose that the ability of the agenda setter can come from three sources: (1) experience (learning by doing), (2) study or (3) intrafamily communication. The third case allows for the possibility that agenda-setting wisdom can be passed down from father to son. First, by making the agenda setters' terms very short, the possibility of learning by doing is minimized. Second, by making the agenda setters' terms unpredictable, the private reward for investment in knowing other people's preferences is also minimized. Third, restriction of the monthly agenda setters to one tribe makes communication between sequences of agenda setters more costly. To the extent that knowledge is passed down best within a family, and a family is a proper subset of a tribe, the knowledge of how to be an agenda setter or a log-rolling entrepreneur will be broken up.

The construction above assumes that the Athenians wished that the median voter would control the agenda and argues that randomization of the agenda setters with rapid turnover makes sense as an instrument to this end. There is direct evidence that can support this reconstruction from Plato's *Laws*. The issue is the election of generals; the list of candidates considered is set by the agenda setters. However, anyone could ask to have the candidate list amended by offering an alternative candidate. Moreover, this motion to amend the agenda seems (in Plato's account) to have parliamentary priority:

> at the election of the generals it was open to anyone present in the body of the meeting to propose the substitution of a candidate of his own naming for one who was included in the official list, and to ask for a vote to be held prior to the election itself in order to determine whether such a substitution should be effected.[57]

Thus, changes in the agenda could be made, but (at least in this instance) on a matter germane to the issue, by the majority. Hence, the median voter could revise the agenda on the matter at issue, but not (on this account) bring up a new issue or tie in this issue with another issue.

The Athenian precautions seem to make sense in, and perhaps only in, the context of the modern public choice literature. The importance of randomized, rapid change in agenda setters is apparent in this literature. This is possibly another instance to add to the evolutionary literature as an example of an institution which evolved but could not have been designed because no one understood, in some Platonic sense, its importance until two and a quarter millennia after its demise.

LESSONS FROM THE PAST?

In the context of modern concerns over use of the political process by organized interest groups, the Athenian practice of randomization may have more than antiquarian interest. If legislative boundaries were set at random, would not this help reduce the power of incumbency? If regulators were selected at random for short terms, would not this help reduce the ability of the industry to capture the regulatory process?

Even though the founders of the American constitution were extremely knowledgeable about ancient political matters, the importance of randomization to the Athenian democracy became clear only after the publication in the 1890s of the *Athenian Constitution*. Given the founders' ambivalence toward democracy, this lack of guidance on how Athens actually worked might have not have made much of a difference. However, with our current commitment to democracy, perhaps the employment of a randomization procedure would be worth considering.

Indeed, one can view the recent spate of term limitation legislation in the United States as an attempt to combine the best part of random representation with election by lot. The cost of election by lot is the loss in precision relative to the median voter. The great benefit of election by lot is the guaranteed turnover in incumbents. Perhaps, United States citizens are feeling their way back to the beginning of democratic practice. It is wonderfully amusing that the 'revolt of the median voter' is never connected by scholars with Athenian practice.

CONCLUSION

Statistical techniques are our best empirical devices for discovering an underlying, unknown reality. It is no accident that one of the American Statistical Association's official collections is titled *Statistics: A Guide to the Unknown*.[58] In the context of politics as a discovery process, it is remarkable that many aspects of Athenian constitutional theory and practice can be rationalized as possessing a deep statistical underpinning.

The statistical basis for the Athenian constitutional theory shows up in several important areas. (1) We can talk about the general will or social optimum (in the absence of decision-making costs) without recourse to controversial philosophical claims or the 'what is, is ideal' assertion. (2) For one issue considered in isolation, as the number of independent citizens participating in the process increases, the actual vote approaches the general will. (3) When we take into account decision-making costs, it will not be sensible in general to make optimum decisions in the sense of point 1. Imprecise decision rules are fine when the economic loss suffered by imprecise performance is small.[59] (Philosophers who enjoy disputing would have a different view of this matter than the general population.) (4) We can explain what is 'wrong' with factions by appeal to what mathematical statisticians call an 'influence curve'. What is the marginal impact of one observation on an estimator? When the distribution is bimodal, and the modes are far from center, which might well happen in factional politics, the sample median's influence curve is not well behaved. This fragility of the influence curve can be employed as a prediction of gains from political violence. In this context James Madison rightly deserves to be called the intellectual father of the Constitution. (5) The Athenian randomization procedure for agenda setting makes it more likely that majority rule will generate the median voter than would be expected to occur in the absence of this institution.

Chapter 10

Fame and the supply of heroics

INTRODUCTION

This chapter is very important to my enterprise, for in it I propose an account in canonical form of how an ordinary person's theory of conduct might influence the provision of public goods. The line of attack I shall take is to work from the insights of ordinary people, as expressed by their accounts of the gods, to obtain a specification of the model. The desire for approbation – fame or honor – or the equivalent desire to avoid disapprobation – infamy or shame – is critical to this account.

A quick reading of the Homeric epics may give a very narrow view of the relation between fame and public goods. While everyone notices that in the *Iliad* the foresight of fame motivates soldiers voluntarily to chance death for their friends and family,[1] it may not be so obvious that fame comes to a wider class of action. In the *Odyssey*, for example, fame is offered as a payment to singers of heroic tales who have been blessed by divinity.[2]

Looking back at even older tradition, it is easy to see just how general is the link between fame and public good provision. Consider *Gilgamesh*. Fame surely comes to a man willing to risk single combat with a god:

> Friend, who can scale [heaven]?
> Only the gods [live] forever under the sun.
> As for men, their days are numbered;
> their achievements are a puff of wind.
> Here you are, afraid of death.
> What of your great strength?
> Let me walk in front of you, . . .
>
> If I fail, I will have made myself a name.
> 'Gilgamesh,' they will say, 'went against fierce Humbaba
> and died.' [They will remember], afterward,
> the child born in my house.[3]

But, there is a less perilous path to immortality:

Section b describes another way in which Gilgamesh sought immortality
– building the walls of Uruk. The building of enduring structures, with
their accompanying foundation inscriptions . . . served to perpetuate the
name of the royal builder.[4]

Four thousand years later, we still remember Gilgamesh and his walls.

But will this really work? Can the fame motive really generate public
goods? While everyone could contribute to finance public goods, everyone
cannot be equally famous.[5] While a fame motive may indeed be important
to produce academic science, this academic economist's reaction is to
dismiss my trade as an extraordinary enterprise.[6] For a fame motive to
generate the private provision of public goods, it is not sufficient to explain
why a few people might provide public goods.[7] But, to foretell all, we will
be setting up one prisoner's dilemma problem to trap another.

FAME AND CONTROVERSY

It is important to recognize that the desire for fame is a controversial
motive. There was controversy among the Greeks because the desire for
fame seemed to them a contest with the gods:

> Unfortunately, the *psyche* usually lost creative powers after death, and so
> was helpless in comparison with divinity and nature. This was the source
> of the familiar old quarrel between Simonides and Kleoboulos of Lindos.
> Kleoboulos thought men could make things – a bronze statue, a carved
> stele, a poem – which would not waste away or be extinguished 'so long
> as water flows or the tall trees bloom, so long as the sun goes up to
> shine, and the brilliant moon, so long as rivers flow and the sea-waves
> surge on the shore.' That was immortal memory, fame, *kleos aphthiton*,
> the oldest ambition in Greek poetry. Creativity was a magic drug, a
> *pharmakon* against death and against being forgotten. Simonides thought
> he saw a tougher truth, that rivers, flowers, sun, moon and waves were
> immeasurably stronger than human creation because they were divine. It
> was idiocy to 'set the strength of a stele against the flame of the sun and
> the gold moon and the whirling sea' because our work is inescapably
> mortal. Still, in the short time between the Greeks and ourselves, rivers
> have dried up and oceans shifted while many Greek *pharmaka* against
> death are still potent.[8]

Homer's gods realize that fame confers the shadow if not the substance of
immortality. These shadows, cast by men who used to be, can eclipse the
gods' own luster. Death puts men beyond the reach of the gods; the gods
themselves now are in harm's way, and they are afraid:

> 'Do you not see now these flowing haired Achaians
> have built a wall landward of their ships, and driven about it

a ditch, and not given to the gods any grand sacrifice?
Now the fame of this will last as long as dawnlight is scattered,
and men will forget that wall which I and Phoibos Apollo
built with our hard work for the hero Laomedon's city.'[9]

So even in the *Iliad* – what Simone Weil called 'The Poem of Might' – city walls, the great public good in an era of bandits with arrows and spears, generate fame. The stone walls of Troy, built by two of the high immortals to be hard enough to withstand a ten-year siege, can be overshadowed by a wooden barrier thrown up overnight by men desperate to cling to life for just another day.

Perhaps, it is not just the Homeric gods who worry:

And the whole earth was of one language, and of one speech. . . . And they said, Go to, let us build us a city and a tower, whose top *may reach* unto heaven; and let us make us a name, lest we be scattered abroad upon the face of the whole earth. And the Lord came down to see the city and the tower, which the children of men builded. And the Lord said, Behold, the people *is* one, and this they begin to do: and now nothing will be restrained from them, which they have imagined to do. Go to, let us go down, and there confound their language.[10]

Here is an old textual problem: why is God angry? Is the desire for fame such an evil thing? After all, God Himself offers fame to Abraham as part of the covenant.[11] Perhaps there is a difference between taking fame by one's own deeds and having God give it to you.

Indeed, when we find an explanation for the production of public goods by a desire for fame, we see religious controversy lurking in the background. A wonderful example is provided by Douglass Adair's celebrated *Fame and the Founding Fathers*, in which he sketches the motivation of the founders of the American republic as they themselves understood it:

The love of fame is a noble passion because it can transform ambition and self-interest into dedicated effort for the community, because it can spur individuals to spend themselves to provide for the common defense, or to promote the general welfare, and even on occasion to establish justice in a world where justice is extremely rare.[12]

To the references cited by Adair as informing the founders' opinions on such matters one should surely add Polybius' comparison of the Roman constitution with other constitutions. The Romans recognize the importance of fame to motivate public services:

the Romans through their customs provide many incitements to develop these qualities among their young men. One instance will be sufficient proof of the interest shown by the state in developing men of such character as to endure all in order to gain a reputation in their country for courage.[13]

Although specialist opinion is divided, there is some evidence for the existence of what economists might consider an exchange theory of politics in the teaching of the remarkable Greek atomist Democritus. Here is what Democritus wrote about motivation inside a republic:

> To good men, it is not advantageous that they should neglect their own affairs for other things; for their private affairs suffer. But if a man neglects public affairs, he is ill-spoken of, even if he steals nothing and does no wrong. And if he is negligent and does wrong, he is liable not only to be ill-spoken of but also to suffer bodily harm. To make mistakes is inevitable, but men find it hard to forgive.[14]

It is startling that those classical texts, Polybius' and Lactantius', to which colonial historians have pointed as particularly important to the American founding, are the same classical texts to which classical scholars have independently pointed as having roots in Democritus' writings.[15]

The classical republican tradition, as it is called, concerns itself with the conditions under which free people can be self-governing. One does not have to read very far in this literature without encountering the claim that republicanism requires voluntary service in the public good. One possibility is that individuals are, in fact, motivated by the common good or out of a sense of benevolence. What if we take a hard-headed Scottish attitude and agree that we do not expect individuals to act but in a self-regarding manner. Is there any hope for republicanism?

A tradition which stresses civic virtue will regard the claims of fame with considerable difficulty. There is no reason why lusting after fame should be regarded as virtuous. In what sense is the desire for fame connected with the common good if everyone cannot be famous?[16] It is not altogether clear that on judgment day one would wish to associate with defenders of the importance of fame. The problem is not the ancient spokesmen. For example, Heracleitus said this:

> The best men choose one thing rather than all else: everlasting fame among mortal men. The majority are satisfied, like well-fed cattle.[17]

But he was one of the first explicit monotheists among Greek philosophers and he had hard words for the morality of Greek ritual.[18] Even Democritus has had admirers in high places.[19] Thomas Hobbes presents a problem:

> Desire of Praise, disposeth to laudable actions, . . . Desire of Fame after death does the same . . . yet is not such Fame vain; because men have a present delight therein, from the foresight of it, ...[20]

As does Bernard Mandeville:

So that the most insatiable Thirst after Fame that ever Heroe was inspired with, was never more than an ungovernable Greediness to engross the Esteem and Admiration of others in future Ages as well as his own; and . . . the great Recompence in view, for which the most exalted Minds have with so much Alacrity sacrificed their Quiet, Health, sensual Pleasures, and every Inch of themselves, has never been any thing else but the Breath of Man, the Aerial Coin of Praise. . . . To define then the Reward of Glory in the amplest manner, the most that can be said of it, is, that it consists in a superlative Felicity which a Man, who is conscious of having perform'd a noble Action, enjoys in Self-love, whilst he is thinking on the Applause he expects of others.[21]

Mandeville could not be clearer what the isssue is. Approbation does not require the gods:

For as soon as it was found out, that many vicious, quarrelsome, and undaunted Men, that fear'd neither God nor Devil, were yet often curb'd and visibly with-held by the Fear of Shame . . . they had made a Discovery of a real Tie, that would serve many noble Purposes in the Society.[22]

ALTERNATIVES SOURCES OF IMMORTALITY

The fact of the religious controversy over fame is important. To this economist controversy hints at the possibility of a close substitute for fame. This is important for a number of reasons. If everyone cannot be famous, then fame cannot be 'basic' to life the way water is. This is suggestive of how the problem is to be structured.

Before this suggestion is exploited, I propose to give three striking instances of controversy between those who hold that immortality comes through fame and those who hold that immortality comes through survival of the soul. Fame can be seized by human hands; real immortality comes as a gift of the gods. I propose to consider fame and the smiles of the gods as alternative sources of approbation. The first instance is an interpretation of Homer associated with Erwin Rohde's book *Psyche*. The second instance is the line of attack which important Christian apologists took upon pagan religion. The third instance fleshes out the bones of one of the strangest performances in the body of economic theory, Bentham's mummification program.

Rohde's hypothesis: out of sight, out of mind

Few moralists have had good words to say about the Homeric gods as exemplars for mankind. One who did defend them, and who looked at the moralists' attacks in terms of *their* self-interest, Friedrich Nietzsche, had a considerable influence on German philology. Indeed, the competitive, self-interested aspect of Greek poetry/philosophy which Nietzsche pointed to seems to have strongly influenced Erwin Rohde's famous *Psyche*.[23] Crudely put, Rohde's hypothesis is that the Homeric poems are an active polemic against a previous 'cult of the soul'. There is something after death in the Homeric account, but it is not life.[24] The funeral practices recognized in the poems are aimed at making certain that the dead stay away from the living.[25]

The grave in Homer has ceased to be an instrument to attain material immortality; rather, it has become an instrument to attain fame:

> If we ask the Homeric poet for what purpose a mound was heaped up over the grave of the dead and a gravestone set upon it, he will answer us: in order that his fame may remain imperishable among men, and that future generations may not be ignorant of his story. That sounds truly Homeric. When a man dies his soul departs into a region of twilit dream-life; his body, the visible man, perishes. Only his glorious name, in fact, lives on. His praises speak to after ages from the monument to his honour on his grave-mound – and in the song of the bard. A *poet* would naturally be inclined to think such things.[26]

The last sentence in the quotation is not an accident. Rohde was a friend of Nietzsche, who did not know that philologists were not supposed to advance interest-group arguments to explain institutions. Rohde finds the great challenge to the Homeric vision to be the 'cult of the hero', the claim that the dead could bring physical harm or benefit to worshipers. For this too he finds an interest-group explanation:

> We, indeed, may be permitted to inquire what motive the shrewd Delphic priesthood may have had in the creation or renewal of so many Hero-cults. There is very evident method in their promotion of the belief in Heroes, as there is in all the activities of the oracle in religious and political matters. Was it ecclesiastical policy that made the priests of Delphi, in this as in so many other cases, search out and multiply to the greatest possible extent the objects of belief and cult? The more widespread and the more deeply ingrained was the uneasy dread of an invisible all-powerful spirit-world, the greater became the authority of the oracle that alone could give guidance in the confused turmoil of ghostly activities. Superstition had achieved a power that the Homeric age never knew.[27]

There are many problems with the evidence which Rohde musters to defend his hypothesis. Perhaps most obvious, to those who live post-Milman Parry, is Rohde's confidence that we can use the Homeric epics to see behind Homer, e.g., the notion that Patroklos' funeral is testimony to a pre-Homeric cult of the soul.[28] To the extent that one subscribes to the oral, evolutionary hypothesis of the Homeric epics it is difficult to believe that one can find strata in Homer without appeal to the formulaic structure of the language.[29]

Suppose we take a weaker version of the Rohde hypothesis which makes the following claim: the Homeric epics assert that 'life' after death through survival of the soul is made of the same sort of stuff as fame. This claim can be defended simply by considering the Homeric language. How does fame create immortality? Obviously, by memory of great deeds carried through song, by physical memorial, and the like. Our heirs carry our immortality by their memory of what collides with their senses. Consider the Homeric word εἴδωλον, which describes the soul after death. With a root (Liddell and Scott) εἶδος, 'that which is seen', and traditionally translated as 'image' or 'phantom', the claim to reality for εἴδωλα is that we see them.[30] What we know about εἴδωλα, in addition to our sense perception, is that they fade; the real images of the dead are of a weaker sort than those conjured up by song or memorial.[31] Fame gives immortality, nothing else which men can control does. εἴδωλον fade too fast to be permanent. As the proverb has it, out of sight, out of mind.

It is in this context that I would read Plato's attack on Homer in Book 10 of *The Republic*. Plato's myth of Er offers the favor of the gods as an incentive to escape from the hazards of competition for fame. Even the famous Odysseus would choose to throw in the towel:

> And it fell out that the soul of Odysseus drew the last lot of all and came to make its choice, and, from memory of its former toils having flung away ambition, went about for a long time in quest of the life of an ordinary citizen who minded his own business, and with difficulty found it lying in some corner disregarded by the others, and upon seeing it said that it would have done the same had it drawn the first lot, and chose it gladly.[32]

Christians v. pagans

Of the few anti-Christian attacks launched by pagan antiquity, one which has survived in substantial form is Celsus' *True Discourse*. Surely it survived because later Christians rightly believed that a comparison of Celsus' attack and Origen's defense would make it obvious who had the better part of the argument. Selectivity bias rears its ugly head because no Christian philosopher of Origen's stature, admittedly an exclusive club, produced a similarly detailed response to Porphyry's attack. How do we deal with the bias in evaluating the arguments of school A when the members of school B picked which texts survive? I propose that pagan arguments can often be found, presumably unfiltered, in authors who avowed Christianity, but who have been convicted of various degrees of unorthodoxy. Similarly, philosophers like Plato have been elected by Christians to survive presumably in part because of the close family resemblance of their philosophy to Christianity.

We can see the objections of real pagan philosophers to religious systems with some resemblance to Christianity by attending to Democritus' strictures about the importance of fame and the irrelevance of one's after-death state:

> Marks of honour are greatly valued by right-thinking men, who understand why they are being honoured.[34]

> Some men, not knowing about the dissolution of mortal nature, but acting on knowledge of the suffering in life, afflict the period of life with anxieties and fears, inventing false tales about the period after the end of life.[35]

In this context one should note Celsus' charge that Christianity allows people to gain immortality even when they fail in their civic duty:

> And that I am not criticizing them any more bitterly than the truth compels me, anyone may see also from this. Those who summon people to the other mysteries make this preliminary proclamation: Whosoever has pure hands and a wise tongue. And again, others say: Whosoever is pure from all defilement, and whose soul knows nothing of evil, and who has lived well and righteously. Such are the preliminary exhortations of those who promise purification from sins. But let us hear what folk these Christians call. Whosoever is a sinner, they say, whosoever is unwise, whosoever is a child, and, and in a word, whosoever is a wretch, the kingdom of God will receive him.[36]

Of course, it is quite wrong to suppose that this charge is exclusively a pagan attack on Christianity. Obviously, it is a charge which bears upon any religion which offers salvation through grace or ritual and is as applicable to the Eleusinian mysteries as it is to some forms of Christianity:

> 'Pataikion the thief will have a better fate after his death because he has been initiated at Eleusis than Agesilaos or Epameinondas,' sneered Diogenes the Cynic.[37]

We have noted above the oddity that an unorthodox Christian father, Lactantius, was selected independently by classical scholars as an heir to Democritus and by colonial historians as offering guidance to those who wished to seek fame inside a Christian world.[38] Lactantius' *Divine Institutes* contains a statement of the relation between the immortality offered by Christianity and that offered by heroics. The sentence to which the italics draw attention is a gracious epitaph to pagan heroics:

Finally, no one would have ever existed who despised this very same brief life or who underwent death unless it were with the hope of a longer life. Those who voluntarily offered themselves to be slain for the safety of the citizens, as Menoeceus of Thebes, Codrus of Athens, and Curtius and the two Mures of Rome, would never have preferred death to the advantage of life, unless they had thought that they would gain immortality in the minds of their people. *Although these did not know the way of immortality, they were not deceived as to the thing itself.*[39]

Since the pagan gods, in Lactantius' account, are simply good men rewarded for their service to society, their worship is an understandable error, easily corrected. Moreover, Lactantius views the honor paid to civic service as perfectly sensible:

So men fashioned representations of them, in order to draw some solace from looking at their images, and going even further in their love, they began to reverence the memory of the departed to such an extent that they seemed to render thanks to those who merited well and aroused in their successors the desire to rule well.

Cicero teaches this about the nature of the gods when he says: 'The life of man and common customs have accepted that by fame and will they should exalt to the sky men excelling in kind deeds. Hence we have Hercules, Castor, Pollux, Aesculapius, Liber.' And in another place he states this fact: 'In most states it can be understood that for the sake of increasing virtue or that all the best may approach danger more willingly for the sake of the republic, the memory of brave men is consecrated by honor due the immortal gods.' Surely, the Romans consecrated their Caesars and the Moors their kings for this reason. So, little by little, such religions began to exist.[40]

This should be compared to St Augustine's orthodox distinction between honor and virtue. Virtue, in his account, is something which is done without regard for worldly rewards of any sort:

Cato is rightly praised more than Caesar, for, as Sallust says of him: 'The less he sought for glory the more it followed him.' However, the only kind of glory they were greedy for was merely the reputation of a good name among men; whereas, virtue rests not on others' judgments but on the witness of one's own conscience, and therefore, is better than a good name. Hence, the Apostle says: 'For our glory is this, the testimony of our conscience'; and in another place: 'But let everyone prove his own work, and so he shall have glory in himself only, but not in another.' Therefore, virtue should not pursue the glory, honor, and dominion which they sought, even though their good men sought to reach these ends by good means, but these things should follow virtue.[41]

Elsewhere, we find that the pagan gods are not just great men of old, misunderstood, but demons snatching the souls of men by luring them to false worship.[42] Honor is now private vice, and we return to Mandeville's results.

Bentham reorganizes the afterlife

If Hobbes is the high priest of anti-Christian tradition and Mandeville its jester, all we lack to close this circle of unbelief is a great engineer. For this we turn to Jeremy Bentham and his *Auto-Icon*. When historians of economic theory tell their students about Bentham's mummy in the London School of Economics, how many of us tell them that Bentham's method of disposal of his remains is an exercise in the economics of fame? In fact, Bentham proposes in his *Auto-Icon*, to establish both a positive and a negative 'Temple of Fame'. This pamphlet is a remarkable attempt to set up, in utilitarian terms, a Christian afterlife. Bentham is quite explicit that his proposal attempts to lengthen the horizon over which individuals optimize:

> It would diminish the horrors of death, by getting rid of its deformities
> . . .
>
> New motives will thus be brought into the field of thought and action, – motives both moral and political. What will be said of my Auto-Icon hereafter? The good report obtained by good conduct will attach to the man after death, – he will not be consigned to oblivion, – he must anticipate the judgment of his fellow man.[43]

The pamphlet is as careful about details as we would expect from anything Bentham writes. He, for example, makes allowances for the possibility of error in reputation:

> Sometimes for honour, sometimes for reproach, will Auto-Icons be preserved . . . .
> If injury had been done to the reputation of an Auto-Icon placed in the temple of dishonour . . . might transfer the sufferer to the temple of honour; and, perhaps, some Auto-Icons, whom the interests and prejudices of our age had transferred to the temple of honour, might, when those interests and prejudices had passed away, be placed prominently in the temple of dishonour. How instructive would be the vibrations of the Auto-Icons between the two temples![44]

He suggests that auto-icons might make interesting artifacts for country gentlemen:

> If a country gentleman had rows of trees leading to his dwellings, the Auto-Icons of his family might alternate with the trees.[45]

Is it necessary to cite the fact that Bentham discusses the waterproofing problems?

FAME AND AN ORDINARY PERSON'S THEORY OF CONDUCT

Fame is supposed to be an instrument to obtain approbation. Fame itself results from behavior which diverges from the average. Thus, to build an economic theory of the importance of fame, the subjects of my theory must also be theorists; they must have an idea about average behavior. After the great work of John Muth, this is an undemanding requirement if we assume that individuals have costless computing capability or they can ask me about average behavior.[46] Of course, I have renounced such devices.

By now, perhaps, it will be no surprise that we find ourselves walking in Adam Smith's footsteps. Smith treats heroic behavior as that which flies in the face of what we know about human nature. We have already quoted his account in *Theory of Moral Sentiments*. Those who succeed in attaining fame act contrary to what run-of-the-mill mankind see as natural inclination. Those who succeed see themselves as rivaling the gods themselves.[47]

Such machinery appears in the familiar context of wage theory in *Wealth of Nations*. Public admiration is an alternative to material income, and it seems to suffice to generate a supply of a certain type of public goods. Public admiration is generated by behavior far from the central tendency of mankind:

> To excel in any profession, in which but few arrive at mediocrity, is the most decisive mark of what is called genius or superior talents. The publick admiration which attends upon such distinguished abilities, makes always a part of their reward; a greater or smaller in proportion as it is higher or lower in degree. It makes a considerable part of that reward in the profession of physick; a still greater perhaps in that of law; in poetry and philosophy it makes almost the whole.[48]

Here is what Smith writes about how sailors pay to take risks:

> Common sailors, therefore, more frequently get some fortune and preferment than common soldiers; and the hope of those prizes is what principally recommends the trade. Though their skill and dexterity are much superior to that of almost any artificers, and though their whole life is one continual scene of hardship and danger, yet for all this dexterity and skill, for all those hardships and danger, while they remain in the condition of common sailors, they receive scarce any other recompence but the pleasure of exercising the one and of surmounting the other.[49]

Needless to say, the facts, and the explanation which Smith offers for these facts, are consistent with the paradox which Frank Knight so enjoyed.[50]

People do some things precisely because they are difficult. The trick in game-like behavior is not how some absolute measure of performance comes out, but how you do, relative to the average. Frank Knight's joke about the folly of the efficiency 'expert' who would make up football teams with twenty-two players on one side is exactly to the point.

Fame, we will suppose, following dutifully in the lines sketched out above, is produced by unusual behavior. Suppose we have an economic model such that there is only one activity over which there is choice. Let us take the issue as to how much time is employed in the production of public goods. If we know what is anticipated and what really occurs then surprise can be defined by the difference between actual and expected. This is a standard ploy: surprise is the residual of theory.

In the simplest case, where fame is simply a residual in the theory, we can write the fame anticipated by individual i as the difference between his public good contribution, PB-time$_i$, and what i thinks, m_i, to be the average. Then, we know the fame he anticipates is

$$\text{Fame}_i = F(\text{PB-time}_i - m_i) \tag{10.1}$$

To make (10.1) tractable we write this anticipated fame in linear form, supposing that the representative individual, the mediocre, cannot be famous. θ is taken as a positive constant for all M individuals.

$$\text{Fame}_i = \theta \cdot (\text{PB-time}_i - m_i) \tag{10.2}$$

With positive surprise comes fame; with negative surprise comes infamy; with mediocrity comes oblivion.

It is obvious that if we wish to introduce fame into the model, we cannot count on everyone behaving the same. If they did, there would be a universe of zero fame and we might as well forget about fame. But if there will be considerable difference in the population, how will the ordinary person know what the average is? I shall presume that the ordinary person engages in a sampling exercise to determine this average. Now, if everyone engaged in the same amount of public good production, then one could efficiently determine the average by the 'pick one' method of sampling. But this will not work here if we insist that the sampling procedure have some sensible outcome, such as unbiasedness.

We shall inquire into how the ordinary person comes to know what the average is. The digression is both technical and rather unproductive. A rigorous approach depends upon a vast amount of information which I despair of obtaining. A less rigorous approach gets a glimpse of a result. So much machinery, so little to show for it. The difficulties are documented in an easily ignored appendix.

A MODEL OF THE PRODUCTION OF APPROBATION

There are M individuals in our society each of whom maximizes his utility function subject to constraints without regard to the actions of others. We suppose that individuals have two ultimate arguments in their utility functions, approbation and nutrition. These are Beckerian Z goods where each of M individuals in society possesses a common utility function

$$\text{Utility}_i = U(A_i, N_i) \text{ for } i = 1 \ldots M \tag{10.3}$$

This utility function is supposed to be the usual sort, with one proviso. This restriction is that A and N are taken to be basic goods, that is, without at least a real positive amount of each of A and N, $U(\ ,\ )$ itself is less than some positive infinitesimal. When $U(\ ,\ )$ is infinitesimal, the individual ceases to exist by choice or necessity. Without enough food one cannot live; without enough approbation one does not want to live.[51]

Corn is the one physical good in society. To address such an ancient problem it seems fitting that we should employ a Ricardian corn model, the oldest reputable device which economists have to display. Corn can be produced by two different methods of employing one's time. An individual can plant his own land, and so produce a private good, or study the weather, and so produce a public good. How much corn is produced by individual $i = 1 \ldots M$ depends upon the total amount of time all individuals $j = 1 \ldots M$ employ in the alternative time uses. We measure the time employed by an individual i in private production of corn as PR-time$_i$ and in public production of corn as PB-time$_i$. The ultimate resource constraint in the system is the fact that:

$$\text{PR-time}_i + \text{PB-time}_i = 24 \tag{10.4}$$

We allow differences in the production of private goods, but suppose everyone equally competent at the production of public goods. Thus the corn production for individual i depends upon the amount of time i applies to his own farm and the total time applied by all individuals to the production of public goods. This we write in fairly general factor-augmenting form, where the constant $\varkappa$ is the amount which a unit of time spent producing public goods augments everyone's production function:

$$\text{Corn}_i = C_i(\text{PR-time}_i(1 + \varkappa \sum_{j=1}^{M} \text{PB-time}_j)) \tag{10.5}$$

With little loss of generality, and to make certain we confront the full force of a large numbers prisoner's dilemma, we assume that the increment to i's corn production from i's time employed in public production is always smaller than the increment to i's corn production from his time employed in private production. In terms of the function specified in (10.5), this specification requires that the constant $\varkappa$ is small.

The individual can do two things with the corn produced, feed himself,

N_i, or sacrifice to the gods, S_i, in return for which they will approve of him. It is assumed for the present that these exchange rates are in constant proportions to corn expenditures; thus:

$$N_i = \eta C_i \tag{10.6}$$
$$S_i = \gamma C_i \tag{10.7}$$

The prices are exogenously determined. This assumption is too important to take for granted; it will be reconsidered after the competitive implications are developed.

Approbation is the basic good, but approbation does not only come from the gods. To make the case more dramatic than is necessary, we posit that the basic good approbation is simply the sum of S and Fame, or:

$$A_i = S_i + F_i \tag{10.8}$$

The texts quoted above have given us reason to believe that F and S are substitutes; (10.8) posits they are perfect substitutes.

The model is to be solved iteratively, so we shall examine how the model proceeds from one iteration to the next. The only question addressed in detail is whether there will be equilibrium at the production of zero time employment in public goods. There are only two problems in this economy for each individual: how much public good to produce, and how to allocate the corn produced between nutrition and the gods.

We start with the assumption that each individual takes the average public good production to be zero. The first order of business is to check whether this is an internally consistent solution to the model. After we

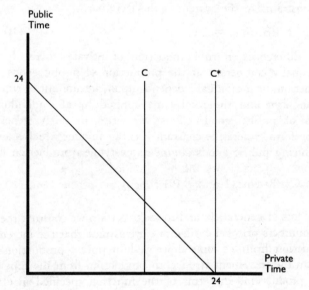

Figure 10.1   Two time uses

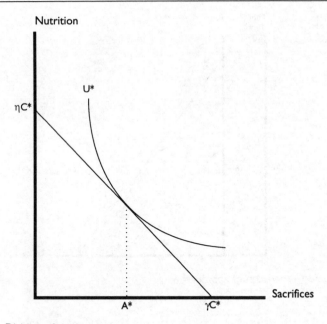

Nutrition

ηC^*

U*

Sacrifices

A* γC^*

Figure 10.2   Division of the corn

have established that it is, we ask if this is the solution which maximizes utility.

From our specification of the production function, the method of maximizing private corn output is to put all one's time into private production. (The result isn't quite as tautological as it sounds, but close.) Hence, C^* corn is produced. This is shown in Figure 10.1 where we draw vertical isoquants between public and private time use in the production of *private* corn. From a private point of view, time spent studying the weather is wasted on the neighbors. This C^* can then be expended between nutrition and sacrifices. The budget constraint is deduced immediately from the linearity specifications of (10.5) and (10.6): the maximum amount of nutrition is ηC^* and the maximum approbation from the gods is γC^*. Equilibrium over these goods follows immediately when indifference curves between nutrition and approbation are added in Figure 10.2. A^* is the utility-maximizing of approbation, all of which is obtained by sacrifice to the gods.

Thus, a solution without fame is consistent; hence, the initial stipulation that no public good was expected to be produced is also consistent. Moreover, any sampling procedure – including the 'pick one' method – employed by the ordinary person as statistician will quickly discover this result.

Now, we ask the more interesting question. Is this zero production of

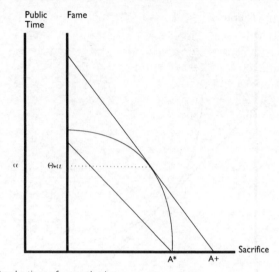

Figure 10.3   Production of approbation

public goods equilibrium? Consider Figure 10.3. By working twenty-four hours in his own garden, our individual has C^* to divide between food and sacrifice. We have found that by dealing with the gods at their posted prices he obtains A^* of approbation. To answer the question whether this is an equilibrium, we ask: can the individual obtain more approbation and the same amount of nutrition by reallocating his time use? By Ricardian principles, the last minutes of time in corn production bring less corn than the first minutes of time. We can look at sacrificial corn as the marginal corn. Is there a cheaper way to obtain approbation?

If the individual were to take some time away from his own garden and produce public goods, he would lose only the most costly corn and startle his neighbors. This would confer fame. Now, the issue is clear. As long as the marginal increment in fame from the production of public goods exceeds the marginal decrement in the favor of the gods from corn production forgone, public goods production will be a sensible way to produce approbation.

Figure 10.3 carries the burden of the choice of how an individual earns approbation. It has been assumed that the individual is indifferent between approbation from fame or approbation from the favor of the gods; hence, all we require are linear iso-approbation lines summing fame and god-granted favors. By (10.2) the fame expected by an individual depends linearly upon the difference between the time input in public goods and his own time input. The concavity of the production of approbation follows immediately from diminishing returns to time in private corn production and a positive fixed corn cost of the favor of the gods.

Figure 10.3 was drawn assuming that *any* amount of production of public goods will seem remarkable. Call the time input to production α; the resulting fame is $\theta \cdot \alpha$. By sacrifice the individual earns approbation $A*$; by a mix of sacrifice and contribution to public goods, he earns a greater amount, $A+$.

Thus, we have given a standard production-theoretic reason to believe that the condition of a public goods time input of zero will not be an equilibrium. Next, we consider the iterative steps necessary to go to equilibrium. We shall assume that the sampling procedure used by individuals is unbiased. The pseudo-justification for this assumption is found in the appendix.

Now, the average individual who in this iteration received positive fame, $\theta \cdot (\alpha - 0)$, for time input α because the common theory said zero was expected, would receive zero fame if the theory was revised to anticipate an average amount of public goods time input α. If the individual employed less than α in public goods production, he would have to bear negative fame, shame or infamy. This process should remind us of profit in a competitive industry: entry bids it away.

Now with the representative public goods production equal to α, the production function for corn shifts out for all members of society. By (10.5) they expect to receive $C_i(24 - \alpha)$ but actually receive, on average, a higher amount $C_i((24 - \alpha)(1 + \varkappa M \alpha))$. This changes the trade-off between the two methods of obtaining approbation from that pictured in Figure 10.3. The new equilibrium results from two effects. First, as the expected public goods time input changes from 0 to α the maximum amount of fame falls from $\theta \cdot (24 - 0)$ to $\theta \cdot (24 - \alpha)$; second, by (10.6), since the price of the favors from the gods is constant in corn, it falls in time forgone because the marginal product of time in private corn production has increased. The change in public goods production changes the relative price of our two methods to obtain approbation. Let us suppose the new average public goods time input is $\beta < \alpha$. If this were equilibrium the average individual would bear shame, since $\theta \cdot (\beta - \alpha) < 0$. This is not the solution, since the sample will be revised to reflect the change in behavior. Iteration continues.

There may be many equilibria to this model. The equilibria will surely be sensitive to the method of sampling. However, our substantive concern is only whether the production of public goods falls back to zero as the iterative procedure continues. At equilibrium the representative individual will be 'trapped' into producing a positive amount of public goods even though he now receives no fame for it. He produces public goods out of a fear of shame.

The attentive reader, who may also grow corn, will immediately note that we have a prisoner's dilemma problem. And is not one of the purposes of this book to explain how ideas get us *out* of the prisoner's dilemma? If everyone stopped the foolish competition for honor, couldn't everyone relax and be better off at the same time? Oh, wait. Of course, how easy! Yes, a prisoner's dilemma can beat a prisoner's dilemma. Positively Mandevillian.

Can our now enlightened representative individual not reduce his public goods output? If he does, he can always obtain more corn, but he must consider whether the extra corn in his wallet can buy expiation from the gods to compensate for the negative fame he receives for doing less than the representative amount of public goods provision. Concavity of the production of approbation offers a standard reason to believe that public goods production will not fall back to zero.

The model predicts that the fear of shame and the love of fame will help generate a positive voluntary amount of public goods of all sorts. The production equilibrium conditions, supposing that the maximizing behavior occurs at an interior, are straightforward and obvious.

Stipulating that the favors of the gods are fixed in terms of corn, those with more fertile land will find that the favors from the gods are cheaper in terms of time than those with less fertile land. Hence, we would expect those with less fertile land would be more famous than those with more fertile land.

WITHOUT COMPETITION IN RELIGION

We have seen above how much Smith worries about monopoly religion. Dictates of religion, in Smith's account, can trump the dictates of duty. In the context of the model above, it is easy to demonstrate what the problem will be. The providers of religion can make an 'all or none' offer of approbation from the gods which can induce the individual to put all his time into private corn production. Suppose in equilibrium there is a mix of sacrifice and fame to produce approbation. Each individual will have some maximizing amount of approbation; let our individual maximize at $A+$.

A monopoly religion, seeing sacrifice forgone, might decide to offer a small discount, such that this individual could obtain a greater amount of approbation, $A++ > A+$, by giving up all public goods production. Thus, a discriminating religion can destroy the incentive to provide public goods.

It is in this context that I would read Plato's concern in *Laws* 10 about the third type of atheist, those who believe the gods can be bribed. In Plato's world the gods grant salvation only for the production of public goods. In Plato's world, would you need to worry about the fame incentive? Could not we found morality on other than competitive grounds? We return to this issue in Chapter 14.

APPENDIX. THE ORDINARY PERSON AS STATISTICIAN

How do ordinary people engage in statistical inference?[52] There is a closely related research area in economics, the statistical theory of discrimination, which points out that individuals form stereotypes of racial or sexual characteristics as a method of economizing on information.[53] Suppose we look at the question of anticipation or stereotyping as a problem of estimation. The ordinary person we study needs to make inferences about an underlying population from a limited number of observations. We know the number of observations will be limited because, after one has exhausted immediate neighbors, extra observations cost something. This of course is the standard sampling problem where we take into account the cost of processing this information.[54]

To be more particular, in the model sketched above, the ordinary person needs a location statistic to estimate the center of the distribution of time use. Which one is it? As far as I know, the question of what sort of estimator is employed to form or update a stereotype has not been systematically studied. While this is a disappointment, it is not surprising, because in the statistical discrimination literature employers have stereotypes about workers; workers do not have stereotypes about other workers. Let us see what consequences follow from this.

If the cost flowing from the difference between the actual observations and the location statistic used swamps computational costs, then we come back to the standard statistical issues. Employers can probably afford to buy the same statistics textbooks an economist can, so they might very well use the same devices as we would. We and they ask about the underlying distribution and then generate some sort of optimal estimator from the answer to the distributional question. In the context of asking about how ordinary people form their theories, this usually attractive approach is precluded.

To see why I believe this to be so, we begin at a very rigorous level from which we will soon depart. Suppose each individual has a loss function which he attempts to minimize.[55] At a minimum the loss depends upon some three considerations. The first cost component comes when there is a difference between location statistic, say, m, chosen to estimate the underlying population parameter μ and the actual observations. The absolute or the squared error might be a reasonable approximation to this component of cost.[56] This is the standard component of the loss function. The second cost component comes from the unpleasant fact that sampling costs will be nonlinear: the neighbors are observed for nothing, others are not. There is no reason to believe that the sampling costs are ever unbounded as N increases. The third component of loss will depend upon the computational complexity. Ordinary people, perhaps without the concept of zero, let alone an electronic calculator, may have great difficulty computing many plausible estimators. Standard estimators may simply be infeasible.

Consider the three classical estimators of location: the mean, the median and the mode. What sort of resources does it take to carry out these computations? Let us call the raw materials for computation 'registers'. At our disposal we have the following instruments: (1) registers for storage, (2) addition (accumulation) registers, (3) division registers, (4) the capability of exchanging the value in a register on the basis of an inequality test. There is good reason to believe that each of these instruments will be employed at a different cost. There are K observations to consider.

The sample mean's great attraction is that it only requires two accumulation registers and none for additional storage. In the first register, the algorithm accumulates $K-1$ sums of the values of the observations, in the second register it accumulates the number of observations. Finally, a division of the value in one register by the value in another is required.[57] From the point of view of electronic technology ca. 1990 this is surely the minimum-cost estimator. We know this because one can obtain a calculator to carry out this computation for next to nothing. One cannot find the same disposable calculators giving the sample mode or the sample median; either of these requires K storage registers. However, the mix of operations in computations for the median and the mode differs considerably from those required for the mean. While the median uses a minimum of K storage registers and many exchanges, it does not require addition or division.[58] Thus, to know just one component of the loss function, we shall require a vector of register prices. Without this information we make little headway.

Let us reformulate the general loss function problem into a much more tractable form. For a fixed number of K observations, can we find an unbiased estimator of location with a variance which falls with the square root of the sample size, which minimizes computational cost?[59] Generations of econometrics students have been drilled into appreciating the virtues of a question which asks for the unbiased linear estimator which minimizes sampling variance. It comes as a shock to them if they discover that the linearity restriction serves to constrain the costs of computation and analysis.[60] Thus, we are exchanging the constraint and the objective function in an optimization problem. Alas, duality fails.

There is a little-used estimator of location, the midrange, which deserves our attention. It is unbiased in a general setting and, at least with an underlying normal distribution, has a small-sample standard error which declines with the square root of the number of observations.[61] If computational costs increase without limit as the number of observations increase, then we need not worry about what happens with an infinite number of observations. Hence, the usually important property of consistency, per se, is unlikely to matter much in our formulation. The fact that the midrange is not generally a consistent estimator is neither here nor there. Hence, this estimator satisfies our constraints.

The midrange's computations require two registers, $2K-2$ logical operations to compare the new observation with the previous minimum and maximum, one accumulation and one division by 2. The main reason, in fact, a midrange would be used is because of its computational attraction.[62] If logical operations are much cheaper than addition — do you find it harder to tell which of two numbers is larger or to add them together? — then it will be difficult to find an unbiased estimator with a standard error falling with the square root of the number of observations which is cheaper to compute.

The influence curve of the sample midrange is zero between the sample minimum and the sample maximum.[63] This zero influence would allow us to work with a theory based on samples and, even for the current iteration, treat the theory as exogenous to the actor over some range. Of course, one would encounter discontinuities at the minimum or the maximum.

If, in fact, ordinary people use the midrange as a data-organizing principle, it explains why 'great men' might be very important to form expectations or stereotypes. The extremes of one's sampled experience would be all that mattered.

Part V

A competitive episode: the Malthusian controversy

We have been discussing religious competition in the abstract at considerable length, so it is a good time to work through a real-world example. Most religious controversy concerns matters which are so remote from the working experience of this economist as to be practically inaccessible. There is an exception. This is the controversy which is associated with the name of T. R. Malthus and concerns matters which are central to the distribution theory of the classical economists.

Unfortunately, it is hard for modern readers to appreciate the moral radicalism of Malthus' writings. Malthus is a subtle writer and he has no desire to play up the controversy. It is a disaster that readers of this controversy have become almost completely tone-deaf to traditional moral voices. As witness to the religious issues, let me introduce two writers who called Malthus master.[1] The first is Charles Bradlaugh. The Neomalthusian movement became legal in Great Britain in 1877 as an outcome of the trial of Bradlaugh and co-defendant Annie Besant for the crime of distributing explicit birth-control material. Long before this trial, Bradlaugh wrote a tract called *Jesus, Shelley, and Malthus*. Yes, the title is ambiguous, so here is a flavor of the text:

> Jesus, Shelley, and Malthus, also represent three conditions of thought. The first, that of thought fettered. The second, Freethought: − learning, but not yet learned; honest, but sometimes erring. The third, the special application of educated thought to the relief of the human family from at least some of the many evils under which its members suffer.[2]

The second is the great wild man of the American birth-control movement, Moses Harman.[3] Harman published a newspaper, *Lucifer the Light-Bearer*. Could one imagine a more explicit name to announce an anti-Christian position? Yes, his perhaps unlettered neighbors called it *Satan*; they got the point.

Scholars, learned enough to decorate universities founded as memorials to rich men, have frequently asserted − apparently seriously, since there isn't much laughter in these books − that the wider Malthusian movement served the vested interests of the ruling classes. These ruling classes thought so highly of a candid discussion of marital rape Harman published in *Lucifer* that, at age seventy-five, he spent the winter of 1906 as guest of the state of Illinois, breaking large rocks into gravel. So subtle and far-reaching were these ruling classes that they controlled both the Church of England and the Malthusian movement which opposed its teaching; they controlled those arrested for passing out birth-control literature and those who made the arrests. I suppose that if I were an activist opponent of a ruling class with such ability I too would have neither the time to laugh nor the time to read.

What is Malthus, the arch-conservative of Marxist demonology, doing with friends like these? Part of the difficulty which noneconomists have with Malthus is that he was a good economist. You think not? How would you like to be a co-discoverer of the law of diminishing marginal productivity? Non-economists do not see the large numbers prisoner's dilemma trap which Malthus sprang on the communism proposed by his contemporaries and so miss out on the action. Another part of the difficulty, which economists face, is that when Malthus wrote that usually men and women had a choice of 'vice or misery', he acknowledged that people talk about choice and sometimes they say choice is 'vicious'. Until economists get this straight, it is hard to believe that Malthus can be read correctly. What Malthus recommended was changing the words we use to judge a certain class of actions. Later, the birth-control movement in America and the Neomalthusian movement in Britain proposed to widen the range of action judged acceptable.

It is important to recall that economists went up against Christian doctrine, and all but the Catholic church blinked. The victory over Protestant teaching was so complete that it now seems that there never was a controversy. Unlike wars in the ancient world, where the victors would sow salt in the ground of the vanquished, the vanquished here seem to have sown salt in the ground of memory.

These chapters carry a radical rereading of the economics of T. R. Malthus and David Ricardo from days in which I was too young to be frightened. In the important aspects my reading is consistent, I am pleased beyond measure to point out, with that offered by the greatest living historian of economics.[4]

Chapter 11

Ricardo and the iron law

The thrust of what follows is that the natural wage which appears so prominently in the commentary on Ricardian economics is endogenously determined by the working of David Ricardo's model. That is to say, it is that wage which sets population growth equal to zero: 'that price which is necessary to enable the labourers, one with another, to subsist and to perpetuate their race, without either increase or diminution'.[1] It is not, I shall argue, an exogenous specification from T. R. Malthus' population theory. Nor, I shall argue, has it any function in Ricardo's argument when the population is growing.

To make this case I shall combine a model of Malthusian labor-supply theory and a model of Ricardian labor-demand theory to specify Ricardo's distribution theory. Although the model is presented in more or less modern terms, it purports to be a useful model only of the Ricardian texts. I hope that it is judged on Chicago School criteria: how well routine manipulation by the rules of modern economics generates Ricardo's conclusions.[2] No one, I think, confuses an economic model of behavior with the behavior itself. Thus, there should be no difficulty in distinguishing between the terminology used in a model to explain/predict the texts and the terminology used in the texts themselves.

It is widely held in the standard commentary on Ricardo that the natural rate of wages is used by Ricardo in his analysis of all positions of equilibrium, not just the stationary state. Specifically, it is asserted that Ricardo used the assumption of an infinitely elastic supply of labor at the natural wage, even for short-period problems where this specification is clearly unwarranted.[3]

To explain Ricardo's distribution theory, the standard commentary reads Malthus' population theory as assuming that the demand for sexual intercourse is constant. It does not matter much whether sexual passions result in marriage or not; the population will grow whether births are legitimate or not. From this assumption, it is argued, and the American evidence, Malthus deduced that there is a constant birth rate which would cause population to double every twenty-five years if the positive checks to population growth did not enter.[4] Adjustments in population take place, in the large, in the form of variation of the rate of death. Consequently, the notion of a natural rate of wages as a specification of what one could expect the laborer to earn comes from Malthus' population theory.[5]

Stanley Jevons, Leon Walras, Frank Knight and Joseph Schumpeter argued that Ricardo's theory requires the natural rate of wages to produce a determinant distribution theory: without an exogenous natural rate of wages, Ricardo's theory has two unknowns and three equations.[6] Jevons and Knight[7] asserted that Ricardo did not believe in the natural wage doctrine; thus, his distribution theory is read as mathematically absurd.

It is clear that the doctrine of the exogenously determined natural rate of wages would be required to justify Ricardo's reported result that the working class cannot be taxed. This reading dates at least from James Mill's *Elements*: 'Mr. Ricardo, throughout his disquisitions on political economy . . . [asserts that] no tax can fall upon the labourer; and if any tax is imposed upon wages, it is easy to trace in what way it must produce a corresponding rise in wages.'[8] Among the distinguished commentators who have reported that Ricardo asserted that the working class cannot be taxed are M. Longfield, J. Cairnes, F. Y. Edgeworth, W. Ashley, E. Cannan, W. C. Mitchell, Lionel Robbins, Mark Blaug and D. P. O'Brien.[9]

My reading of Malthus' population theory is that it is a theory of choice: individuals choose when they marry.[10] What makes the marriage decision *per se* important for population theory is that without effective contraception it is reasonable to assume that on average children will regularly follow marriage.[11] Conversely, sexual intercourse outside of marriage is unlikely to contribute significantly to population growth, since one prostitute – an important classical substitute for marriage[12] – can have sex with quite a number of men. Hence, the decision of people to marry earlier will increase the birth rate and, other things being equal, increase the rate of population growth.[13]

To explain the costs of marriage we must explain the costs of a child. The higher the wages which children can earn and contribute to the family, the less they will cost their parents. Higher wages paid to parents will mean a higher income. In Figure 11.1 the feasibility conditions are described for two distinct levels of corn wages ($w_1 > w_0$). The higher corn wages of w_1 mean that an unmarried worker could consume more corn; the same higher wages mean that his children cost him less, so the flatter the boundary of the feasibility set. With preferences between the age of marriage and corn described by the indifference curves in Figure 11.1 we can solve for the utility-maximizing consumption decision: at w_1 people marry at (say) twenty-five; at w_0 people marry at (say) thirty. If wages are high enough, children have a positive net present value, and the feasibility set will have a positive-sloped boundary. This condition existed in the

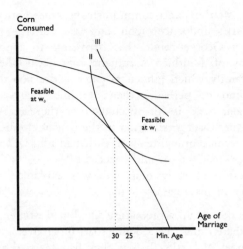

Figure 11.1   Cost of children and age at marriage

American colonies, according to Adam Smith; thus Americans married earlier than Europeans.[14]

In terms of Malthus' argument, one can look at the slope of the feasibility set's boundary as measuring the strength of the preventive check to population growth. Under a William Godwin type of communism where everyone gets an equal share of the communal pie, the private cost of marriage and the social cost diverge widely. The private cost – how much less material goods a man or woman consumes as a result of their marriage – is almost zero. If there are N people in the community, and NNP is the goods and services produced by the community members, then before marriage a man and woman obtain NNP/N. If N is large, even if children make no contribution to output, then the private cost of a family of (say) twenty children to each parent is small: $NNP/N - NNP/(N + 20)$. This is, of course, the reason Malthus argued that the communal systems would break down; they would abolish the preventive check to marriage. Regardless of how poor the members of the community became, they would have no incentive to postpone marriage. As Malthus put it:

> I cannot conceive a form of society [Godwin's] so favourable upon the whole to population . . . as we are supposing no anxiety about the future support of children to exist, I do not conceive that there would be one woman in a hundred, of twenty-three years of age, without a family.[15]

This not very difficult application of the principle that private costs differ from social costs when there are no property rights has systematically baffled the commentary on Malthus. It is easy to appreciate why Karl Marx would not wish to read Malthus this way. In Marx's political interpretation, Malthus' anti-communism becomes anti-progress.[16] It is a tribute to Marx's influence upon how we see the past that neither Schumpeter nor George Stigler has been able to appreciate the simple microeconomics of Malthus' argument that it is the private cost of supporting a family which influences parents' decision to have a family.

Less well known, perhaps, than Malthus' analysis of subsidies to children by poor laws is his discussion of the factory employment of children. In either case, a reduction in the cost of children, by poor law or by the possibility of employing them earlier in life, will induce individuals to marry earlier than they would otherwise.[17]

The importance of early marriages was explained by Malthus with tolerable clarity in his *Summary View*:

(By 'early' is not meant a premature age; but if women marry at nineteen or twenty, there cannot be a doubt that, on an average, they will have a greater number of births than if they had married at twenty-eight or thirty.)[18]

And in fact this makes a considerable difference in population growth:

[it is] obvious to common observation, by which we can scarcely fail to see that numbers delay marriage beyond the period when the passions most strongly prompt to it, but it is proved by the registers of different countries, which clearly shew, either that a considerable number of persons of a marriageable age never marry, or that they marry comparatively late, and that their marriages are consequently less prolific than if they had married earlier.[19]

The important result from all this is simply that the supply of labor is upward-sloping: the wages required to support a population growing 3 percent per annum are higher than those required to support a stationary population.[20]

I read Ricardo as following Adam Smith in devoting much of his attention to explaining why some countries grow more rapidly than others, and the importance of such differences in the rate of growth on wages and profits.[21] Such a cross-section model cannot, I think, separate conditions of growth from distribution theory.

A good deal of Ricardo's analysis makes perfect sense if he is read as assuming fixed proportions between inputs of labor and capital applied to a constant amount of land in a one-industry (corn) model.[22] It is, I think, important to make the one-industry assumption, since Ricardo, unlike Edward West,[23] clearly stated that an increase in productivity outside of the production of wage goods will have no impact on profits.[24] If we assume fixed proportions between inputs of labor and capital, then we cannot define the marginal product of labor or the marginal product of capital. An increase in either of the inputs, holding the other constant, will have no impact on output, but a decrease in one input will reduce output.[25] To use Milton Friedman's apt example, we cannot define a marginal product of a person's right hand or the marginal product of the left hand because they come in fixed proportions. Thus, we cannot, using marginal productivity theory, construct a determinant distribution between a right and a left hand. We can, however, treat a two-handed person as the economic entity and define the marginal product of a person.[26]

Although we cannot define the marginal product of separate factors of production if proportions are fixed, we can define the marginal product of a composite input of labor (L) and capital (K) which we will call $L\&K$. Thus, we can ask what happens to output, and to the distribution of output, when inputs of labor and capital are increased in proportion on land (D) in corn production.

Given a production function for corn, Corn $= C(L\&K,D)$, on standard neoclassical grounds, if we treat $L\&K$ as one factor, we can define the fund out of which labor and capital are paid:

$$\partial C/\partial(L\&K) = \text{Corn wages} + \text{Corn profits}.$$

This is, of course, the famous Ricardian residual: that part of the marginal product of labor and capital, in corn units, which does not go to the capitalist goes to the worker.[27]

Ricardo, of course, did not talk about 'marginal product', so we must translate the above argument, which is in terms of neoclassical theory, to concepts which are found in Ricardo's text. The link between the two is Ricardo's value theory. If the marginal product of labor and capital in agriculture falls, then more labor and capital will be required at the margin of cultivation of corn. Ricardo generally assumes that gold is produced in an industry with constant returns to scale, so that the labor and capital required to produce a unit of gold is unchanged over time.[28] Thus, there will be more labor and capital required to produce a unit of corn relative to what is required to produce a unit of gold. In terms of Ricardo's cost-of-production theory of exchange value, the exchange value of corn relative to gold will rise. Thus, as the marginal product of labor and capital falls in agriculture, the price of corn rises.[29] This critical relation – the higher the price of corn (measured in gold), the less corn there will be to divide between the laborer and the capitalist – is shown in Figure 11.2. The numbers come from Ricardo's illustrative chart.[30]

If we restrict our attention to economies with the same security of property, so that we may neglect savings in hoards of precious metals,[31] the higher the profits of the capitalist, his share of the marginal product of labor and capital, the more he will save and the faster capital grows.[32] If we wish to compare economies in different states of development, it is most useful to work in percentage rates of growth. This is shown in Figure 11.3.

Since the stock of capital provides the subsistence for the laborer during

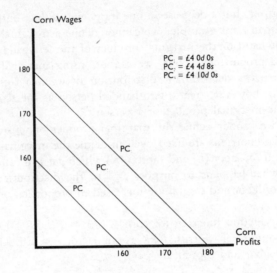

Figure 11.2 Marginal product of labor and the exchange value of corn

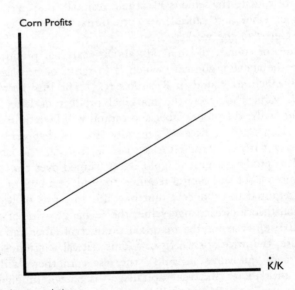

Figure 11.3 Capital accumulation

the annual period of production, if we know the relation among corn wages, the price of corn and the rate of capital accumulation, we know the labor-demand conditions.[33] This solution is carried out in Figure 11.4. $LD(PC_i)$ specifies the locus of combinations of corn wages and capital growth rates, for each price of corn, i, which is consistent with equilibrium in the labor-demand sector.

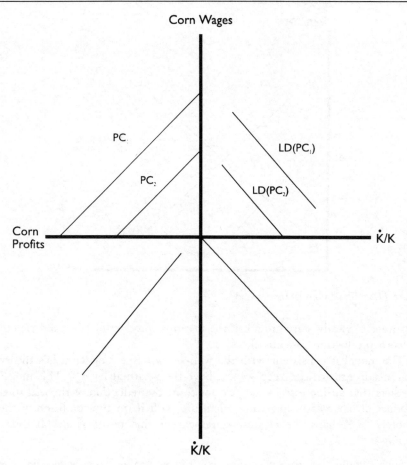

Figure 11.4 Labor demand

The locus of all possible states of equilibrium with respect to the demand for labor is drawn in Figure 11.5. This is combined with an upward-sloping labor supply curve $\dot{L}/L = f(\text{corn wages})$. This is not specified as $\dot{L}/L = f(W_m - W_n)$, where W_m is the market wage and W_n is the natural wage, since W_n is *defined* as that wage which sets population growth equal to zero. The latter specification makes sense only if the natural wage is assumed to be a constant, at least with respect to the labor-supply equation.

If the rate of growth of capital exceeds that of labor, corn wages will rise.[34] If the rate of growth of labor exceeds that of capital, corn wages will fall.[35] For equilibrium in the model the percentage rates of growth of labor and capital are equal.[36] In Figure 11.5 each price of corn corresponds to a distinct equilibrium corn wage. The numbers are again drawn from Ricardo's illustrative chart.[37] All the positions of equilibrium are potential

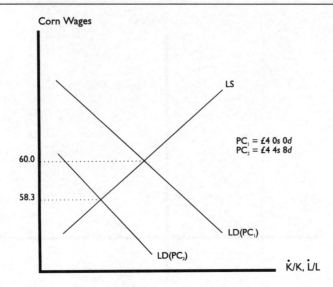

Figure 11.5   Equilibrium labor demand

positions of steady-state growth if the marginal product of labor and capital in corn production remains the same.[38]

The model is consistent with the well-known aspect of Ricardo's theory that steady growth can keep wages above their natural level.[39] This model predicts that an increase in the price of corn, the reduction of the marginal product of labor and capital in agriculture, will harm the condition of the laborers.[40] Perhaps the clearest statement of this result is in Malthus's *Principles*:

> Such would be the necessary course of profits and wages in the progressive accumulation of capital, as applied to the progressive cultivation of new and less fertile land, or the further improvement of what had before been cultivated; and on the supposition here made, the rates both of profits and of real wages would be highest at first, and would regularly and gradually diminish together, till they both came to a stand at the same period, and the demand for an increase of produce ceased to be effective.[41]

Ricardo accepted this statement.[42]

This model predicts that the natural wage is only relevant when the economy is at the stationary state. This point was made vigorously by Malthus:

> Mr. Ricardo has defined the natural price of labour . . . This price I should really be disposed to call a most unnatural price; because in a natural state of things, that is, without great impediments to the

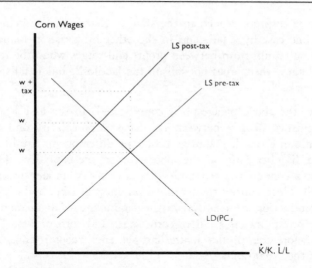

Figure 11.6   The effect of taxation

progress of wealth and population, such a price could not generally occur for hundreds of years.[43]

The same point was made by West and Longfield.[44] Clearly, there is sufficient evidence to conclude that if Ricardo used the natural wage when the economy was growing, such use was not warranted by the population theory understood by Malthus.

The question is, of course, whether Ricardo used the notion of a natural wage as a simplification for such applications as the incidence of taxation.[45] This model can be tested by its predictions with Ricardo's text. A tax on wages would increase the cost of supporting a family, reduce the income of the parents, hence delay marriage. This would reduce the rate of population growth; labor would grow more slowly than capital. This would increase wages, reduce profits and slow the rate of capital accumulation. Wages would not rise to offset the tax completely, since the supply curve is upward sloping. This is shown in Figure 11.6. A tax on profits would have the same result of reducing both post-tax profits and wages. This result is found in the text:

> This principle of the division of the produce of labour and capital between wages and profits, which I have attempted to establish, appears to me so certain, that excepting in the immediate effects, I should think it of little importance whether the profits of stock, or the wages of labour, were taxed. By taxing the profits of stock, you would probably alter the rate at which the funds for the maintenance of labour increase, and the wages would be disproportioned to the state of that fund, by being too high. By taxing wages, the reward paid to the labourer would

also be disproportioned to the state of that fund, by being too low. In the one case by a fall, and in the other by a rise in money wages, the natural equilibrium between profits and wages would be restored. A tax on wages, then, does not fall on the landlord, but it falls on the profits of stock.[46]

Clearly, the above paragraph is complicated. In the first sentence Ricardo distinguishes sharply between the legal responsibility and the economic incidence of a tax: it makes no economic difference in equilibrium whether the tax liability falls on the laborer or on the capitalist. The next three sentences contain the economic results of a tax: money wages and profits will fall. Since neither the marginal products of labor and capital in corn or gold production are changed in the argument, a fall in money wages and money profits means a fall in corn wages and corn profits. The lack of an 'only' before the 'profits' in the last sentence keeps it consistent with the rest of the paragraph.

This is not an isolated result. Ricardo asserted elsewhere that the slowing of growth caused by taxation will reduce the workers' well-being.[47] Ricardo noted that an increase in taxation and a decrease in the marginal product of labor and capital in agriculture would have the same impact on wages and profits.[48] Ricardo does emphasize that workers cannot pay much in taxes.[49]

In the first two editions of the *Principles* Ricardo stated that the working class cannot bear any taxation:

> The whole produce of the land and labour of every country is divided into three portions: of these, one portion is devoted to wages, another to profits, and the other to rent. It is from the two last portions only, that any deductions can be made for taxes, or for savings.[50]

This, I believe, is inconsistent with the rest of Ricardo's text. Ricardo seems to have thought so too, because he corrected his argument in the third edition:

> Perhaps this is expressed too strongly, as more is generally allotted to the labourer under the name of wages, than the absolutely necessary expenses of production. In that case a part of the net produce of the country is received by the labourer, and may be saved or expended by him; or it may enable him to contribute to the defense of the country.[51]

It is only, I think, when the economist corrects himself that we can easily distinguish between his slips and ours.

Ricardo asserted that subsidies on earlier marriages would reduce the well-being of those workers not subsidized.[52] In terms of the model this is what a rightward shift in the supply curve of labor would predict.

META-HISTORICAL APPENDIX

I am deeply indebted to a reader who drew my attention to an article by G. S. L. Tucker in the 1961 *Economica*. In his argument the following appears:

> It is worth noting that Ricardo's 'Malthusianism' in this connection was not logically inconsistent with his desire, resting partly on welfare grounds, that Britain's capital should continue to increase as rapidly as possible. Although the effects upon real wages of a rapid accumulation of capital would be largely offset by an expansion of population, they would not be *wholly* offset. To induce population (or the supply of labour) to grow at a higher rate, corresponding to a higher rate of growth of capital (or demand for labour), real wages would have to improve to some extent; and they would remain at this level so long as the higher rate of population growth was called for. This would be necessary in order to give a greater incentive to marriage and to permit labouring families to rear successfully larger numbers of children. In other words, if we imagine a schedule showing the various levels of real wages required to ensure different rates of growth of population, the resultant curve would not be horizontal but upward sloping. It may be objected that this simply means, in conditions of rapid economic growth, that the higher real wage obtained by each workman would be spread over a larger family. Perhaps so; but it would have been thought an improvement, surely, if men could witness a decline of mortality-rates among their own children.[53]

This is of course very close to my reading of Ricardo. I would rather emphasize that marriage enters into the preference orderings of the workers.

The interesting question is, I suppose, why Tucker's argument did not make a dent in the standard reading. I would conjecture that as long as it was assumed that Ricardo asserted that the working class could not be taxed, his hopes for higher wages through higher growth were assumed to be extratheoretical.

Chapter 12

Some normative aspects of the Malthusian controversy

If it is the case that the Malthusian message is that the working class is doomed to some ill-defined, socially determined minimum of subsistence by its child-bearing decisions, then the widespread reading of the Malthusian controversy as one between economic reactionaries and their humanitarian critics is plausible.[1] For what if Malthusian population theory entails not an infinitely elastic supply of labor at some exogenously determined wage, but rather an upward-sloping supply curve?

I propose that part of the difficulty that economists have had with the controversy is that T.R. Malthus insisted that normative questions were important.[2] Modern economists have of course constructed normative models, but these are characteristically utilitarian. An economist maps from what he observes an individual choosing to what the economist judges desirable in such a fashion as to preserve rank ordering.[3] I will argue that, to reconstruct the normative aspects of the Malthusian controversy, it will be necessary to formulate a nonutilitarian model of moral judgment.

Modern welfare economics takes as primitive an observational, choice-theoretic relation of preference, R, read as 'preferred or indifferent to', to implicitly construct a judgmental relation 'judged better or no worse by the observing economist'. It will be necessary in the argument to make the judgmental relation independent of R, so I will denote an explicitly judgmental relation by B. Inside standard welfare economics B is constructed in the following manner. If S is the set of all possible states of affair for all $a, b \in S$, then

$a \, R \, b$ iff $a \, B \, b$

if we neglect costs of transactions.[4]

Consider a possible nonutilitarian normative specification such that in a two-commodity world one of the commodities is exogenously specified to be sacred, or of 'infinite value' with respect to the other valuable commodity. In such a world a lexicographic order to judgment is defined. We may specify that X is the sacred commodity, Y is the non-sacred commodity; then for all ordered pairs $a, b \in S$ $[a = (x(a), y(a))]$,

if $x(a) > x(b)$ then $a\ B\ b$
or if $x(a) = x(b)$ and $y(a) > y(b)$ then $a\ B\ b$

In such a model it is, of course, not generally possible to map from choice to moral judgment about choice in a manner which will preserve ranks, since, as will be seen, what is preferred will not characteristically be what is judged better.

The genesis of the Malthusian controversy does not hinge upon the positive model of the child-bearing decision. William Godwin and Malthus follow Adam Smith in treating the child-bearing decision as entailed by the marriage decision.[5] In order to explain the decision to marry, the classics argued, we must explain the costs of children, since in a world without effective mechanical contraception children will regularly follow marriage.

The costs of children can be modeled in terms of the consumption of corn forgone by the parents. In Figure 11.1 two distinct indifference curves are drawn, specifying the locus of commodity pairs of equal utility to an individual, i.e., corn consumed by the possible parents and the age of marriage. The more corn consumed, other things being equal, and the earlier a marriage, other things being equal, the higher the utility. Also in Figure 11.1 two distinct feasibility sets are drawn under the assumption that an individual is responsible for the children resulting from a marriage. The earlier a marriage, the more numerous the children that will result.

The higher the wages which children can earn and contribute to their parents, the less a child will cost in terms of corn consumption forgone. The higher the wages ($w_1 > w_0$) paid to adults, the more corn an unmarried worker could consume: the 'corn' intercept of what is feasible at w_1 is higher than at w_0 in Figure 11.1. The same higher wages mean that children more nearly pay their own way; hence, the flatter the boundary of what is feasible at w_1 than at w_0.

The utility-maximizing solution is such that (at least for the classical analysis) at w_1 the worker would marry earlier and consume more corn in the form of food or drink than at w_0. It is important to note that there is both a wealth effect of higher wages (the higher intercept) and a substitution effect (the flatter slope), since Malthus will spend much time considering a problem in which an institutional reform would change the slope from a substantial negative number to approximately zero.

In *Political Justice* Godwin accepted a theory of such a structure to explain marriage and population growth under private property:

So long as there is a facility of subsistence, men will be encouraged to early marriages, and to a careful rearing of their children. . . . In such countries the wages of the labourer are high. . . . In many European countries, on the other hand, a large family has become a proverbial expression for an uncommon degree of poverty and wretchedness. . . . It is impossible where the price of labour is greatly reduced, and an added population threatens a still further reduction, that men should not be considerably under the influence of fear, respecting an early marriage, and a numerous family.[6]

For a consistent utilitarian, Figure 11.1 would contain both the positive and normative aspects of the discussion. It might be plausible to describe an individual who married at thirty as practicing 'moral restraint'. Indeed, the modern analytical commentaries of George Stigler and Joseph Schumpeter insist that this is what Malthus means by 'moral restraint'.[7] However, Malthus is at least as emphatic in asserting that this is not *all* he means by the term:

> It will be observed that I here use the term *moral* in its most confined sense. By moral restraint I would be understood to mean a restraint from marriage from prudential motives, with a conduct strictly moral during the period of this restraint; and I have never intentionally deviated from this sense. When I have wished to consider the restraint from marriage unconnected with its consequences, I have either called it prudential restraint, or a part of the preventive check, of which indeed it forms the principal branch.[8]

The normative aspect of the problem which is obliterated if Malthus is read as a straightforward utilitarian is that it is quite literally Gospel that individuals who could not remain chaste outside of marriage ought to marry. This point was made in stark clarity by St Paul:

> Now concerning the things whereof ye wrote unto me: It is good for a man not to touch a woman. Nevertheless, to avoid fornication, let every man have his own wife, and let every woman have her own husband . . . For I would that all men were even as I myself. But every man hath his proper gift of God, one after this manner, and another after that. I say therefore to the unmarried and widows, It is good for them if they abide even as I. But if they cannot contain, let them marry: for it is better to marry than to burn.[9]

Pauline doctrine was clearly expressed in the Anglican marriage service in the Book of Common Prayer.[10]

The point with which Malthus dealt obliquely was trumpeted in an earlier literature. Early marriage was to be encouraged because it increased population and reduced prostitution. We read in Dean Tucker's argument:

> The Natives of *England* likewise do not *increase* so fast, as those of other Countries; our common People being much more *abandoned* and *debauched*. The *marriage State* also is not sufficiently encouraged among Us: and ten Thousand *common Whores* are not so fruitful (setting aside the *Sin* of the *Parents*, the *Diseases* of the *few* Children that are *born*, and their want of a *proper* and *virtuous* Education) I say, 10,000 common Whores

are not so fruitful as *fifty* healthy young married Women, that are *honest* and *virtuous*: By which Means, the State is defrauded of the Increase of upwards of 199 Subjects out of 200, every year.[11]

Robert Wallace was somewhat more discreet:

> Hence, in a debauched nation, addicted to sensuality and irregular amours, and where luxury and an high taste of delicate living prevail, the number of people must be proportionably small; for their debauchery will hinder many from marrying. . . . For the same reason, a nation shall be more populous in proportion as good morals . . . prevail.[12]

Hence, *de facto* birth control was practiced by delay of marriage. The male part of the population coupled this celibacy with consumption of the services of prostitutes.

Hence, overlaid on a problem of choice is a consideration of the moral judgment to be made about the choice. If the dispute were solely among utilitarians, judgments made about choice would follow from the choices themselves. Malthus, himself, accepted the Christian judgment that individuals ought not to engage in extramarital sexual gratification, at least if other things remain the same.[13] This is not the same as accepting a judgment that individuals ought not to engage in extramarital sexual gratification regardless of the consequences. In Figure 12.1 we can specify the unconditional Christian normative judgment about the choice. In Christian normative terms the judgment is made that the individual ought to marry as early as possible, regardless of the consequences in terms of the corn income. This judgmental relation is specified by pseudo-indifference curves of judgment with respect to these choices, where we use pseudo-Roman numerals to rank the choices (JJ B J). Clearly, if these moral judgments do not change either what is feasible or the preferences of individuals, then the individuals described in Figure 12.1 will not do what Christian moral doctrine says ought to be done.[14] In our notation t B s, s R t, and not t R s.

Godwin proposed in *Political Justice* that it would be desirable that a communal society be founded where each individual was entitled to an equal share of the communal income.[15]

Malthus, in his first *Essay*, pointed out that, under such institutions, each individual would be encouraged to marry very early in life because the private costs of marriage would be abolished.[16] The private cost of marriage, the corn forgone by the parents, would be small under a system of distribution where individuals received an equal share of the communal income. An extra child, or twenty, would not substantially reduce the corn consumed by their parents.[17] This criticism Godwin accepted, given a low state of human development:

> It is true, the ill consequences of a numerous family will not come so

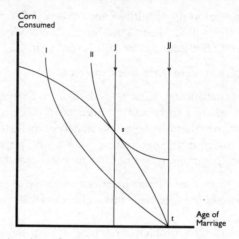

Figure 12.1 The Christian view of extramarital sex

coarsely home to each man's individual interest, as they do at present. It is true, a man in such a state of society might say, If my children cannot subsist at my expense, let them subsist at the expense of my neighbour.[18]

The short-run result of a communal system is specified in Figure 12.2. The individual worker would be judged better on either utilitarian or Christian criteria, since he has moved up indifference curves of choice and pseudo-difference curves of judgment.

Malthus argued that this equilibrium, described in Figure 12.2 (point *r*), was to be heartbreakingly brief. The resulting increase of population in a world where the marginal private cost of a family was nearly zero would not be matched with an equal increase in food production.[19]

Figure 12.3 specifies the long-run equilibrium for communism and private property. The individual in a communal state would find himself on a lower indifference curve, since the preventive check of delaying marriage in anticipation of the future costs of a family would not bind men and women.[20] Godwin could only hope that human nature would improve so that people would act out of regard for the social consequences of their choice.

Figure 12.3 specifies the choice offered to society by Malthus in the first edition. Population will be restrained either at point *s* by prudential considerations and casual sexual gratification, or at point *q* by misery.[21] This aspect of the discussion is assumed away if Malthus's normative model is forced into a utilitarian context where vice and misery would both mean lower indifference curves.

The addition in the later editions of the possibility of moral restraint –

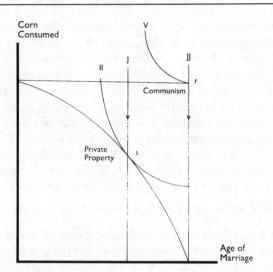

Figure 12.2   Short-run equilibrium

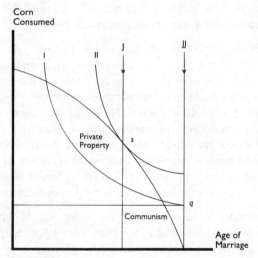

Figure 12.3   Long-run equilibrium

the possibility of a chaste life outside of marriage – is not important for the positive economics, since neither Malthus nor his critics believed that the period before marriage could be spent chastely.[22] It is, however, important for the normative purposes. In keeping with Christian terminology, Malthus could recommend 'moral restraint'; however, he tolerated immoral restraint as the lesser of two evils. Hence, Malthus found himself in a classical ethical bind of conflicting duties. This dilemma is observed in Malthus' reply to Arthur Young:

Mr. Young has asserted that I have made perfect chastity in the single state absolutely necessary to the success of my plan; but this surely is a misrepresentation. Perfect virtue is, indeed, necessary to enable man to avoid *all* the moral and physical evils which depend upon his own conduct; but who ever expected perfect virtue upon earth? I have said, what I conceive to be strictly true, that it is our duty to defer marriage till we can feed our children; and that it is also our duty not to indulge ourselves in vicious gratifications; but I have never said that I expected either, much less both, of these duties to be completely fulfilled. In this, and a number of other cases, it may happen that the violation of one of two duties will enable a man to perform the other with greater facility.[23]

Malthus' radicalism results from his practical conclusions:

Whatever I may have said in drawing a picture *professedly* visionary, for the sake of illustration, in the practical application of my principles I have taken man as he is, with all his imperfections on his head. And thus viewing him, and knowing that some checks to population must exist, I have not the slightest hesitation in saying, that the prudential check to marriage is better than premature mortality.[24]

It is, I think important to take into account the non-utilitarian normative aspects of the discussion if we wish to understand why Malthus was charged with deicide. If God gave man a choice of only vice or misery, would anyone continue to worship him?[25]

Judgment need not follow choice. None the less, as modeled in Figure 12.3, Christian normative judgments require that the poor be judged better, i.e., the poor have been raised to higher pseudo-indifference curves of judgment even while recognizing that institutions which encourage early marriage would eventually reduce the poor to lower indifference curves. This possibility was developed at length by James Grahame:

That the worth or happiness of the poor would be promoted by abstinence from matrimonial connections, is a proposition totally incompatible with the notions commonly entertained in the meaning of worth and happiness, and of the comparative effects of matrimony and celibacy. A celibacy exempt from vice has been esteemed a state of so difficult attainment, that many have regarded marriage in no other light than as the preventive of vice . . . The relations and ties created by marriage, however embarrassing they may prove to many of the poor, add at least as much to the worth of their character, as they can possibly detract from the ease of their circumstances.[26]

The incompatibility of Malthus' recommendation, that prudential restraint ought to be encouraged, with Christian moral doctrine was frequently mentioned in the books written against Malthus.[27]

Malthus, in the later editions, suggested in a pseudo-Swiftian chapter that it would be possible to allow individuals to marry as early as their parsons desired if the death rate were high enough:

> To act consistently, therefore, we should facilitate, instead of foolishly and vainly endeavouring to impede, the operations of nature in producing this mortality . . . If by these and similar means the annual mortality were increased . . . we might probably every one of us marry at the age of puberty, and yet few be absolutely starved.[28]

Malthus was led to consider the consequences of traditional morality:

> I certainly cannot think that the vices which relate to the sex are the only vices which are to be considered in a moral question; or that they are even the greatest and the most degrading to the human character . . . there are other vices the effects of which are still more pernicious; and there are other situations which lead more certainly to moral offences than the refraining from marriage. Powerful as may be the temptations to a breach of chastity, I am inclined to think that they are impotent in comparison of the temptations arising from continued distress . . . there will be found very few who pass through the ordeal of squalid and hopeless poverty . . . without a great moral degradation of character.[29]

Malthus boldly confronted Pauline doctrine:

> Universally, the practice of mankind on the subject of marriage has been much superior to their theories; and however frequent may have been the declamations on the duty of entering into this state, and the advantage of early unions to prevent vice, each individual has practically found it necessary to consider of the means of supporting a family before he ventured to take so important a step. That great *vis medicatrix reipublicæ*, the desire of bettering our condition, and the fear of making it worse, has been constantly in action, and has been constantly directing people into the right road, in spite of all the declamations which tended to lead them aside.[30]

If the above reconstruction is correct, then we must attend to Malthus' radicalism. Malthus found an anomaly in traditional morality such that, characteristically, it was not possible for a poor man to do his duty to both his children and to God. This anomaly forced Malthus to take the fundamental step in ethical radicalism: to choose amongst competing ethical systems.[31]

I find no evidence that Malthus was personally radical. It is, of course, true that Malthus emphatically rejected mechanical contraception for fundamentally theological reasons.[32] For this he was attacked by Francis Place, who argued that mechanical contraception would allow early marriage, relatively high corn consumption and a reduction of prostitution:

If means were adopted to prevent the breeding of a larger number of children than a married couple might desire to have, and if the labouring part of the population would thus be kept below the demand for labour, wages would rise so as to afford the means of comfortable subsistence for all, and all might marry. Marriage, under these circumstances, would also be, by far, the happiest of all conditions, as it would be the most virtuous . . . Much even of that sort of promiscuous intercourse carried on by means of open prostitution, now so excessively and extensively pernicious, would cease.[33]

Still, the radicalism of Malthus' step is not recognized even today in mainline economic theory. First-rate economists write of a trade-off between equity and efficiency. Surely, equity is a word of moral judgment. If what we want to do is 'inequitable', why cannot we change our morality? Changing our morality so that what we want to do is now 'equitable' produces the same material goods but with more 'equity'. This is not what is usually meant by a trade-off.

Chapter 13

Libertarian communists, Malthusians and J. S. Mill – who is both

INTRODUCTION

Our understanding of J. S. Mill's social philosophy has been obscured by the failure of historians to come to grips with the issues in the debate between William Godwin and T. R. Malthus over the desirability of private property, familial responsibility, marriage and kindred social institutions. The debate seems to begin with the thesis advanced by David Hume. As part of his dispute with John Locke, Hume puts forward a theory of property establishing that property exists, and only exists, in conditions of limited benevolence and scarcity; that is, in situations either with benevolence or without scarcity we do not observe property.[1] What if, Godwin argues, as if in opposition to part of Hume's argument, scarcity is artificial, a creation of property itself? If the rest of Hume's analysis were correct, would not abolishing property create general benevolence? This is the Godwinian challenge to a system of private property, the claim that an egalitarian distribution of income and an other-regarding morality could be simultaneously created by a radical piece of social engineering.[2]

Not fitting neatly into any of the modern 'isms', there is an interesting problem in giving Godwin's social philosophy a name which does not misrepresent its subtlety. Since Godwin's proposal to share communal resources equally without regard to production is advanced to free people from the constraints both of government and of property, perhaps it is not inappropriate to characterize his philosophy as 'libertarian communism'. An alternative characterization, 'philosophical anarchism', requires a supplementary proviso that Godwin opposes property as well as government.[3] Making his case against property to unbind the constraint he sees to human development, Godwin does not defend redistribution which is not accompanied by a corresponding change in the motivation of individuals.[4]

Malthus attacks Godwin on the grounds that scarcity is natural because human motivation is not a policy variable, that human wants are insatiable, and cannot be bound by social concern. Waiving consideration of communism's reduction of the incentive to labor, Malthus bases his attack on what we know about the sexual passions of men and women and about the possibility of agricultural production. A libertarian communism abolishes the individual material responsibility for marriage by making each responsible for everyone's children. If human motivation is a given, the constraints to appropriation of resources to support children provided by a moral law are ephemeral without the supplement of the constraints inherent in a system of private property.

The fascinating paradox of Mill's social philosophy is that, as the great spokesman for Malthusianism in the latter half of the nineteenth century, he defends a libertarian communism on the Godwinian grounds that the abolition of private property would bring with it a moral law strong enough to provide the requisite constraints to appropriation. The burden of Mill's argument is to show that a successful libertarian communism would inculcate an altruistic motivation replacing self-regarding motivation. He defends libertarian communism by denying the foundations of economic reductionism – the approach to social theory which posits that the goals to which individuals aspire are constant.

The Malthusian background is vital to understand why the institutional framework for Mill's proposed reform of public opinion has such a strong religious cast. When we see that Malthus shows that Christianity encourages the sort of irresponsibility which would doom a libertarian communism, we can understand Mill's argument that Christianity must be replaced or reformed to serve as the moral basis for the new order. Mill looks for a day in which individuals are motivated only by general benevolence, so the constraints of property become obsolete.[5]

Arthur Lovejoy has called attention to the vast importance of combinatory originality, new theory built by selection and rearrangement from the common stock of ideas.[6] Mill's response to Malthus is an example of such combinatory originality. He secularizes theological utilitarianism by specifying the infinite importance of moral development. Seeing no reason why a competitive process would lead to such a development, Mill draws upon the theory of an endowed, culture-diffusing class to effect the morality of social unity.[7] To allow these theories to guide reality, rather than be falsified by reality, Mill relies upon a developmental philosophy of social theory in an Aristotelian teleology.[8] Combined with some of the technical aspects of Malthusian theory, these pieces serve as the basis for Mill's defense of libertarian communism as an institutional reform to force moral, motivational development. The Malthusian controversy comes to rest with Mill where it began in Godwin: a controversy over the desirability of libertarian communism.

Although the issues in the Malthusian controversy seem to be of interest today mainly to historians of economic theory, the ramifications of this dispute are considerably wider. At its foundation the libertarian communist quarrel with Malthus is a quarrel with the economic–philosophical tradition of economic reductionism which posits that the goals to which people aspire are fixed. In this reductionist tradition, the only thing which differentiates people across time and space is differential access to means to attain fixed goals. The problem facing reductionists is to explain systematically how differences in these means (knowledge, prices, income, time) predict differences and similarities in behavior.[9]

It is important to notice what the reductionist tradition precludes: the influence of an individual's beliefs about how he ought to behave on these goals. An individual's beliefs presumably influence his choice of means to these goals, so the reductionists do not deny the influence of morality on choice. However, this fixed goal assumption allows theorists to distinguish sharply between social theory and the reality which social theory describes. If goals were not assumed to be fixed, the social theory which is held by these individuals would influence their goal; hence, we could not separate social reality from the theory describing that reality. Mill's response to the reductionist tradition is important because the tradition is important, and because Mill's response is not marred by technical deficiencies.

THE MALTHUSIAN BACKGROUND

There are two aspects of Malthus' work which provide an important background for Mill's work. First, Malthus shows that the traditional economic theory of population could be used to analyze the consequences of a state which abolished familial responsibility and private property without replacing them with some institution imposing responsibility on individuals' decisions to have children. Second, Malthus shows that the dictates of traditional Christianity conflict with the dictates of humanitarianism. These aspects have been discussed in the previous two chapters.

Malthus further claims that some forms of poor laws allow individuals to pass the cost of supporting a family on to society, encouraging population growth. Malthus' analysis establishes the possibility of perverse poor relief: those forms of poor laws which approximate a libertarian communistic income distribution encourage rapid increase in population; hence, they benefit the subsidized poor *at the expense* of the independent poor; that is, those poor who support themselves without parish relief.[10] However, he conjectures that it would be possible to design a poor law which did not produce a substantial divergence between the private and social costs of children. If poor relief were imposed under stringent sumptuary controls, individuals would not marry expecting to receive poor relief.[11] If Malthus's conjecture were correct, it would be possible to provide some assistance for distress without financing poor relief by making independent laborers poorer.

Mill's Malthusianism is shaped by Nassau Senior's contributions to population theory and policy. Senior's study leading to the New Poor Law of 1834 provides the cutting, empirical edge of later Malthusian policy proposals and theory. Senior's study provides the evidence that it is possible to design a non-perverse poor law along the lines of Malthus' long-forgotten conjecture. Moreover, his study shows it to be possible to explain behavior in different societies by variation in incentives.

Senior is hardly an uncritical disciple of Malthus. In his first exposition of classical population theory, he points out that the terminology which Malthus uses suggests both the empirically false propositions that wages could not persist above subsistence and that living standards have not risen in the course of economic development.[12] This terminological confusion is at issue in the exchange between Senior and Malthus,[13] an exchange which does not jeopardize Senior's good standing as a Malthusian.[14]

Senior's investigation of the European and American experience with poor relief discovers that British experience of rapidly increasing expenditure for poor relief is almost unique.[15] This intersocial difference could be explained by the private cost of availing oneself of poor relief in these different societies. Where poor relief is sufficiently unpleasant, societies do not suffer the British experience.[16] Thus Malthus' conjecture is confirmed.

The economics literature of the period following the New Poor Law's establishment stresses the importance of the quantitative divergence between the private and social costs of a family on population growth. As an empirical matter, it seems that it is unnecessary to allow poor people or their children to starve to impress upon others the desirability of being able to support themselves before they marry. Poor assistance provided with sumptuary controls has the same effect on the marriage decision. Thus, Senior's study marks an important development in both Malthusian theory and policy. It leads economists to stress the quantitative issues involved in poor law controversy.[17] For example, Mill uses Senior's finding to argue against Harriet Martineau's statement of David Ricardo's position that all forms of poor relief are perverse.[18] Indeed, Mill's *Political Economy* contains a lengthy summary and exposition of the findings of Senior's study.[19]

Towards the end of the nineteenth century, the Malthusian position forms a stock objection to libertarian communism.[20] Alfred Marshall points out that the dispute between Godwin and Malthus has a classical analogy:

> well-meaning enthusiasts, chiefly under French influence, were proposing communistic schemes which would enable people to throw on society the responsibility for rearing their children. [Note to the text] It is interesting to compare Malthus' criticism [of Godwin] with Aristotle's comments on Plato's *Republic* (see especially *Politics*, II, 6).[21]

MILL'S RESPONSE TO ECONOMIC REDUCTIONISM

A defining characteristic of economic reductionism is a claim that the goals to which all individuals aspire are constant. Variation in access to means to these ends is thus necessary and sufficient to explain variation in behavior. To analyze the future course of society, reductionists presume that human motivation, the goals to which individuals aspire, is the one stable feature.[22] Malthus locates himself in this tradition when he criticizes Marquis de Condorcet's conjecture of the perfectibility of man:

> It may perhaps be said that the world is yet so young, so completely in its infancy, that it ought not to be expected that any difference should appear so soon.
>
> If this be the case, there is at once an end of all human science. The whole train of reasonings from effects to causes will be destroyed. We may shut our eyes to the book of nature, as it will no longer be of any use to read it. The wildest and most improbable conjectures may be advanced with as much certainty as the most just and sublime theories, founded on careful and reiterated experiments. We may return again to the old mode of philosophising and make facts bend to systems, instead of establishing systems upon facts.[23]

Godwin's and Mill's defense of libertarian communism operates within an opposing philosophy of social theory where indeed 'facts bend to systems'. In his first response to Malthus, Godwin depends critically upon the assertion that under libertarian communism moral, motivational development would occur spontaneously. Godwin provides no reason to believe this would be the case.[24] Mill provides, if not a reason, at least an elaboration of the issues.

Mill's social teleology

The issue between the reductionists and the libertarian communists is whether it is probable that under libertarian communism individuals would act out of social concern in their family-forming decision. Mill knows from Senior's study that individuals show no sign of doing so. The empirical issue is whether human motivation is set or whether it can be expected to 'develop' in response to social change. Although standard accounts characterize Mill as an empiricist, his approach to social philosophy and economics is much closer to Aristotle's teleology than Hume's Newtonianism. Teleology specifies a goal independent of observed choice; moreover, it specifies that evidence can be dismissed from falsifying the theory. That is, there are divergences between theory and reality which are the fault of the reality, not the theory. These are the 'mistakes' of nature.[25] For example, an Aristotelian would not regard the observation of an irrational individual as falsifying the proposition that all men are rational. The irrational individual is defective, he has not attained his potential.[26]

Mill finds in Coleridge a technique to defend the *potential* of social institutions, here an established culture-diffusing class:

> That such a class is likely to be behind, instead of before, the progress of knowledge, is an induction erroneously drawn from the peculiar circumstances of the last two centuries, and in contradiction to all the rest of modern history.[27]

It is a shock to note the teleological confidence with which Mill dismisses the evidence of two centuries. But, Mill is concerned with the potential of social institutions, not with what is actually observed: 'If we have seen much of the abuses of endowments, we have not seen what this country might be made by a proper administration of them'.[28]

The importance of the methodological prescriptions in Mill's *Logic* for understanding Mill's social philosophy has been rightly insisted upon by J. M. Robson.[29] Mill regards the laws of the formation of character as critical; none the less, they 'cannot be ascertained by observation and experiment'. Although Mill proposes an approach which Karl Popper would make famous, that a deductive model be constructed which generates implications then to be compared to reality,[30] Mill simply frees his speculations on character development from any empirical constraint. If humans develop, what we learn from observation now may not be applicable tomorrow.[31]

On forcing moral, motivational development

We learn from everything Mill writes the importance he assigns to moral development. In sharp contrast to the reductionist claim that effective morality only redirects the means to satisfy given passions, Mill looks for morality to change human desires.[32] The reductionists examine observed morality; what Mill considers morality is vital to his defense of libertarian communism.

Mill's explicit statement of the Greatest Happiness Principle in *Utilitarianism* contains a distinction between 'higher' and 'lower' pleasures.[33] Although acute critics have asserted otherwise, this distinction is made not on the basis of observed choice,[34] but on the basis of the judgment of the most developed creatures. It is certainly true that Mill writes in places as if individuals who can attain both will actually choose the higher pleasure over the lower.[35] None the less, it seems unduly harsh to read Mill as making this vital distinction on actual, observed choice. The absurdity of such an argument had been long exposed by any number of philosophers who could write with their eyes open.[36] In fact, he admits that even more highly developed individuals do not behave the way their judgments would suggest. This revealed non-preference does not, at least for Mill, prove their judgments false.

> It may be objected, that many who are capable of the higher pleasures, occasionally, under the influence of temptation, postpone them to the lower. But this is quite compatible with a full appreciation of the intrinsic superiority of the higher. Men often, from infirmity of character, make their election for the nearer good, though they know it to be the less valuable; and this no less when the choice is between two bodily pleasures, than when it is between bodily and mental. They pursue sensual indulgences to the injury of health, though perfectly aware that health is the greater good.[37]

Indeed, if Mill were arguing that we know what is moral by observing what moral men do, then he indeed would be advancing a transparent circularity.[38] Mill defines 'higher' pleasure in terms of *judgments* of fully developed individuals, regardless of how they themselves behave.

The 'higher'/'lower' distinction has consequences for Mill's social philosophy which we explore next. Indeed, in a nutshell, Mill's normative social philosophy is how to induce individuals to choose the 'higher' pleasure. How do we produce moral, motivational development?

Agreeing with Godwin, Mill's hope for social unity is the heart of his support of communism:

> Mankind are capable of a far greater amount of public spirit than the present age is accustomed to suppose possible. History bears witness to the success with which large bodies of human beings may be trained to feel the public interest their own. And no soil could be more favourable to the growth of such a feeling, than a Communist association, since all the ambition, and the bodily and mental activity, which are now exerted in the pursuit of separate and self-regarding interests, would require another sphere of employment, and would naturally find it in the pursuit of the general benefit of the community.[39]

The Malthusian challenge is acknowledged; if libertarian communism continues to exist, it must produce moral, motivational development:

> Another of the objections to Communism is similar to that, so often urged against poor-laws: that if every member of the community were assured of subsistence for himself and any number of children, on the sole condition of willingness to work, prudential restraint on the multiplication of mankind would be at an end, and population would start forward at a rate which would reduce the community, through successive stages of increasing discomfort, to actual starvation. There would certainly be much ground for this apprehension if Communism provided no motives to restraint, equivalent to those which it would take

away. But Communism is precisely the state of things in which opinion might be expected to declare itself with greatest intensity against this kind of selfish intemperance . . . The Communistic scheme, instead of being peculiarly open to the objection drawn from dangers of over-population, has the recommendation of tending in an especial degree to the prevention of that evil.[40]

Since libertarian communism requires moral, motivational development, we cannot say what the future organization will be like.[41] This may explain why Mill does not worry over the details of the future communistic organization.

Mill has relied upon his teleology to 'prove' the vital issue. That is, given that a libertarian communism is stable, then moral development must occur. What if the Malthusian nightmare comes to pass? To consider the gains and losses from a communist experiment, it is necessary to consider the importance which Mill assigns to social unity.

Under libertarian communism the Greatest Happiness Principle with its distinction of higher and lower pleasures might be taught as an imperative from a created religion. Mill believes that religion has the ability to mold character; a situation not without its dangers. However, there will be no dangers in the new order, since the doctrine of this new religion is that the highest of all pleasures is unity with one's fellow creatures:

In an improving state of the human mind, the influences are constantly on the increase, which tend to generate in each individual a feeling of unity with all the rest; which feeling, if perfect, would make him never think of, or desire, any beneficial condition for himself, in the benefits of which they are not included. If we now suppose this feeling of unity to be taught as a religion, and the whole force of education, of institutions, and of opinion, directed, as it once was in the case of religion, to make every person grow up from infancy surrounded on all sides both by the profession and by the practice of it, I think that no one, who can realize this conception, will feel any misgiving about the sufficiency of the ultimate sanction for the Happiness morality.[42]

We note that both in *On Liberty* and elsewhere Mill explicitly considers moral development a higher-order good than even liberty:

It is, perhaps, hardly necessary to say that this doctrine is meant to apply only to human beings in the maturity of their faculties . . . we may leave out of consideration those backward states of society in which the race itself may be considered as in its nonage . . . Despotism is a legitimate mode of government in dealing with barbarians, provided the end be their improvement, and the means justified by actually effecting that end. Liberty, as a principle, has no application to any state of things anterior to the time when mankind have become capable of being improved by free and equal discussion. Until then, there is nothing for them but implicit obedience to an Akbar or a Charlemagne, if they are so fortunate as to find one.[43]

The gamble which Mill is willing for society to take is to free society from all constraints other than the new morality. If the gamble fails, nothing important has been lost, since moral, motivational development is a higher-order good than anything which might be lost. Mill has secularized Blaise Pascal's wager; any gamble to attain the infinite good is worthwhile for any finite probability of success. Any costs of the gamble vanish because of the hierarchy of his moral universe.

CONCLUSION: MALTHUSIANISM AS AN INDICATOR OF HUMAN DEVELOPMENT

Now we can understand the paradox of Mill's Malthusianism. Mill's *Political Economy* serves as an important forum to diffuse Senior's result that variation in self-regarding incentives across societies is necessary and sufficient to explain variation in the effects of poor relief. When behavior can be reduced to considerations of self-regarding incentives, people are in a deplorable state of development. Here, they behave as Malthusian theory describes.[44] Under libertarian communism the choice is: develop or starve. Given Mill's hierarchical morality, the choice presented by libertarian communism is an acceptable gamble. We who still feel the costs paid in illiberal attempts to create a 'New Man' might feel otherwise.

Part VI

Objections and applications

The idea that there is a competition for approbation has appalled many great thinkers. Indeed, starting with Plato one can find systematic attempts to replace the motive of competition for approbation with something more seemly. The first chapter sketches the effort common to Plato and John Locke to replace competition for approbation with belief. What if the gods only provide approbation for those who produce public goods? Do we need to compete for fame? We also provide Bernard Mandeville's devastating attack on the particulars of John Locke's version of the Platonic argument.

To be fair to the Platonic position, we must allow someone to speak against competition. To this end we consider in some detail the great anti-competitive statement by S. T. Coleridge. Coleridge writes explicitly against Adam Smith, so the argument is joined. Coleridge asserts that words are much more important than the Scots would allow. Words operate more directly on social reality in Coleridge's view than many of his readers have understood. None the less, it is a fact beyond debate that many who have read Coleridge have found his results convincing. And even if he had persuaded only John Stuart Mill, it would be necessary that his arguments be examined seriously.

The two chapters following examine, in detail, arguments that students of ordinary people's choice do not need to consider the ideas of ordinary people. The first of the pair considers F. A. Hayek's position; the second considers Benedict Spinoza's. One counter-example works against both their arguments: the case of imperfect knowledge. We have found above that imperfect knowledge *suffices* to explain why ordinary people's ideas are important in some maximizing problems. If the Spinoza–Hayek position holds outside the case of imperfect knowledge – it is my opinion that it does – then imperfect knowledge is a necessary condition for us to attend to ordinary people's ideas. Thus, imperfect knowledge is necessary and sufficient to attend to the ideas of ordinary people.

Finally, as the book opens with the question of how a 'false' theory might be serviceable to a maximizer, it is only fitting that it close with the same abstract question in a different guise. The theory in question will be achingly familiar to my fellow economists: single-priced monopoly is inefficient. Then how is it, some have asked, that we observe them?

Chapter 14

Must one believe to obey?

INTRODUCTION

At base the Platonic enterprise proposes that the passionate, competitive aspect of human nature ought to be controlled by the reflective.[1] The author of this book is in a particularly perilous position to argue with Plato about whether ideas matter to choice. What is open for debate is the position taken by the speakers in Plato's dialogues that ordinary people have the wrong sort of ideas. We have glanced at this assertion before, but now we will confront a very sharp statement of the thesis that something is dreadfully wrong with what people believe. This is the statement of the Athenian Stranger in Plato's *Laws*:

> No one who believes, as the laws prescribe, in the existence of the gods has ever yet done an impious deed voluntarily, or uttered a lawless word: he that acts so is in one or other of three conditions of mind — either he does not believe in what I had said; or, secondly, he believes that the gods exist, but have no care for men; or, thirdly, he believes that they are easy to win over when bribed by offerings and prayers.[2]

This is the origin of the argument that crime is the result of atheism.[3] Those who do not believe may themselves not be criminals, but they corrupt others and ought therefore to be punished.[4]

At its basis the Platonic principle that where there is no proof there is no true knowledge is a terrifically powerful attack on the whole idea of a competitive process in morality. The Platonic principle is that those who cannot prove it is to their interest to be moral cannot be counted on to be moral.[5] Can atheists — those who do not believe in a divine accounting mechanism — be counted on to be moral? If they cannot, ought not atheism to be suppressed as a method to fight crime and immorality?

The importance of a required proof for morality is important. The moral atheist cannot say, 'Look, it is my interest to be moral', to prove his good nature; the obvious response is: what if conditions change to make it to your interest to be immoral? From a Platonic point of view, the good atheist has been moral without a principled reason to be so, and so there is no reason to believe that he will be moral tomorrow. There is no reason to disbelieve that some terrible temptation might occur which would cause the previously good atheist to become criminal.

In spite of the hoary tradition characterizing John Locke as the intellectual father of the United States constitution, we find the same Platonic doctrine mandating belief advanced by Locke in his theoretical writings and his proposed constitution for Carolina. The latter is a particularly nasty version:

> No man shall be permitted to be a freeman of Carolina, or to have any estate or habitation within it, that doth not acknowledge a GOD; and that God is publickly and solemnly to be worshipped.[6]

One must be very careful in calling Locke a Platonist; Plato's *Laws* would be far too liberal for Locke's constitutional setting. It is itself a searching discussion of the laws and Locke has this to say about such activity:

> Since multiplicity of comments, as well as of laws, have great inconveniences, and serve only to obscure and perplex; all manner of comments and expositions, on any part of these Fundamental Constitutions, or any part of the common or statute law of Carolina, are absolutely prohibited.[7]

A *jihad* was launched against Platonic doctrine during the seventeenth and eighteenth centuries. One front of this onslaught – an attack on the Platonic enterprise on its own metatheoretical grounds – has been very thoroughly studied. Inside the rules of the Platonic enterprise, it is certainly reasonable to ask Platonists to prove that the divine accounting mechanism, about which one must believe, exists. On what basis do we believe these principles that will keep us moral? Prove *this*, if you can. The fame, lasting as long as daylight is scattered over free people, which David Hume and Immanuel Kant earned for demolishing all such proofs demonstrates the importance of their efforts.

Another front of this attack has been less thoroughly studied. This calls into question the presumed link between a particular form of religious belief and moral behavior. The Platonic principle was revived with considerable force by Blaise Pascal in his famous wager over behavior when one is uncertain about the existence of God. This was later employed by John Locke and George Berkeley. Pascal was a great philosopher and a great mathematician. Bernard Mandeville was neither. None the less, Mandeville found a trick and won the throw. Although the offense begins with Pierre Bayle's claim that a society of atheists would behave no differently than a society of believers, we attend to Bernard Mandeville's pungent version.[8] In Mandeville's attack we find him portraying men and women confronting the commands of absolute morality and the lusts of the flesh. What is worthy of remark is that he treats the dictates both of absolute morality and of the flesh seriously.

JOHN LOCKE, PLATONIST

Under what conditions will men be moral? Locke provides the same answer to this question in many places. Only when the morality is self-enforcing, only when morality provides a motive to influence choice. For Locke, this motive is provided by Christian revelation of the reality of Heaven and Hell. In Locke's polemical account, classical philosophy does not provide a foundation for such behavior.[9] That is, not only do classical philosophers fail to give a complete account of morality, but knowledge of morality does not *per se* provide an incentive to moral behavior.[10] Christianity, suitably reformed to focus on incentives to morality, would provide such a motive.

> The generality could not refuse her [virtue] their esteem and commendation, but still turned their backs on her, and forsook her, as a match not for their turn. But now there being put into the scales, on her side, 'an exceeding and immortal weight of glory,' interest is come about to her; and virtue now is visibly the most enriching purchase, and by much the best bargain. . . . The view of heaven and hell will cast a slight upon the short pleasures and pains of this present state, and give attractions and encouragements to virtue, which reason and interest, and the care of ourselves, cannot but allow and prefer. *Upon this foundation, and upon this only, morality stands firm, and may defy all competition. This makes it more than a name, a substantial good, worth all our aims and endeavours* . . .[11]

The passage to which my italics draw attention ought to be considered very carefully by those who hold that in Locke we find an answer to Hobbes. Isn't it the cornerstone of Hobbes's doctrine that words are inconsequential unless they carry with them a promise of pleasure or pain? Words without swords are just names. Locke says just that.

In Locke's version of Pascal's wager, moral choice is utility-maximizing when the infinite value of the side-payments promised in Christian revelation are taken into account.[12] Locke considers belief in the existence of a supernatural accounting mechanism vital to the social order, since those who do not believe in heaven and hell will not obey the law. Locke refuses toleration for atheists precisely because their behavior cannot be depended upon.[13] Similarly, Locke condemns government policy which induces individuals to take false oaths and thus reduce their sanctity.[14]

Locke's proposed reform of Christianity is an attempt to focus men's attention on doctrinal aspects which would modify their behavior. If a doctrine stands in the way of understanding the rewards of virtue, then it is not required dogma. Hence, Locke argues that it is not important to require belief that the soul is immaterial – belief in the immortality of the soul provides sufficient motive for good behavior on earth. The great debate which follows involves more than questions of theology; it raises the question of whether religious doctrine is a policy variable.[15]

DOCTOR MAN-DEVIL

The Platonic enterprise is to wire belief and behavior together. If you 'truly' believe that God gives infinite punishments and rewards, then you never act contrary to the will of God for merely finite pleasure. Bernard Mandeville asks the particularly useful question: does anyone actually have such a true belief? Do we observe such a linkage between belief and behavior in the world?

> The greatest Difficulty of our Religion is to live up to the Rules of Christianity. To conquer our Passions, and mortify our darling Lusts, is, what few of us earnestly set about; and as to higher and heroick Virtues they are very scarce to be met with.[16]

> The chief Duty then of real Religion among Christians consists in a Sacrifice of the Heart, and is a Task of Self-denial, with the utmost Severity against Nature to be perform'd on our selves.[17]

> Should it be objected, that I was not in Earnest, when I recommended those mortifying Maxims, I would answer, That those, who think so, would have said the same to St *Paul*, or JESUS CHRIST himself, if he had bid them sell their Estates and give their Money to the Poor.[18]

Mandeville strikes at the heart of social Platonism by questioning the linkage between belief about what is utility-maximizing behavior and utility-maximizing behavior itself. Suppose we agree that irrational acts will not be systematically observed. What Mandeville demonstrates is that acceptance of the theorem 'Sin is irrational' does not imply that sin is irrational, if as we have agreed, irrational means not observed systematically. Here is where Mandeville's Paradox is very important. One cannot pass from normative theorems to positive predictions precisely because the important normative theorems are not 'true'. We have demonstrated that this does not raise any serious difficulties for an absolutist morality; it does hit Mandeville's target.

When the Platonist asked the good atheist for a 'reason' that he would be good tomorrow, the answer demanded was to take the form 'Because it is always utility-maximizing to be good'. Mandeville finds people – Christians – who believe as the Platonists require, but do not behave differently than anyone else. Behavior does not tag along after belief even when the beliefs are of transfinite reality.

This is a very narrow argument. Mandeville does not deny that approbation is important; on the contrary, he revels in the glory of approbation. But it is man-made approbation that counts for behavior:

> Men are better paid for their Adherence to Honour, than they are for their Adherence to Virtue: The First requires less Self-denial; and the Rewards they receive for that Little are not imaginary but real and palpable. But Experience confirms what I say: The Invention of Honour has been far more beneficial to the Civil Society than that of Virtue, and much better answer'd the End for which they were invented. . . . The Persuasions to Virtue make no Allowances, nor have any Allurements that are clashing with the Principle of it; whereas the Men of Pleasure, the Passionate and the Malicious, may all in their Turns meet with Opportunities of indulging their darling Appetites without trespassing against the Principle of Honour.[19]

Unfortunately, Bishop Berkeley's exchange with Mandeville raises no new issues.[20]

There is an old debate – is Mandeville an immoralist? – which we need not enter. On the question whether society can create its own morality or whether morality needs to come from outside by revelation, Mandeville's position is quite clear.

If society is capable of evolving its own morality then of course there is no *a priori* reason to require belief.

TO BE CONTINUED

The great Platonic counter-attack on competitive morality would have to wait until Mandeville, Hume and Smith had had their say. Then the great Platonist of the nineteenth century, S. T. Coleridge, comes into the picture with words which can bind and release. This is the next chapter, which requires special technical machinery.

Chapter 15

S. T. Coleridge replies to Adam Smith's 'pernicious opinion'

THE PUZZLE

The problem can be stated simply enough: how did Samuel Taylor Coleridge persuade a generation and more of competent social thinkers to share his disapprobation of a free market in culture and to disregard Adam Smith's analysis of the consequences of the endowments of intellectuals? The fact is that he did.[1] In the history of economic theory Adam Smith has few peers; here is testimony from one of them:

> we honour Coleridge for having rescued from the discredit in which the corruptions of the English Church had involved everything connected with it, and for having vindicated against Bentham and Adam Smith and the whole eighteenth century, the principle of an endowed class, for the cultivation of learning, and for diffusing its results among the community. That such a class is likely to be behind, instead of before, the progress of knowledge, is an induction erroneously drawn from the peculiar circumstances of the last two centuries . . .[2]

That Coleridge had an influence seems clear. What troubles me is why. My difficulty is very simple: Smith's argument against endowments is a valid deduction from the first principles of economic analysis, what economists today call 'the law of demand'. In particular, if an endowment reduces the rewards for success and the penalties for failure in intellectual pursuits, we can expect less excellence to be forthcoming.[3] Smith's position hardly requires a long chain of technical reasoning; consequently, as Mill writes, Smith's position is scarcely unique. If anything, Samuel Johnson made the more compelling case for the free market in the production of literature:

> A man (said he) who writes a book, thinks himself wiser or wittier than the rest of mankind; he supposes that he can instruct or amuse them, and the publick to whom he appeals, must, after all, be the judges of his pretensions.[4]

It should come as no surprise then that Smith and Johnson were coupled together in Coleridge's eyes as opponents to his position:

> A pernicious Opinion that of Dr Johnson's & Dryden's & Adam Smith's &c that Authors by compulsion in the profession are likely to be the best i.e. professional musicians &c.[5]

Not only is this analysis of endowments an easy inference from a principle of great empirical power, Oxford and Cambridge stood mute testimony to the disastrous effect of the withdrawal of incentives to diligence.[6] Now, if the Smith–Johnson argument is valid and there is evidence to substantiate the conclusion, how did Coleridge escape the inference they drew?

What does the commentary say about this issue? Here, I find little guidance either from the studies which deal with classical British economics or from those which consider Coleridge's political philosophy. Modern historians of economics have paid little attention to the 'romantic' critics of the classical economics, so lack of guidance from this literature is expected.[7] None the less, I was surprised to discover that many famous analyses of Coleridge's political philosophy do not even mention the fact that Coleridge writes in opposition to Smith's analysis.[8]

In spite of the gap in the commentary on this particular issue, one broad point of agreement which does emerge from various studies of Coleridge's social philosophy is his desire to engender spiritual improvement through institutional reform.[9] Of course this raises a technical question: just how is one supposed to go about making spiritual improvement through institutional reform? Answering this technical question can, I shall argue, illuminate the mechanics of Coleridge's response to Smith and Johnson.

Coleridge actually made two important proposals for institutional reform: the egalitarian Pantisocracy in the 1790s and the endowed cultural class in the 1830s. Coleridge switched philosophical positions in the time period which separates these proposed reforms. In his Pantisocratic days, he subscribed to the tenets of philosophical materialism.[10] By the years he proposed an endowed status for intellectuals, he had converted to Neoplatonism.[11] Before we turn to the hard problem of the mechanics of endowing intellectuals, we shall deal with the easy problem of looking at what wrecked Coleridge's Pantisocratic hopes. The case will be made that Coleridge's later proposal came to grips with the lessons taught by the early failure. In the Pantisocratic failure Coleridge discovers the importance of creating new men and women to act as the founders of a new order. How this can be done will be examined when we look at the role that Neoplatonic social engineering plays in the argument.[12]

AN INTERPRETATIVE THESIS

Before we confront the texts, we can consider the problem which confronts anyone who is to deflect the free-market conclusion which Smith and Johnson drew from their analysis. This will tell us – at least in outline form – how Coleridge must proceed. Understanding what case he had to press will help considerably. First, it is necessary for Smith and Johnson that human nature is fixed. Without such an assumption, there is no inferential path from the past to the future. Even if past endowments were failures, why would this bear on the future? Perhaps human nature has changed in the meantime.[13] Second, it is necessary that the judgments in the marketplace of ideas are compelling. Smith refers to the 'current opinions of the world' and Johnson speaks of how the public must judge the 'pretensions' of authors to instruct them.

By this analysis we know what Coleridge requires to make his case. First, an institutional reform can remake human nature itself in some predictable fashion; or, second, those ideas which are ultimately important are not something about which the masses of mankind can judge. We know, thus, what patterns to look for in Coleridge's writings. Not to keep the reader in suspense, I shall argue that Coleridge relies upon the Hermetic model of man to defend both the claims at issue: first, institutional reform can remake mankind itself and, second, judgments from the marketplace of ideas are systematically flawed.

Reading Coleridge's proposal for constitutional reform as resting on somewhat occult premises is, of course, hardly novel.[14] It is, however, a rather controversial interpretation; indeed, a recent attempt has been made to mechanize Coleridge, to collapse what he calls 'Ideas' into ur-public opinion. In this view, Coleridge holds that the masses are dominated by the producers of philosophical truths.[15] In this interpretation, Coleridge's position is as straightforward as that of J. M. Keynes.[16] This interpretation suffers from, I think, a terrible shortcoming. Coleridge's argument would be strangled at birth by the Smith–Johnson analysis.[17] Judging the performance of educational institutions by the acceptance in the marketplace of ideas – which is all the Keynes position authorizes – gives the game to Smith and Johnson. Who could deny the unendowed Scottish universities dominated their endowed English rivals in the eighteenth century?

I shall argue that Coleridge found in the Hermetic tradition two theses: first, all the important ideas are within us and, second, these ideas are self-actualizing. These theses meet both parts of the Smith–Johnson challenge. The first gives us a method of judging what ideas are worthwhile independently of what the world thinks; the second tells us that human nature can be changed in lawlike fashion.

In a structural sense, one part of Coleridge's answer to Smith and

Johnson is the same as the answer which the Hermetic philosophers gave to those who claimed that the world was governed by fate. How can we possibly change what will be? The Hermetic answer is to remember that we are God, brother to the creator[18] but, while fate dominates our material self, God dominates fate; so we become God to escape fate.[19] A concise Hermetic statement of the relation between religious behavior and knowledge was recovered from Nag Hammadi within living memory:

> the pious who are counted are few. Therefore wickedness remains among (the) many, since learning concerning the things which are ordained does not exist among them. For the knowledge of the things which are ordained is truly the healing of the passions of matter.[20]

My thesis is that Coleridge works within the logical presuppositions of the Hermetic world view to answer Smith and Johnson: free an elite from material preoccupations, they will contact the divine within and creativity will flourish. Hermetism provides the key to unlocking creativity because creativity results from uncaused activity;[21] to open the door to the uncaused world, essentially we must coerce the divine. What we might call Hermetic 'social engineering' has a long history, as we have been taught by various Warburg Institute studies over the last three decades. Coleridge's endowment proposal, as I shall demonstrate, makes sense inside this tradition. And, conversely, only inside this tradition is his argument compelling. There are thus two parts of the exercise. My case, that, if Coleridge accepted the Hermetic presuppositions, then his proposed endowment is sensible, can be made on straightforward textual grounds. The converse – only inside the Hermetic view of the world does Coleridge's proposal make sense – cannot of course be made on textual grounds, but it is a simple case to make on history of philosophy grounds: Hermetism allows certain operations which no other ontological system allows.

MORAL REFORM BY CHANGE IN INCENTIVES

In Coleridge's Pantisocratic discussion in the 1790s, we find him attending to a fundamental issue – the vicious circle between personal immorality and evil institutions – which his endowment proposal seeks to evade. In the materialist tradition where human nature is assumed fixed moral reform is mainly a matter of changing incentives.[22] Following the libertarian communism of William Godwin, Coleridge claims property is a barrier to moral conduct. In a letter we read:

> The real source of inconstancy, depravity, & prostitution, is *Property*, which mixes with & poisons every thing good – & is beyond doubt the Origin of all Evil.[23]

Coleridge's defense of his proposed communal experiment is clearly offered in the spirit of philosophical materialism – to change behavior one must first change incentives:

> Wherever Men *can* be vicious, some *will* be. The leading Idea of Pantisocracy is to make men *necessarily* virtuous by removing all Motives to Evil – all possible Temptations.[24]

In his emotional divorce from Robert Southey, he states that his communistic hopes are for spiritual improvement:

> I returned to Cambridge hot in the anticipation of that happy Season, when we should remove the *selfish* Principle from ourselves, and prevent it in our children, by an *Abolition* of property: or in whatever respect this might be impracticable, by such similarity of Property, as would amount to a *moral Sameness*, and answer all the purposes of *Abolition*.[25]

In Godwin's account, institutions are unambiguously the *cause* of moral evil in people. Contrary to this, even in the midst of his Pantisocratic fever, Coleridge worried about the moral fiber of the founders of the new order and, in so doing, spelled out an awareness that the evil in institutions could be caused by the evil in people. In a letter to Southey he writes:

> I was challenged on the subject of Pantisocracy, which is indeed the universal Topic at the University – A Discussion began and continued for *six* hours. In conclusion, Lushington and Edwards declared the System impregnable, supposing the assigned Quantum of Virtue and Genius in the first Individuals.[26]

In the same letter, these concerns are spelled out in graphic detail. The stability of the moralizing society would be undermined by immoral founders:

> there are *Children* going with us. Why did I never dare in my disputations with the Unconvinced to *hint* at this circumstance? Was it not, because I knew even to certainty of conviction, that it is subversive of *rational* Hopes of a permanent System? These children – the little Fricker for instance and *your* Brothers – Are they not already *deeply* tinged with the prejudices and errors of society? Have they not learnt from their Schoolfellows *Fear* and *Selfishness* – of Hatred? *How* are we to prevent them from infecting the minds of *our* Children?[27]

Consequently, Coleridge's earliest thoughts on institutional reform confront the delicate problem of mutual causality of evil. Institutions corrupt people, but without virtuous individuals to act as founders of the new society, what hope is there to purge vice? And, where can we find those uncorrupted by their society? Coleridge is left with Archimedes' problem: where is there a place outside the world by which to move it?

Only a little after he had discarded his Pantisocratic hopes, Coleridge wrote that he had discovered the Hermetic branch of the Neoplatonic tradition:

> Metaphysics, & Poetry, & 'Facts of mind' – (i.e. Accounts of all the strange phantasms that ever possessed your philosophy-dreamers from Tauth [Thoth], the Egyptian to Taylor, the English Pagan), are my darling Studies.[28]

The burden of the argument below is that inside the Hermetic tradition Coleridge breaks out of a circle of vice. Reform can first moralize an elite who then moralize the rest.

COULD HERMETISM SURVIVE CASAUBON?

In my interpretation, Coleridge's proposal to create an endowed learned class (the clerisy) in *Constitution of Church and State According to the Idea of Each* is an attempt to rip apart the chains binding effects with material cause, to create by a change in legal institutions a vacuum in time and space for spiritual activity, for what he authorizes us to call the supernatural.[29] Sheltered from the causal nexus, spiritual activity by this clerisy could create a new reality: a reality where men no longer confounded wealth with welfare, where no longer would the worse be chosen over the better.

In brief, I shall argue that Coleridge's proposal to endow a learned class through institutional change, an instance of what we would today call social engineering, takes on meaning within what we now know to be the 'Hermetic tradition' where efforts to expand the scope of personal spiritual activity are commonplace. Our guides for this tradition are, of course, Paul O. Kristeller, A.-J. Festugière, D. P. Walker and Frances Yates. What I find most particularly helpful in Yates' series of studies on the Hermetic tradition is her reconstruction of an engineering school within the broad Neoplatonic point of view.[30] Knowing first-hand so much of the excitement from the triumphs of modern engineering within our Einsteinian–Newtonian tradition in astrophysics and microelectronics, we can more easily empathize with the Neoplatonic engineers. Raymond Lull's symbolic constructs are only a world view away, artificial intelligence under paradigm shift, from Charles Babbage's analytical engine and H. A. Simons's theorem-proving programs.[31] Similarly, the pictures on our television of Jupiter and Saturn, which the engineers at Cal Tech's Jet Propulsion Lab have arranged to appear, prepare us, at least to some degree, for the sort of result expected to flow from a Neoplatonic memory theater.[32]

In broad brush, the scope of Coleridge's interest in the Neoplatonic supernatural is too well known to belabor. Thomas Carlyle's icily contemptuous caricature,[33] John Livingston Lowe's classic study of the

Ancient Mariner,[34] and now in our time Thomas McFarland's examination of Coleridge's place in the pantheistic tradition[35] and Kathleen Coburn's study of the notebooks and marginalia,[36] all carry the same message: the Coleridgean world view ventures into neighborhoods where occult sympathy still rules, where ideas carry power to bind and release.

The obvious objection to my thesis must be first considered. Who took the critical texts of the Hermetic revival seriously after Isaac Casaubon's demolition of the *Corpus Hermeticum*'s claims to antiquity? After all, Coleridge wrote in the clear light of the nineteenth century.[37] In fact, Coleridge seems to have accepted the historicity of some of the key texts of the Hermetic tradition[38] but I place no real weight on this. Today, learned philologists still argue about the confusion of texts and religious traditions in the ancient world. For my purposes, such evidence can be waived because Coleridge took the Bible very seriously and, although it is often neglected in modern studies of the occult, it is a very magical book. This is central to my argumentative strategy.[39] For if one takes the literal truth of the Bible as given[40] then one could accept, as Ralph Cudworth and Henry More did, the philological demonstration that the Hermetic treatises were contaminated by frauds of the Christian era, yet still save Hermetism from the ash heap.[41] The More–Cudworth position that the *Corpus Hermeticum* (*CH*) – albeit contaminated with Christian era frauds – contains genuine Egyptian teachings rescues considerable Hermetism for Jews and Christians.[42] The fact is that in Exodus the highest of all possible authority attests to the prowess of the Egyptian magicians. For Jews or Christians reading the *Corpus Hermeticum*, the wonder-working passages simply corroborate the Mosaic account of the competence of Egyptian magicians.[43]

Because my argument depends upon the seemingly incredible proposition that someone of Coleridge's dates and stature took Hermetism seriously, it is important for me to establish that the Bible gives credence to the Hermetic engineering claims. In fact, in Exodus the Egyptian magicians provide independent, albeit hostile, testimony for the majesty of God's works.[44] For their testimony to be compelling, they cannot be incompetent. This they are not. Indeed, in competition with God, the first few exchanges are rather close. The magicians almost matched God in turning rods to snakes, although God had the larger snakes.[45] God and the magicians run dead heats exterminating fish[46] and generating frogs.[47] While it is true that God removes the frogs first, any fair reading would consider this part of the contest called for lack of vermin.[48] At the beginning of the fourth round God is ahead on points, but the magicians still stand. Then, class tells:

> And the Lord said unto Moses, Say unto Aaron, Stretch out thy rod, and smite the dust of the land, that it may become lice throughout all the land of Egypt.

And they did so . . .

And the magicians did so with their enchantments to bring forth lice, but they could not: so there were lice upon man, and upon beast.

Then the magicians said unto Pharaoh, This *is* the finger of God . . .[49]

In any such contest there is a simultaneity of prowess. Just as the magicians explicitly testify for God's power, God implicitly testifies for theirs. While it is true that when the magicians are last seen they are not standing,[50] Pharaoh would have been well advised to heed his Council of Occult Advisers. Coleridge was not the only one who drew some interesting conclusions from this report and others like it.[51]

If there is genuine Egyptian doctrine which can be extracted from the Hermetic texts, then all is not lost to the Hermetist. Because the power of natural or dæmonic Egyptian magic can be established independently, by the best of all possible authority, the only real problem is how to tap this power. To the extent that there is ancient Egyptian doctrine mixed with the frauds, there is still information to be gained from the Hermetic tradition. Philology is not destiny.

THE NEOPLATONIC TRADITION

The critical presuppositions which we must accept to work within a Neoplatonic world view are these:

1 True knowledge is found in Ideas (Plato's archetypes) which are the thoughts of God.[52]
2 Human beings have within them a divine spark (soul, mind) which allows them potentially to contemplate these Ideas directly. (Trivially, 1 and 2 imply that, in so doing, a human being can contemplate God directly.)[53]
3 Human beings rarely are able to achieve this contemplative feat because they are distracted by Matter, in particular pleasure and pain of the body.[54]
4 Ideas are self-actualizing; they are more than images of reality, they cause reality itself.[55]

It follows immediately that, to attain this True knowledge, one must free oneself from the lures of the flesh, that one cannot attain union with the divine lusting after money and fame.[56] Equally immediately it is clear why the doctrine of Thomas Hobbes presents such a challenge to this tradition: for Hobbes there is no life without striving, no quiet from the passionate storm in which to contemplate and reflect.[57]

A particularly lovely statement of this Neoplatonic vision is found in *The Platonic Philosopher's Creed* by Coleridge's contemporary Thomas Taylor:

> I believe that the human soul essentially contains all knowledge, and that whatever knowledge she acquires in the present life is nothing more than a recovery of what she once possessed; and which discipline evocates from its dormant retreats, . . .[58]

In what I take to be the majority view of the commentary, the Hermetic contribution to the Neoplatonic tradition is the startling claim that the activity of the divine can be changed by means of a formula taught to the not-so-gifted, in a word by a science. This seems to me a critical distinction between the orthodox Neoplatonists and the Hermetic school.

There are two cases to consider. (1) Can prayer move the divine? (2) Can magic move the divine? In this context prayer is a weak form of magic, asking the divine to do such-and-such. Magic is prayer which does not have to say 'please'.

The first case is easy to answer for any thinker within the broad orthodox Platonic tradition. Prayer cannot have an effect upon the divine.[59] Belief that the will of God can be moved by prayer and supplication is of course Plato's definition of the third type of atheism.

Prayer will not work, but what about magic? This is a complicated case to make, in part, because there is no doubt that Plotinus, the founder of Neoplatonism, believed magic to be an empirical discipline.[60] The critical difference between Plotinus and the Hermetist, as I read the texts, is that for Plotinus one escapes magic by turning inward. Entrapment by magic seems to me to be Plotinus' metaphor for life in the material world:

> For everything that looks to another is under spell to that: what we look to, draws us magically. Only the self-intent go free of magic. Hence every action has magic as its source, and the entire life of the practical man is a bewitchment: we move to that only which has wrought a fascination upon us.[61]

The life of the mind is immune to magic:

> Contemplation alone stands untouched by magic; no man self-gathered falls to a spell; for he is one, and that unity is all he perceives, so that his reason is not beguiled but holds the due course, fashioning its own career and accomplishing its task.
>
> In the other way of life, it is not the essential man that gives the impulse; it is not the reason; the unreasoning also acts as a principle, and this is the first condition of the misfortune. Caring for children, planning marriage – everything that works as bait, taking value by dint of desire – these all tug obviously . . .[62]

Just as the Egyptian magicians are made to testify to God's power in Exodus, so too an Egyptian magician is made to testify to Plotinus' immunity to magic.[63] When one can attain union with the Divine, what power can the material world bring to bear?[64]

But there is a dissenting tradition which reads Hermetism as a purely contemplative doctrine, akin to Plotinus'. In particular, Hermetism (in this reading) claims no power to operate on 'the physical world or upon other human beings for one's own advantage'.[65] If this is so then the Hermetic philosopher does not claim an ability to influence activity. Thus, there can be no social engineering claims made from a Hermetic framework. In this interpretation of the Hermetic philosopher, 'his object is not power but enlightenment'.[66] I don't think this is a correct reading of the Hermetic texts, where knowledge of the divine is power. Knowledge of the divine drives magic, it does not laugh the siege to scorn. What I find to be critical are the passages in *CH* which describe the creation of powerful idols by the divine power within us. Here is A.-J. Festugière's translation:

> De même que le Seigneur et le Père ou, pour lui donner son nom le plus haut, Dieu, est le créateur des dieux du ciel, ainsi l'homme est-il l'auteur des dieux qui résident dans les temples et qui se satisfont du voisinage des humains: non seulement il reçoit la lumière (vie), mais il la donne à son tour, non seulement il progresse vers Dieu, mais encore il crée des dieux. Admires-tu, Asclépius, ou manques-tu de foi toi aussi, comme la plupart?
>
> – Je suis confondu, ô Trismégiste . . .
>
> – . . . les images des dieux que façonne l'homme ont été formés des deux natures, de la divine qui est plus pure et infiniment plus divine, et de celle qui est en deçà de l'homme, je veux dire de la matière qui a servi à les fabriquer; en outre, leurs figures ne se bornent pas à la tête seule, mains ils ont un corps entier avec tous ses membres. Ainsi l'humanité, qui toujours se souvient de sa nature et de son origine, pousse-t-elle jusqu'en ceci l'imitation de la divinité, que, comme le Père et Seigneur a doué les dieux d'éternité pour qu'ils lui fussent semblables, ainsi l'homme façonne-t-il ses propres dieux à la ressemblance de son visage.
>
> – Veux-tu dire les statues, ô Trismégiste?
>
> – Oui, les statues, Asclépius. Vois comme toi-même tu manques de foi! Mais ce sont des statues pourvues d'une âme, conscientes, pleines de souffle vital, et qui accomplissent une infinité de merveilles; des statues qui connaissent l'avenir et le prédisent part les sorts, l'inspiration prophétique, les songes et bien d'autre méthodes, qui envoient aux hommes les maladies et qui les guérissent, qui donnent, selon nos mérites, la douleur et la joie.[67]

Granting, then, the Hermetic world view that men and women are in a world sprinkled with divinity, the technical problem remains: how to go about contacting the divine? There seem to have been basically two points of view, not necessarily mutually exclusive: one which emphasized the possibility of contacting divinity within us purely through meditation, another which emphasized external possibilities to contact the divine 'out there'. Walker summarizes these Neoplatonic research traditions as follows:

The tradition, as Ficino left it, comprised two kinds of magic, the natural, spiritual magic . . . and the demonic magic . . . The tradition, therefore, was likely to grow in two divergent directions; which it did. The demonic magic, combined with mediaeval planetary magic, led to the overtly demonic, recklessly unorthodox magic of Agrippa and Paracelsus. The spiritual magic tended to dissolve into something else: music and poetry, . . .[68]

COLERIDGE, HERMETICALLY CONSIDERED

Let me take it as demonstrated that Coleridge has sympathy for the Hermetic tradition.[69] We can draw a consequence out of this which can sharpen a distinction between the Hermetic tradition and Neoplatonism more generally.[70] The non-Hermetic Neoplatonist would claim that it is possible to encounter the divine within without accepting the possibility that this can have any consequence upon the empirical world. Mystical union does not allow us to turn our neighbor into a frog. For if it can, this means we can coerce the divine; we can operate on the divine in the same way we can operate the telephone in Paris. Any occultist will acknowledge a random component.

We can bring out the metaphysical difference if we can temporarily adopt Kantian terminology. Divinity is clearly a property of things-in-themselves, not of appearance. Hermetism makes causal statements about things-in-themselves; that is, under such-and-such conditions so-and-so will probably occur. A non-Hermetic Neoplatonist needs to make no causal statements about the divine. It exists but we have no science to control it.[71]

We know what to look for now. If Coleridge participates in the Hermetic tradition, he is allowed to make causal statements about the divine, in Kantian terms, about things-in-themselves.

We know that Coleridge regards intellectual inquiry for its own sake as an ideal[72] – study for its own sake is an aspect of *uncaused* activity. Here Coleridge contrasts work for reward with work for its own sake:

But this is the worst sort of Slavery: for herein true Freedom consists, that the outward is determined by the inward, as the alone self-determining Principle – what then must be the result, when in the vast majority of that class in which we are most entitled to expect the *conditions* of Freedom, and Freedom itself as manifested in the *Liberal* Arts and Sciences, all Freedom is stifled & overlaid from the very commencement of their career, as men – namely, in our Universities, Schools of Medicine, Law &c?[73]

Here we have a suggestion of what Coleridge found attractive in the proposal of an endowed cultural class: it would free the learned from the thrall of the material world itself.

It is important for us to recognize that Coleridge knew of both Hermetic traditions which Walker has called our attention to and explicitly renounced any attempt to engage in external dæmonic magic. Many references to the ms. of the Huntington Library, with its wonderfully revealing, redundant title, *On the Divine Ideas*,[74] have appeared in the last fifty years, but the significance of the moral constraints which Coleridge puts on himself has gone unremarked. If Coleridge here distances himself from Thomas Taylor, who wished to sacrifice a bull to Zeus, as he distances himself from the dæmonic tradition of Neoplatonism in *Philosophical Lectures*,[75] it is not completely out of conviction that their approach will not work.

> I cannot commence this subject more fitly than by disclaiming all wish and attempt of gratifying a speculative refinement in myself, or an idle presumptuous curiosity in others. I leave the heavenly hierarchies with all their distinctions 'Thrones, Dominations, Princedoms, Virtues, Powers', Names, Fervours, Energies with the long et cetera of the false Dionyius, and the obscure students of Cornelius Agrippa. All pretence, all approach to particularize on such a subject involves its own contradiction . . . Or had the evident contradiction implied in the attempt failed in preventing it[,] the fearful abuses, the degrading idolatrous superstitions, which have resulted from its applications . . . form too palpable a warning not to have deferred me even from motives of common morality.[76]

In this same ms. Coleridge gives a very clear definition of the Idea, a definition which locates him firmly in the Neoplatonic tradition:

> An Idea is not simply knowledge or perception as distinguished from the thing perceived: it is a realizing knowledge, a knowledge causative of its own reality, in it is Life . . .[77]

Can we read this definition of an Idea – self-actualizing knowledge, knowledge which creates reality – back into the *Constitution of Church and State According to the Idea of Each*?

If so, then we may have some insight into why an endowed learned class was so important. The Ideas are accessible through meditation, what Walker and Yates have taught us to call 'spiritual astrology'. Since the important truths are in us, study of our inner self is a vastly more appealing route to knowledge for Coleridge than study of the external world.[78] The efficient creation and dissemination of new knowledge about the physical universe, a claim which Smith uses to justify a competitive educational system, is for Coleridge a far from unmixed blessing. The material reward for study of the new ideas may lead people to forsake the old. Thus, one part of the Smith–Johnson challenge is addressed. The new ideas which are produced under material incentives are not as important as those which have been forgotten as a consequence.[79]

We gain insight in what attracted Coleridge to an endowed culture if we attend to the facts which Smith presents both about the origin of the new ideas and about the fate of the old in the competitive market for ideas:

> The improvements which, in modern times, have been made in several different branches of philosophy, have not, the greater part of them, been made in universities; . . . several of those learned societies have chosen to remain, for a long time, the sanctuaries in which exploded systems and obsolete prejudices found shelter and protection, after they had been hunted out of every other corner of the world.[80]

Smith's previous discussion of school learning gives a good picture of what sorts of 'systems' might have been hunted out:

> . . . if subtleties and sophisms composed the greater part of the Metaphysics or Pneumatics of the schools, they composed the whole of this cobweb science of Ontology, . . .[81]

The description which Coleridge gives in *Aids to Reflection* of some of the new methodological developments in education stands in sharp contrast to Smith's high opinion.

> He only thinks who reflects. [Note] The indisposition, nay, the angry aversion to think, even in persons who are most willing to attend, and on the subjects to which they are giving studious attention, as political economy, biblical theology, classical antiquities, and the like, – is the phenomenon that forces itself on my notice afresh, every time I enter into the society of persons in the higher ranks.[82]

Coleridge asserts that the new ideas are substituting study of what is 'out there' for study of what is 'in here':

> Distinction between thought and attention. – By thought is here meant the voluntary reproduction in our minds of those states of consciousness or . . . of those inward experiences, to which, as to his best and most authentic documents, the teacher of moral or religious truth refers us. In attention we keep the mind passive: in thought, we rouse it into activity . . . but self-knowledge, or an insight into the laws and constitution of the human mind and the grounds of religion and true morality, in addition to the effort of attention requires the energy of thought.[83]

What remains to be demonstrated is that Coleridge thought an endowed cultural class would offer a better chance for study for its own sake (remember: this is uncaused activity) of ideas of real importance. Here it helps a great deal to remember that some critical passages in *Church and State* are explicitly reproduced from *Biographia Literaria*.

THE CLERISY, OR FREEDOM OF AN INTELLECTUAL ELITE FROM MOTIVE

The preliminary sketch of the idea of a clerisy, as noted in *Church and State*, is found in *Biographia Literaria*. This occurs in a context which emphasizes Coleridge's contention that literature should be produced without motivation from either money or 'immediate' fame.[84] This contention is a vital link in the Neoplatonic chain. Matter must not corrupt spiritual things:

> I would address an affectionate exhortation to the youthful literati, grounded on my own experience . . . NEVER PURSUE LITERATURE AS A TRADE . . . Three hours of leisure, unannoyed by any alien anxiety, and looked forward to with delight as a change and recreation, will suffice to realize in literature a larger product of what is truly *genial*, than weeks of compulsion. Money, and immediate reputation form only an arbitrary and accidental end of literary labor. The *hope* of increasing them by any given exertion will often prove a stimulant to industry; but the *necessity* of acquiring them will in all work of genius convert the stimulant into a *narcotic*. Motives by excess reverse their very nature, and instead of exciting, stun and stupefy the mind . . . he should devote his *talents* to . . . some known trade or profession, and his genius to objects of his tranquil and unbiased choice;[85]

True knowledge, in Coleridge's idealism, cannot result from activity generated by material incentives. Johnson and Smith, across their political–religious divide, both hold the 'pernicious opinion' that the production of literature requires substantial motivation: desire of money or fame.[86]

Of course, Coleridge would have been negligent if he did not suggest a profession which allowed a regular income, sufficient leisure time and minimal motive for the production of literature. All these conditions could be satisfied by working for the established church:

> the church presents to every man of learning and genius a profession, in which he may cherish a rational hope of being able to unite the widest schemes of literary utility with the strictest performance of professional duties[87]

Coleridge also noted that the emoluments of the profession were quite handsome, and went on to suggest that the presence of an established clergyman provides social benefits to the neighborhood:

> a neighbour and a family-man, whose education and rank admit him to the mansion of the rich land-holder, while his duties make him a frequent visitor of the farm-house and the cottage.[88]

In *Church and State* Coleridge uses Hermetic machinery to argue that motiveless study ('thinking' as defined in *Aids to Reflection*) will be co-extensive with religious study. Two critical issues are clear: we contact the divine within us and the Ideas in which divinity is embodied are self-actualizing. In the next passage the former is clear, the latter is hinted, although this too will be clear in later passages.

> That in all ages, individuals who have directed their meditations and their studies to the nobler characters of our nature, to the cultivation of those powers and instincts which constitute the man, at least separate him from the animal, and distinguish the nobler from the animal part of his own being, will be led by the *supernatural* in themselves to the contemplation of a power which is likewise super-*human*; that science, and especially moral science, will lead to religion, and remain blended with it . . .[89]

The group who compromise the clerisy are defined:

> The CLERISY of the nation, or national church, in its primary acceptation and original intention comprehended the learned of all denominations; – the sages and professors of the law . . . medicine and physiology; of music; of military and civil architecture; of the physical sciences; with the mathematical as the common *organ* of the preceding;

and, linked to the Neoplatonic research tradition, 'the doctrine and discipline of ideas'. When we look inside ourselves, what do we see? We see the divine. 'Theology' is, of course, simply a transliteration of the Greek for 'study of god':

> [Theology] . . . was indeed, placed at the head of all; and of good right did it claim the precedence. But why? Because under the name of Theology, or Divinity, were contained [the substantive issues] . . . and lastly, the ground-knowledge, the prima scientia as it was named, – PHILOSOPHY, or the doctrine and discipline of ideas.[90]

Thus, in *Church and State*, the links between theology and the pursuit of knowledge for its own sake are connected far more tightly than they are in *Biographia Literaria*. Finally, the self-actualizing property of the divine is appealed to:

> The Theologians took the lead, because the SCIENCE of Theology was the root and the trunk of the knowledges that civilized man, because it gave unity and the circulating sap of life to all other sciences.[91]

When we recall the material conditions under which the Ideas can be contemplated, Coleridge's elitism does not seem unnatural; the many are in no position to free themselves from material interests. The philosophical truths unearthed through contemplation are self-enforcing. This is just another way of saying they are Ideas, not simple opinions:

> NATIONAL EDUCATION, the *nisus formativus* of the body politic, the shaping and informing spirit, which *educing, i.e.*, eliciting, the latent *man* in all the natives of the soil, *trains them up* to citizens of the country, free subjects of the realm . . . And of especial importance is it to the objects here contemplated, that only by the vital warmth diffused by these truths throughout the MANY, and by the guiding light from the philosophy, which is the basis of *divinity*, possessed by the FEW, can either the community or its rulers fully comprehend, or rightly appreciate, the permanent *distinction*, and the occasional *contrast*, between cultivation and civilization; . . .[92]

We see how the Ideas are recalled and how they are self-actualizing. The freedom from material incentives is obvious when we examine the details of the proposed endowment. Coleridge's three-tiered proposal to be financed by the national endowment[93] of the national church – (1) national universities, (2) a '*parson* in every parish' and (3) a 'school-master in every parish' – makes explicit provision for incentives in the lowest tier: the schoolmaster 'who in due time, and under condition of a faithful performance of his arduous duties, should succeed to the pastorate'.[94]

The formal argument now stands complete. It is an elegant, spare construction. Each of the Hermetic premises has been employed and the validity of the enterprise is clear. The obvious question is whether this system would actually do what it was supposed to do. Coleridge offers as evidence the history of previous experiments in Hermetic social engineering. The critical text here is Coleridge's chapter 7 of *Church and State*, 'Regrets and Apprehensions'. It contains a review of the 'moral history of the last 130 years', a history of gloom caused by the mechanical philosophy,[95] 'Ouran Outang theology of the origin of the human race',[96] 'hardness of heart, in political economy',[97] the 'Guess-work of general consequences substituted for moral and political philosophy'[98] and the 'gin consumed by paupers'.[99] By contrast Coleridge recalls the bright episodes before 1660. The episodes worth remembering occurred when Hermetism was at the center of culture. Here is what he says about Ficino's social engineering:

> the remarkable contrast between the acceptation of the word, Idea, *before* the Restoration, and the *present* use of the same word. *Before* 1660, the magnificent SON OF COSMO was wont to discourse with FICINO, POLITIAN and the princely MIRANDULA on the IDEAS of Will, God, Freedom. SIR PHILIP SIDNEY, the star of serenest brilliance in the glorious constellation of Elizabeth's court, communed with SPENSER, on the IDEA of the beautiful: and the younger ALGERNON – Soldier, Patriot, and Statesman – with HARRINGTON, MILTON, and NEVIL on the IDEA of the STATE: . . .[100]

It seems clear that Coleridge's clerisy is the proposed rebirth, in Christian guise and on a national scale, of Ficino's academy.[101] The vision of endowed intellectuals freed from motive penetrating the divine as a technique to provide moral uplift to the masses helps put what Coleridge found attractive in a clerisy into much sharper focus. Thanks to modern historical work in many fields, we now know a great deal about previous Neoplatonic social engineering, government-sponsored academies and masques recalling to life the ancient mysteries in an attempt to change the morals of people. On what economists call revealed preference grounds, we must take this activity seriously. For instance, English kings spent vast amounts of their money, and caused others to spend vast amounts, on masques to uplift court morals.[102] Moreover, Yates has shown us the depth of the Elizabethan court's involvement in Hermetic social engineering;[103] it is consequently no surprise that Coleridge would see this as a bright spot in history. Joe Dee, the grand *magus*, is, of course, Sidney's teacher.[104]

ONCE AGAIN: IN LIGHT OF THE PHILOSOPHICAL LECTURES

We can summarize our argument supported by independent passages from the *Philosophical Lectures*. In the Neoplatonic world view, one must be purified before one can contemplate the divine, the source of Ideas, self-actualizing knowledge of real worth. Coleridge's debt to engineering Neoplatonism, the Hermetic tradition, is clear in his use of the most famous of all Hermetic phrases:

> At once the most complex and the most individual of creatures, man, taken in the idea of his humanity, has been not inaptly called the microcosm of the world.[105]

To break the thrall of this material world, Coleridge proposes to free an elite from material motive, thus bringing about the requisite purification. Here we can contact the divine within us:

> which exists in all men *potentially* and in its germ, though it requires both effort from within and auspicious circumstances from without to evolve it into effect − by this third and higher power he places himself on the same point as Nature, and contemplates all objects, himself included, in their permanent and universal being and relations.[106]

Coleridge cites Francis Bacon's views on purification:

> He tells us that the mind of man is an edifice not built with human hands, which needs only to be purged of its idols and idolatrous services to become the temple of the true and living light.[107]

These are, of course, 'idols of the den, of the theatre, and of the market place'.[108]

Coleridge draws the reader's attention to the past glories of Neoplatonic policy, to Ficino's academy, where the divine within us was tapped, even if in a pagan context. These, we are led to believe, were magical times:

> yet there was the power felt, and and [*sic*] with the power the grace and the life and the influence of Platonic philosophy. This was under the auspices of Lorenzo the Magnificent . . . There the mighty spirit still coming from within had succeeded in taming the untractable matter and in reducing external form to a symbol of the inward and imaginable beauty.[109]

Ficino's academy seems to be the paradigm of Coleridge's social engineering. Here was an institution which quite literally worked magic. When Coleridge discusses the good times, he is talking about Ficino. Yates and Walker have taught us to understand what this means.

CLOSING THE ARGUMENT

Let me not pretend that the argument above accomplishes more than it does. I have attempted to demonstrate that Coleridge's argument against Smith's and Johnson's anti-endowment position is coherent inside the Hermetic tradition. What is special about the Hermetic tradition is the claim that under well-specified conditions we can control the divine within us and, by so doing, control the material world. What I claim to have shown is that *if* Coleridge were a social engineer in the Hermetic tradition, *then* his argument follows. Coleridge proposes we create an institutional setting inside which we can let the divine speak through us.

The next step in my argument is to demonstrate the converse to my claim: if Coleridge were not a social engineer in the Hermetic tradition, then his argument does not follow. This is a logical, not a textual, argument and we consider a special case first.

Suppose Coleridge were developing his argument from a Kantian point of view. Would the argument be valid? Would freeing individuals from incentives allow them to obtain self-actualizing knowledge, to break free of determinism? For Kant, determinism is necessary to think about appearances; free will is only sensible for things-in-themselves.[110] Obviously, in a Kantian framework we cannot conduct social policy to determine things-in-themselves. The Kantian split between the determined world and the free world will not support Coleridge's claims *because Coleridge needs to make causal statements about self-actualizing events*. This can be done in a Hermetic system – the paradigm is that if we free individuals from material concern, they will obtain *gnosis* and this event takes an individual outside fate, outside determinism, outside the chain of cause and effect. I think it clear that Coleridge knew that Kant's construction would not suffice for his result. Things-in-themselves cannot be coerced.[111]

The general case is now easy. For Coleridge's argument to hold, we must be able to coerce the divine within us. In particular, we want to create an institutional setting in which all sorts of good things would be created outside material causality. We are the operators on the divine. This is a defining characteristic of theurgy, and the link between theurgy and the *Chaldean Oracles* is well known.[112] Thus, we find ourselves back in the Hermetic tradition. This establishes the converse as required.

If the above reconstruction of Coleridge's political economy is correct, we can break the silence in the commentary on *Church and State* about how Coleridge comes to grips with Smith and Johnson. Further, we find reason to believe that Coleridge's claimed debt to the Neoplatonics is quite real and not a sham throwing sand over his debt to Kant. Indeed, if we are willing to grant the Hermetic view, Coleridge's construction is absolutely first-rate. At bottom, however, we must ask whether the game is worth the effect, whether there is reason to believe that such social engineering would work. The proper question was asked long ago by Coleridge's great master:

Glendower. I can call spirits from the vastie deepe.
Hotspur. Why, so can I, or so can any man: But will they come, when you doe call for them?[113]

And, it really makes no difference whether the spirits are in here or out there; will they come when we call?

Chapter 16

The impossibility of a complete methodological individualist

INTRODUCTION

F. A. Hayek is uniquely responsible for his fellow economists' grasping the importance of the decentralization of knowledge: as Hayek shows in his pathbreaking 'Use of Knowledge in Society', knowledge nowhere exists as a coherent whole and to pretend otherwise is a most serious error.[1] Hayek also shares responsibility for the popularity of a strong form of the methodological individualist research program which asserts that, since collectives *as such* have no impact on the choices of individuals, we ought to purge any reliance on collectives from our analysis.[2]

There are many versions of methodological individualism which are not at issue here. Many economists, for example, work to construct a theory of the firm grounded in individual choice, just as many of us try to give an individualist account of the political process. To this research program I have nothing to say here. Indeed, is not a demonstration that the behavior of a firm or a government is explained by the decisions of individuals evidence of scientific progress? Have not we reduced the number of independent entities required for the analysis? Who would deny that this is the heart of scientific progress? What concerns me is only the very strong position that collectives *as such*, because they are only theoretical entities, can have no impact on individual choice and consequently we can ignore them.

Ultimately, the assumption with which I shall take issue is that economic analysis, and other forms of language usage, are outside the economic process. We must confront the difficulty that those who analyze and those who are analyzed are both language users. Hayek claims we can dichotomize economic theory and the subjects of economic theory:

> It is very important that we should carefully distinguish between the motivating or constitutive opinions on the one hand and the speculative or explanatory views which people have formed about the wholes; confusion between the two is a source of constant danger. Is it the ideas

which the popular mind has formed about such collectives as society or the economic system, capitalism or imperialism, and other such collective entities, which the social scientist must regard as no more than provisional theories, popular abstractions, and which he must not mistake for facts? That he consistently refrains from treating these pseudo-entities as facts, and that he systematically starts from the concepts which guide individuals in their actions and not from the result of their theorizing about their actions, is the characteristic feature of that methodological individualism which is closely connected with the subjectivism of the social sciences.[3]

I am not disagreeing with the claim which many take to be the defining characteristic of methodological individualism, the claim that only individuals make choices.[4] Indeed, I shall take it for granted that only individuals make choices and ask whether collectives as theoretical entities have an impact on such choices.[5] This is really the question at issue: does it follow from the claim that only individuals make choices that collectives as theoretical entities can have no impact on choice? As I read Hayek's words this is precisely his position.[6]

REDUCTION UNDER IMPERFECT INFORMATION

The thesis of this chapter is that the version of methodological individualism which asserts that collectives as theoretical entities can have no impact on individual choice is inconsistent with the requirement that knowledge is imperfect. More precisely, whenever knowledge is imperfect we cannot dispense with collective terms to the extent that our explanations of individual activity are grounded on individuals' knowledge and belief. Of course, an adherent of methodological individualism with whom I was taking issue would not deny that references to collectives are valuable labor-saving devices; rather, the methodological individualist would wish to be able to replace a collective term by its individual components whenever the need arises.[7] The stumbling block to the reduction from collective to individualist terms is a hoary consideration in the philosophy of language. The denotation of a name and its meaning are not the same thing. Moreover, names of any sort cannot, in general, be replaced by equivalents in an intentional sentence without altering the truth value of the sentence.[8] Consider the following illustrative sentence:

1   Mr A knows that Willie Mays played centerfield for both the New York and the San Francisco Giants.

As a matter of record, Willie Mays was the only major league baseball player to hit fifty-one home runs in the 1955 season. If we were to substitute this fact into (1) we would obtain:

2 Mr A knows that the only major league baseball player to hit fifty-one home runs in the 1955 season played centerfield for both the New York and the San Francisco Giants.

Even if (1) is true, we cannot be sure of the truth value of (2) because Mr A may not have the requisite piece of baseball trivia at his disposal. If not, the substitution which transformed (1) to (2) can alter the sentence from true to false. In the theory of language and intentionality such a consideration has a venerable place indeed.

Now, let us apply this point to our problem. Consider an individual, Ms B, who makes a decision on the basis of the state of a collective, such as GNP, so that the following is true:

3 Ms B expands her sheet metal factory because she knows that GNP rose 10 percent in the last year.

Ms B may very well have found that a rise in what the newspapers call GNP does very nicely forecasting what her sheet metal sales will be, holding other things equal. Of course, we have no reason to believe that Ms B knows what GNP really is. She knows 'GNP' (a name) but not what GNP is. However, those economists who specialize in national income accounting know that GNP is the inner product of the quantity of n goods and services and the prices of these goods and services. Thus

4
$$GNP = \sum_{i=1}^{n} p_i q_i$$

To follow methodological individualism, we could purge the reference to the collective term GNP in (3) by using its individualist decomposition in (4). This would result in:

5 Ms B expands her sheet metal factory because she knows that:

$$\sum_{i=1}^{n} p_i q_i \text{ rose 10 percent in the last year.}$$

By hypothesis that only specialists know (4) and that Ms B is not one of these, we have no reason to know that (3) and (4) entail (5). Ms B simply does not know that

$$\sum_{i=1}^{n} p_i q_i \text{ rose 10 percent last year.}$$

Thus, in a decentralized state of knowledge where only specialists in technical areas know how to reduce some collective term to its individual components, methodological individualism which we are considering cannot ultimately succeed. To the extent that we wish to explain how individuals behave, and their behavior is influenced by their knowledge of the state of a decomposable collective, we cannot dispense with collective terms when the acting individuals do not know how to effect the decomposition. Collectives as theoretical entities can influence an individual's choice when the individual does not know what the collective means.

There are some objections which have been advanced by my friends[9] which may interest the skeptical reader because they sharpen the point at issue. (1) Doesn't methodological individualism only involve rejection of entities which cannot be directly observed by an individual? Of course, much of what individuals directly observe is the product of collectives, e.g., crowd noise, the production of firms, etc. Moreover, these are collectives which the acting individual does not know how to reduce unless it is a particular research interest of that individual.

I have no quarrel with this position, especially since the friend concerned is the last economist who would claim that we can dichotomize people's choices and their theories. However, it should be noted that we then have no *a priori* warrant to disregard such macroeconomic indices as the consumer price index or gross national product when we explain individual choice. Empirically, they may not matter, but this is another matter.

(2) Isn't Hayek really saying: if no one can make sense of a term in a particular context, ought we not to stop using it? For example, Hayek claims 'social justice' is meaningless inside a market economy because of the game-like feature of the market: there is no interesting game where the winners are known in advance, so 'distributive' or 'social' justice is senseless in this context.

My answer is easy: no. Social justice may or may not exist, but 'social justice' surely does. Even if we could prove that social justice is at best a fuzzy concept, what leads us to believe that it has no influence on people's behavior?

Both of these objections raise exactly the point with which I wish to take issue. What *a priori* warrant do we have for ruling out the impact on individual behavior of an individual's theorizing about behavior? Does it matter whether it is first or *n*th-hand theorizing? It may very well be that the impact of theorizing is not uniform over sectors of social organization, but this is a nice technical question to which the elegant tools developed in modern economics and mathematical statistics might be usefully applied.

If the argument advanced above is correct, do we still have warrant to reject, on methodological grounds, Aristotle's claim that the state is prior to the individual?[10] If individuals *believe* that they are born into a constitutional setting which changes only at the margin during their lifetime, then their actions may reflect this belief. If individuals believe that their family has an existence separate from the individuals who are members of their family, can we still conclude that on *a priori* grounds such a belief can have no influence on their conduct? I think not. Whatever influence this belief has is an empirical issue. We know that rational ignorance has a vital role to play in public choice theory; why not in more general contexts?

CONCLUSION

Even if we are methodological individualists, if the people we study are methodological collectivists for the sensible reason that methodological individualism is a very costly way of looking at the world, what theoretical justification do we have for rejecting collectives from our analysis? One interesting implication of the line of argument developed above is that there well may be macroeconomic foundations of microeconomics. That is to say, the individuals for whom our preference axioms are so lovingly crafted may make decisions on the basis of states of collectives which they are told about by the merchants of theory. Merely because macroeconomics has microfoundations does not allow us to conclude that microeconomics has no macrofoundations.

The consequence I would draw is not to abandon methodological individualism, for I think that Hayek is correct that it has been at the foundation of much scientific progress. Rather, I would urge my fellow participants in this tradition to recognize that there are really no *a priori* limits to what might influence an individual's choice; hence, we have no reason to exclude a class of information from consideration. This is so even when this information is the product of government statistical agencies or Greek philosophers of antiquity.

I do not think that I have said anything with which most adherents of methodological individualism or subjectivist economics would disagree. What is at issue is the role of economic theory in market activity and I see no reason why a subjectivist would not wish to take theoretical entities into account if there is empirical reason to do so. Obviously, we must address the factual problem of whether such information is important.

Chapter 17

Spinoza and the cost of thinking

INTRODUCTION

The one feature supposed to distinguish modern social theory from ancient is the modern's hypothesis that man is 'inside' nature. This is a common theme in the discussions of many otherwise disparate thinkers. Suppose that human behavior is indeed inside the world, and is subject to natural law. Let us now ask is one characteristic form of human activity, that of theorizing about human behavior, inside the world? Splitting the social world into full-time theorists of the social world and ordinary people, we can then ask a further question along these lines: why are the theories of these two groups so different?

Benedict Spinoza was acutely aware of such a problem and, moreover, did a quite remarkable job of solving it by recognizing that thinking is a costly activity. His argument is the more remarkable because only recently has the notion of a positive cost of thought been formally introduced into statistical decision theory.[1] Positive costs of thinking allow fundamental economic insights to be brought to bear on traditional philosophical imperatives to consistent thinking. Much is made in philosophical disputes about the 'pain' of inconsistency. As long as there are alternative employments of one's mind, there are also pains, or at least opportunity costs, of consistency and so one can question whether avoiding the cost of inconsistency is worth the trouble. When thinking has no cost, then there is no trouble to avoid.[2]

None the less, Spinoza stumbles over an implication of his theoretical construct: if costs of thinking are negligible, people can be expected to think correctly. It is interesting that this contradiction was caught by Bernard Mandeville. To preclude misunderstanding, I have no evidence that Mandeville here is responding to Spinoza there.[3] However, the issue is touched upon in Pierre Bayle's massive polemic against Spinoza, and Mandeville's debt to Bayle is both obvious and openly acknowledged.

The contradiction can be generated by either of two approaches. First, I shall utilize a device due to Leo Strauss which brings the 'form' of how something is written to bear upon the 'content' of what is written. While the Straussian technique is terrifically powerful – it is thought that some interpretative results cannot be obtained without it – it is far from being universally accepted by competent authorities.[4] Hence, I shall provide a second proof on grounds which only depend upon the explicit content of the texts. The second proof explicitly develops the cost of thinking aspect of Spinoza's *Ethics*.

A STRAUSSIAN PROOF

In *Ethics* Spinoza is good enough to tell us what he wants to do, and how his research program is more interesting than what others have done before. It is a famous passage, but let me quote it at length:

> Most who have written on the emotions, the manner of human life, seem to have dealt not with natural things which follow the general law of nature, but with things which are outside the sphere of nature: they seem to have conceived man in nature as a kingdom within a kingdom. For they believe that man disturbs rather than follows the course of nature, and that he has absolute power in his actions, and is not determined in them by anything else than himself. They attribute the cause of human weakness and inconstancy not to the ordinary power of nature, but to some defect or other in human nature, wherefore they deplore, ridicule, despise, or, what is most common of all, abuse it: and *he that can carp in the most eloquent or acute manner at the weakness of the human mind is held by his fellows as almost divine*. Yet excellent men have not been wanting (to whose labour and industry I feel myself much indebted) who have written excellently in great quantity on the right manner of life, and left to men counsels full of wisdom: yet no one has yet determined, as far as I know, the nature and force of the emotions and what the mind can do in opposition to them for their constraint. . . . For I wish to revert to those who prefer rather to abuse and ridicule the emotions and actions of men than to understand them. It will doubtless seem most strange to these that I should attempt to treat on the vices and failings of men in a geometrical manner, and should wish to demonstrate with accurate reasoning those things which they cry out against as opposed to reason, as vain, absurd, and disgusting. This, however, is my plan. Nothing happens in nature which can be attributed to a defect of it: for nature is always the same and one everywhere, and its ability and power of acting, that is, the laws and rules of nature according to which all things are made and changed from one form into another are everywhere and always the same, and therefore one and the same manner must there be of understanding the nature of all things, that is, by means of the universal laws and rules of nature.[5]

While positivists have read this as a model statement of the positive research program,[6] I would like to argue that Spinoza's statement is contradictory on its face.

Let me parse the claims which I shall consider:

1   Many previous thinkers have said, 'Mankind stands outside of natural law and can act rationally'.
2   Many previous thinkers have said, 'Mankind does not act rationally'.
3   The response of these previous thinkers when their theory (1) is falsified by evidence, (2), is to blame the evidence; we see that because these thinkers ridicule mankind.

These all seem correct to me. Spinoza certainly has his texts right here. So we proceed with his argument:

4   I say, 'Mankind stands inside of natural law'.
5   I say, 'Mankind's behavior is explicable'.
6   I say my theory, (4), corresponds to the evidence, (5); consequently, 'Mankind's behavior can be treated in a geometrical manner with all the dignity which this confers'.

How could I quarrel with this? From a positivist point of view, this seems to me to be the most profitable way to proceed with social analysis.

So what's the problem? And what's wrong with the usual positivistic reading of this? Spinoza's words, as I read them, ridicule and abuse, albeit gently, previous social analysis. Consider what Spinoza implies by his sarcasm:

7   I say that 'Many previous thinkers' behavior is worthy of ridicule'.

And so by applying (3):

8   I say that 'Many previous thinkers' behavior is inexplicable'.

Oops! We have a problem. We have just proven (5 and 8) that inside Spinoza's system 'Many previous thinkers are not members of mankind'.[7] What I'm afraid has happened is that we have read Spinoza's fine compelling positivism, and ignored his wonderfully funny abuse and ridicule, and thus not thought through the consequence of his ridicule. If Spinoza is correct that abuse and ridicule in social analysis give compelling evidence of erroneous social theory, then Spinoza's abuse and ridicule of previous social analysis give compelling evidence that he is doing erroneous social theory. It is erroneous at least when it comes to giving an account of previous social theory.[8]

This problem is related to one noted by Bayle in remark N, 'Spinoza', in his *Dictionary*:

First, I would like to know what he means when he rejects certain doctrines and sets forth others. Does he intend to teach truths? Does he wish to refute errors? But has he any right to say that there are errors? The thoughts of ordinary philosophers, those of Jews, and those of Christians, are they not modes of the infinite being, as much as those of his *Ethics*? Are they not realities that are as necessary to the perfection of the universe as all his speculations? Do they not emanate from the necessary cause? How then can he dare to claim that there is something to rectify?[9]

Bayle's charge is that inside Spinoza's technical system all sentences are true. Because everyone is within God, in Bayle's reading, what everyone says is true. By freeing Spinoza from this charge, I make my case on standard grounds.

ON STANDARD GROUNDS

Cannot one evade my claim of contradiction by asserting that the abuse and ridicule I find in the passage are only in my mind? Without an unambiguous interpretative tradition, irony may only be in the mind of the amused.[10]

This is, indeed, a possible escape route, so let us sharpen the problem by noticing what is emphasized above in what Spinoza wrote. A social theorist who says these false things about human failings gets well rewarded for this activity; that is, he is 'held by his fellows as almost divine'.[11] Fame is no less scarce than money, so payment in fame is no less interesting than payment in money. We could state this in a modern economics context with the paradox that maximizing agents pay people to tell them not to maximize. This is the content of what we have called 'Mandeville's Paradox'. This sharpens the problem because we no longer have isolated theorists to contend with – a few who could be dismissed as 'outliers' if not out-and-out liars – but the mass of mankind who are after all, paying these theorists something of value to teach them falsehoods.

To obtain this sort of a contradiction within Spinoza's technical system in *Ethics*, without reference to *how* Spinoza said what he did, the strategy I shall employ is formulating Spinoza's system to evade Bayle's challenge – in Spinoza's system all sentences must be true – and then derive a contradiction. Then it will be easy enough to show how Mandeville struggles with this issue.

The argument will be formulated inside an ontology with only one stuff; 'stuff' will be a technical term inside my reconstruction of Spinoza by which I propose to roll up God, nature and all that.[12] There is an enormous technical advantage within such an ontology: theory and the subject of theory are made of stuff, if they are made of anything, so establishing the rules of correspondence is trivial. On the contrary, within a set-up with different stuffs, this correspondence is frightfully difficult to formalize. Abraham Wald's point bears repeating:

> In order to apply the theory to real phenomena, we need some rules for establishing the correspondence between the idealized objects of the theory and those of the real world. These rules will always be somewhat vague and can never form a part of the theory itself.[13]

The internal citation style I shall employ is x:Py for the yth proposition in the xth part of the *Ethics* and x:Dy for the yth definition in the xth part.

Spinoza puts truth judgments into his stuff in a nice binary, Democritean way.[14] First, truth is claimed to be in stuff:

> 2:P32.   All ideas, in so far as they have reference to God, are true.

This is proved by the following observation, which replies upon the supposition that stuff has, what might be called by a dualist, sentences and observation in correspondence:

> *Proof.*   Now all ideas which are in God must entirely agree with their ideals . . . and therefore . . . they are true.

To bring out some of the power of this approach, let us make Spinoza's 'see clearly' or 'see adequately' equivalent technical terms within our reconstruction. If we see clearly, we see the correspondence of the manifestation of stuff as 'sentences' and the manifestation of stuff as 'things':

> 2:P34.   Every idea in us which is absolute, or adequate and perfect, is true.
>
> *Proof.*   When we say that an adequate and perfect idea is granted in us, we say nothing else than that . . . there is granted in God an adequate and perfect idea in so far as he constitutes the essence of our mind, and consequently . . . we say nothing else than that such an idea is true.

The power of monostuffism to deal with falsity is apparent immediately because falsity occurs when the 'clear sight' condition fails.[15]

> 2:P33.   There is nothing positive in ideas, wherefore they could be called false.
>
> 2:P35.   Falsity consists in privation of knowledge which is involved by inadequate or mutilated and confused ideas.

Failure of the clear sight conditions is, within a dualist ontology, almost equivalent to the noncorrespondence of sentences and the things about which the sentences speak. A dualist cannot exactly get noncorrespondence, but the difference is only truth by chance, and Spinoza need not worry overly much about truth by randomness.[16]

Think about Democritus again. Can atoms be said to 'collide' with the void? Or do they just penetrate the void? Then ,in Spinoza's set-up, what happens when truth stuff collides with falsity nonstuff? Obviously, penetration of nonstuff by stuff:

4:P1.   Nothing positive, which a false idea has, is removed by the presence of what is true in so far as it is true.

This formulation of Spinoza's lets him escape part of Bayle's charge: it is not the case that all sentences are true. The only true sentences will be those where the clear sight condition is fulfilled, a condition we have no reason to believe will be very frequent. Since the argumentative strategy at work is to pin Spinoza between Bayle's charge and mine, let us work out the details of his escape from Bayle. Recall that Spinoza wishes to claim that we can explain falsity as easily as truth:

2:P36.   Inadequate and confused ideas follow from the same necessity as adequate or clear and distinct ideas.

Consider Spinoza's explanation why his view of stuff is so different than other people's? In the Appendix to the First Part, Spinoza gives his explanation on a 'desire to know' basis which seems both perfectly straightforward and consistent. He starts simply enough:

It will suffice here for me to take as a basis of argument what must be admitted by all: that is, that all men are born ignorant of the causes of things, and that all have a desire of acquiring what is useful; that they are conscious, moreover, of this.[17]

The theory which men have is determined by what they find useful:

Whence it comes to pass that they always seek out only the final cause of things performed, and when they have divined these they cease, for clearly then they have no cause of further doubt.[18]

Spinoza sketches an account of the heuristics of human problem-solving which nicely incorporates a cost of thinking aspect. Contradictions do not cost ordinary people very much, so why should anyone worry a lot about purging them?

. . . and although experience daily belied this, and showed with infinite examples that conveniences and their contraries happen promiscuously to the pious and impious, yet not even then did they turn from their inveterate prejudice. For it was easier for them to place this among other unknown things whose use they knew not, and thus retain their present and innate condition of ignorance, than to destroy the whole fabric of their philosophy and reconstruct it.[19]

If this argument passes muster, and I think there is much to be said for it, then we can explain the distinction between clear and confused sight on the basis of the cost of thinking.

The final technical device employed in our reconstruction is Spinoza's equivalent to the modal box, the mark of necessary truth in modern philosophy of language. The modal box is called for when a sentence can only take on the truth value 'true'. To represent this eventuality in Spinoza's system, we write 'necessarily stuff'. This condition is in force when the clear sight condition *always* holds. When does this happen?[20] In terms of the argument above, when the cost of thinking is zero, when knowledge comes from being alive.

> 2:P38.   Those things which are common to all, and which are equally in a part and in the whole, can only be conceived adequately.

One example Spinoza gives of a proposition which is necessarily stuff is that a man chooses more than less. This is what we might call the maximizing assumption:

> [Corollary 2 to 4:P35] For the more each man seeks what is useful to him and endeavours to preserve himself, the more he is endowed with virtue . . . , or, what is the same thing, . . . the more power he is endowed with to act according to the laws of his nature, that is . . . , to live under the guidance of reason.

Because this choosing the better instead of the worse is a requisite of human life, Spinoza claims that everyone knows it:

> In other words, of two goods everyone will choose the one which he thinks the greater, and of two evils the one which he thinks the lesser. I say expressly, 'which he (the chooser) thinks the greater or lesser'; not that his judgement is necessarily correct. Now this law is graven so deeply upon human nature that it must be set among the eternal truths which everyone must know.[21]

This is the first statement of revealed preference that I know. Moreover, Spinoza takes this to be necessarily stuff. It is 'set among the eternal truths which everyone must know'. This is important momentarily because Spinoza sees maximizing behavior everywhere we look.

Rational choice in Spinoza depends on understanding:

> 4:P26.   Whatever we endeavour to do under the guidance of reason is nothing else than to understand; nor does the mind, in so far as it uses reason, judge anything useful to itself save what is conducive to understanding.

Further, Spinoza uses the necessarily stuff condition to define Good and Bad, or at least so I read 'we certainly know':

4:D1.   By Good [*bonum*] I understand that which we certainly know to be useful to us.

4:D2.   But by Bad [*malum*] I understand that which we certainly know will prevent us from partaking of any good.

'Good' requires that we know for certain, we have clear sight of how choice maps to desire.

Reflecting on these principles, we find that usefulness comes from acting in accord to the laws of nature, which is the same thing as the guidance of reason. The guidance of reason is nothing but understanding — understanding is, of course, stuff. Now, we get an important implication; to wit: no individual will knowingly accept the bad.

Consider a situation where an individual accepts a theory, and does something on the basis of this theory. The individual can, we suppose that Spinoza allows, detect the impact of the theory on his desires; desire has some element of consciousness.

Desire is the very essence of man in so far as it is conceived as determined to do something by some given modification of itself.[22]

In case the impact of theory is positive, desire augmenting, the individual has enough information to declare the theory stuff. In case the impact is negative, desire decrementing, the individual has enough information to declare the theory nonstuff. Hence, the individual has enough information to know whether the theory is Good or Bad. If Bad, it pays to discard.

Now the contradiction arises because Spinoza has asserted previously that bad theory is so commonly accepted you can trip over it. And those who produce this theory are well paid. Approbation is valued in Spinoza's system:

Honour or glory [*gloria*] is pleasure accompanied by the idea of some action of ours which we imagine others to praise.[23]

Thus, maximizers are choosing not to maximize. Hence, the irrationality of *popular* moralists is evidence, within Spinoza's technical system, that the populace at large is irrational. The route out which claims significant costs of thinking is blocked by Spinoza's own words that people see clearly how the world can be of service to them.

Again we obtain a contradiction. In this approach we have paid no attention to how Spinoza wrote what he did. The Straussian proof, in my opinion, is a good deal neater.

THAT'S EASY TO FIX, YOU JUST . . .

There are several possible escape routes which I consider in turn.

1 *Deny that people maximize.* That's fine but not for Spinoza. Spinoza

takes the revealed preference maximizing postulate as a necessary truth.

2 *Ignore what people say. Who are they to argue with us?* I suppose that this is really Spinoza's escape route. This approach avoids an inconsistency within his system at the expense of an acknowledged gap in understanding of people's own theories about their choice. And, to the extent that these theories influence their choice, we misunderstand their nonverbal behavior too.

3 *Write down the problem in canonical form and solve it.*

But all this is very much in line with Mandeville's own research program to show that one can explain both choice and bizarrely false theories about choice, e.g.:

> *Cleo.* Whence came the *Dryades* and *Hama-Dryades?* how came it ever to be thought impious, to cut down or even to wound, large venerable Oaks, or other stately Trees; and what Root did the Divinity spring from, which the Vulgar, among the ancient Heathens, apprehended to be in Rivers and Fountains?
>
> *Hor.* From the Roguery of designing Priests and other Imposters, that invented those Lies, and made Fables for their own Advantage.
>
> *Cleo.* But still it must have been want of Understanding; and a Tincture, some Re-mainder of that Folly, which is discover'd in young Children, that could induce, or would suffer Men to believe those Fables. Unless Fools actually had Frailties, Knaves could not make Use of them.
>
> *Hor.* There may be something in it; . . .[24]

Merely because a theory is false on its face does not make a compelling case that it is nonstuff. If maximizing agents knowingly 'buy' false theory, then there must be something in it for them. One point of this book has been to argue that such a principle is not tautological. Ridicule of the theory is compelling evidence only that we do not understand it. I learned this from Spinoza.

Chapter 18

The myth of monopoly

INTRODUCTION

It has been argued above, obliquely to be certain, that the foundations of neoclassical economics are not very well established. Because neoclassical economics has neither a well-established theory of property nor a theory of self-restraint, our devices do not explain why people trade and rats do not. I have suggested that inattention to the fact that approbation can be carried by language is involved in this difficulty. I now return to this theme and consider a particularly interesting controversy over whether one can observe an inefficient institution in the real world. Again, I shall argue that the difficulty is founded in our inattention to the complicated ways of approbation within a language community.

There seem basically two schools of thought about the possibility of observing an inefficient institution. Over the last two decades, the discussion has gone something like this:

N. Can we observe an inefficient institution? There in the real world is a single-price monopoly. [*Points to the world.*] OK? Now, go to the board and draw a profit-maximizing, single-price monopoly. Note that there is a difference between price and marginal cost; therefore there is a loss in consumer's surplus relative to competition. QED.

C. The picture on the board has a potential income stream which no one has realized. If one purchased the monopoly and then engaged in price discrimination, the social loss would be turned into profit. Hence, you Ns are finding inefficiency only because you do not allow individuals to maximize. But since individuals do maximize, your picture cannot be true.

N. Of course, if you assume zero transaction's costs, what you say is a simple result of Ronald Coase's work. But this was cleared up a long time ago because the Coasean result does not go through without zero transaction's costs.

C. Hold it. Who said anything about zero transaction's costs? Certainly it will cost something to turn the social loss from monopoly into private property. Call this a transaction's costs. There are two cases. (1) The transaction's costs are less than the gain realized, in which case either the transaction is effected or someone is not maximizing utility. (2) The transaction's costs are more than the gain realized, in which case we would not want the transaction effected – it is actually efficient to have what you call 'inefficient' institutions.

N. That's absurd. You are simply defining 'efficiency' as that which exists and then proving that what exists is efficient.[1]

The argument I shall make is that the members of these two schools are taking advantage of theorists' ability to vary the assignment of praise and blame. What one school of thought sees as an 'inefficient' institution another sees as a 'false' theory. It is the same reality and the same theory, but the assignment of approbation differs. The operation of approbation is a decision with opportunity cost.

FIRST, MAKE IT SIMPLE

The structure of my argument is to work within Abba Lerner's model of monopoly, which is widely viewed as a successful reformulation of Alfred Marshall's model.[2] Conversations of the sort reported above often seem to depend upon the distinction between choice *within* an institution and choice *between* institutions. While the Ns of my acquaintance would agree – insist might be the correct word – that there is always an efficient choice made within an institution, this is not the case for choice between institutions. Lerner's model can be easily extended to allow us to analyze a choice within an institution as well as a choice between institutions. The extension we make is to distinguish between choice within an institution and choice between institutions on the basis of transaction's costs. Inside an institution, we suppose transaction's costs small enough to neglect whereas we cannot neglect the costs of moving from one institution to another.

There are several aspects to the argument below. First, we recall with utmost brevity Lerner's discussion of the inefficiency of monopoly relative to competition and the interpretation which Lerner made of this analysis. Second, we formulate a minimal condition of dynamic economic rationality. Third, it is easy to demonstrate that Lerner's model of monopoly fails to pass this test of minimal economic rationality. This failure would surely not surprise Lerner because, fourth, an easy repair of his discussion – the explicit introduction of the transaction's costs of moving from one institution to another – makes it consistent with minimal economic rationality. Fifth, and finally, the normative conclusion which Lerner drew, if applied to the repaired model of monopoly in point four, has the same structure as a canonical model of choice in traditional ethics.

From a technical point of view the repaired version of Lerner's model is an instance of nonconvex optimization. At the current institution there are short-run transaction's costs incurred when we move to any other institution. We fall off a utility cliff when we bear the costs of a move from one institution to another.[3] The problem of nonconvex optimization, as we have seen above, has historically drawn the attention of moralists. This attention in other contexts is suggestive.

LERNER ON MONOPOLY'S INEFFICIENCY

Lerner, dissatisfied with Marshall's discussion of the social losses from monopoly, which employs the concept of consumer's surplus, gave a proof which requires only indifference curves.[4] In Lerner's model consider the productive possibility set with respect to goods X and Y. There are two interesting equilibria: a monopolistic equilibrium *ME* and a competitive equilibrium at *CE*.[5] The market price facing firms producing X and Y is not influenced by the quantity supplied in competition, so the relative price equation facing firms, *P*, is linear; hence *CE* results. On the contrary, under monopoly of X and competition of Y, the price equation facing firms is influenced by the quantity supplied of X, so the (omitted) relative price equation is non-linear; hence *ME* results. From this analysis, Lerner draws the familiar conclusion that there is a social loss from monopoly.

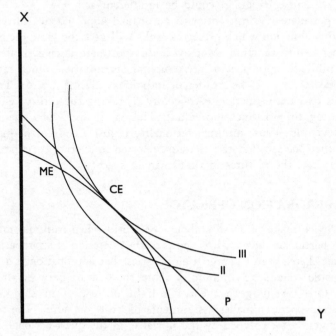

Figure 18.1   Competitive and monopolistic equilibria

A WEAK CONDITION OF DYNAMIC RATIONALITY

Lerner's graphical argument has two explicit dimensions: good X and good Y; even so, a conclusion about movement in time is offered. The question we address is how to go from static indifference curves to dynamic trajectories. This is a considerable problem in standard neoclassical economics. Consider the treatment in Michael Intrilligator's fine textbook. Intrilligator works through standard static ordinal optimization, pointing out that any utility function which preserves rank order is as good as any other utility function.[6] When he considers dynamic optimization, he writes a unique *cardinal* utility function to be integrated over some optimal trajectory.[7] Moreover, even if one can find a unique cardinal utility function, it is not immediately obvious that any sort of dynamic optimization will be consistent.[8]

Let us postulate a very weak rationality condition for dynamic optimization which shall be called 'minimal rationality'. If for any two intertemporal trajectories, A and B, for any t if $B(t)$ is not preferred to $A(t)$, and for at least one t, $A(t)$ is preferred to $B(t)$, then trajectory A is preferred to B. Choosing A in lieu of B can be said to be minimally rational. Obviously, for trajectories A and B, there will be no Strotz reversals; once an individual begins a journey through time on A, there is no incentive to switch to B. If A is preferred to B at t, B cannot be preferred to A at $t + i$, $i > 0$. Of course, B and A could be indifferent at $t + i$.

This postulate is consistent with an ordinal approach to utility theory. Any utility function which preserves ranks will give the same prediction as any other utility function. Moreover, this postulate is consistent with an almost nihilistic approach to intertemporal optimization which regards an individual at time i to be a different individual at time j, $i \neq j$. Trajectory A would be Pareto-superior to trajectory B, taking the utility at each t to be accruing to a distinct individual. This is, in fact, why there are no Strotz reversals. Thus, minimal rationality is just a convenient method of stating that one social state is Pareto-preferred to another social state. It is easier to draw the pictures in time than in space.

THE APPROBATION OPERATOR

What do we make of a story about the world when minimal rationality fails? In particular, how shall we employ the operation of approbation? The argument sketched in Chapter 4 emphasizes that approbation is a decision made inside a language community about the relation between theory and reality. One can judge a theory in light of reality; in this case, the approbation operator makes assignments of 'true' or 'false'. The school of thought gently stereotyped by the initial C in the quasi-fictional dialogue recounted above would accept this interpretation of approbation. But, this is only one possible use of approbation, because reality itself can be caught in the web of judgment and said to be 'efficient' or 'inefficient'. Economists do not like, it seems, to use the traditional words 'right' and 'wrong'. No matter. As long as 'inefficient' does not signify that there is something amiss with our theory the way 'false' does, the line of argument is unmoved.

Let me spin a variation on Don McCloskey's example here.[9] Walk into a bar during the American Economic Association convention and accost two economist-like persons. Ask us what we make of the following story. 'A person, walking along the street, comes to a stop. He bends over and picks up what looks like a $100 bill. He says 'Wow! A $100 bill.' He puts it back on the ground and walks on.'

My guess is that the reaction would be something like this: 'That's a lie!' or 'So, you saw the tooth-fairy did you?' In a word, 'false'. Your story will be rejected out of hand because it conflicts with minimal rationality. Or, in McCloskey's own version, that is why we don't find $100 bills on the sidewalk. Any transaction which satisfies this characteristic of minimal rationality will be grabbed at the first opportunity.

Another city, another convention, another bar. Tell your story to two members of the 'caring professions'. 'The man needs help' or 'Isn't it a shame that we have lost the ability to take care of sick people?' Someone who fails minimal rationality has a problem. It is his fault or it is society's fault. The story might well be 'true', because we live in a 'sick' world.

When we encounter Lerner's model of monopoly, we have to make the decision how to use our approbation operator. Do we take the account of monopoly to be 'true' so there is an 'inefficiency' in society? Or do we say Lerner's account of monopoly is 'false' because it offers someone a free $100 bill and no one has picked it up? Either decision is possible.

If we reject as 'false' all models which fail minimal rationality, then we are left with (1) nothing at all or, if something remains, (2) those models which do not fail minimal rationality. But, if the only normative principle we accept is minimal rationality – the Paretian principle in one convenient guise – by rejecting as 'false' theories which fail minimal rationality, we have ruled out all 'inefficient' states of affairs.

This does not seem to me the same as defining as 'efficient' that which exists. Rather, it seems to me to be an inexorable consequence of using one model to both describe and prescribe. If we reject all models which do not correctly describe the world as 'false', then we are left with nothing more than 'right', because 'true' differs from 'right' only by interpretation of the operation of approbation.

Notice what we have done. We have come back to the question with which this book started: how can 'false' theory be useless? Demonstrating that a theory is descriptively 'false' does not make it prescriptively useless. Or so I've argued above.

LERNER'S MODEL OF MONOPOLY FAILS MINIMAL RATIONALITY

Let us work through the dynamic trajectory which Lerner's model offers to the consumer who finds himself at the monopoly equilibrium, *ME*. The most obvious trajectory is staying at the monopoly equilibrium, which, without loss of generality, we assume generates a constant amount of utility for each time period. This is one trajectory in Figure 18.2. The other trajectory is to move from monopoly equilibrium to competitive equilibrium at *CE*. With the curvature assumptions as specified by Lerner, the rational consumer moves *up* indifference curves as he leaves the monopoly equilibrium and draws nearer competitive equilibrium. This generates the trajectory to *CE* in Figure 18.2. It is important that local movement with convex indifference curves and a convex production possibility set generates a nondecreasing level of utility over time as we move from *any* nonoptimum to the optimum.

If there is any monopoly which continues to exist – so revealing a preference for trajectory *ME* – then Lerner's consumer has failed the test of minimal rationality. Minimal rationality requires that the movement to competitive equilibrium be taken.

THAT'S EASY TO FIX, YOU JUST . . .

The reaction of anyone who has read this far is surely one of impatience at what seems a simple implication of the most naive version of the Coase theorem.[10] With no transaction's costs, we would surely have an efficient

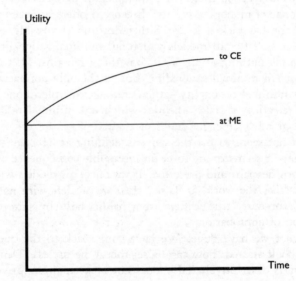

Figure 18.2 An easy choice of trajectories

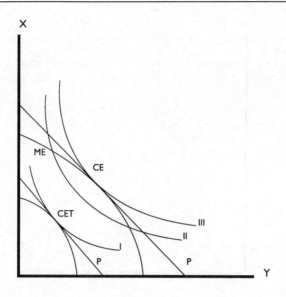

Figure 18.3   Costs to attain competitive equilibrium

equilibrium. But, of course, we do have costs of transactions.

Transaction's costs can take many forms. Perhaps, the consumers do not understand economic theory and cannot figure out that a reform can make them better off. If this is the problem, then James Buchanan has given us the answer.[11] The economist *qua* reformer explains to other people how we can all gain from reform.[12] The proposed reform can be treated as a hypothesis in welfare economics – if you move from monopoly to competition, you will be better off – which can be tested. Do we move? If so, that's the answer. Buchanan has it right.

Let us suppose we do not move, what can we conclude? In fact, this is where the analysis gets dicey, so we have to move with caution. Suppose that we view transaction's costs as 'temporary costs'. That is to say, to take into account transaction's costs, one simply pushes in the production possibility set, temporarily to be sure, so that a movement from monopoly equilibrium to temporary competitive equilibrium, *CET*, puts the individual on a lower indifference curve, say, *I*. This is shown in Figure 18.3.

CET is a temporary competitive equilibrium which persists until the production possibility set expands back to the competitive equilibrium without transaction's costs. Supposing that the production possibility set changes by an infinitesimal amount in an infinitesimal period of time, the utility trajectory will be a continuous function of time. The alternate trajectories facing the individual are shown in Figure 18.4. At time τ the

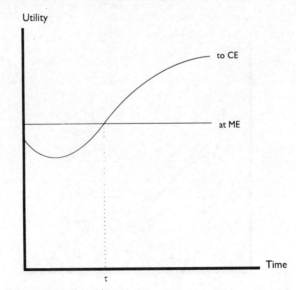

Figure 18.4   Two costly trajectories

trajectory toward *CE* has overtaken the trajectory of remaining at *ME*. Costs are paid and benefits accrue.

One trajectory is, as before, remaining at monopoly equilibrium. The other is moving to competitive equilibrium, taking into account that there must be an initial depression of utility to pay for the transaction's costs. Choosing a trajectory which holds to *ME* does not fail the standards of minimal rationality and so the continued existence of monopoly does not falsify the revised Lerner model. Nor, of course, would a choice of moving to *CE*.

The trajectory to *CE* in Figure 18.4 has been encountered before. To gain utility in the 'long run' we must give up utility in the 'short run'. This might be employed as a defining characteristic of nonconvex optimization problems.

AND SO?

When the Buchanan test fails, and there is no such thing as a free reform, what conclusion are we to draw? Which trajectory is higher?

Here again we demonstrate the malleability of approbation. Suppose that we observe an individual remaining at *ME*. What conclusion do we draw? Do we conclude that Figure 18.1 is 'false' and that there is really more utility at a monopoly if we take into account transaction's costs? Or do we conclude that because Figure 18.1 is 'true' the choice of remaining at *ME* is 'inefficient'?

Let us deepen the paradox. The economists who say that there is nothing wrong with Figure 18.1 – it isn't the fault of the picture that transaction's costs get in the way – are being paid by society to say such things. We are back to where we started. We find 'false' theory – on one interpretation – to be useful. And where do we expect to find 'false' theory? The time trajectory we encounter is the same trajectory we found the Greek poets and philosophers worrying about.

Our faithful companion, through the winding byways of this book, has been the problem of time preference. Here it is again. The pictures tell us nothing about how far is down and how far is up but yet we conclude that there is only the Way. With nothing other than the pictures to go on, we can only count on the trajectory to *CE* having a greater present value than remaining at *ME* under the conditions of an infinite horizon and zero time preference.

We leave the realm of revealed preference and enter the realm of classical ethics when we conclude from the overtaking picture that any rational individual will prefer the trajectory which is eventually higher. That such a choice should always be preferred is the content of one aspect of classical myth and morality. It is not that of Bellman's principle of optimality.

This is not to say that the myth does not have the important feature of changing the world. For example, it might well preclude society from ever choosing a monopoly. In that case the myth has created its own efficiency.

THE LONG RUN AND THE SHORT

Thus, the proof that an observed monopoly is inefficient requires an infinite horizon and zero time preference to go through. There are many names which have been given for such considerations which throw us outside an Archimedian framework in which there are no absolute values. Pagans speak of immortality from 'fame' and Christians talk about 'Heaven'. Economists are wont to speak of the 'long run'.

> Now this habit of taking the long view is not only characteristic of the orthodox economic theorist, but in the discussion of matters of economic policy it is often the principal characteristic by which he can be distinguished from other professional economists or even from the intelligent layman.[13]

By whatever name, this point of view is a most austere one. What one chooses is not what one ought because we do not behave as if we had zero time preference and an infinite horizon. Bernard Mandeville taught us this. But Mandeville also taught us that preaching austerity is an observed choice; a well-paying profession, he might insist!

The dynamic characterization of the proof that monopoly is 'inefficient' is the same dynamic characterization we have recovered from ancient Greek moral advice. The paradigm of the ancient Greek morality was Hercules.

His decision to lead a life of virtue and duty so impressed later Christians that he was allowed to live again in new religion.[14] It is a grand story to tell our children, but sometimes one might wonder whether we are up to it. Here is Richmond Lattimore's reflection on Hercules' choice of the austere way:

> Now here began a succession of sick and disastrous years
> for the tough, the greedy, the cruel and sly of the world, here began
> a most pitiable outcry, thumping and struggle as he laid them all by
>   the ears.
> The strenuous little man
> who fought from grinning helm with spear or bare with his bones, club
>   wrenched broad boles,
> mashed snake heads, speared pounded butted or strangled lion and bull,
> outsized pig, giant and ogre, and the monsters crawled away and hid in
>   their holes.
> Much done. But a thin ragged life. Who has told how scarred and
>   twisted, how pitiful
>
> and used, the hero who walked the grand peaks in the end of his time?
> A sad strong man, remembering every fight
> and harsh from sour triumphs, fears and sickness, the gift of his prime,
> and bare night
> alone in the slum of the mind, the inward niggle of doubt.
> Had he chosen right at the fork of the ways? Was it worth
> the beating it took to pacify and set right a world torn inside out,
> and fight his way to being the best man on earth?
>
> This is a moral and momentous story I tell,
> Here is the Y-shape of tragic choice, Hecate's fork, out sprung
>   three-piece cross;
> the trails to heaven and hell.
> Yes, but which is which? [15]

THE CIRCLE IS COMPLETE

The book began with a problem of how ordinary people's 'false' theory could aid optimization problems. The book closes with a problem of how professional economists' 'false' theory could aid optimization problems. We know who we are.

Notes

A preface to word-taking behavior

1 By Jack Wiseman, whose relation to the Jack of the conversation is a possibility without potential surprise in even a Shacklean world.
2 It is a phrase Tyler Cowen coined for this occasion.
3 Friedrich Nietzsche, *The Portable Nietzsche*, translated by Walter Kaufmann (New York: Viking Press, 1968). p. 96.

PART I INTRODUCTION AND BACKGROUND

Chapter 1 Why worry about the economic ideas of ordinary people?

1 George J. Stigler, *The Theory of Price* (New York: Macmillan, third edition, 1966), p. 8.
2 Frank H. Knight, *The Ethics of Competition* (New York: Augustus M. Kelley, 1951), p. 74: 'Thus we appear to search in vain for any really ethical basis of approval for competition as a basis for an ideal type of human relations, or as a motive to action. It fails to harmonize either with the Pagan ideal of society as a community of friends or the Christian ideal of spiritual fellowship. Its only justification is that it is effective in getting things done; but any candid answer to the question, "what things," compels the admission that they leave much to be desired.'
3 Frank H. Knight and Thornton W. Merriam, *The Economic Order and Religion* (New York: Harper & Brothers, 1945), p. 240.
4 Knight, *Ethics of Competition*, p. 83.
5 Knight, *Ethics of Competition*, p. 86.
6 Bernard Mandeville, *Free Thoughts on Religion, the Church, and National Happiness* (London, 1720), pp. 18–19.
7 Edward O. Wilson, *Sociobiology* (Cambridge, Mass.: Belknap Press, 1975), p. 561: 'The enduring paradox of religion is that so much of its substance is demonstrably false, yet it remains a driving force in all societies'.
8 Paul A. Samuelson, *The Collected Scientific Papers*, edited by Joseph E. Stiglitz (Cambridge, Mass.: M.I.T. Press, 1966), 1:3–114.
9 Stigler, *Theory of Price*, p. 68. The Mandeville reference is *The Fable of the Bees*, edited by F. B. Kaye (Oxford: Clarendon Press, 1924), 1:151–2. After a lapse of many years, Kaye's great edition of Mandeville's *Fable of the Bees* is now back in print through Liberty Classics.
10 George J. Stigler, *Five Lectures on Economic Problems* (London: London School of Economics, 1949), pp. 12–24.

11 The attentive reader will now ask: how long will it take me to invoke this principle?
12 Richard P. Feynman, '*What Do You Care What Other People Think?*' (New York: Bantam Books, 1989), pp. 126–7, explains the role of the ●.
13 Martin Buber, *I and Thou*, translated by Ronald Gregor Smith (New York: Collier Books, second edition, 1987), p. 51, revels in the indeterminacy of the dialogue. 'Here *I* and *Thou* freely confront one another in mutual effect that is neither connected with nor coloured by any causality'.
14 Jürgen Habermas, *Moral Consciousness and Communicative Action*, translated by Christian Lenhardt and Shierry Weber Nicholsen (Cambridge, Mass.: M.I.T. Press, 1990), pp. 87–8. Habermas considers the consistency and universality purely semantic, non-ethical rules. Surely, consistency requires an incredible expenditure of resources upon thinking. Why would this be sensible? Such consistency claims are considered in Chapter 17.
15 Stephen K. White, *The Recent Work of Jürgen Habermas* (Cambridge: Cambridge University Press, 1990), pp. 13–21. This is not to say that the standard rational choice approach is any better. Obviously, I am attempting to change this situation.
16 The attentive reader now knows.
17 No one seems to escape the sirens of tractability, not even G. L. S. Shackle, *Epistemics and Economics* (Cambridge: Cambridge University Press, 1972), p. 249: '*Economizing* can be idealized and represented in the ultimate degree of formal perfection by means of the calculus. The calculus furnishes for it a ready-made apparatus of thought which is precisely apt, not only to the requirements of expression and manipulation, but to the nature of the intuitive act by which people everywhere, never having heard of the differential calculus, correctly adjust their budgets so as to get the most satisfaction from their means'.
18 There exist cases such that one can prove that *a* and *b* exactly agree. In these cases adding the constraint is a sensible estimation procedure because our proofs are more reliable than our numerical procedures. The details are found in David M. Levy, 'Increasing the Likelihood Value by Adding Constraints', *Economics Letters* 28 (1988): 57–61.
19 Figure 1.1 was first drawn to explain some 'counter-intuitive' results in a technical optimizing problem. Susan Feigenbaum and David M. Levy, 'Hypothesis Testing When Constraints Increase the Likelihood Value', paper presented at Western Economic Association, San Diego, July 1990.
20 Kenneth J. Arrow and F. H. Hahn, *General Competitive Analysis* (San Francisco: Holden-Day, 1972), p. 173.
21 James M. Buchanan, *The Demand and Supply of Public Goods* (Chicago: Rand McNally, 1968), p. 210 has the index entry: 'Indivisibility, as characteristic of public goods'.
22 Milton Friedman, *Essays in Positive Economics* (Chicago: University of Chicago Press, 1953), pp. 30–9.
23 It is useful for Americans to be reminded by intelligent visitors how remarkably religious we were. V. S. Naipaul, *A Turn in the South* (New York: Alfred A. Knopf, 1989).
24 Milman Parry, *The Making of Homeric Verse*, edited by Adam Parry (Oxford: Clarendon Press, 1971).
25 Hao Wang, *From Mathematics to Philosophy* (New York: Humanities Press, 1974), p. 324, was authorized by Kurt Gödel to present the following interpretation of what has been rigorously proven: 'The human mind is incapable of formulating (or mechanizing) all its mathematical intuitions. . . . on the basis of what has been proven so far, it remains possible that there may exist (and even be empirically discoverable) a theorem-proving machine which in fact *is* equivalent to mathematical intuition, but cannot be *proved* to be so, nor even to proved to yield only *correct* theorems of finitary number theory'.

26 *The Aeneid of Virgil*, translated by Allen Mandelbaum (Berkeley: University of California Press, 1982), 9:243–6.

27 Sappho, *Archilochos, Sappho, Alkman*, translated by Guy Davenport (Berkeley: University of California Press, 1980), No. 151.

28 Frederick Nietzsche, *The Birth of Tragedy and the Case of Wagner*, translated by Walter Kaufmann (New York: Vintage Books, 1967), p. 43: 'The same impulse which calls art into being, as the complement and consummation of existence, seducing one to a continuation of life, was also the cause of the Olympian world which the Hellenic "will" made use of as a transfiguring mirror. Thus do the gods justify the life of man: they themselves live it – the only satisfactory theodicy!'

29 Nahum M. Sarna, *Understanding Genesis* (New York: Schocken Books, 1970), pp. xvii–xix, makes clear the link between those books which became canonical and those books which survived by laborious copying and preservation.

30 Richard Smith, 'Afterword: The Modern Relevance of Gnosticism', *The Nag Hammadi Library*, edited by James M. Robinson (San Francisco: Harper & Row, third edition, 1988) gives a riveting history of how intellectuals have long lamented that the Gnostic texts did not survive. The evidence provided by the Nag Hammadi collection convinces me that the most frightening words in the English language are 'You have three wishes'.

31 Franz Rosenzweig, *The Star of Redemption*, translated by William W. Hallo (Boston: Beacon Press, 1971), p. 265.

32 In a reference which I have managed to lose!

33 Frank H. Knight, 'The Ricardian Theory of Production and Distribution', *Essays on the History and Method of Economics* (Chicago: University of Chicago Press, 1956).

34 George J. Stigler, *Memoirs of an Unregulated Economist* (New York: Basic Books, 1988), p. 175: 'Frank Knight once proposed that a professor should be allowed to publish a piece for public consumption only after it had met the approval of his colleagues at the university. He argued that a professor should not be allowed to influence the lay public if he could not get his colleagues' approval of the professional quality of his ideas. Knight's proposal was viewed indulgently as a cute piece of creativity, and I have no doubt that it was pointed out at the time that this particular proposal had not been approved by his colleagues in the Department of Economics of the University of Chicago'.

PART II THE DEMAND FOR IDEAS

Chapter 2 Adam Smith and the Texas A&M rats

1 This is an understatement; the long-looked-for Giffen effect has been observed among animal consumers. Raymond C. Battalio, John H. Kagel and Carl A. Kogut, 'Experimental Confirmation of the Existence of a Giffen Good', ms., 1989.

2 I lament that only when this book is finished do I discover David Lewis, *Convention* (Cambridge, Mass.: Harvard University Press, 1969). His link of language to non-cooperative games will be of interest to anyone wishing to pursue this line of inquiry. This approach is implemented in important directions by Karl Wärneryd, *Economic Conventions* (Stockholm: Economic Research Institute, 1990). Wärneryd uses signals to give information about the structure of the game; I use approbation to modify the pay-offs of the game. It will be interesting to see whether these approaches are ultimately complements or substitutes.

3 Charles J. Lumsden and Edward O. Wilson, *Promethean Fire* (Cambridge, Mass.: Harvard University Press, 1983), p. 36: 'Human beings are unique in their possession of a fully symbolic language, an enlarged memory, and long-term contracts upon

which elaborate forms of reciprocity can be based'.

4 The two names one need mention are G. L. S. Shackle and James M. Buchanan. G. L. S. Shackle finds unpredictable choice in the question of decision-making under uncertainty. A characteristic expression can be found in his *Expectation, Enterprise and Profit* (Chicago: Aldine Publishing Company, 1970), p. 106: 'Decision is choice amongst rival available courses of action. We can choose only what is still unactualized; we can choose only amongst imaginations and figments. Imagined actions and policies can have only imagined consequences, and it follows that we can choose only an action whose consequences we cannot directly know, since we cannot be eye-witness of them'. Buchanan often discusses the problem of creative choice in the context of Shackle's work. He notes, *Cost and Choice* (Chicago: Markham Publishing, 1969), pp. 36–7, Shackle's unwillingness to carry through the unpredictability argument in the context of 'certainty'. Here is Buchanan's judgment on Shackle's work, 'The Domain of Subjective Economics', *Method, Process, and Austrian Economics*, edited by Israel M. Kirzner (Lexington, Mass.: Lexington Books, 1982), p. 18: 'Any attempt, however, to carry over the modern analysis of individual choice under uncertainty to the genuine choice making that is the subject of subjective economic theory reflects intellectual confusion. How can anything remotely resembling a probabilistic calculus be applied to choices that are among alternatives that only come into being through the act of choice itself? The human beings whose choices occupy the thoughts of G. L. S. Shackle could never be reduced to the status of rats, even superintelligent ones. In my view, no economist other than Shackle works exclusively within the domain of subjective economic theory, as I have defined it here. Any methodological advance must build on the work of Shackle. But as many scholars have already found, the next steps are not easy. The advances themselves will, of course, be genuine choices in the full Shackleian sense. They cannot be predicted'.

5 Roger Penrose, *The Emperor's New Mind* (New York: Oxford University Press, 1989), pp. 30–73, gives a very accessible description of the theory of algorithms due to Alan Turing and on pp. 140–6 a description of the difference between problems which can be solved in polynomial time and those which cannot. (This statement, and others in the text, suppose that *NP*-complete algorithms cannot be solved in polynomial time. This mathematical problem is still open.) This identification of a precise *formal* classification of *NP* algorithms with the heuristic of hard or intractable is controversial. In one sense the identification is too strong because the simplex, the workhorse of linear programming, is known not to be a polynomial time algorithm. In another sense, the identification is too weak because polynomial time can be very long indeed. Hao Wang, *Reflections on Kurt Gödel* (Cambridge, Mass.: M.I.T. Press, 1988), p. 170, makes the latter point.

6 If the real-world choices which confront the starting-point problem turn out to be chaotic, then Shackle's location of the creative aspect of choice in uncertainty may be deeper than one might think. For although the chaotic equations can be written in deterministic form, there is a type of randomness arising from the multiplicity of solutions which brings back uncertainty in a particularly nasty form.

7 Christos H. Papadimitriou and Kenneth Steiglitz, *Combinatorial Optimization* (Englewood Cliffs, N.J.: Prentice-Hall, 1982), pp. 454–81, give the results for local search for discrete optimization problems when there exists a polynomial time algorithm for *each* starting point. Obviously, if *any* starting point requires a nonpolynomial computation then the situation is even less appealing.

8 Shackle's model of uncertainty has proven very difficult for economists to work with because it is built up from hypotheses (theories made of words), not subsets of *N*-dimensional Euclidean space. Thus, in Shackle's framework, we need to confront language. G. L. S. Shackle, *Imagination and the Nature of Choice* (Edinburgh: Edinburgh University Press, 1979), p. 120: 'My theme has argued that the rival choosables are

original arrangements by the chooser of elements suggested by reports from the field. The elements themselves are necessarily works of imaginative thought. The stream of impressions can be resolved by the chooser in many and perhaps indefinitely many ways into a scene made up *alphabetically*, that is, composed of characters, 'letters', forming a spelling system, as words, sentences, whole presentations of complex thought can be built of the letters of the alphabet'.

9 Lumsden and Wilson, *Promethean Fire*, p. 55: 'So there is a kind of genetic destiny, one that nevertheless steered evolving mankind away from a frozen fate and towards the creation of free will.' From this they conclude that St Augustine was wrong; therefore, 'We are perfectible according to our own will' (p. 56).

10 Susan Feigenbaum and David M. Levy, 'Hypothesis Testing When Constraints Increase the Likelihood Value,' presented at the Western Economic Association, San Diego, June 1990.

11 Penrose, *New Mind*, p. 108, stresses the importance of Gödel's theorem to his enterprise. One can prove within some axiomatic system, that there exist true theorems which cannot be proven from these axioms.

12 Penrose, *New Mind*, p. 405: 'What *selective advantage* does a consciousness confer on those who actually possess it?'

13 James M. Buchanan, 'The Domain of Subjective Economics', *Method, Process and Austrian Economics*, edited by Israel M. Kirzner (Lexington: D. C. Heath, 1982), p. 9: 'An economy (if indeed it could be called such) in which all persons respond to constraints passively and in which no one engages in active choice could never organize itself through exchange institutions. Such an economy would require that the constraints be imposed either by nature or by beings external to the community of those participants who are the passive responders. In either case, such an economy would be comparable in kind to those whose participants are the "animal consumers" examined by John Kagel and Raymond Battalio, and their coworkers'.

14 Adam Smith, *An Inquiry into the Nature and Causes of the Wealth of Nations*, edited by W. B. Todd (Oxford: Clarendon Press, 1976), p. 25. The *first* glitch? Cf. George J. Stigler, *The Theory of Price* (New York: Macmillan, third edition, 1966), pp. 8–10.

15 *Wealth of Nations*, p. 25.

16 Edward O. Wilson, *Sociobiology* (Cambridge, Mass.: Belknap Press, 1975), p. 551: 'only man has an economy. His high intelligence and symbolizing activity make true barter possible'.

17 *Wealth of Nations*, p. 30: 'Those different tribes of animals, however, though all of the same species, are of scarce any use to one another. The strength of the mastiff is not, in the least, supported either by the swiftness of the greyhound, or by the sagacity of the spaniel, or by the docility of the shepherd's dog. The effects of those different geniuses and talents, for want of the power of disposition to barter and exchange, cannot be brought into a common stock, and do not in the least contribute to the better accommodation and conveniency of the species'.

18 *Wealth of Nations*, p. 26.

19 Aristotle, *Rhetoric*, translated by W. Rhys Roberts, *The Complete Works of Aristotle*, edited by Jonathan Barnes (Princeton: Princeton University Press, 1984), 1355b27–8: 'Rhetoric may be defined as the faculty of observing in any given case the available means of persuasion'.

20 Adam Smith, *Lectures on Jurisprudence*, edited by R. L. Meek, D. D. Raphael and P. G. Stein (Oxford: Clarendon Press, 1978), p. 352. Also, pp. 493–4. This is surely a high point of the semiotic theory of money: money as capitalized language. At the critical point in the early draft of the *Wealth of Nations*, reprinted in the Glasgow edition of *Lectures on Jurisprudence*, pp. 570–1, Smith has nothing to say about 'reason and speech'. Rather this is what he says: 'This is a propensity, common to all men, and to be found in no other race of animals, a propensity to truck, barter and exchange one

thing for another'. It seems that here Smith is treating this as a primitive propensity.

21 The revealed preference approach is simply the converse of NCT. If NCT fails then, obviously, its converse must be reconsidered.

22 John H. Kagel, Raymond C. Battalio, Howard Rachlin and Leonard Green, 'Demand Curves for Animal Consumers', *Quarterly Journal of Economics* 96 (1981): 1–16.

23 I owe my knowledge of the 'failed' experiment to Gordon Tullock, John Kagel and Vernon Smith. The impact of publication bias toward 'significant' results upon hypothesis testing is discussed in Frank T. Denton, 'Data Mining as an Industry', *Review of Economics and Statistics* 57 (1985): 124–7.

24 Raymond C. Battalio, John H. Kagel and Don N. McDonald, 'Animals' Choices over Uncertain Outcomes: Some Initial Experimental Results', *American Economic Review* 75 (1985): 597–613. The statement in the text only means that the Allais paradox holds for animal consumers too.

25 This point was clarified in conversation by Gil Harman and Charlie Plott, who saw the corrected neoclassical theorem before I did.

26 Jack Wiseman taught me that they have our devices to emulate. But they don't learn from us in the way we can learn from them.

27 The difference between John Locke's much more famous theory of property and Hume's theory of property will be discussed in detail in Chapter 7 below. Interest in Hume's theory of property was revived by Arnold Plant, *Selected Economic Essays and Addresses* (London: Routledge & Kegan Paul, 1974), pp. 30–116. The importance of Plant's work has been stressed by F. A. Hayek, *Constitution of Liberty* (Chicago: University of Chicago, 1960), p. 455. Harold Demsetz, 'The Exchange and Enforcement of Property Rights', *Journal of Law and Economics* 7 (1964): 11–26, develops a scarcity-based theory of property independently of Hume's work.

28 Winston Bush, 'Individual Welfare in Anarchy', *Explorations in the Theory of Anarchy*, edited by Gordon Tullock (Blacksburg, Va.: Center for the Study of Public Choice, 1972) and Robert J. Mackay, *Winston Bush's Contribution to Public Choice* (Fairfax, Va.: Center for Study of Public Choice, 1990). (Yes, we have dropped the 'the'.)

29 One example, an econometric one, is provided in David M. Levy, 'Estimating the Impact of Government R&D', *Economics Letters* 32 (1990): 169–72.

30 I owe this example to Ron Heiner.

31 Wilson, *Sociobiology*, p. 264, reports on the expansion of a territory as the number of competing species increases.

32 Susan Feigenbaum and Jennifer Roback have emphasized this to me. Variations on this theme have been urged by Jack Wiseman, Ron Heiner, Charles Plott, Tom Ireland and David Rose. Ireland's and Rose's objections were reported by Susan Feigenbaum.

33 John T. Bonner, *The Evolution of Culture in Animals* (Princeton: Princeton University Press, 1980), pp. 23–5; Lumsden and Wilson, *Promethean Fire*, pp. 30–1.

34 Jane Goodall, *The Chimpanzees of Gombe* (Cambridge, Mass.: Belknap Press, 1986), p. 204: 'In chimpanzee society the closest bonds, as we have seen, are those between family members . . .'.

35 Penrose, *New Mind*, pp. 423–34, makes a sharp distinction between language and pictures. Mathematicians, he points out, often think in terms of pictures and not words. Perhaps, I should emphasize theory instead of language. The pictures which mathematicians draw are surely theoretical artifacts even if they are not part of our language. And rats don't draw Venn diagrams.

36 This possibility was stressed in conversation, independently, by Gordon Tullock, James Buchanan and Roger Congleton.

37 Wilson, *Sociobiology*, pp. 300–13.

38 Body language will do. If you speak only English and I speak only FORTRAN, we might be able to get by with grunts, gestures and flow-charts.

39 Goodall, *The Chimpanzees of Gombe*, p. 667, index entry 'Grooming'.

40 R. Mark Isaac and James M. Walker, 'Communication and Free-riding Behavior', *Economic Inquiry* 26 (1988): 585–608.

41 Lumsden and Wilson, *Promethean Fire*, p. 112, emphasize how language constrains us.

42 St Augustine, *Confessions*, quoted by Ludwig Wittgenstein, *Philosophical Investigations*, translated by G. E. M. Anscombe (Oxford: Basil Blackwell, 1972), No. 1 [p. 2^e].

43 Noam Chomsky, *Cartesian Linguistics* (New York: Harper & Row, 1966), pp. 4, 10–11.

44 Goodall, *The Chimpanzees of Gombe*, p. 144, reports considerable local variation in chimpanzee communication.

45 The initial enthusiasm for ape-language experiments was shattered when Herbert Terrace reported the ability to explain the use of signs by Nim Chimpsky by a small number of decision rules. H. S. Terrace, 'A Report to an Academy, 1980', *The Clever Hans Phenomenon*, edited by Thomas A. Sebeok and Robert Rosenthal, *Annals of the New York Academy of Sciences* 364 (1981), pp. 94–114, is widely cited as a disreplication of the entire ape-language research enterprise. However, this study, in turn, seems to have now been disreplicated, E. Sue Savage-Rumbaugh *et al.*, 'Ape-language Research beyond Nim', in E. Sue Savage-Rumbaugh, *Ape Language* (New York: Columbia University Press, 1986). An examination of Terrace's experimental procedure is found in Chris O'Sullivan and Carey Page Yeager, 'Communicative Context and Linguistic Competence', *Teaching Sign Language to Chimpanzees*, edited by R. Allen Gardner, Beatrix T. Gardner and Thomas E. Van Cantfort (Albany: State University of New York Press, 1989).

46 A chimpanzee who knows how to sign will sign to other chimpanzees whether or not there are humans around, R. Allen Gardner and Beatrix T. Gardner, 'A Cross-fostering Laboratory', *Teaching Sign Language to Chimpanzees*. Chimpanzees can teach each other signs, Roger S. Fouts, Deborah H. Fouts and Thomas E. Van Cantfort, 'The Infant Loulis Learns Signs from Cross-fostered Chimpanzees', *Teaching Sign Language to Chimpanzees*.

47 Goodall, *The Chimpanzees of Gombe*, pp. 369, 372–6.

48 Savage-Rumbaugh, *Ape Language*, pp. 206–28.

49 Brain size in animals and humans is discussed by Bonner, *Culture in Animals*, pp. 47–51.

50 John C. Eccles cites a study of a girl deprived of language until the age of 13.5 years. The result was a 'functional atrophy of the left hemisphere because of the enormously prolonged absence of linguistic usage'. Karl R. Popper and John C. Eccles, *The Self and its Brain* (New York: Springer International, 1978), p. 309. Bonner, *Culture*, p. 37, cites a demonstration that learning in rats increases the number of connections in the brain. Alfonso Caramazza and Argye E. Hillis, 'Lexical Organization of Nouns and Verbs in the Brain', *Nature* 349 (February 28, 1991): 788–90 provide evidence that the grammatical structure of language is intimately related to the brain's physical structure. This finding provides wonderful support for Chomsky's view of the inate structure of language.

51 To make evolution explosive, just make it recursive and tweak the parameters. Suppose there is something genetic which makes the brain more or less elastic with respect to language. If brain size at time $t - 1$ determines language complexity at time t; language complexity at t assists survival for those with more language-elasticity brains than for those with less language-elasticity brains; language complexity at t determines brain size at t, then it is easy to generate an explosive evolutionary process.

52 Monboddo believed that apes and humans fall in the class of tool-using animals. Lord Monboddo, *Of the Origin and Progress of Language* (Menston, UK: Scolar Press [1773]), 1:272: 'And if there were nothing else to convince me that the Ouran Outang belongs to our species, his using sticks as a weapon would be alone sufficient.' Apes differ from us by lack of language, *Origin*, 1:289: 'They live in society, build huts. Apes are the

member of the class without language: joined in companies attack elephants, and no doubt carry on other joint undertakings for their subsistence and preservations; but have not yet attained the use of speech'. David Hume recommended to Smith the first volume of *Origin and Progress of Language, Correspondence of Adam Smith*, edited by Ernest Mossner and Ian Ross (Indianapolis: Liberty Classics, 1989), pp. 166–7. I know three reliable accounts of Monboddo's doctrine: Arthur O. Lovejoy, 'Monboddo and Rousseau', *Essays in the History of Ideas* (Baltimore: Johns Hopkins University Press, 1948); Gladys Bryson, *Man and Society* (Princeton: Princeton University Press, 1945); E. L. Cloyd, *James Burnett Lord Monboddo* (Oxford: Clarendon Press, 1972). Of these fine scholarly works, only Bryson's even hints at the Hermetic context inside which many of Monboddo's positions are routine. Only Cloyd could have taken advantage of D. P. Walker's or Frances Yates's Hermetic research, but, to our loss, did not.

53 *Philosophical Investigations*, No. 268 [p. 94^e].

54 Some of this discussion is involved in what is now called the 'paradox of value'. A reconstruction is found in David Levy, 'Diamonds, Water and Z Goods', *History of Political Economy* 14 (1982): 312–22.

55 Saul A. Kripke, *Wittgenstein on Rules and Private Language* (Cambridge, Mass.: Harvard University Press, 1982), pp. 112–13.

56 Even so, the economics literature which grandly conceded the case to market socialism forgot to worry about the incentives of the price setters. David M. Levy, 'The Bias in Centrally Planned Prices', *Public Choice* 67 (1990): 213–36.

57 Edward O. Wilson, *Sociobiology*, p. 274. In class George Stigler illustrated the case of negative returns by pointing out that one day's labor applied to a square mile of land produces only a very brisk walk.

58 I owe this point to Charlie Plott in a memorable conversation at Cal Tech.

59 Wilson, *Sociobiology*, pp. 274–5, gives the following account of a three-stage theory of territory: '*Level 1*. At the lowest population density, territories are not circumscribed by competition. No individual is prevented from settling in the best habitat. *Level 2*. As the population density rises, some individuals are excluded from the optimal habitats and are forced to establish territories in the poorer habitable areas. *Level 3*. At the highest densities, some individuals are prevented from establishing territories altogether.'

60 Dæmon is a technical term in Monboddo's system meaning someone in the chain of being between God and us. So it is that Monboddo, *Antient Metaphysics* (New York: Garland Publishing [1779–99]), 4:267, explains the origin of language: 'That men do not speak naturally, but must have learned it by teaching or imitation, is evident; and it is as evident, that they could not have taught themselves, any more than dumb men could teach themselves. They must, therefore, have been taught by others; but these others must have been first taught themselves. Now, who taught them, since they could not teach themselves? And, I say, it was not men such as they were, or such as we are, but superior intelligences, such as the Dæmon Kings of Egypt were'. Also, *Origin*, 1:474, for the same point more delicately, since he does not claim that Thoth is dæmonic. In this context the fact that Monboddo neither accepts nor denies the Hebraic account of God giving language to Adam and Eve, Monboddo, *Origin*, 1:191–2 (on the grounds that he does not read Hebrew!), is not evidence for Monboddo's hard-headed skepticism but only for his participation in the Hermetic tradition.

The High One of the Hermetic tradition has better things to do with Her time than to teach language to beings such as us. Indeed, our world itself was not created by the Highest but by some dæmon. Remarkably enough, this story is the basis of David Hume's devasting attack on the 'proof' of God's existence from the evidence of design. The Creator, in Hume's counter-story, spent many years trying to live down this particular fiasco.

61 Donald Johanson and James Shreeve, *Lucy's Child* (New York: William Morrow, 1989), pp. 262–3, sketch a plausible cost/benefit calculus of why a species usually will not evolve a big brain. 'What a big brain gives you is *flexibility*. With a brain you are no longer a creature dependent on the moment, doomed to programmed responses that may or may not be equal to the task posed by the new challenges you face. . . . their cost is prohibitive. Modern humans spend about 20 percent of their metabolic energy keeping their brains running, as opposed to about 10 to 13 percent in a relatively cerebral nonhuman like a monkey'.

62 Robert Axelrod, *The Evolution of Cooperation* (New York: Basic Books, 1984), finds that 'tit for tat' is a winning strategy in part because his scoring system does not distinguish between early points and later points. If my time preference is such that I only care about the first round, 'tit for tat' always loses.

63 John Kagel, 'Giffen Goods and Intertemporal Consumption', Public Choice Wednesday Lecture, May 1989.

64 This is Charlie Plott's suggestion. And since Charlie has contributed so much to this chapter – he introduced me to experimental economics – he gets the last word.

65 The procedures to employ when one uses the data both to formulate and to test a hypothesis are described in Frederick Mosteller and John W. Tukey, *Data Analysis and Regression* (Reading, Mass.: Addison-Wesley, 1977).

Chapter 3 Utility-enhancing consumption constraints

1 Suppose one were to construct the indifference relation between consumption bundles by defining it in terms of a perception failure; that is, if there is no discernible difference (NDD) between states a and b, or aNDDb, then aIb. As intuitively plausible as this may be, it is flatly inconsistent with the usual axioms. Indifference so defined is not transitive. To see why this is so, consider a 'heap' of a commodity which, over a range, remains a 'heap' without discernible difference if one grain is removed. Let us start with a heap of size b, remove one grain at a time until n are removed, at which time the heap has become noticeably smaller. Although bNDD$b - 1$ NDD$b - 2$ . . . NDD$b - n$, it is not the case that bNDD$b - n$. This demonstrates intransitivity of NDD and hence indifference.

2 Oscar Morgenstern, 'Thirteen Critical Points in Contemporary Economic Theory', *Journal of Economic Literature* 10 (1972): 1163–89, considers the revealed preference approach one of the 'critical points' in modern economic theory.

3 The occurrences of 'ατη in early Greek literature are tabulated and discussed by Richard E. Doyle, *'ATH: Its Use and Meaning* (New York: Fordham University Press, 1984).

4 The bracketed Greek is from Homer, *Iliad*, edited and translated by A. T. Murray (Cambridge, Mass.: Loeb Classical Library, 1925).

5 Homer, *The Iliad of Homer*, translated by Richmond Lattimore (Chicago: University of Chicago Press, 1961), 19:86–95. E. R. Dodds, *The Greeks and the Irrational* (Berkeley: University of California Press, 1951), pp. 1–27, gives a widely cited analysis of 'psychic intervention' in the Homeric epics. Hugh Lloyd-Jones, *The Justice of Zeus* (Berkeley: University of California Press, 1971), pp. 8–27, discusses these texts from a different vantage.

6 *The Odyssey of Homer*, translated by Richmond Lattimore (New York: Harper Torchbook, 1967).

7 Gary Becker [1965], 'A Theory of the Allocation of Time', G. S. Becker, *The Economic Approach to Human Behavior* (Chicago: University of Chicago Press, 1976).

8 I provide a history of the Beckerian approach and a proposal to tighten the definition of Z goods in 'Diamonds, Water and Z Goods', *History of Political Economy* 14 (1982):

312–22. The results in the text are independent of the proposed redefinition.

9 It is useful to note that perceived real-income constant demand curves will be downward-sloping. This follows from the result which confines error to movement along the budget constraint. Changes in the budget constraint will change consumption in the usual direction.

10 Abraham Robinson, *Non-standard Analysis* (Amsterdam: North-Holland, revised edition, 1974).

11 Paul A. Samuelson, 'A Note on the Pure Theory of Consumers' Behavior' [1938], *Collected Scientific Papers*, edited by Joseph Stiglitz (Cambridge, Mass.: M.I.T. Press, 1966).

12 The supposition that the individual will not move outside the range of knowledge or perception, coupled with these continuity assumptions, allows us to show that when an individual moves along the budget constraint through space which must be explored, z is a continuous function of time.

13 Vernon Smith, 'Experimental Study of Exchange', Public Choice Seminar, October 1986.

14 R. Tyrrell Rockafellar, *Convex Analysis* (Princeton: Princeton University Press, 1970).

15 The weak axiom of revealed preference does not hold because the individual who chooses c at j but moves to a after arriving at c could have moved direct to a initially.

16 Once again we encounter perception failing; troubles befall mankind when the advice of Prometheus is disregarded. Liddell and Scott translate προμήθεια as 'foresight or forethought'.

17 Hesiod, *Works and Days*, translated by Richmond Lattimore (Ann Arbor: University of Michigan Press, 1959).

18 Kathleen Freeman, *Ancilla to the Pre-Socratic Philosophers* (Oxford: Blackwell's, 1971), p. 18.

19 The Presocratic fragments are from Freeman's *Ancilla*. Freeman provides a translation of the B fragments in H. Diels, *Die Fragmente der Vorsokratiker* so I shall provide the traditional Diels numbers, marked by ¶ in lieu of a page reference.

20 Democritus' notion of pleasure is discussed by J. C. B. Gosling and C. C. W. Taylor, *The Greeks on Pleasure*. (Oxford: Clarendon Press, 1984), pp. 27–37.

21 Democritus ¶9: 'Sweet exists by convention, bitter by convention, colour by convention; atoms and Void (*alone*) exist in reality . . . We know nothing accurately in reality, but (*only*) as it changes according to the bodily condition, and the constitution of those that flow upon (*the body*) and impinge upon it.'

22 Doubts expressed, Zeph Stewart, 'Democritus and the Cynics', *Harvard Studies in Classical Philology* 53 (1958): 179–91, about the reliability of Democritus' fragments depend, in part, on the assertion that Democritus' outlook differs radically from the main schools'. The account offered in the text finds Democritus' voice in harmony with the emphasis on constraint as an instrument to human goals.

23 Gosling and Taylor, *Greeks on Pleasure*, pp. 255–83, argue that Aristotle did not really escape Eudoxus' pleasure principle.

24 Joseph A. Schumpeter, *History of Economic Analysis* (New York: Oxford University Press, 1954), p. 57: '[Aristotle] therefore refused assent to the pleasure-and-pain doctrines about behavior that were gaining ground in the Greece of his day. But though he did not give a utilitarian definition of happiness, he placed the concept of happiness in the center of his social philosophy. Whoever does this has taken the decisive step and has committed the original sin: whether he then emphasizes virtue and vice or pleasure and pain is secondary – the way is smooth from the one to the other'.

25 Aristotle, *Nicomachean Ethics*, translated by H. Rackham (Cambridge, Mass.: Loeb Classical Library, 1934), 1097a31–b7.

26 The same translation is provided in Aristotle, *Nicomachean Ethics*, translated by W. D.

Ross and revised by J. O. Urmson, *The Complete Works of Aristotle*, edited by Jonathan Barnes (Princeton: Princeton University Press, 1984).

27 *N Ethics* 1111b7–10.

28 The example is Glaucus' trading gold armor for bronze, *Iliad* 6:236, discussed by Aristotle at *N Ethics*, 1136b10–13. What Dodds treats as divine intervention, *Greeks and the Irrational*, p. 4, Aristotle treats as 'unrestrained' action.

29 *N Ethics* 1111b13–16.

30 *N Ethics* 1112a15.

31 *N Ethics* 1139a22–30.

32 *N Ethics* 1172a25–b5.

33 *N Ethics* 1172b20–25.

34 *N Ethics* 1174a8–12.

35 *N Ethics* 1107a1–2.

36 *N Ethics* 1106b27–7a4.

37 Heraclitus ¶85.

38 Democritus ¶236.

39 *N Ethics* 1146a10–12: 'But a self-restrained man must necessarily have strong and evil desires; since if a man's desires are good, the disposition that prevents him from obeying them will be evil, and so Self-restraint will not always be good; while if his desires are weak and not evil, there is nothing to be proud of in resisting them; nor is it anything remarkable if they are evil and weak'.

   N Ethics 1146b31–b2: 'The profligate yields to his appetites from choice, considering it right always to pursue the pleasure that offers, whereas the man of defective self-restraint does not think so, but pursues it all the same'.

40 The quotation marks indicate that words of judgment are employed to describe the choice. Right conduct may or may not exist: for our empirical purposes all that matters is that 'right' conduct exists; that is, there is conduct which is described as 'right'. It would make no difference if the space inside the cone was said to be 'rational' and that outside was said to be 'irrational'. What is critical from a formal point of view is a determination of the issue when there is a violation of the P-cone, where the blame is laid. Is the P-cone rejected as a 'false' theory? Or is the choosing agent blamed for his action? Only in the latter case, where the P-cone is exempt from falsification by the existence of choices outside it, can it provide a guide to conduct.

   The theory which claims that the P-cone is 'rational' functions as normative theory as long as choice outside the P-cone is not cited as falsifying the hypothesis that only choice inside the P-cone is rational. Chapter 4 treats this consideration in detail.

41 Mike McPherson noted that in earlier versions I had not given a reason to preclude the individual from remaining at c, a point which appears to be a constrained maximum. To the extent that my account escapes this difficulty, this sort of morality cannot function simply as a mute constraint upon conduct. However, Chapter 6 considers another constraining morality which might function this way.

42 Even with convexity, a moral code could speed the time to equilibrium and thus reduce the costs to the consumer.

43 Abraham Charnes and William W. Cooper, 'Goal Programming and Multiple Objective Optimizations', *European Journal of Operational Research* 1 (1977): 39–54, and Abraham Charnes, William W. Cooper, Arie P. Schinnar and Nestor E. Terleckyj, 'A Goal Focusing Approach to Analysis of Trade-offs among Household Production Outputs', *Production of Well-being* (Washington: National Planning Association, 1979).

44 Arnold Kaufmann, *Introduction to the Theory of Fuzzy Subsets*, translated by D. L. Swanson (New York: Academic Press, 1975).

45 Kaufmann, *Fuzzy Subsets*, pp. 22–3.

46 The best known example of nonconvexity occurs in public goods problems and the associated prisoner's dilemma and is addressed elsewhere in the book. See also Jon

Elster, 'Weakness of Will and the Free-rider Problem', *Economics and Philosophy* 1 (1985): 231–65.

47 Thomas C. Schelling, *Choice and Consequence* (Cambridge, Mass.: Harvard University Press, 1984). Nonconvexity gives good reason to believe that consumption patterns will not be unimodal. This seems consistent with casual observation with regard to cigarette consumption. While many people do not smoke at all and many people smoke a pack a day, very few may smoke one cigarette a week. This prediction allows a test of the hypothesis that addiction problems are ultimately nonconvexities.

48 Jon Elster, *Ulysses and the Sirens* (Cambridge: Cambridge University Press, revised edition, 1984). Unfortunately, one of Elster's examples – 'Investment is perhaps the simplest example of a global maximization that requires bypassing a local maximum: one step backwards in order to take two steps forward' (p. 10) – is not correct with a capital market in which one can borrow on the future value of the investment. The details are found in Jack Hirshleifer, *Investment, Interest, and Capital* (Englewood Cliffs, N.J.: Prentice-Hall, 1970).

49 Needless to say, a society composed of Kantians would not be a full participant in this particular conversation because the utility-maximizing model cannot be easily employed for moral issues within a Kantian framework.

50 It is obvious that the improper integral of utility from now over the end of life diverges for any real valued utility. In some contexts, this is another way of saying that life has an infinite value.

51 Plato, *Protagoras*, translated by C. C. W. Taylor (Oxford: Clarendon Press, 1976). The argument is discussed by Martha C. Nussbaum, *The Fragility of Goodness* (Cambridge: Cambridge University Press, 1986), pp. 113–17, who stresses the importance of the claim that pleasure is homogeneous, that pleasure can be added up and moral issues reduced to what Jeremy Bentham would have called a hedonic calculus. This claim is necessary for Socrates' argument, but it is far from sufficient. The homogeneity condition would be satisfied with any rate of time preference: one could add up present and future pleasures with a rate of time preference of 100 percent as well as with a rate of time preference of 0 percent. Socrates' argument fails with a nonzero rate of time preference.

52 Ronald A. Heiner, 'The Origin of Predictable Behavior', *American Economic Review* 83 (1983): 560–95.

53 Alasdair MacIntyre, *After Virtue* (South Bend, Ind.: University of Notre Dame Press, 1981).

Chapter 4 Ethics and the basis of logic

1 Adam Smith, *Theory of Moral Sentiments*, edited by D. D. Raphael and A. L. Macfie (Oxford: Clarendon Press, 1976), pp. 17, 19.

2 *Correspondence of Adam Smith*, edited by Ernest Mossner and Ian Ross (Indianapolis: Liberty Classics, 1989), pp. 220–1.

3 Arthur Prior, *Logic and the Basis of Ethics* (Oxford: Clarendon Press, 1947), pp. 66–7. Prior's criticism, as far as I know, has never been challenged before. Could this answer Gilbert Harman's question of why philosophers have not paid all that much attention to Smith's moral theory? Gilbert Harman, *Moral Agent and Impartial Spectator* (Lawrence: University of Kansas Press, 1986).

4 *Logic and the Basis of Ethics*, p. 67.

5 *Logic and the Basis of Ethics*, p. 67.

6 Hao Wang, *Reflections on Kurt Gödel* (Cambridge, Mass.: M.I.T. Press, 1988), p. 188.

7 A participant in some of these debates, Hao Wang, *Beyond Analytic Philosophy* (Cambridge, Mass.: M.I.T. Press, 1986), p. 133, confesses puzzlement over exactly

what the issues were, who did what first, and asks for the services of a historian to clarify the issue! Good luck.

8 Ludwig Wittgenstein, *Tractatus Logico-philosophicus*, translated by D. F. Pears and B. F. McGuinness (London: Routledge & Kegan Paul, second edition, 1971), 6.113.

9 Rudolf Carnap, *Meaning and Necessity* (Chicago: University of Chicago Press, second edition, 1956), p. 175. More recently, Arthur W. Burks, *Chance, Cause, Reason* (Chicago: University of Chicago Press, 1977).

10 Rudolf Carnap, *Introduction to Semantics* (Cambridge, Mass.: Harvard University Press, 1948), p. 8: 'An investigation of a language belongs to *pragmatics* if explicit reference to a speaker is made; . . .'

11 Clarence Irving Lewis, *Collected Papers of Clarence Irving Lewis*, edited by John D. Goheen and John L. Mothershead, Jr. (Palo Alto: Stanford University Press, 1970), pp. 238–9. I owe this reference to Jeremy Shearmur.

12 Burks, *Chance, Cause, Reason*, p. 4 gives 'All swans are white' as an instance of an empirically false statement.

13 John G. Kemeny, 'Analyticity versus Fuzziness', *Form and Strategy in Science*, edited by John R. Gregg and F. T. C. Harris (Dordrecht: D. Reidel, 1964), pp. 125–6. Karl R. Popper, *Realism and the Aim of Science*, edited by W. W. Bartley, III (Totowa, N.J.: Rowman & Littlefield, 1983), p. xxi: 'Suppose, however, that there is someone who, when a non-white swan is shown to him, takes the position that it cannot be a swan, since it is "essential" for a swan to be white. Such a position amounts to holding non-white swans as logically impossible structures (and thus also as unobservable). It excludes them from the class of potential falsifiers. Relative to this *altered* class of potential falsifiers the statement "All swans are white" is of course unfalsifiable. In order to avoid such a move, we can demand that anyone who advocates the empirical–scientific character of a theory must be able to specify under what conditions he would be prepared to regard it as falsified . . .' Also, Karl R. Popper, *The Philosophy of Karl R. Popper*, edited by Paul Arthur Schilpp (La Salle, Ill.: Open Court, 1974), p. 982.

14 Carnap gave up his position very late in his life upon seeing a formal difficulty inside his system. David Kaplan, 'Homage to Carnap', *Rudolf Carnap, Logical Empiricist*, edited by Jaakko Hintikka (Dordrecht: D. Reidel, 1975), pp. xlvii–xlix: 'Then, with evident enthusiasm, he reflected that he had been quite wrong for about thirty years, and his critics who had been arguing that theories must be accepted or rejected as a whole (he mentioned at least Quine and Hempel) were very likely correct'. One burns candles to such integrity.

15 Pierre Duhem, *The Aim and Structure of Physical Theory*, translated by Philip P. Wiener (Princeton: Princeton University Press, 1954), pp. 183–90. Duhem's account of the history of physics is called by Karl Popper 'conventionalism' and labeled the strongest challenge to his own theory because it suffers from no internal inconsistencies. Karl R. Popper, *The Logic of Scientific Discovery*, translated by Karl R. Popper, Julius Freed and Lan Freed (London: Hutchinson & Co., 1974), pp. 78–81.

16 Willard Van Orman Quine, *From a Logical Point of View* (Cambridge, Mass.: Harvard University Press, second edition, 1961). Charles King started me reading Quine; it will be obvious to all what a difference this has made.

17 Alfred Tarski, *Logic, Semantics, Metamathematics*, translated by J. H. Woodger (Oxford: Clarendon Press, 1956), pp. 418–20. Tarski was, indeed, the one with whom Carnap was first arguing for his thesis. Carnap, *Semantics*, p. vii: 'I stress the distinction between factual truth, dependent upon the contingency of facts, and logical truth, independent of facts and dependent merely on meaning as determined by semantical rules. I believe that this distinction is indispensable for the logical analysis of science . . . Here again, Tarski seems to doubt whether there is an objective difference or whether the choice of a boundary line is not more or less arbitrary'. Popper, *Philosophy*,

p. 1096, discusses his attempt in 1946–8 to find a method of distinguishing factual and logical. As of 1974 Popper's position is 'I now think that Tarski's scepticism concerning a clear demarcation between logical and descriptive signs is well founded'.

18   Wang, *Gödel*, p. 65. F. P. Ramsey, *Philosophical Papers*, edited by D. H. Mellor (Cambridge: Cambridge University Press, 1990), p. 51.

19   Thomas S. Kuhn, *The Structure of Scientific Revolutions* (Chicago: University of Chicago Press, second edition, 1970); Imre Lakatos, 'Falsification and the Methodology of Scientific Research Programmes', *Criticism and the Growth of Knowledge*, edited by Imre Lakatos and Alan Musgrave (Cambridge: Cambridge University Press, 1970).

20   For example, in *Logic of Scientific Discovery*, Popper offers his view of science as a normative model of conduct and compares how conventionalists, those described by Duhem, and Popperians might respond to scientific shocks, p. 80: 'And periods when science develops slowly will give little occasion for conflict – unless purely academic – to arise between scientists inclined toward conventionalism and others who may favour a view like the one I advocate. It will be quite otherwise in a time of crisis. Whenever the 'classical' system of the day is threatened by the results of new experiments which might be interpreted as falsifications according to my point of view, the system will appear unshaken to the conventionalist. He will explain away the inconsistencies which may have arisen; perhaps by blaming our inadequate mastery of the system. Or he will eliminate them by suggesting *ad hoc* the adoption of certain auxiliary hypotheses, or perhaps of certain corrections to our measuring instruments. In such times of crisis this conflict over the aims of science will become acute. We, and those who share our attitude, will hope to make new discoveries; and we shall hope to be helped in this by a newly erected scientific system. Thus we shall take the greatest interest in the falsifying experiment'.

What is remarkable is how much of the discussion of 'normal' science and 'revolutionary' science which Thomas Kuhn made famous is found in this brief criticism of Duhem's work. Indeed, not-so-veiled accusations about Kuhn's debt to Duhem have been made. Stanley L. Jaki, *Uneasy Genius: The Life and Work of Pierre Duhem* (The Hague: Martinus Nijhoff Publishers, 1984), p. 370. Priority fights sprout like weeds here and such fights provide good evidence of the importance of these results to the philosophical literature.

21   Melvin W. Reder, 'Chicago Economics: Permanence and Change', *Journal of Economic Literature* 20 (1982): 1–38.

22   Abraham Hirsch and Neil de Marchi, *Milton Friedman, Economics in Theory and Practice* (Ann Arbor: University of Michigan Press, 1989). A 'rational reconstruction' of Ludwig von Mises' position along these lines is offered by Mario Rizzo, 'Mises and Lakatos', *Method, Process, and Austrian Economics*, edited by Israel M. Kirzner (Lexington, Mass.: Lexington Books, 1982).

23   A most instructive example is the von Neumann–Morgenstern 'expected utility' axioms which upon dramatic falsification by the Allais paradox became normative. See, for example, Mark J. Machina, '"Expected Utility" Analysis Without the Independence Axiom', *Econometrica* 50 (1982): 277–323, who struggles with the switch from positive to normative theorizing.

24   David M. Levy, 'Smith and Kant Respond to Mandeville', *Studies in Early Modern Philosophy* 2 (1988): 25–39.

25   Abraham Robinson, *An Introduction to Model Theory and the Metamathematics of Algebra* (Amsterdam: North-Holland, 1963).

26   Abraham Wald, *On the Principles of Statistical Inference* (South Bend, Ind.: University of Notre Dame Press, 1942), p. 1.

27   One of the most interesting controversies in recent years has been Abraham Charnes and W. W. Cooper's attack on econometric methodology, which usually supposes, without being willing to risk the supposition with a test, that optimization solutions leave tracks in the data. Operations researchers often can observe both the objective function

and the feasibility set. The operations research problem is precisely to find the minimum cost solution. One cannot suppose that it can be found in the world absent the intervention of operations researchers. A. Charnes, W. W. Cooper, T. Sueyoshi, *More on Breaking up Bell* (Austin: Center for Cybernetic Studies, 1988).

28 Willard Van Orman Quine, *From a Logical Point of View* (Cambridge, Mass.: Harvard University Press, second edition, 1961).

PART III THE SUPPLY OF IDEAS

Chapter 5 Adam Smith's 'natural law' and contractual society

1 The virtue of formulating the problem so is that we are not tempted to conclude that Smith believed that all free societies are harmonious; that they can survive without civil war. Smith clearly recognized that civil war was a fact of an earlier time in England when he discussed Hobbes's contributions to ethics: Adam Smith, *Theory of Moral Sentiments*, edited by A. L. Macfie and D. D. Raphael (Oxford: Clarendon Press, 1976), p. 318: 'The laws of the civil magistrate, therefore, ought to be regarded as the sole ultimate standards of what was just and unjust, of what was right and wrong. It was the avowed intention of Mr. Hobbs, by propagating these notions, to subject the consciences of men immediately to the civil, and not to the ecclesiastical powers, whose turbulence and ambition, he had been taught, by the example of his own times, to regard as the principal source of the disorders of society. . .'. If, in fact, the peace of society depends upon certain institutional facts, such as competition among religions, then readings of Smith which suppose him to argue for an organic society have neglected to explain how a society can be organic at times and mechanistic at other times. It is difficult to conceive of an organic society in formal terms (individual *i*'s mind depends upon the mind of individual *j*); it is even more difficult to conceive how an atomistic society (where individual *i*'s mind depends at most on the physical, hence observational, state of individual *j*) switches to and from an organic society. The classic statements of the organic society reading of Smith are L. A. Selby-Bigge, *British Moralists* (Oxford: Clarendon Press, 1897), 1:lix–lx; Glenn R. Morrow, *The Ethical and Economic Theories of Adam Smith* (New York: Longmans Green, 1923), p. 84. That reading has been revived by J. Ralph Lindgren, *The Social Philosophy of Adam Smith* (The Hague: Martinus Nijhoff, 1973), pp. 58–9.

2 Hayek has long emphasized that a common element among philosophers as diverse as Bernard Mandeville, David Hume and Adam Smith is their opposition to Hobbes's analysis, e.g., F. A. Hayek, *Law, Legislation, and Liberty* (Chicago: University of Chicago Press, 1973), 1:29–34; also, Jacob Viner, *The Role of Providence in the Social Order* (Philadelphia: American Philosophical Society, 1972), pp. 64–5.

3 Hume's opposition to any teleological connotation given to the word 'natural' is clear in his letter to Francis Hutcheson in July 1739: 'I cannot agree to your Sense of *Natural*. Tis founded on final Causes; which is a Consideration, that appears to me pretty uncertain & unphilosophical. For pray, what is the End of Man? Is he created for Happiness or for Virtue? For this Life or for the next? For himself or for his Maker? Your Definition of *Natural* depends upon solving these Questions, which are endless, & quite wide of my Purpose. I have never call'd Justice unnatural, but only artificial. . .'. *The Letters of David Hume*, edited by J. Y. T. Greig (Oxford: Clarendon Press, 1932), 1:33.

4 Frank Knight, *Ethics of Competition* (New York: Augustus M. Kelley, 1951), p. 20: 'If human wants are data in the ultimate sense for scientific purposes, it will appear that there is no place for ethical theory in the sense in which ethicists have conceived that subject, but that its place must be taken by economics'.

5 *Theory of Moral Sentiments*, p. 204. 'The different situations of different ages and countries, are apt, in the same manner, to give different characters to the generality of those who live in them, and their sentiments concerning the particular degree of each quality, that is either blameable, or praise-worthy, vary according to that degree, which is usual in their own country, and in their own times'. Adam Smith, *An Inquiry into the Nature and Causes of the Wealth of Nations*, edited by W. B. Todd (Oxford: Clarendon Press, 1976), p. 28. 'The difference of natural talents in different men is, in reality, much less than we are aware of; and the very different genius which appears to distinguish men of different professions, when grown up to maturity, is not upon many occasions so much the cause, as the effect of the division of labour.'

6 Hobbes, *Leviathan*, edited by C. B. Macpherson (Harmondsworth, England: Penguin Books, 1972), p. 186.

7 *Leviathan*, pp. 223–4. Emphasized by Viner, *Role of Providence*, pp. 62–3.

8 *Leviathan*, p. 190.

9 *Leviathan*, p. 223.

10 *Leviathan*, pp. 120–1.

11 *Leviathan*, pp. 169–70.

12 *Leviathan*, p. 75: 'But yet, me thinks, the endeavour to advance the Civill Power, should not be by the Civill Power condemned; nor private men, by reprehending it, declare that they think that Power too great . . .' Hobbes, p. 727, justifies the lack of classical citations on the ground that he is engaged in normative disputes: 'the matters in question are not of *Fact*, but of *Right*, . . .'. Thus, p. 728: 'Therefore I think it may be profitably printed, and more profitably taught in the Universities, in case they also think so, to whome the judgment of the same belongeth. For seeing the Universities are the Fountains of Civill, and Morall Doctrine, . . . there ought certainly to be great care taken, to have it pure, both from the Venime of Heathen Politicians, and from the Incantation of Deceiving Spirits. And by that means the most men, knowing their Duties, will be the less subject to serve the Ambition of a few discontented persons, in their purposes against the State; . . .'.

13 *Leviathan*, pp. 636–7.

14 *Leviathan*, pp. 691–2.

15 *Leviathan*, pp. 704–15.

16 *Leviathan*, pp. 177–8.

17 *Leviathan*, pp. 699–700.

18 *Theory of Moral Sentiments*, pp. 340–1.

19 Hobbes, *Leviathan*, p. 160: 'For there is no such *Finis ultimus*, (utmost ayme,) nor *Summum Bonum*, (greatest Good,) as is spoken of in the Books of the old Morall Philosophers. Nor can a man any more live, whose Desires are at an end, than he, whose Senses and Imaginations are at a stand. Felicity is a continuall progresse of the desire, from one object to another; . . .'.

20 *Leviathan*, p. 166.

21 *The Fable of the Bees*, edited by F. B. Kaye (Oxford: Clarendon Press, 1924), 2:128.

22 *Fable*, 2:220. Hector Monro's excellent work, *The Ambivalence of Bernard Mandeville* (Oxford: Clarendon Press, 1975), pp. 148–77, has gathered Mandeville's arguments on religion and cast a good deal of doubt on his sincerity. If, however, Mandeville did not accept the truth of Christian doctrine for the sake of the argument, his position that men are not influenced by Christian religion would lose much of its cogency. For example, what could be made of the following if Christian revelation were not accepted as true? Bernard Mandeville, *Free Thoughts on Religion, the Church and National Happiness* (London, 1720), pp. 146–7: 'CHRIST was the first, who plainly taught Men, that this World would be destroy'd and succeeded by another, where according as their behaviour was in this Life, they would be punish'd or rewarded for ever. . . . no Argument could be invented more cogent, to make Men of sound Reason to bear for so

short a space with any Suffering, that might be serviceable to attain such a Bliss, and reject all Pleasures, that might lead to such Miseries'. The thesis that Mandeville attacks a position that no one holds gives evidence of insufficient familiarity with John Locke's doctrine on this matter. These texts are discussed in Chapter 14.

23 Mandeville, *Free Thoughts*, p. 19: 'The worst of Sinners have their Fits of Devotion, and many of them will not only be very angry at a prophane Jest, or hearing any Thing ridicul'd they have a Religious Veneration for; but would likewise be desirous to make an atonement to GOD for their Crimes at any rate, except parting with their darling Lust. CHRISTIANS then are not bad for want of Faith, or of wishing to be Good; but because they are not able to overcome their Appetites, and curb their Passions . . .'.

24 *Fable*, 1:41–57, on the origin of moral virtue.

25 *Fable*, 1:151: 'I expect to be ask'd why in the Fable I have call'd those Pleasures real that are directly opposite to those which I own the wise Men of all Ages have extoll'd as the most valuable. My Answer is, because I don't call things Pleasures which Men say are best, but such as they seem to be most pleased with; . . .'

26 Hume argues that if there were general benevolence, justice would not be required. *A Treatise of Human Nature* (Oxford: Clarendon Press, 1888), p. 494.

27 *Treatise*, p. 480. T. D. Campbell, *Adam Smith's Science of Morals* (London: Allen and Unwin, 1971), p. 188, notes that Smith deals only with Hume's restricted concept of justice.

28 Hume, *Treatise*, p. 481.

29 *Treatise*, p. 484.

30 *Treatise*, pp. 478–80.

31 *Treatise*, pp. 478–80. To appreciate the argument, see David Lewis, *Convention* (Cambridge, Mass.: Harvard University Press, 1969).

32 *Treatise*, p. 490.

33 *Treatise*, p. 497.

34 *Treatise*, p. 521.

35 *Treatise*, p. 538: 'There is no quality in human nature, which causes more fatal errors in our conduct, than that which leads us to prefer whatever is present to the distant and remote, and make us desire objects more according to their situation than their intrinsic value'.

36 *Treatise*, p. 537: 'Here then is the origin of civil government and society. Men are not able radically to cure, either in themselves or others, that narrowness of soul, which makes them prefer the present to the remote. They cannot change their natures. All they can do is to change their situation, and render the observance of justice the immediate interest of some particular persons, and its violation their more remote'.

37 E.g., as argued in the entire *Dialogues Concerning Natural Religion*.

38 Examples abound in Hume's *History of England* (London, 1762), e.g., 1:80–2, 89–90, 166–8.

39 Hume, *Treatise*, p. 500.

40 Viner, *Role of Providence*, pp. 77–82.

41 *Theory of Moral Sentiments*, p. 136.

42 *Theory of Moral Sentiments*, p. 136.

43 *Theory of Moral Sentiments*, pp. 12–13.

44 *Theory of Moral Sentiments*, pp. 52–3.

45 Campbell, *Smith's Science*, p. 236.

46 This presupposes an expressive theory of voting. Susan Feigenbaum, Lynn Karoly and David Levy, 'When Votes are Words not Deeds: Evidence from the Nuclear Freeze Referendum', *Public Choice* 58 (1988): 201–16.

47 *Theory of Moral Sentiments*, p. 82: 'As every man doth, so shall it be done to him, and retaliation seems to be the great law which is dictated to us by nature'. Noted in Campbell, *Smith's Science*, pp. 158–9, 186.

48 *Theory of Moral Sentiments*, pp. 87–8.
49 *Theory of Moral Sentiments*, pp. 70–1.
50 *Theory of Moral Sentiments*, p. 91. The last sentence quoted in the text is not in the second edition, the edition which contains Smith's responses to Hume's criticism.
51 At least Smith's calculating criminal is not seriously bothered by the fear of Hell, *Theory of Moral Sentiments*, pp. 116–17.
52 *Theory of Moral Sentiments*, p. 319: 'The general maxims of morality are formed, like all other general maxims, from experience and induction. We observe in a great variety of particular cases what pleases or displeases our moral faculties, what these approve or disprove of, and, by induction from this experience, we establish those general rules'. This argument is improved in the *Wealth of Nations*, pp. 768–70, where specialization of moral philosophers brings well formulated moral systems.
53 *Theory of Moral Sentiments*, p. 163.
54 *Theory of Moral Sentiments*, p. 164.
55 *Theory of Moral Sentiments*, p. 116.
56 *Theory of Moral Sentiments*, p. 127.
57 *Theory of Moral Sentiments*, pp. 163–4.
58 *Theory of Moral Sentiments*, p. 170.
59 *Theory of Moral Sentiments*, p. 170.
60 *Theory of Moral Sentiments*, p. 176.
61 *Wealth of Nations*, p. 793.
62 *Wealth of Nations*, pp. 788–90.
63 *Wealth of Nations*, p. 759.
64 *Wealth of Nations*, pp. 266–7.
65 *Wealth of Nations*, pp. 785–8.
66 The majority of the population, laborers as well as landlords, have no incentive, in Smith's argument, to acquire information about the impact of the political process. *Wealth of Nations*, pp. 265–6.

Chapter 6 Who monitors the monitors?

1 Rent-seeking was introduced into the modern economics literature by Gordon Tullock, 'Charity of the Uncharitable', *Western Economic Journal* 9 (1971): 379–91.
2 Adam Smith, *An Inquiry into the Nature and Causes of the Wealth of Nations*, edited by W. B. Todd (Oxford: Clarendon Press, 1976), p. 791.
3 George Akerlof, 'The Market for "Lemons"', *Quarterly Journal of Economics* 84 (1970): 488–500.
4 *Wealth of Nations*, p. 808. Emphasis added.
5 *Wealth of Nations*, pp. 792–3. Emphasis added.
6 In particular, the previous chapter and Gary J. Anderson, 'Mr. Smith and the Preachers', *Journal of Political Economy* 96 (1988): 1066–88.
7 *Wealth of Nations*, p. 796. Jeremy Shearmur saw the highly visible hand of the state in this argument long before we did. Jeremy Shearmur, 'Adam Smith and the Cultural Contradictions of Capitalism', *Adam Smith's Legacy* (London: Adam Smith Institute, 1990).
8 *Wealth of Nations*, p. 796.
9 George J. Stigler, 'Smith's Travels on the Ship of State', *Essays on Adam Smith*, edited by Andrew S. Skinner and Thomas Wilson (Oxford: Clarendon Press, 1975).
10 We are thinking of Jacob Viner in particular. Viner read Smith as holding a harmony of interest doctrine in *Theory of Moral Sentiments* without counterpart in *Wealth of Nations*. Jacob Viner, 'Adam Smith and Laissez Faire', in J. M. Clark *et al.*, *Adam*

Smith 1776–1926 (Chicago: University of Chicago Press, 1928); *Guide to John Rae's 'Life of Adam Smith'* in John Rae, *Life of Adam Smith* [1895] (Fairfield, Ct.: Augustus M. Kelley, 1977); *The Role of Providence in the Social Order* (Philadelphia: American Philosophical Society, 1972).

11 Adam Smith, *Theory of Moral Sentiments*, edited by A. L. Macfie and D. D. Raphael (Oxford: Clarendon Press, 1976), pp. 134–6. Emphasis added.

12 *Wealth of Nations*, p. 124.

13 *Wealth of Nations*, pp. 124–5. Smith's otherwise puzzling defense of usury laws is intimately related to this supposed perception failure. David Levy, 'Adam Smith's Case for Usury Laws', *History of Political Economy* 19 (1987): 387–400.

14 *Theory of Moral Sentiments*, pp. 158–9.

15 *Theory of Moral Sentiments*, pp. 163.

16 *Theory of Moral Sentiments*, p. 159.

17 *Theory of Moral Sentiments*, p. 170.

18 *Theory of Moral Sentiments*, p. 176.

19 David Hume, *The History of England* (Indianapolis: Liberty Classics, 1983), 1:5–6: 'The religion of the Britons was one of the most considerable parts of their government; and the Druids, who were their priests, possessed great authority among them. . . . No species of superstition was ever more terrible than that of the Druids. Besides the severe penalties, which it was in the power of the ecclesiastics to inflict in this world, they inculcated the eternal transmigration of souls; and thereby extended their authority as far as the fears of their timorous votaries. They practised their rites in dark groves or other secret recesses; and in order to throw a greater mystery over their religion, they communicated their doctrines only to the initiated, and strictly forbad the committing of them to writing, lest they should at any time be exposed to the examination of the profane vulgar'. The same point was at issue in the debate over whether to provide the Bible in the vernacular, *History*, 3:231–3.

20 Hume has great respect for the time horizon considered by the Popes, *History* 1:214–15. Thus, a policy of encouraging superstition is something which cannot be taken casually; the Popes are not likely to act systematically contrary to their interests. He finds their power is augmented by ignorance and superstition. Writing about the First Crusade, *History* 1:237: 'Europe was at this time sunk into profound ignorance and superstition: The ecclesiastics had acquired the greatest ascendant over the human mind: The people, who, being little restrained by honour, and less by law, abandoned themselves to the worst crimes and disorders, knew of no other expiation than the observances imposed on them by their spiritual pastors . . .'. Thus it is that Hume is so interested in John Wickliffe, *History*, 2:326: 'He seems to have been a man of parts and learning, and has the honour of being the first person in Europe, that publicly called in question those principles, which had universally passed for certain and undisputed during so many ages.'

When the competition of ideas starts, there is no stopping it. In Hume's view, Henry VIII made a terrible mistake in stooping to theological controversy. Debating with Martin Luther was perilous in itself; however, even if Henry had triumphed in their exchange, the very fact that he had opened theology to debate posed a danger to the authority of future rulers of England, *History*, 3:290: 'he encouraged the people, by his example . . . to the study of theology; and it was in vain afterwards to expect . . . that they would cordially agree in any set of tenets or opinions prescribed to them'.

Monopoly power may also allow income extraction by the straightforward method of going on strike. Hume discusses the policy of interdict, *History*, 1:425–6. The clergy shut down public religion, relics were grounded, mass was stopped. The king's response, *History*, 1:426: 'to distress the clergy in the tenderest point, and at the same time expose them to reproach and ridicule, he threw into prison all their concubines, and required high fines as the price of their liberty'.

21 *Wealth of Nations*, pp. 266–7: 'Their superiority over the country gentleman is, not so much in their knowledge of the publick interest, as in their having a better knowledge of their own interest than he has of his. It is by this superior knowledge of their own interest that they have frequently imposed upon his generosity, and persuaded him to give up both his own interest and that of the publick, from a very simple but honest conviction, that their interest, and not his, was the interest of the publick.'

22 *Wealth of Nations*, p. 794.

23 *Theory of Moral Sentiments*, pp. 163–4.

24 *Wealth of Nations*, pp. 794–5.

25 *Wealth of Nations*, pp. 784–5.

26 E. R. Dodds, *The Ancient Concept of Progress* (Oxford: Clarendon Press, 1973), p. 142, discusses Greek religious organization. Henry Chadwick, *The Role of the Christian Bishop in Ancient Society*, edited by Edward C. Hobbs and Wilhelm Wuellner (Berkeley: Center for Hermeneutical Studies in Hellenistic and Modern Culture, 1980) details the monitoring activities of bishops.

27 *Wealth of Nations*, p. 795.

28 *Wealth of Nations*, p. 794.

29 *Wealth of Nations*, p. 796.

30 *Theory of Moral Sentiments*, pp. 202–3.

31 *Wealth of Nations*, p. 771.

32 *Wealth of Nations*, p. 794: 'In the liberal or loose system, luxury, wanton and even disorderly mirth, the pursuit of pleasure to some degree of intemperance, the breach of chastity, at least in one of the two sexes, &c. provided they are not accompanied with gross indecency, and do not lead to falsehood or injustice, are generally treated with a good deal of indulgence, and are easily either excused or pardoned altogether. In the austere system, on the contrary, those excesses are regarded with the utmost abhorrence and detestation'.

33 *Wealth of Nations*, p. 771.

34 *Wealth of Nations*, pp. 768–9.

35 *Wealth of Nations*, p. 770.

36 *Wealth of Nations*, p. 796.

37 *Wealth of Nations*, p. 795.

38 *Theory of Moral Sentiments*, p. 17: 'To approve of another man's opinions is to adopt those opinions, and to adopt them is to approve of them. If the same arguments which convince you convince me likewise, I necessarily approve of your conviction; and if they do not, I necessarily disapprove of it . . .'.

39 *Theory of Moral Sentiments*, p. 155.

40 This part of the argument is consistent with rational expectations theory. John F. Muth, 'Rational Expectations and the Theory of Price Movements', *Rational Expectations and Econometric Practice*, edited by Robert E. Lucas, Jr., and Thomas J. Sargent (Minneapolis: University of Minnesota Press, 1981).

41 Hume, *History*, 2:326: 'Wickliffe . . . was distinguished by a great austerity of life and manners, a circumstance common to almost all those who dogmatize in any new way, both because men, who draw to them the attention of the public, and expose themselves to the odium of great multitudes, are obliged to be very guarded in their conduct, and because few, who have a strong propensity to pleasure or business, will enter upon so difficult and laborious an undertaking'. *History*, 1:30: 'Augustine . . . attracted their attention by the austerity of his manners, by the severe pennances to which he subjected himself, by the abstinence and self-denial which he practised: And having excited their wonder by a course of life, which appeared so contrary to nature, he procured more easily their belief of miracles . . .'. *History*, 1:104: 'The monks were able to prevail in these assemblies . . . having been so fortunate as to obtain, by their pretended austerities, the character of piety, their miracles were more credited by the populace'.

42 *History*, 1:275: 'The cardinal, in a public harangue, declared it to be an unpardonable enormity, that a priest should dare to consecrate and touch the body of Christ immediately after he had risen from the side of a strumpet: For that was the decent appellation which he gave to the wives to the clergy. But it happened, that the very next night, the officers of justice, breaking into a disorderly house, found the cardinal in bed with a courtezan; an incident which threw such ridicule upon him, that he immediately stole out of the kingdom: The synod broke up; and the canons against the marriage of clergymen were worse executed than ever.' Martin Luther's break with the established order was set off by monks of his order selling indulgences. Here is what Hume tells us the money went for, *History*, 3:138: 'the collectors of this revenue are said to have lived very licentious lives, and to have spent in taverns, gaming-houses, and places still more infamous, the money, which devout persons had saved from their usual expences, in order to purchase a remission of their sins'.

43 *Wealth of Nations*, p. 769.

44 *Wealth of Nations*, pp. 769–70.

45 *Theory of Moral Sentiments*, pp. 238–9.

46 William Feller, *An Introduction to Probability Theory and its Applications* (New York: John Wiley, third edition, 1966).

47 Peter J. Huber, *Robust Statistics* (New York: John Wiley, 1981).

48 *Wealth of Nations*, pp. 793–4.

49 *Wealth of Nations*, pp. 792–3.

Chapter 7 Property, justice and judgment

1 Robert Nozick, *Anarchy, State, and Utopia* (New York: Basic Books, 1974), pp. 174–82.

2 W. W. Cooper once remarked that 'in one hundred years, no one will know why Professor So and So won a Nobel Prize, but then they didn't have to argue with him'. There is a similar puzzle: why was so little of Frank Ramsey's work taken seriously outside Cambridge until it was rediscovered piece by piece?

3 Testimony of the surprise is provided by Gordon Tullock, 'Theoretical Forerunners', James M. Buchanan and Gordon Tullock, *The Calculus of Consent* (Ann Arbor: University of Michigan Press, 1962), pp. 336–7.

4 Anthony Down, *An Economic Theory of Democracy* (New York: Harper & Row, 1957), p. 244.

5 As evidence of the vilification consider the scholarly debate over whether Filmer was attacked as a feint from the real issues. This affirmative is put forward by James Daly, *Sir Robert Filmer and English Political Thought* (Toronto: University of Toronto Press, 1979). The relevance of Filmer is defended by Blair Worden, 'The Commonwealth Kidney of Algernon Sidney', *Journal of British Studies* 24 (1985), p. 21: 'If we follow the findings of the most recent study of Filmer, by James Daly, then the concentration by those three writers, and by other Whig polemicists, on the author of *Patriarcha* seems puzzling. For Filmer, argues Daly, was "decidedly unimportant" in the Tory thought of the early 1680s. . . . The Whigs, in summoning so much heavy information against Filmer, were "busy getting him a reputation," in order to discredit mainstream royalism by association – although Daly implies that Sidney's attention to Filmer is to be explained by obtuseness rather than, as in Locke's case, by cunning'. Even though Worden dissents from Daly's charges of Locke's bad faith and Algernon Sidney's worse thinking in selecting Filmer for their target, even he, p. 21n107, worries: 'It is true that, after 1688, Sidney's concentration on Filmer came to seem a puzzle'. Richard Ashcraft, *Revolutionary Politics and Locke's 'Two Treatises of Government'*

(Princeton: Princeton University Press, 1986), p. 187, has useful things to say about this debate.

6 Robert Filmer, *Patriarcha*, edited by Peter Laslett (Oxford: Blackwell's, 1949), p. 92. Filmer, pp. 54–5, assumes that the government knows its own interests just as he might assume 'an implicit faith is given to the meanest artificer in his own craft'. Filmer's assumption that the offices are annual means only that he takes the practice of election by lot as characteristic of a democracy. He has the authority of Aristotle that this is so. A detailed discussion of the Athenian practice will be found below in Chapter 9.

7 J. A. W. Gunn, *Politics and the Public Interest in the Seventeenth Century* (London, 1969), p. 226, glances at this point, but, by smuggling group interest into the argument, misses the import of an argument from the large number prisoner's dilemma: 'In his best-known tracts, Robert Filmer derided the new idea that the public interest concerned as much the interests of ordinary men as it did the king's.'

8 Algernon Sidney, *Discourses Concerning Government* (London, 1696), p. 215, or Algernon Sidney, *Discourses Concerning Government*, edited by Thomas G. West (Indianapolis: Liberty Classics, 1990), p. 270.

9 Sidney, *Discourses*, p. 218.

10 Peter Laslett's evidence for the conjecture that Locke wrote the *Second Treatise* first is, in part, that in the *Second Treatise* Locke does not seem to know *Patriarcha*. Peter Laslett, 'Introduction', *Locke's Two Treatises of Government*, edited by Peter Laslett (Cambridge: Cambridge University Press, second edition, 1970), p. 58: 'it looks as if Locke must have been using the 1679 volume when he wrote ¶22 of the *Second Treatise* . . . And it looks as if he had reached that paragraph before even reading *Patriarcha*; indeed the text of the *Second Treatise*, although written against patriarchalism, could have been originally composed without his having seen *Patriarcha* at all'. Willmoore Kendall had 'guessed', 'John Locke Revisited', *Willmoore Kendall contra Mundum* (New Rochelle: Arlington House, 1971), p. 440, at this compositional order in 1941. Richard Ashcraft, *Locke's Two Treatises of Government* (London: Allen & Unwin, 1987), pp. 286–97, summarizes his long-standing dissent from Laslett's dating.

The relation between Laslett's conjecture and Locke's silence is very simple. The claim of rational ignorance is made late in *Patriarcha* and not, as far as I can see, in his other writings. The relevant chapter in Gordon J. Schochet, *Patriarchalism in Political Thought* (New York: Basic Books, 1975), pp. 115–35, considers material mainly outside *Patriarcha* and finds not a whiff of 'rational ignorance'. Thus, if Locke did not know *Patriarcha* until very late in the composition of the *Two Treatises* then he might not even have noticed the argument, or even if he had, he might not have had time to think it through.

11 There are, of course, other reasons given by Thomas G. West, 'Introduction', *Discourses Concerning Government*.

12 The commentary by Laslett in his edition is, in my opinion, decisive.

13 Robert Filmer, *Observations Concerning the Origin of Government* in *The Free-holder's Grand Inquest* (London, 1679), pp. 45–9, 70.

14 John Locke, *Locke's Two Treatises of Government*, edited by Peter Laslett (Cambridge: Cambridge University Press, second edition, 1970), *Second Treatise* ¶6: 'For Men being all the Workmanship of one Omnipotent, and infinitely wise Maker; . . . sent into the World by his order and about his business, they are his Property, whose Workmanship they are, made to last during his, not one anothers Pleasure. . . . Every one as he is *bound to preserve himself*, and not to quit his Station wilfully; so by the like reason when his own Preservation comes not in competition, ought he, as much as he can, *to preserve the rest of Mankind*'. Laslett's edition comes with many different page numbers so we adhere to the traditional section numbers. Thus 2dT¶x is to be decoded as *Second Treatise*, Section number x.

15 2dT¶25: 'God, as King *David* says . . . *has given the Earth to the Children of Men*, given it to Mankind in common'.

16 2dT¶26: 'God, who hath given the World to Men in common, hath also given them reason to make use of it to the best advantage of Life, and convenience'.

17 2dT¶28: 'And will any one say he had no right to those Acorns or Apples he thus appropriated, because he had not the consent of all Mankind to make them his? Was it a Robbery thus to assume to himself what belonged to all in Common? If such a consent as that was necessary, Man had starved notwithstanding the Plenty God had given him'.

18 2dT¶27: 'For this *Labour* being the unquestionable Property of the Labourer, no Man but he can have a right to what that is once joyned to, at least where there is enough, and as good left in common for others'.

19 2dT¶32: 'But the *chief matter of Property* being now not the Fruit of the Earth, and the Beasts that subsist on it, but the *Earth it self*; as that which takes in and carries with it all the rest: I think it is plain, that *Property* in that too is acquired as the former'.

20 2dT¶131: 'For no rational Creature can be supposed to change his condition with an intention to be worse'.

21 2dT¶33: 'Nor was this *appropriation* of any parcel of *Land*, by improving it, any prejudice to any other Man, since there was still enough, and as good left; and more than the yet unprovided could use'.

22 2dT¶37: 'To which let me add, that he who appropriates land to himself by his labour, does not lessen but increase the common stock of mankind'.

23 2dT¶39–40: 'supposing the *World* given as it was to the Children of Men *in common*, we see how *labour* could make Men distinct titles to several parcels of it, for their private uses; wherein there could be do doubt of Right, no room for quarrel. Nor is it so strange, as perhaps before consideration it may appear, that the *Property of labour* should be able to over-ballance the Community of Land. For 'tis *Labour* indeed that puts the *difference of value* on every thing . . . I think it will be but a very modest Computation to say, that of the *Products* of the Earth useful to the Life of Man 9/10 are the *effects of labour* . . .'.

24 2dT¶37: 'But if they perished, in his Possession, without their due use . . . he offended against the common Law of Nature, and was liable to punished; he invaded his Neighbour's share, for he had *no right, farther than his Use* called for any of them'.

25 David Hume, *A Treatise of Human Nature*, edited by L. A. Selby-Bigge (Oxford: Clarendon Press, 1888), p. 493. John Dunn, 'The Politics of Locke in England and America', in John W. Yolton, editor, *John Locke: Problems and Perspectives* (Cambridge: Cambridge University Press, 1969), pp. 60–2, holds that Hume's objections are nothing more than a quarrel with the realism of the state of nature model.

26 *Treatise*, p. 494.

27 *Treatise*, p. 494.

28 *Treatise*, p. 495.

29 The same theory is present in *History*. Hume often emphasizes the importance of making land holdings stable, e.g., *History*, 1:46: 'Ina, his successor, inherited the military virtues of Ceodwalla, and added to them the more valuable ones of justice, policy, and prudence . . . he treated the vanquished with a humanity, hitherto unknown to the Saxon conquerors. He allowed the proprietors to retain possession of their lands . . .'. Also, *History*, 1:457–8.

30 Hume, *Treatise*, p. 537: 'men cure their natural weakness, and lay themselves under the necessity of observing the laws of justice and equity, notwithstanding their violent propension to prefer contiguous to remote . . . the utmost we can do is to change our circumstances and situation, and render the observance of the laws of justice our nearest interest, and their violation our more remote . . . Here then is the origin of civil government and allegiance'. There is a wonderful argument in the *History* that criminal

fines paid to the government increased its concern for the administration of justice, 1:175–6: 'The magistrate, whose office it was to guard public peace . . . conceived himself to be injured by every injury done to any of his people; and beside the compensation to the person who suffered, or to his family, he thought himself entitled to exact a fine . . . The numerous fines which were levied, augmented that revenue of the king: And the people were sensible, that he would be more vigilant in interposing with his good offices, when he reaped such immediate advantage from them . . .'. Hume defends pecuniary punishment against 'a false appearance of lenity' at 1:359. Although he does not comment on the issue, it is hard to imagine what benefit the government received from amputation, the new form of punishment for criminals.

31 Adam Smith, *An Inquiry into the Nature and Causes of the Wealth of Nations*, edited by W. B. Todd (Oxford: Clarendon Press, 1976), p. 65: 'In that early and rude state of society which precedes both the accumulation of stock and the appropriation of land, the proportion between the quantities of labour necessary for acquiring different objects seems to be the only circumstance which can afford any rule for exchanging them for one another.' And at p. 67: 'As soon as the land of any country has all become private property, the landlords, like all other men, love to reap where they never sowed, and demand a rent even for its natural produce. The wood of the forest, the grass of the field, and all the natural fruits of the earth, which, when land was in common, cost the labourer only the trouble of gathering them, come, even to him, to have an additional price fixed upon them. He must then pay for the licence to gather them; and must give up to the landlord a portion of what his labour either collects or produces'.

For some true radicalism, Smith, 'Early Draft of Part of *The Wealth of Nations*', *Lectures on Jurisprudence*, edited by R. L. Meek, D. D. Raphael and P. G. Stein (Oxford: Clarendon Press, 1978), pp. 563–4: 'But with regard to the produce of the labour of a great society there is never any such thing as a fair and equal division. In a society of an hundred thousand families, there will perhaps be one hundred who don't labour at all, and yet, either by violence or by the more orderly oppression of law, employ a greater part of the labour of society than any other ten thousand in it'.

32 Gladys Bryson, *Man and Society* (Princeton: Princeton University Press, 1945), p. 11, and Garry Wills, *Inventing America* (Garden City: Doubleday, 1978), pp. 149–50.

33 [Francis Hutcheson], *An Inquiry into the Original of our Ideas of Beauty and Virtue* (London, 1725), p. 111.

34 *Beauty and Virtue*, p. 129.

35 *Beauty and Virtue*, p. 170.

36 *Beauty and Virtue*, pp. 129–30.

37 *Beauty and Virtue*, p. 176.

38 *Beauty and Virtue*, p. 159.

39 [Francis Hutcheson], *An Essay on the Nature and Conduct of the Passions and Affections* (London, 1728), p. xv.

40 *Passions and Affections*, p. 65.

41 *Passions and Affections*, p. 201.

42 [Lord Kames, Henry Home], *Essays on the Principles of Morality and Natural Religion* (Edinburgh, 1751), p. 55.

43 *Principles*, p. 105.

44 *Principles*, p. 381.

45 Francis Hutcheson, *A System of Moral Philosophy* (Glasgow, 1755), p. 320.

46 *Moral Philosophy*, p. 321.

47 *Moral Philosophy*, p. 329.

48 *Moral Philosophy*, p. 314.

49 Adam Smith, *Theory of Moral Sentiments*, edited by A. L. Macfie and D. D. Raphael (Oxford: Clarendon Press, 1976), pp. 137.

50 *Theory of Moral Sentiments*, p. 82.

51 *Theory of Moral Sentiments*, p. 175. The passage continues, contrasting the sharp rules of justice with fuzzy rules of other moral virtues.

52 R. Mark Isaac and James M. Walker, 'Communication and Free-riding Behavior', *Economic Inquiry* 26 (1988): 585–608.

53 Henry Chadwick, *The Role of the Christian Bishop in Ancient Society*, edited by Edward C. Hobbs and Wilhelm Wuellner (Berkeley: Center for Hermeneutical Studies in Hellenistic and Modern Culture, 1980), p. 5: 'His [the bishop's] share (normally a quarter of the offerings of the faithful) of the church treasury was also the resource on which he called for supporting the poor, the protection of whom was one of his prime responsibilities. In the fifties of the third century the community in Rome had on its payroll one bishop, 46 presbyters, 7 deacons, 7 sub-deacons, 42 acolytes, 52 exorcists, readers, and door-keepers, and more than 1500 widows and distressed persons'.

54 Chadwick, *Role of the Christian Bishop*, p. 13: 'A rich man might build a splendid church and then seem a natural candidate for election to the bishopric'.

55 For those who know his present stature in Christian theology, it will seem yet another irony that the great opponent of this practice was Origen. Indeed, evidence of how widespread the practice of 'auction' was comes, in part, from Origen's recommendation that office seekers be selected by lot as a device to cut down the costs of bribes, Robin Lane Fox, *Pagans and Christians* (New York: Alfred A. Knopf, 1986), p. 514.

56 Chapter 18 goes through these problems.

57 A. K. Sen, *Ethics and Economics* (Oxford: Blackwell's, 1987).

PART IV EQUILIBRIUM IDEAS

Chapter 8 Rational choice in the Homeric epics

1 The early controversy is studied in David M. Levy, 'Rational Choice and Morality', *History of Political Economy* 14 (1982): 1–36.

2 In a Sather lecture, M. I. Finley considers Greek discussions of both private and public activity. Here is his report of the analysis of private activity. M. I. Finley, *The Ancient Economy* (Berkeley: University of California Press, 1973), pp. 19–20: 'In Xenophon, however, there is not one sentence that expresses an economic principle or offers any economic analysis, nothing on efficiency of production, "rational" choice, the marketing of crops. The Roman agricultural manuals (and no doubt their lost Greek forerunners) do occasionally consider marketing and soil conditions and the like, but they never rise above rudimentary common-sense observations (when they do not simply blunder or mislead)'. Public issues fare no better, pp. 20–1: 'Since revenues loom so large in the affairs of a state, it is not surprising that occasionally *oikonomia* also was used to mean the management of public revenues. The one Greek attempt at a general statement is the opening of the second book of the pseudo-Aristotelian *Oikonomikos*, and what is noteworthy about these half a dozen paragraphs is not only their crashing banality but also their isolation in the whole of surviving ancient writing'.

3 Joseph A. Schumpeter, *History of Economic Analysis*, (New York: Oxford University Press, 1954), pp. 53–4: 'They merged their pieces of economic reasoning with their general philosophy of state and society and rarely dealt with an economic topic for its own sake. This accounts, perhaps, for the fact their achievement in this field was so modest, especially if compared with their resplendent achievement in others . . . most statements of fundamental facts acquire importance only by the superstructures they are made to bear and are commonplace in the absence of such superstructures. Such as they were, the scientific splinters of Greek economic thought that are accessible to us may

be gleaned from the works of Plato . . . and Aristotle'. Even a sharp critic of the Finley and Schumpeter approach does not dispute their result that there is no neoclassical economics to be found in the Greek texts, Scott Meikle, 'Aristotle and the Political Economy of the Polis', *Journal of Hellenic Studies* 99 (1979): 52–73.

The full-scale attempt by S. Todd Lowry, *The Archaeology of Economic Ideas* (Durham, N.C.: Duke University Press, 1987) to establish a Greek economics gives definitive evidence of the importance of utility-maximizing considerations to the Greek discussion. All else is a matter of details.

4 Donald N. McCloskey, 'The Rhetoric of Economics', *Journal of Economic Literature* 21 (1983): 481–517, and *If You're So Smart* (Chicago: University of Chicago Press, 1990).

5 The relation between narrative style and the requirements for memorization are discussed in Eric A. Havelock, *The Greek Concept of Justice* (Cambridge, Mass.: Harvard University Press, 1978). Below, we quote the sad tale of a singer who dared compare himself favorably with the Muses. For his punishment he was made a singer without memory.

6 Samuel Eliot Bassett, *The Poetry of Homer* (Berkeley: University of California Press, 1938), p. 130: 'Homer's rule is this: in the nexus of important actions, to make the most careful preparations and the most convincing explanations; but in details, especially when these merely heighten the effect of an otherwise impressive moment, to neglect motivation and often to omit it altogether . . . Homer *makes the listener supply the motivation*'.

7 M. M. Willcock, 'Some Aspects of the Gods in the *Iliad*', *Essays on the Iliad*, edited by John Wright (Bloomington: Indiana University Press, 1978).

8 Walter Burkert, *Structure and History in Greek Mythology and Ritual* (Berkeley: University of California Press, 1979).

9 Richmond Lattimore, 'Introduction', *The Iliad of Homer* (Chicago: University of Chicago Press, 1951), p. 54: 'The gods of Homer are mainly immortal men and women, incomparably more powerful than mortals, but like mortals susceptible to all human emotions and appetites . . .'

10 Sappho, No. 151, translated by Guy Davenport, *Archilochos, Sappho, Alkman* (Berkeley: University of California Press, 1980): 'To die is evil/The gods think so,/Else they would die.'

11 Martin P. Nilsson, *A History of Greek Religion* [1925], translated by F. J. Fielden (Oxford: Clarendon Press, 1952), p. 158: 'In point of fact there are in Homer three anthropomorphic classes. The distinction between the two lower, the nobility and the people, is no less clear than the distinction between the two upper, the nobility and the gods.' Martin Persson Nilsson, *Greek Piety*, translated by Herbert Jennings Rose (Oxford: Clarendon Press, 1948), p. 20: 'It has been said that in Homer there are three classes of human beings, the common people, the nobles, and the gods. This would be correct if the gods were not immortal. A sharp distinction is made between gods and men, and to try to overstep it is *hybris*, . . . any such attempt being severely punished'.

12 George J. Stigler and Gary S. Becker, 'De Gustibus Non Est Disputandum', *American Economic Review* 67 (1977): 76–90.

13 Jenny Strauss Clay, *The Wrath of Athena* (Princeton: Princeton University Press, 1983), p. 236.

14 James George Frazer, *The Golden Bough* (London: Macmillan, third edition, 1917), 1:31: '[. . . in] ancient religion in general [t]he gods stood as much in need of their worshippers as the worshippers in need of them. The benefits conferred were mutual. If the gods made the earth to bring forth abundantly, the flocks and herds to teem, and the human race to multiply, they expected that a portion of their bounty should be returned to them in the shape of tithe or tribute'.

15 *The Odyssey*, translated by Richmond Lattimore (New York: Harper Torchbooks,

1967), 13.128–9: The reaction of the gods to human competition will be documented below.

16 Hesiod, *Theogony* 391ff. Aeschylus, *Prometheus Bound*, translated by David Greene, *The Complete Greek Tragedies*, edited by David Greene and Richmond Lattimore (Chicago: University of Chicago Press, 1959), 36–8 (Might to Hephaestus): 'Why is it that you do not hate a God whom the Gods hate most of all? Why do you not hate him, since it was your honor that he betrayed to men?'.

17 The competition for cities is clear; there seems controversy about who adjudicated between the gods: men or gods. Apollodorus, *The Library*, translated by James George Frazer (Cambridge, Mass.: Loeb Classical Library, 1921), III.xiv.1: 'the gods resolved to take possession of cities in which each of them should receive his own peculiar worship. So Poseidon was the first that came to Attica, and with a blow of his trident on the middle of the acropolis, he produced a sea . . . After him came Athena, . . . planted an olive-tree . . . But when the two strove for possession of the country, Zeus parted them and appointed arbiters, not, as some have affirmed, Cecrops and Cranaus, nor yet Erysichton, but the twelve gods. And in accordance with their verdict the country was adjudged to Athena . . . Poseidon in hot anger flooded the Thriasian plain and laid Attica under the seas'. Frazer, 'Note 1' to this passage: 'The unlucky Poseidon also contested the possession of Argos with Hera, and when the judges gave a verdict against him and in favour of the goddess, he took revenge, as in Attica, by flooding the country'.

18 *Iliad* 24.28–30. *Cypria*, translated by Hugh G. Evelyn-White, *Hesiod, The Homeric Hymns and Homerica* (Cambridge, Mass.: Loeb Classical Library, 1977), p. 491: 'The three are led by Hermes at the command of Zeus to Alexandrus on Mount Ida for his decision, and Alexandrus, lured by his promised marriage with Helen, decides in favour of Aphrodite'. Since I suppose below that those parts of the epic cycle which did not become part of the Homeric canon are evolutionary failures, it is important to verify all the stories in the cycle with texts in the canon. Cf. Malcolm Davies, 'The Judgement of Paris and *Iliad* Book XXIV', *Journal of Hellenic Studies* 101 (1981): 56–62.

19 Apollodorus, *Library*, I.viii.2: 'In sacrificing the firstfruits of the annual crops of the country to all the gods Oeneus forgot Artemis alone. But she in her wrath sent a boar of extraordinary size and strength, which prevented the land from being sown and destroyed the cattle and the people that fell in with it'.

Is this why actual Greek community sacrifices were to groups of gods? The larger the offering to a single god, the more this individual god would move up status and the more gods would move down status ranks and thus be offended. Walter Burkert, *Greek Religion*, translated by John Raffan (Cambridge, Mass.: Harvard University Press, 1985), pp. 216–17: 'The facts of the cult are unmistakable: at festivals of the gods, sacrifice is regularly made not to one god but to a whole series of gods. The Attic calendars of sacrifices in particular show this even for the individual villages and even more so for the city as a whole'. Burkert, p. 150, discusses Euripides' *Hippolytos*: 'But his exclusive devotion to [Artemis] is in violation of the rules which govern human life, and so he falls victim to Aphrodite'.

20 *Odyssey* 5.99–103. Homer can do 'comparative static' analysis. Here is what would happen if people had different time use constraints, *Odyssey* 10.82–6: 'one herdsman, driving/his flocks in hails another, who answers as he drives/his flocks out; and there a man who could do without sleep could earn him/double wages, one for herding the cattle, one for the silvery/sheep'.

21 Zeus faces other, more complicated constraints. He cannot bed Thetis without risking the prophecy that she will have a son who is greater than his father, Aeschylus, *Prometheus Bound* 768. Night, a power from an older regime, has power over the newer gods which Zeus cannot ignore, *Iliad* 14.259.

22 Emily Vermeule, *Aspects of Death in Early Greek Art and Poetry* (Berkeley: University of California Press, 1979), pp. 123–4: 'Caged in their unending existence, the Homeric gods still manage to join men in suffering from fear, anger, spite, lack of discipline, overwhelming erotic impulses, greed and anxiety. In epic, the gods have . . . a sense of not knowing the right course of action because the future is unclear . . . When men are extremely depressed . . . they can wish for death to end a life of misery, but the gods are not so lucky. Zeus cannot always control events or protect his children'.

23 Later poets in the monotheistic tradition had an easy answer for this: lies, all lies. *Callimachus*, translated by Stanley Lombardo and Diane Rayor (Baltimore: Johns Hopkins University Press, 1988), 'Hymn to Zeus', 80–3: 'Old poets lie when they say that the lot/assigned triplicate homes to the sons of Kronos./Who would play dice for Olympos and Hades/except a green novice?' The notes to this translation do not remark how bizarre it is that this legendary scholar cannot remember this text from the *Iliad*; Olympos was not part of the gamble, it was to be held in common by all the gamblers. This textual inexactitude does help the argument flow at 85–7: 'A poet's fiction should at least be plausible./Not the luck of the draw made you shah of the gods/but Strength in your hands'. The use of the Persian word in the translation does help emphasize how foreign is this autocratic account of Zeus.

24 Chapter 9 goes into this in detail.

25 *Iliad*, translated by Richmond Lattimore (Chicago: University of Chicago Press, 1951), 14.237–41. Malcolm M. Willcock, *A Companion to the Iliad* (Chicago: University of Chicago Press, 1976), p. 160: 'The common prayer formula (cf. 1.39) comes rather strangely from the queen of the gods'.

26 *Odyssey* 8.344–8, 355–6: 'there was no laughter for Poseidon, but he kept entreating/Hephaistos, the famous craftsman, asking him to set Ares/free, and spoke aloud to him and addressed him in winged words:/"Let him go, and I guarantee he will pay whatever/you ask, all that is approved among the immortal deities/ . . . if Ares goes off and escapes, not paying/anything he may owe you, then I myself will pay it"'.

27 *Iliad*, 1.35–41. The consequences of not sacrificing are discussed at 9.497–512. Richard Posner, 'The Homeric Version of the Minimal State', *The Economics of Justice* (Cambridge, Mass.: Harvard University Press, 1983), notes that the government does not enforce security of property or persons. Why should it while the gods are willing to carry out the enforcement for thigh bones?

28 *Iliad* 1.43–52. Apollo's action surely cannot result from any great concern over the fate of men, 21.462–6.

29 *Iliad* 2.514–15: 'a modest maiden; she went into the chamber/with strong Ares, who was laid in bed with her secretly'. Also, *Odyssey* 11.241–5.

30 Poseidon to Zeus, *Iliad* 7.448–53: 'Do you not see now how these flowing-haired Achaians/have built a wall landward of their ships, and driven about it/a ditch, and not given to the gods any grand sacrifice?/Now the fame of this will last as long as dawnlight is scattered,/and men will forget that wall which I and Phoibos Apollo/built with our hard work for the hero Laomedon's city.' Zeus allows Poseidon to destroy the wall at 7.459–63, which he does at 12.17–33.

31 *Iliad* 2.597–600: 'for he boasted that he would surpass, if the very Muses,/daughters of Zeus who holds the aegis, were singing against him,/and these in their anger struck him maimed, and the voice of wonder/they took away, and made him a singer without memory . . .' Apollodorus, *The Library*, I.iv.2: 'Apollo also slew Marsyas, the son of Olympus. For Marsyas, having found the pipes which Athena had thrown away because they disfigured her face, engaged in a musical contest with Apollo.' I.iv.3: 'He first married Side, whom Hera cast into Hades because she rivalled herself in beauty.' I.vii.4: 'These perished by reason of their pride; for he said that his wife was Hera, and she said that her husband was Zeus'.

Clay, *Wrath*, explains the wrath of Athene by divine fear of Odysseus' wit, p. 209:

'To put it simply, if not too crudely, *Odysseus is too clever; his intelligence calls into question the superiority of the gods themselves.*' If Odysseus could trick the gods for more life, this motivates Athene's outrage, contra to the explanation presented in *The Sack of Ilium* and *Trojan Women*.

32 *Iliad* 1.261–72: 'in my time I have dealt with better men than/you are, and never once did they disregard me. Never/yet have I seen nor shall see again such men as these were,/ . . . These were the strongest generation of earth-born mortals,/the strongest, and they fought against the strongest, the beast men/living within the mountains, and terribly they destroyed them./ . . . against such men no one/of the mortals now alive upon earth could do battle'.

33 *Iliad* 21.441–54: 'Can you not even/now remember all the evils we endured by Ilion,/you and I alone of the gods, when to proud Laomedon/we came down from Zeus and for a year were his servants/for a stated hire, and he told us what to do, and to do it?/Then I built a wall for the Trojans about their city,/ . . . But when the changing seasons brought on the time for our labour/to be paid, then headstrong Laomedon violated and made void/all our hire, and sent us away, and sent threats after us./For he threatened to hobble our feet and to bind our arms,/to carry us away for slaves in the far-lying islands'. This and other citations are provided by Vermeule, *Aspects of Death*, pp. 125–6. Posner, 'Homeric Version', p. 124, cites the fact that the gods built the wall as evidence that the Trojan government did not provide public defense. Surely, what is relevant is who financed the wall, not the identity of the contractor.

34 Book 5 of the *Iliad* is full of examples of mortals who have imposed pain on immortals.

35 *Odyssey* 10.573–4: 'Whose eyes can follow the movement/of a god passing from place to place, unless the god wishes?'

36 *Iliad* 5.127–8: 'I have taken away the mist from your eyes, that before now/was there, so that you may well recognize the god and the mortal'. The latter condition is important because once the mist is back in place, what is to prevent him from being destroyed, *à la* Lykourgos, after a temporary victory? C. M. Bowra, *Homer* (New York: Scribner, 1972), pp. 34–5.

37 E. R. Dodds, *The Greeks and the Irrational* (Berkeley: University of California Press, 1951), pp. 29–30.

38 *Iliad* 15:193–5.

39 An example of this sort of holistic analysis is found in James M. Redfield, *Nature and Culture in the 'Iliad'* (Chicago: University of Chicago Press, 1975), p. 132: 'Men and cities are the counters in a game played between the gods. The game can become absorbing, but it is never really worth a quarrel. The gods can always repair their differences by allowing the destruction of another ephemeral human thing. The fall of Troy thus becomes an emblem of the fall of Mycenaean civilization; all the cities will perish as, one after another, they happen to become the objects of divine anger. Whatever man does, in prayer and sacrifice, temples and feasting, is in the end not enough.'

40 Cedric H. Whitman, *Homer and the Heroic Tradition* (Cambridge, Mass.: Harvard University Press, 1958), p. 225: 'It is commonly observed that Zeus in the *Odyssey* defends universal justice, while in the *Iliad* he is arbitrary, even violent, and controlled by nothing, except "fate", . . . The impression of arbitrary force and irresponsibility rests upon one, and only one, thing which Zeus does: his defense of Achilles' cause'. A similar conclusion is reached by Hugh Lloyd-Jones, *The Justice of Zeus* (Berkeley: University of California Press, 1971).

41 *Iliad* 1.396–401, 407. Willcock, *Companion*, p. 11: 'Homer requires a reason for Zeus to be under an obligation to Thetis and therefore creates one . . .'. G. S. Kirk, *The Iliad: A Commentary* (Cambridge: Cambridge University Press, 1985), p. 93, discussing 1.399: 'There is no other reference in Homer or in later poets to this particular act of *lèse-majesté*, which has one or two points in common with the tale of

Ares being tied up in a jar for thirteen months (although by mortals) at 5.385–91'. Also, p. 94: 'Homer, naturally, concentrates on Zeus's eventual supremacy rather than on the details of his early struggles; even so, Thetis' reminiscence is unusual, and there is no hint in Zeus's confident remarks elsewhere that the gods had ever presented a real threat to him, as the present passage suggests'.

42 Some commentators, disturbed by Zeus' failure to enforce the oath in the near term, see the sack of Troy as its eventual punishment. Unfortunately, this reading would allow Paris' rape of Helen to escape without punishment. Troy can only be sacked for one crime; the others are accounts left unsettled. Posner, 'Homeric Version', p. 131, claims that Hektor and Priam do not have sufficient authority to extricate the Trojans from the war by returning Helen. Nevertheless, they force Paris to duel with Menelaos to settle the issue. Zeus has a debt to pay, so divine intervention keeps the war going.

43 *Iliad* 3.298–302. Jasper Griffin, *Homer on Life and Death* (Oxford: Clarendon Press, 1980), p. 169: 'Even grimmer, when both sides pray for a just outcome to the duel between Paris and Menelaos, "So they spoke, but Zeus did not yet grant their prayer." The plans and purposes of gods can be inscrutable'. Redfield, *Nature and Culture*, p. 131, finds the gods frivolous: 'We, who see the gods among themselves, can follow the shifting but coherent process which gives rise to their interventions; we find the gods less erratic but more willful, more frivolous. It is a part of the terror of the *Iliad* that it shows us a world in which human action is conditioned by powers and purposes less serious and less moral than our own'.

44 *Iliad* 18.394–8, 406–8. Willcock, *Companion*, p. 208: 'this is an invented story, to give Hephaistos an obligation to Thetis that will cause him to accede to her request. In this it is exactly parallel to the obligation of Zeus created in 1.396–406.' Kirk, *Commentary*, p. 113, discussing 1.586–94: 'The exegetical scholium in A reminds us that there were "two throwings of Hephaistos", since at 18.394–9 he thanks Thetis for saving him when his mother Here . . . threw him out of Olumpos because he was lame. There were presumably two variant and in fact contradictory stories to account for his lameness; the monumental composer uses both of them, at a long interval in the poem, to motivate first Hephaistos' role as mediator between Here and Zeus, and then his special gratitude to Thetis'.

45 In Carpenter's reconstruction of the *Cypria* this debt is settled at the wall of Troy. Rhys Carpenter, *Folk Tale, Fiction and Saga in the Homeric Epics* (Berkeley: University of California Press, 1946), p. 56: 'In the *Iliad*, Athena assumes the likeness of the Trojan Deiphobos and in this guise persuades Hector to take his stand against Achilles, then promptly vanishes, leaving her dupe to face his destroyer alone. In the Teuthranian version, Dionysos magically causes a vine to spring and trip the fleeing Telephos, so that Achilles can overtake and sorely wound him'.

46 *Iliad* 6.130–6.

47 *Odyssey* 24.73–6. This transaction is discussed in isolation from payment for Thetis' other obligations by Walter F. Otto, *Dionysus*, translated by Robert B. Palmer (Bloomington: Indiana University Press, 1965), pp. 56–7. Patroklos' ghost requests interment of this vase at *Iliad* 23.91–2.

48 G. S. Kirk, *The Songs of Homer* (Cambridge: Cambridge University Press, 1962), p. 248: '"Aristophanes and Aristarchus make this the end of the Odyssey": that is the scholiast's comments on 23.296. So far as book 24 is concerned it is hard not to agree. From our point of view the poem ends perfectly naturally at the point indicated by the ancient critics, whose judgement is important if not decisive'. E. R. Dodds, 'Homer', *Fifty Years (and Twelve) of Classical Scholarship*, edited by Maurice Platnauer (New York: Barnes & Noble, 1968), p. 7: 'there is virtual unanimity [among analysts] on certain points, such as the lateness of Book XXIV . . .'. Is it so obvious that an ending at 23.296 is natural? F. A. Wolf, *Prolegomena to Homer 1795*, translated by Anthony Grafton, Glenn W. Most and James E. G. Zetzel (Princeton: Princeton University

Press, 1985), p. 133: 'Anyone with common sense can see that if the last part of this poem were missing, we would go away worried for Ulysses, who had conquered such great difficulties. For at that point we would be quite fearful for him because of the parents and relatives of the 108 slain noble youths, if an amnesty and peace were not brought about by a sudden intervention of the gods'.

49 Bassett, *Poetry*, p. 175: 'But every prominent Greek whose story was left unfinished in the *Iliad* finds a place either in the Telemachy or in one of the two Necyias'.

50 Minna Skafte Jensen, *The Homeric Question and the Oral-formulaic Theory* (Copenhagen: Museum Tusculanum Press, 1980), p. 74: 'The very idea of letting Odysseus be his own singer derives, I think, from the standpoint of oral poetics. If the real thing, the true story, is what you are after, it is elegant to let the main character tell his own story . . . There are no Olympic scenes in Odysseus' tale, and at the only point where he tells something of the gods' decisions, he conjures up Calypso as his (not too likely) source: Hermes told Calypso who told me, and that is how I know'. Also, Clay, *Wrath*, pp. 24–5.

51 *Odyssey* 9.477–9: '"your evil deeds were to catch up with you, and be/too strong for you, hard one, who dared to eat your own guests/in your own house, so Zeus and the rest of the gods have punished you."' Posner, 'Homeric Version', p. 138, accepts both that 'the Cyclops is severely punished for his abuse, as a host, of the guest relationship' and that, p. 132, 'the ultimate cause of the disaster is Odysseus's own act in taunting the Cyclops'.

52 Zeus' interest in human justice is vital to what is seen as the theodicity in the *Odyssey*; in particular, *Odyssey* 22.413. B.C. Dietrich, *Death, Fate and the Gods* (London: Athlone Press, 1965), p. 217: 'From this passage emerge two important points which had only been hinted at in Zeus' apology in Book i. First, the person or persons who committed a crime did this against their fellow men and not against the gods. That means the gods are actively interested in maintaining human laws that have little to do with themselves'. A vigorous dissent is registered in Clay, *Wrath*, pp. 215–21.

53 *Odyssey* 9.252–5. The question is formulaic; Nestor asks the same question of Telemachos at 3.71–4. This shakes the reading in Clay, *Wrath*, p. 117: '[Polyphemos] immediately accuses them of being pirates. For those who lack all notions of commerce or communal enterprise, whether hostile or peaceable, outsiders can only be private trouble-makers – pirates'.

54 Precedent is also on his side, Apollodorus, *Library*, II.iv.9: 'When he was tried for murder, Hercules quoted a law of Rhadamanthys, who laid it down that whoever defends himself against a wrongful aggressor shall go free . . .'.

55 Norman Austin, 'Name Magic in the *Odyssey*', *California Studies in Classical Antiquity* 5 (1972):4: 'Poseidon fulfills the curse exactly according to Polyphemos's terms . . .'.

56 Carpenter, *Folk Tale*, p. 146: 'The curious prophecy which Teiresias makes to Odysseus on the manner of his ultimate death is probably an original element in the legend . . . but it fills no place in the Odyssey story as Homer tells it, and it seems not to interest its hero in the slightest degree, . . . It was, no doubt, these gaping seams in the composition and this none-too-skillful patching of the narrative which moved Wilamowitz to brand the underworld scene in the Odyssey as an Orphic interpolation'. Odysseus certainly remembered Teiresias' instructions; indeed, they are his last words to Penelope before they resume their old ritual (*Od.* 23.266–84). The Orphic claim was abandoned by even Wilamowitz, cf. Dodds, *Greeks and the Irrational*, p. 158.

57 Does this claim ignore the fact that Poseidon is lord of *all* waters? John H. Finley, Jr., *Homer's Odyssey* (Cambridge, Mass.: Harvard University Press, 1978), p. 115: 'As a pre-Greek god of all waters, not of the sea only, Poseidon was worshipped in inland places'. Lewis Richard Farnell, *The Cults of the Greek States* (Oxford: Clarendon Press, 1907), 4.5: '[Although] leader of the Nymphs, the god of fresh water . . . he was never able to absorb the special cults of the various rivers and springs . . .' In the first

place Poseidon's fresh water role does not seem important in Homeric worship. Walter F. Otto, *The Homeric Gods*, translated by Moses Hadas (New York: Pantheon, 1954), p. 156: 'But the men of the *Iliad* and *Odyssey* think of Poseidon only when they have to do with the sea. For them his power does not operate within the earth, in vegetation, or in animals, or in the abundant water of rivers'. George M. Calhoun, 'Polity and Society', *A Companion to Homer*, edited by Alan J. B. Wace and Frank H. Stubbings (London: Macmillan, 1962), p. 446: 'If one lives near a river, he makes frequent offerings to the god . . . if near a mountain, to Zeus . . . if on the seacoast, to Poseidon . . . and few live far enough removed from the grottoes and groves and springs where dwell the nymphs to neglect due homage to these gracious beings . . .' In the second place people who know of Poseidon only from inland waters will surely underestimate his true power. Inland people may know of Poseidon as lord of horses, but again, if they have never seen the sea, how can they gauge his power?

58 *Odyssey* 23.267–75, recalling 11.121–30. Ann L. T. Bergren, 'Odyssean Temporality: Many (Re)Turns', *Approaches to Homer*, edited by Carl A. Rubino and Cynthia W. Shelmerdine (Austin: University of Texas Press, 1983), p. 54: 'There he will plant this instrument of both commerce at sea and cultivation of the land, and by this act at last resolve his conflict with Poseidon . . .'.

59 Walter Burkert, *Homo Necans*, translated by Peter Bing (Berkeley: University of California Press, 1983), p. 133: 'The fact that Odysseus' rescue action provokes the Cyclops' curse and Poseidon's anger, an incomprehensible moral paradox, rests on a ritual foundation'.

60 Burkert, *Homo Necans*, p. 133: 'the structure of Odysseus' "sufferings" quite obviously corresponds to the werewolf pattern that turns up again and again from Delphi to Mount Lykaion'. The werewolf identification was questioned years ago by Carpenter, *Folk Tale*, p. 131: 'There appears to be some deep-seated contamination among the Indogermanic words for wolf, fox (and bear?), perhaps due to taboo or to an undifferentiated generic epithet. Hence the trouble with Lykaon–Kallisto–Arkas on Mount Lykaion, where the bear and not the wolf is worshipped, the "wrongly" formed words *Lykaios* and *Lykosoura*, and the confusion of the disappearing bear votary with a werewolf . . .'.

61 Carpenter, *Folk Tale*, pp. 125–9. If this identification were accepted, Clay's explanation for Athene's wrath (note 31) would gain considerable support, since Sisyphos cheated death for a while (note 69).

62 Nilsson, *History*, pp. 163–4; Dodds, *Greeks and the Irrational*, pp. 1–21; Richard E. Doyle, *'ATH: Its Use and Meaning* (New York: Fordham University Press, 1984).

63 Cost/benefit terminology has been employed by James M. Redfield to describe Odysseus' conduct, 'The Economic Man', *Approaches to Homer*, pp. 218–47. Since Odysseus is described by the gods as the man beyond other men in mind, *Odyssey* 1.66, 13.297–9, it would seem an easy inference that the gods, if anything, do better cost/benefit analysis. Redfield, however, accepts a Platonic–Christian view of the matter (p. 224): 'Thus many traditions see economic activity as the mark of our fallen condition, between god and beast'. Do the Homeric epics see it this way? To the extent that the gods engage in economic activity, the answer is 'no'.

64 This is discussed by Aristotle, *Nicomachean Ethics*, translated by H. Rackham (Cambridge, Mass.: Loeb Classical Library, 1934), 1136b10–13. What Dodds treats as divine intervention, *Greeks and the Irrational*, p. 4, Aristotle treats as 'unrestrained' action.

65 Chapter 3 above.

66 Such imperatives can be found in Homer, e.g., *Odyssey* 7.310: 'Always moderation is better' and *Odyssey* 15.71: 'In all things balance is better'. Darrell Dobbs, 'Reckless Rationalism and Heroic Reverence in Homer's *Odyssey*', *American Political Science Review* 81 (June 1987): 491–508, gives a decision-theoretic treatment of Odysseus' shipmates'

choice to eat the cattle of the sun, and finds that Homer quarrels with their rationality even though they find a dominant strategy in eating the cattle. Even dominant strategies in nonconvex surfaces, such prisoner's dilemma games, will generally not lead to group rational outcomes.

67 Nilsson, *History*, pp. 141–2.

68 Frazer cites Callimachus' *The Baths of Pallas*, 'Note 1', Apollodorus, *Library*, III.vi.7: '. . . [he] saw what it was not lawful to see. The goddess cried out in anger, and at once the eyes of the intruder were quenched in darkness. His mother, the nymph, reproached the goddess with blinding her son, but Athena explained that she had not done so, but that the laws of the gods inflicted the penalty of blindness on anyone who beheld an immortal without his or her consent. To console the youth for the loss of his sight the goddess promised to bestow on him the gifts of prophecy and divination, long life, and after death the retention of his mental powers undimmed in the world below'.

69 Apollodorus, *Epitome* ii.1: 'Some say that [Tantalos] is thus punished because he blabbed to men the mysteries of the gods, and because he attempted to share ambrosia with his fellows'. Sisyphos' adventures are discussed by Carpenter, *Folk Tale*, p. 127: 'A scholiast on the Iliad quotes Pherekydes (always a most interesting and valuable source for myths) to the effect that when Sisyphos, after having once escaped from the underworld, died a second time, a stone was set for him to roll, "so that he should not run away again"'.

70 Hence the fate of Asklepios, Apollodorus, *Library*, iii.x.3–4: 'he not only prevented some from dying, but even raised up the dead . . . Zeus, fearing that men might acquire the healing art from him and so come to the rescue of each other, smote him with a thunderbolt.' Why is Asklepios not punished in Hades? Zeus seems concerned mainly to arrest the diffusion of technology and Asklepios has divine friends.

71 Carpenter, *Folk Tale*, p. 125: '[Sisyphos'] crime was not heinous, and his punishment seems illogical'.

72 If human status in general is a function of divine activity, then Posner's finding that there is no special symbol for political authority – a scepter is a generic status symbol – 'Homeric Version', pp. 128–30, only shows that political authority is like any other authority, a grant from the gods.

73 *The Homeric Hymns*, 'To Demeter', translated by Apostolos N. Athanassakis (Baltimore: Johns Hopkins University Press, 1976), 310–12. Zeus quickly yields to her demand to release Persephone from Hades at 335–56.

74 Vermeule, *Aspects of Death*, p. 126: 'When gods are drawn into such tales, they depart from their normal religious role, and raise disturbing questions beyond the reach of any logic but a scholiast's. Are parts of gods immortal, and other parts like ears and noses not? What is god's ambition for wages? Will he lose social standing among the blessed immortals if he has fewer cauldrons, stallions, and gold ornaments? Upon what does Charon spend the obols of the late Greek dead – new steering oars and caulking? A drink in the tavern of the dead who have no appetites?' Of course, in Aristophanes' *Birds*, divine income from sacrifice counts for more than just status.

75 Burkert, *Homo Necans*, p. 7: 'The rite is objectionable, and was already felt to be so early on, because it so clearly and directly benefits man. Is the god "to whom" the sacrifice is made any more than a transparent excuse for festive feasting? All he gets are the bones, the fat, and the gall bladders. Hesiod says that the crafty Prometheus, the friend of mankind, caused this to be so in order to deceive the gods, and the burning of bones became a standard joke in Greek comedy'.

76 Karl Kerényi, *Prometheus*, translated by Ralph Manheim (New York: Pantheon Books, 1963), p. 47: 'By undertaking to "deceive Zeus" mind,' Prometheus shows himself to be one who necessarily remains wanting, who can never be rewarded by complete success. "Zeus, full of eternal counsel, saw through the stratagem and noted it well"

[*Theogony* 550–1]. Seeing through the deception, he lets himself be cheated . . .'.

77 Lowry, *Archaeology*, p. 128: 'Zeus's indignation at being deceived, according to Hesiod, was the cause of his withholding fire from mankind and also of his terrible punishment of Prometheus'. This seems to be a misreading. Aeschylus, *Prometheus Bound*, attributes Prometheus' punishment solely to the theft of fire (lines 8, 109, etc.) whereas the technology of divination is a matter of mutual benefit of men and gods, 492–6: 'also I taught of the smoothness of the vitals and what color they should have to pleasure the Gods and the dappled beauty of the gall and the lobe. It was I who burned thighs wrapped in fat and the long shank bone and set mortals on the road to this murky craft'.

78 A formal distinction between basic goods and counters is given in David Levy, 'Diamonds, Water and Z Goods', *History of Political Economy* 14 (1982): 551–61.

79 Infinitesimals have became reputable numbers owing to the work of Abraham Robinson, *Non-standard Analysis* (Amsterdam: North-Holland, revised edition, 1974).

80 If sacrifices are negative, presumably the gods are harmed. This would be reason to exterminate such mortals, as Hesiod and Plato demonstrate in texts discussed below.

81 Martin P. Nilsson, *Greek Folk Religion* (Philadelphia: University of Pennsylvania Press, [1940] 1972), p. 74.

82 E. R. Dodds, *The Ancient Concept of Progress* (Oxford: Clarendon Press, 1973), p. 150: 'a god in a Greek comedy complains that he gets a helping suitable only for a dog'.

83 Hesiod, *The Works and Days*, translated by Richmond Lattimore (Ann Arbor: University of Michigan Press, 1977), 133–9.

84 Plato, *Symposium*, translated by W. R. M. Lamb (Cambridge, Mass.: Loeb Classical Library, 1983), 190c–d. The first cut does not produce an optimum, so surgery continues at 191b–c. Kenneth Dover, 'Commentary', Plato, *Symposium* (Cambridge: Cambridge University Press, 1980), p. 116: 'Just as a human feels his life in society to be insupportable if his fellows do not display their regard for him, gods are treated as needing the festivals and sacrifices with which they are honoured.' Aristophanes, *The Birds*, translated by William Arrowsmith (Ann Arbor: University of Michigan Press, 1969), p. 94: 'Since the moment/you founded the city of Cloudcuckooland . . ./not a single sacrifice, not even a whiff of smoke,/no savories, no roast, nothing at all/has floated up to heaven. In consequence, my friend,/Olympos is starving to death.'

85 *Works and Days*, 263–4.

86 Plato, *Republic*, translated by Paul Shorey (Cambridge, Mass.: Loeb Classical Library, 1937), 381c.

87 Plato, *Laws*, translated by R. G. Bury (Cambridge, Mass.: Loeb Classical Library, 1926), 885B–C: 'No one who believes, as the laws prescribe, in the existence of the gods . . . believes that they are easy to win over when bribed by offering and prayers.'

88 Burkert, *Greek Religion*, pp. 305–37.

89 Aristotle, *Magna Moralia*, translated St G. Stock, *The Complete Works of Aristotle*, edited by Jonathan Barnes (Princeton: Princeton University Press, 1984), 1208b27–30: 'For there is, people think, a friendship towards gods and towards things without life, but here they are wrong. For friendship, we maintain, exists only where there can be a return of affection, but friendship towards god does not admit of love being returned, nor at all of loving. For it would be strange if one were to say that he loved Zeus'. Was Aristotle correct? Specialist opinion is divided. Contra: Arthur Bernard Cook, *Zeus* (Cambridge: Cambridge University Press, 1925), 2:1167: 'The Greek was capable of rising to greater heights, and the title *Philios* had from the first a moral connotation. True, Aristotle denied the possibility of love (*philia*) between man and God . . . But popular usage was against him'. Pro: Dodds, *The Ancient Concept of Progress*, pp. 140–1: 'Classical Greece had in fact no word for such an emotion: *philotheos* makes its appearance for the first time at the end of the fourth century and remains a rarity in pagan authors'.

90 Griffin, *Life and Death*, pp. 182–3.
91 Griffin, *Life and Death*, pp. 98, 184–5. *Iliad* 1.1: 'Sing, goddess . . .'. *Odyssey* 1.1:
    'Tell me, Muse . . .'. In the *Odyssey*, Odysseus tests a singer's *bona fides*, offering *him*
    fame if he can truly tell the heroic stories, *Od.* 8.496–8. Plato, *Ion*, translated by
    W. R. M. Lamb (Cambridge, Mass.: Loeb Classical Library, 1925), 534b–c: 'it is not
    by art that they compose and utter so many fine things about the deeds of men – as you
    do about Homer – but by a divine dispensation, each is able only to compose that to
    which the Muse has stirred him . . .'. It is instructive to note the difference between
    Homer, through whom the goddess speaks, and Herodotus, who, although naming
    each of the nine sections in *Persian Wars* for a muse, speaks for himself so that the fame
    of Greek and Barbarian will not be lost. If we are effective agents for the divine, is not
    the divine then redundant?
92 *Odyssey* 8.73–4: 'the Muse stirred the singer to sing the famous actions/of men on that
    venture, whose fame goes up into the wide heaven'.
93 Griffin, *Life and Death*, pp. 46–7: 'To deprive the dead of a grave is to abolish his
    memory, to make him as if he had never been; hence, the passionate concern felt in
    Homer for a grave to remain after one's death, to record for posterity one's existence
    and significance'. Telemachos laments the fact that his father is missing in action,
    Odyssey 1.239–42: 'So all the Achaians would have heaped a grave mound over
    him,/and he would have won great fame for himself and his son hereafter./But now
    ingloriously the stormwinds have caught and carried him,/away, out of sight, out of
    knowledge . . .'.
94 Simone Weil, *The Iliad or The Poem of Force*, translated by Mary McCarthy
    (Wallingford, Pa.: Pendle Hill, 1957), contrasts the living person with the dead
    thing. If there were such a radical dichotomy in the *Iliad*, dead matter is dead matter,
    why are corpses more important than armor? Good armor can stop a spear, what use is
    the best of corpses? Hektor, *Iliad* 7.77–91, is very concerned with his corpse, offering
    reciprocity of corpse exchange. He supposes that armor is part of the booty. Homer's
    concern for armor approximates Archilochos' famous concern for his shield, translated
    by Davenport, no. 79: 'Life seemed somehow more precious./It was a beautiful
    shield./I know where I can buy another/Exactly like it, just as round'.
95 *Iliad* 24.23–4: 'The blessed gods as they looked upon him were filled with
    compassion/and kept urging clear-sighted Argeïphontes to steal the body'.
96 An exchange of bodies is part of the duel Hektor proposes at *Iliad*. 7.77–86, recovery
    of bodies is a concern of Nestor at 7.327–43 and Priam at 7.368–78, a truce is
    arranged to collect bodies and perform the funeral rites at 7.407–32, Glaukos defends
    Sarpedon's body at 16.545, Aias defends Patroklos' at 17.128, Glaukos insults Hektor
    for failing to seize Patroklos' body to exchange for Sarpedon's at 17.159–63. Some of
    the fiercest fighting in the book occurs over Patroklos' body.
97 C. W. Macleod, 'Introduction', *Iliad Book XXIV* (Cambridge: Cambridge University
    Press, 1982), p. 18: 'Achilles . . . threatens to cut off Hector's head as Hector had
    threatened to cut off Patroclus' . . . That threat is dropped, and the poet's reason for
    dropping it is clearly that a decapitated body could not be given back for burial.' Also,
    the now classic study, Charles Segal, *The Theme of the Mutilation of the Corpse in the Iliad*
    (Leiden: Mnemosyne Bibliotheca Classica Batava, 1971). Mutilation is called 'shameful'
    at *Iliad*. 17.254 by a man and at *Iliad*. 17.556 by a god.
98 *Iliad*. 16.453–7. Zeus repeats this to Apollo at *Il.* 16.672–5.
99 Griffin, *Life and Death*, p. 99: 'coward and hero are given the same honour . . . why
    should Achilles not toddle home and die in bed?'
100 Milman Parry, *The Making of Homeric Verse*, edited by Adam Parry (Oxford: Clarendon
    Press, 1971), p. 314: 'For the formulas are not only too ingenious to be the work of
    the one poet of the *Iliad* and the *Odyssey*; they are also too good. The epithets, the
    metaphorical expressions, the phrases for the binding of clauses, the formulas for

running the sentence over from one verse into another, the grouping of words and phrases within the clause and within the verse, all this is many times beyond whatever supreme creative genius for words one could imagine for the poet Homer'.

101 Parry, *Homeric Verse*, p. 330: 'A single man or even a whole group of men who set out in the most careful way could not make even a beginning at such an oral diction. It must be the work of many poets over many generations. When one singer (for such is the name these oral poets most often give themselves) has hit upon a phrase which is pleasing and easily used, other singers will hear it, and then, when faced at the same point in the line with the need of expressing the same idea, they will recall it and use it. If the phrase is so good poetically and so useful metrically that it becomes in time the one best way to express a certain idea in a given length of the verse, and as such is passed on from one generation of poets to another, it has won a place for itself in the oral diction as a formula. But if it does not suit in every way, or if a better way of fitting the idea to the verse and the sentence is found, it is straightway forgotten, or lives only for a short time, since with each new poet and with each new generation of poets it must undergo the twofold test of being found pleasing and useful'.

102 Adam Smith, *An Inquiry into the Nature and Causes of the Wealth of Nations*, edited by W. B. Todd (Oxford: Clarendon Press, 1976), p. 770: 'Different authors gave different systems both of natural and moral philosophy. But the arguments by which they supported those different systems, far from being always demonstrations, were frequently at best but very slender probabilities, and sometimes mere sophisms . . . The patrons of each system of natural and moral philosophy naturally endeavoured to expose the weakness of the arguments adduced to support the systems which were opposite to their own. In examining those arguments, they were necessarily led to consider the difference between a probable and a demonstrative argument, between a fallacious and a conclusive one; and Logick, or the science of the general principles of good and bad reasoning, necessarily arose out of the observations which a scrutiny of this kind gave occasion to'. A modern version of this approach to the evolutionary development of scientific knowledge is sketched in Karl R. Popper, *Objective Knowledge* (Oxford: Clarendon Press, revised edition, 1973).

103 Modern economists have learned most from F. A. Hayek's great paper 'The Use of Knowledge in Society', *Individualism and Economic Order* (Chicago: University of Chicago Press, 1949).

104 Eric A. Havelock, *Preface to Plato* (Cambridge, Mass.: Harvard University Press, 1963), p. 209: 'In short, the dialectic, a weapon we suspect to have been employed in this form by a whole group of intellectuals in the last half of the fifth century, was a weapon for arousing the consciousness from its dream language and stimulating it to think abstractly'.

105 This even happens in mathematics and mathematical statistics. For instance, the foundations of the calculus were not secure until two and three hundred years after Newton and Leibniz. In mathematical statistics, efficient estimators were proposed long before the requisite technical devices were available by which to evaluate them, Stephen M. Stigler, 'Simon Newcomb, Percy Daniell, and the History of Robust Estimation', *Journal of the American Statistical Association* 68 (1973): 872–9.

106 Plato's objection to the entire Homeric process, e.g., the transmission of opinion which does not satisfy the requirements of formal abstraction, is the subject of Havelock's *Preface*. If Havelock is correct, the attack on Plato by twentieth century social evolutionary theorists – Karl Popper's is the only name one need mention – is a response to the logical basis of Plato's attack on evolved *doxa* typified by the Homeric epics.

107 Adam Parry, 'The Language of Achilles', *The Language and Background of Homer*, edited by G. S. Kirk (Cambridge: Cambridge University Press, 1967), p. 50: 'The formulaic character of Homer's language means that everything in the world is regularly

presented as all men (all men within the poem, that is) commonly perceive it. The style of Homer emphasizes constantly the accepted attitude toward each thing in the world, and this makes for a great unity of experience'.

108 Plato, *Ion* 535e: 'For I have to pay the closest attention to them; since, if I set them crying, I shall laugh myself because of the money I take, but if they laugh, I myself shall cry because of the money I lose'.

109 Plato's criticism of the Homeric process is precisely that the poems do not embody expert opinion, and that experts are the only fit judges of the various topics covered, e.g, chariot driving, *Ion* 537a, medicine, 538c, piloting a ship, 540b. Which is, of course, to say that there is no knowledge embodied in the poems, only opinion.

110 Charles Griswold, *Self-knowledge in Plato's 'Phaedrus'* (New Haven: Yale University Press, 1986), p. 256: '[Homer] is criticized implicitly here, and explicitly in the *Rep.* (especially in book 10). Socrates implies that Homer, unlike Stresichorus, created images without being able to distinguish them from originals. In the context of the *Rep.* passage (586c), Socrates attacks those whose lives are ruled by the low desire for physical gratification on the basis that they are in love with *images* of true pleasure and reality instead of the things themselves'. Griswold points out, pp. 72–3, that Homer's blindness is used by speakers in the dialogues as evidence for the unsoundness of his views.

111 Jasper Griffin, 'The Epic Cycle and the Uniqueness of Homer', *Journal of Hellenic Studies* 97 (1977): 38–53. I owe my knowledge of this article, and thus the existence of this section, to C. B. R. Pelling.

112 Griffin, 'Uniqueness', p. 42: 'Even more, in the accommodating world of the Cycle death itself can be evaded. In the *Iliad* no rule is more ineluctable than that expounded by Patroclus's ghost . . . the dead do not return. Even Heracles could not evade death.'

113 Griffin, 'Uniqueness', pp. 45–6: 'in the Cycle great heroes would do anything to avoid military service . . . Achilles was hidden among women, and Odysseus pretended to be mad'. However, at *Odyssey* 24.119 it does not seem that Odysseus was all that keen to ship out. Of course, Odysseus turned down a real immortality to return home.

114 Griswold defends myths against reductionist accounts, e.g., *Self-knowledge*, pp. 143–51, on the basis that any translation scheme brutalizes the poetry and plays havoc with our understanding of inner experience. Setting aside the fact that this assumes the Platonic principle that appearances are not real (else why would inner experience differ from outer?), translation schemes can increase information. If the argument in the text is correct, there is a reason why the gods ask for costless sacrifices. Readers have often had recourse to the lame explanation that the gods were stupid. If our understanding of the mechanics is not in order, can we understand the poetry?

Chapter 9 The statistical basis of Athenian and American constitutional theory

1 Kenneth J. Arrow, *Social Choice and Individual Values* (New Haven: Yale University Press, second edition, 1963).

2 A. H. M. Jones, *Athenian Democracy* (Baltimore: Johns Hopkins University Press, 1986), p. 41: 'It is curious that in the abundant literature produced in the great democracy of Greece there survives no statement of democratic political theory'.

3 Jones, *Athenian Democracy*, pp. 46–7. Emphasis mine.

4 Xenophon, *Memorabilia*, translated by O. J. Todd (Cambridge, Mass.: Loeb Classical Library, 1978), I.ii.9. Xenophon does not dispute this charge. Although Karl R. Popper, *The Open Society and its Enemies* (Princeton: Princeton University Press, fourth edition, 1962), would have us understand Socrates as a democrat, Socrates did not offer alternative democratic institutions, merely criticism of existing ones. John Wild, 'Popper's Interpretation of Plato', *The Philosophy of Karl Popper*, edited by Paul Arthur

Schilpp (La Salle, Ill.: Library of Living Philosophers, 1974), p. 870: 'When properly understood, it is difficult to see anything radically non–Socratic in this idea [of the guardians of the *Republic*] that the more intelligent and better trained should govern'. The average Athenian citizen seemed to take a dim view of this teaching; J. A. O. Larsen, *Representative Government in Greek and Roman History* (Berkeley: University of California Press, 1966), p. 14, notes '[the Athenian] belief that the collective judgment of the masses was superior to that of experts . . .'. Also E. S. Staveley, *Greek and Roman Voting and Elections* (Ithaca: Cornell University Press, 1972), p. 55.

5 Is the contrary true? Stephen M. Stigler, *The History of Statistics* (Cambridge, Mass.: Belknap Press, 1986), pp. 25–31, discusses how Euler's unparalleled mathematical abilities directed his intuition toward the wrong track in what was, in retrospect, a statistical problem posing little mathematical difficulty.

6 Aristotle, *Rhetoric to Alexander*, translated by E. S. Forster, *The Complete Works of Aristotle*, edited by Jonathan Barnes (Princeton: Princeton University Press, 1984), 1424a13–16. All further citations of Aristotle will be to this edition via the traditional notation. While this letter is widely held to be spurious, the statement in the text is the most precise statement of the properties of the lot known to me. If Aristotle did not write this, someone as competent did, so I will risk scholarly wrath by citing its author as Aristotle. The passage seems too elliptical to have made an impact on classical scholarship, e.g., Victor Ehrenberg, 'Sortition', *The Oxford Classical Dictionary*, edited by N. G. L. Hammond and H. H. Scullard (London: Oxford University Press, second edition, 1970). 'Except for a few critics like Socrates, the principle of sortition was never discussed. It was, indeed, a necessary and fundamental element of the democratic *polis*'.

7 Jean-Jacques Rousseau, *The Social Contract*, translated by Maurice Cranston (Harmondsworth, England: Penguin Books, 1968). In the public choice literature, Dennis C. Mueller, Robert Tollison and Thomas D. Willett, 'Representative Democracy via Random Selection', *Public Choice* 12 (1972): 57–68, note that the idea for electoral randomization begins in Athens. Scott Gordon, 'Guarding the Guardians' (unpublished manuscript, 1986), discusses the combination of election by lot and by ballot in Venetian politics. Although Gordon notes that Venice was in the Byzantine orbit, he does not connect Venetian with Athenian practice.

8 Aristotle's conjecture is echoed by Rousseau, *Social Contract*, p. 156: 'Election by lot would have few disadvantages in a true democracy, for where all men were equal in character and talent as well as principles and fortune, it would hardly matter who was chosen. But as I have already said, no true democracy exists.

When election by choice and election by lot are both employed, choice should be used to fill places that call for special skills, such as military commands, and lot for those where common sense, justice and integrity are enough, as in the case of political offices, for in a well constituted state, such qualities are found among all the citizens'.

9 James Wycliffe Headlam, *Elections by Lot at Athens*, revised by D. C. MacGregor (Cambridge: Cambridge University Press, second edition, 1933), p. 3. Headlam's dissertation was written before, but published just after, the publication of Aristotle's *Constitution of Athens*, which ended the scepticism about the existence of the Athenian lot.

10 Headlam, *Election by Lot*, p. 11, argues that 'the lot was religious in its origin . . . but that of Athens owing to its constant use for political purposes it was secularised till almost all recollection of its religious origin had disappeared'.

11 Election by lot was in fact practiced by 'heretical' Christians and denounced by the orthodox, Elaine Pagels, *The Gnostic Gospels* (New York: Vintage Books, 1981), pp. 49–51. Pagels reconstructs the Gnostic argument as a belief that the will of God controls the lots. This is consistent with the view of George Grote, *Plato and the Other Companions of Sokrates* (London: J. Murray, new edition, 1888), 4:309–10 who cites

Plato's *Laws* 690C and *Iliad* 7:179.

12 Georg Luck, *Arcana Mundi* (Baltimore: Johns Hopkins University Press, 1985), pp. 244–5. 'Sometimes the will of the god was explored by the casting or drawing of lots . . . This do-it-yourself method could easily be carried out at home, but when important decisions were at stake, the great shrines were still visited'. This pushes the issue back a step; how did the shrines make decisions? The question of lots at Delphi has drawn specialist attention: Joseph Fontenrose, *The Delphic Oracle* (Berkeley: University of California Press, 1981), pp. 237–8, describes them, if I read him correctly, as used for routine matters.

13 Apollodorus, *The Library*, translated by James George Frazer (Cambridge, Mass.: Loeb Classical Library, 1939), I.i.4–ii.1. The more famous passage in Homer, *Iliad* 15.187–92, which testifies to this division by lot, does not reveal the earlier history of settling disputes by violence. Evidence for the antiquity of Apollodorus' version is provided by M. L. West, *The Orphic Poems* (Oxford: Clarendon Press, 1983).

14 Anthony Downs, *An Economic Theory of Democracy* (New York: Harper & Row, 1957).

15 In fact, an example can be produced such that the median voter result minimizes the maximum loss of each individual. David Levy, 'Voting on Voting' (Fairfax: Public Choice Working Papers, 1987). I would conjecture that, relative to other median–unbiased voting procedures, this example could be converted to a theorem.

16 John Rawls, *A Theory of Justice* (Cambridge, Mass.: Harvard University Press, 1971).

17 James Buchanan and Gordon Tullock, *The Calculus of Consent* (Ann Arbor: University of Michigan Press, 1962).

18 Richard D. McKelvey, 'General Conditions for Global Intransitivities in Formal Voting Models', *Econometrica* 47 (1979): 1085–113. McKelvey establishes that, save only when Charles Plott's conditions hold, the outcome of a majority rule process can wander arbitrarily far from the desires of the median voter.

19 Charles R. Plott, 'A Notion of Equilibrium and its Possibility under Majority Rule', *American Economic Review* 57 (1967): 787–806.

20 Kenneth A. Shepsle and Barry R. Weingast, 'Institutionalizing Majority Rule', *American Economic Review* 72 (1982): 367–71.

21 The key term is 'ἄτη which translates as 'disaster', 'blindness' or 'blind folly'. It has been studied by E. R. Dodds, *The Greeks and the Irrational* (Berkeley: University of California Press, 1951), pp. 1–21, and Richard E. Doyle, *'ATH: Its Use and Meaning* (New York: Fordham University Press, 1984).

22 Arnold Kaufmann, *Introduction to the Theory of Fuzzy Subsets*, translated by D. L. Swanson (New York: Academic Press, 1975).

23 The technical and textual aspects are described above in Chapter 3. The problem is not simply one with indifference which could be handled within a revealed preference formulation, Taesung Kim, 'Intransitive Indifference and Revealed Preference', *Econometrica* 55 (1987): 163–7.

24 The machinery is from Susan Feigenbaum, Lynn Karoly and David Levy, 'When Votes are Words not Deeds: Evidence from the Nuclear Freeze Referendum', *Public Choice* 58 (1988): 201–16.

25 Aristophanes, *Ecclesiazusae*, edited by R. G. Ussher (Oxford: Clarendon Press, 1973), lines 197–8. Recent work in the technical literature demonstrates the context in which the preferences for defense expenditure reflect type of property owned. Borimir Jordon, *The Athenian Navy in the Classical Period* (Berkeley: University of California Publications: Classical Studies, 1975), 13:v: 'But the Athenian fleet was more than a tool of Athenian expansionist and defensive policy. Once it began to supplant the hoplite phalanx as the more important and more effective military force, it quickly became the institution which the poorer and underprivileged classes of society . . . made peculiarly their own. Through their service in a navy indispensable to the acquisition and maintenance of power, the lower classes sought to give legitimacy to

their political aspirations, and it was this historical process which provoked the scathing criticism and indignation of the aristocratic and exclusivist writers on political theory of the fifth and fourth centuries'.

26 Can we actually do this? Surely if we assume that an individual's actual choice is random, then the linear expansion path can be estimated by a constrained regression. Needless to say, the linearity assumption aids exposition, but can be weakened by the obvious devices.

27 As I have argued in Chapter 3 above, a fair amount of Greek ethical advice can be formulated in terms of the desirability of moderation.

28 Douglas Maurice MacDowell, 'Ostracism', *The Oxford Classical Dictionary*.

29 D. F. Andrews, P. J. Bickel, F. R. Hampel, P. J. Huber, W. H. Rogers, J. W. Tukey, *Robust Estimates of Location* (Princeton: Princeton University Press, 1972).

30 Equation (9.1) is solved iteratively, starting with the mean as the proposed median. Consider the jth iteration where some median θ is proposed as the true median. This we call the 'jth median'. Inside this iteration, the expression $w_i(\theta_i - j$th median $\theta)$ can take on three and only three values. The 'exceptional' weight of 1 is called to block division by zero; hence, 1 times $0 = 0$ results because $\theta_i - j$th median $\theta = 0$. In all other cases, when $\theta_i - j$th median θ differs from zero, the weight is simply the reciprocal of the absolute value of this term. Consequently, multiplying the weight by $\theta_i - j$th median results in $+1$ or -1.

We know that each term in the series formed by (9.1) is $+1$, -1 or 0. If (1), the sum of these weighted differences, is something other than zero then there are more observations on one side of the jth median than another: the number of plus and minus ones are not equal. Hence, the jth median is not the true median. At some jth median when (9.1) sums to zero the true median is attained; the number of those on one side of the jth median just equals the number of those on the other side: the number of plus ones just equals the number of minus ones. Since the median of zero requires only the same number of positive and negative observations and since the weights do not change the sign, the unweighted median is the same as the weighted median.

31 'Bias' has a longer history in politics than in statistics. James Madison, *The Federalist*, edited by Jacob E. Cooke (Middletown, Ct.: Wesleyan University Press, 1961), p. 59: 'No man is allowed to be judge of his own cause; because his interest would certainly bias his judgment . . .'.

32 *Politics*, translated by Benjamin Jowett, 1281a42–1281b10.

33 Jones, *Athenian Democracy*, p. 46.

34 Martin Ostwald, *From Popular Sovereignty to the Sovereignty of Law* (Berkeley: University of California Press, 1986), p. 82. This is supported by Aristotle, *Constitution of Athens*, translated by F. G. Kenyon, 43.1: 'All the magistrates that are concerned with the ordinary routine of administration are elected by lot, except . . . All military officers are also elected by vote'. Routine duties include checking weights and measures, 50.2, making certain the market goods are pure, 50.1, fixing the price of corn, 51.3, executing convicted criminals, 52.1, serving as a small claims court, 53.1, running the sacrifices, 54.1. Important matters, where votes were taken, include superintending the construction of triremes, 46.1.

35 The sample median minimizes the maximum bias under symmetry and unimodality, Peter J. Huber, *Robust Statistics* (New York: John Wiley, 1981). Huber complains, 'Thus minimizing the maximum bias leads to a rather uneventful theory; for symmetric unimodal distributions, the solution invariably is the sample median.' We drop the unimodality condition later and obtain some very eventful theory.

Only a tenured cynic would say something in public about the value of time and faculty politics.

36 Quoted in Jones, *Athenian Democracy*, p. 47. Aristotle, *Constitution of Athens*, 50.2: 'There are also ten City Commissioners, of whom five hold office in Piraeus and five in

the city. Their duty is to see that female flute- and harp- and lute-players are not hired at more than two drachma, and if more than one person is anxious to hire the same girl, they cast lots and hire her out to the person to whom the lot falls'.

37 Buchanan and Tullock, *Calculus of Consent*.

38 Aristotle, *Politics*, 1303a15–16: 'at Heraea . . . instead of electing their magistrates, they took them by lot, because the electors were in the habit of choosing their own partisans.'

39 Frederick Mosteller and John W. Tukey, *Data Analysis and Regression* (Reading, Mass.: Addison–Wesley, 1977), p. 35.

40 MacDowell, 'Ostracism', pp. 762–3: 'Particularly interesting is a find of 190 *ostraka* all inscribed with the name of Themistocles by only a few different hands . . . Presumably they were prepared for distribution by his opponents. This suggests that he was a victim of an organized campaign, and it illustrates the importance of ostracism as a political weapon in fifth–century Athens'.

41 Aristotle, *Politics*, 1295b35–1296a5.

42 Recall Huber's theorem (cited at note 35) where the nice properties of a sample median depend upon unimodal distributions.

43 Plato, *Republic*, translated by Paul Shorey (Cambridge, Mass.: Loeb Classical Library, 1935), 561D–E: 'And frequently he goes in for politics and bounces up and says and does whatever enters his head. And if military men excite his emulation, thither he rushes, and if moneyed men, to that he turns . . .' Madison, *Federalist*, p. 61: 'Hence it is, that such Democracies have ever been spectacles of turbulence and contention . . .'.

44 Plato, *Republic*, 416D–E: 'none must possess any private property save the indispensable. Second, none must have any habitation or treasurehouse which is not open for all to enter at will. Their food, in such quantities as are needful for athletes of war sober and brave, they must receive as an agreed stipend from the other citizens as the wages of their guardianship . . . And resorting to a common mess like soldiers on campaign they will live together'. Plato, *Republic*, 347D: 'For we may venture to say that, if there should be a city of good men only, immunity from office-holding would be as eagerly contended for as office is now, and there it would be made plain that in very truth the true ruler does not naturally seek his own advantage but that of the ruled . . .'.

45 Plato, *Republic*, 586A–C: 'Then those who have no experience of wisdom and virtue but are ever devoted to feasting and that sort of thing are swept . . . to and fro . . . but they have never transcended all this and turned their eyes to the true upper region nor been wafted there, nor ever been really filled with real things, nor ever tasted stable and pure pleasure, but with eyes bent upon the earth and heads bowed down over their tables they feast like cattle . . .'.

46 Madison, *Federalist*, pp. 57–8.

47 Madison, *Federalist*, pp. 64–5.

48 Smith's texts, and the tradition in which he wrote, are discussed above in Chapters 5 and 6.

49 A. K. Sen, *Collective Choice and Social Welfare* (San Francisco: Holden-Day, 1971).

50 The issues of nonconvex isoquants may occur most dramatically in household production in the problem of addition or other behavior which seems dramatically discontinuous. See Chapter 3.

51 David Schap saw the connection first.

52 Aristotle, *Constitution of Athens*, section 43. My emphasis.

53 McKelvey, 'Global Intransitivities', shows that unless the Plott conditions hold, the outcome of a majority rule vote can wander almost anywhere the agenda setters would like.

54 Plott, 'Equilibrium under Majority Rule'.

55 Staveley, *Voting and Elections*, p. 55, emphasizes the role of rotation in office in the Athenian practice.

56 James Buchanan helped me here.

57 Staveley, *Greek and Roman Voting*, p. 87, quoting Plato's *Laws* 755D.

58 Edited by Judith M. Tanur, *et al.* (San Francisco: Holden-Day, second edition, 1978).

59 I. J. Good, *Good Thinking* (Minneapolis: University of Minnesota Press, 1983), has taken the cost of thinking into account in statistical decision theory.

Chapter 10 Fame and the supply of heroics

1 Homer, *The Iliad*, translated by Richmond Lattimore (Chicago: University of Chicago Press, 1951), 6.444–6: 'I have learned to be valiant/and to fight always among the foremost ranks of the Trojans,/winning for my own self great glory, and for my father.'

2 *The Odyssey of Homer*, translated by Richmond Lattimore (New York: Harper Torchbooks, 1967), 8.496–8: 'If you can tell me the course of all these things as they happened,/I will speak of you before all mankind, and tell them/how freely the goddess gave you the magical gift of singing'. The immortality of poets is one of the great commonplaces of classical poetry. Is there any doubt that this is true?

3 *Gilgamesh*, translated by John Gardner and John Maier (New York: Alfred A. Knopf, 1984), II.vi (Old Babylonian version).

4 Jeffrey H. Tigay, *The Evolution of the Gilgamesh Epic* (Philadelphia: University of Pennsylvania Press, 1982), p. 146.

5 Andy Warhol said this first when he joked that in the future everyone would be famous for fifteen minutes; Leo Braudy, *The Frenzy of Renown* (New York: Oxford University Press, 1986), p. 506.

6 Derek J. de Solla Price, *Science since Babylon* (New Haven: Yale University Press, 1961), p. 48: 'Then again, the motivation for research may be an intellectual itch – indeed, the purpose of education has been defined as the business of making people uncomfortable, making them itch – but a deeper and more specific urge may have made these persons into scientists. By far the most common inner reason is that as youngsters they have wanted to be a Mr. Boyle of the Law. They seek an immortal brainchild in order to perpetuate themselves'. A model of fame production is constructed and tested in David Levy, 'The Economics of Fame and Fortune', *History of Political Economy* 20 (1988): 615–25. The formative work in this area is that of Robert K. Merton *The Sociology of Science*, edited by Norman W. Storer (Chicago: University of Chicago Press, 1973), who explains the importance of 'property rights in ideas'.

7 J. G. A. Pocock, *The Machiavellian Moment* (Princeton: Princeton University Press, 1975), p. 133, worries about whether honor is more than a feudal ethos.

8 Emily Vermeule, *Aspects of Death in Early Greek Art and Poetry* (Berkeley: University of California Press, 1979), p. 23.

9 *Iliad* 7.448–53.

10 Genesis 11:1, 4–7.

11 Genesis 21:12.

12 Douglass Adair, *Fame and the Founding Fathers*, edited by Trevor Colbourn (New York: W. W. Norton, 1974), p. 12. Adair notes a relevant remark from Diderot: 'posterity is for the philosopher what the other world is for the religious man'.

13 Polybius, *The Histories*, translated by Mortimer Chambers, edited by E. Badian (New York: Twayne Publishers, 1966), p. 261.

14 Democritus, *Ancilla to the Pre-Socratic Philosophers*, translated by Kathleen Freeman (Oxford: Blackwell's, 1971), ¶253. There is a charge from antiquity about Plato's hostility to Democritus, Diogenes Laertius, *Lives of the Eminent Philosophers*, translated

by R. D. Hicks (Cambridge, Mass.: Loeb Classical Library, 1979) 9:40.

15 Eric A. Havelock, *The Liberal Temper in Greek Politics* (New Haven: Yale University Press, 1957) and Thomas Cole, *Democritus and the Sources of Greek Anthropology*, Philological Monographs 25 (Chapel Hill: Press of Western Reserve University, 1967). In connection with the American founding, the importance of the euphemistic tradition, for whom Lactantius is an important Christian spokesman, is stressed by Adair, *Fame*. Pocock at various places in *Machiavellian Moment* shows how important Polybius is to the Italian discussion.

16 Pocock, *Machiavellian Moment*, pp. 249–50.

17 Heracleitus, *Ancilla to the Pre-Socratic Philosophers*, translated by Kathleen Freeman (Oxford: Blackwell's, 1972), ¶29.

18 Heracleitus, ¶32: 'That which alone is wise is one; it is willing and unwilling to be called by the name of Zeus.' ¶14: 'Night-ramblers, magicians, Bacchants, Maenads, Mystics: the rites accepted by mankind in the Mysteries are an unholy performance.'

19 Dante Alighieri, *Inferno*, translated by Allen Mandelbaum (Berkeley: University of California Press, 1980), 4:139. 'Democritus, who ascribes the world to chance' is one of the favored companions of Aristotle.

20 Thomas Hobbes, *Leviathan*, edited by C. B. MacPherson (Harmondsworth, England: Penguin Books, 1972), p. 162.

21 Bernard Mandeville, *Fable of the Bees*, edited by F. B. Kaye (Oxford: Clarendon Press, 1924), 1:54–5.

22 Bernard Mandeville, *An Enquiry into the Origin of Honour* (London, 1732), p. 40. Arthur O. Lovejoy, *Reflections on Human Nature* (Baltimore: Johns Hopkins University Press, 1961), is especially instructive on this aspect of Mandeville's work.

23 Friedrich Nietzsche, *The Portable Nietzsche*, translated by Walter Kaufmann (New York: Vintage Press, 1968), pp. 35–6: 'We do not understand the full strength of Xenophanes' attack on the national hero of poetry, unless – as again later with Plato – we see that at its root lay an overwhelming craving to assume the place of the overthrown poet and to inherit his fame'.

24 Erwin Rohde, *Psyche*, translated by W. B. Hillis (London, 1925), p. 9: 'To speak of an "immortal life" of the souls, as scholars both ancient and modern have done, is incorrect. They can hardly be said to *live* even, any more than the image does that is reflected in the mirror; and that they prolong to eternity their shadowy image-existence – where in Homer do we ever find this said? The psyche may survive its visible companion, but it is helpless without it'.

25 *Psyche*, p. 21: 'Since the destruction of the body by fire is supposed to result in the complete separation of the spirit from the land of the living, it must be assumed that this result is also *intended* by the survivors who employ the means in question . . . Cremation, therefore, is intended to benefit the dead, whose soul no longer wanders unable to find rest; but still more the living, for they will not be troubled by ghosts that are securely confined to the depths of the earth'.

26 *Psyche*, p. 43.

27 *Psyche*, p. 130. Rohde separates the Oracle of legend from the historical Oracle in advance of recent scholarship. Joseph Fontenrose, *The Delphic Oracle* (Berkeley: University of California Press, 1981), p. 27, finds that in excess of 50 percent of the 'historical' responses of the Delphic oracle concerned cult foundations (20.3 percent) or sacrifices and offerings (31.1 percent). This is distinguished from less than 22 percent in the 'legendary' category.

28 *Psyche*, pp. 12–15.

29 Milman Parry, *Making of Homeric Verse*, edited by Adam Parry (Oxford: Clarendon Press, 1971).

30 *Psyche*, p. 7: 'That the dream experiences are veritable realities and not empty fancies for Homer is also certain. . . . The figures seen in dreams are real figures, either of the

gods themselves or a "dream spirit" sent by them, or a fleeting "image" (*eidôlon*) that they allow to appear for a moment'.

31 Plato, *The Symposium*, translated by W. R. M. Lamb (Cambridge, Mass.: Loeb Classical Library, 1925), 208C–D: 'Be certain of it, Socrates; only glance at the ambition of the men around you, and you will have to wonder at the unreasonableness of what I have told you, unless you are careful to consider how singularly they are affected with the love of winning a name, "and laying up fame immortal for all time to come." For this, even more than for their children, they are ready to run all risks, to expend money, perform any kind of task, and sacrifice their lives. Do you suppose', she asked, 'that Alcestis would have died for Admetus, or Achilles have sought death on the corpse of Patroclus, or your own Codrus have welcomed it to save the kingdom of his children, if they had not expected to win "a deathless memory for valour," which now we keep?'

32 Plato, *The Republic*, translated by Paul Shorey (Cambridge, Mass.: Loeb Classical Library, 1936), 620c.

33 Robert L. Wilken, *The Christians as the Romans Saw Them* (New Haven: Yale University Press, 1984), pp. 126–63, has an extensive discussion of Christian reaction to Porphyry, emphasizing why there was real reason for his works to be burnt.

34 Democritus, ¶95. Also ¶56 and of course ¶119: 'I would rather discover one cause than gain the kingdom of Persia.'

35 Democritus, ¶297.

36 Origen, *Contra Celsum*, translated by Henry Chadwick (Cambridge: Cambridge University Press, 1980), p. 168.

37 *Psyche*, p. 239. *The Homeric Hymns*, translated by Apostolos N. Athanassakis (Baltimore: Johns Hopkins University Press, 1976), *Homeric Hymn to Demeter* 480: 'Whoever on this earth has seen these is blessed,/but he who has no part in the holy rites has/another lot as he wastes away in dank darkness'. E. R. Dodds, *The Ancient Concept of Progress* (Oxford: Clarendon Press, 1974), p. 149: 'Here, in language discreetly vague, we have the earliest European statement of a religious dogma which has had a long though not very creditable history – the dogma that salvation in the next world depends on taking part in certain rituals in this one'.

38 Adair, *Fame*, p. 18, cites Euhemerism as the way out for Christians who admire the ancients. Lactantius is an interesting Christian father for those with a bent for the unorthodox in any direction. He has attracted renewed interest in recent years for his role in sanctifying the *Corpus Hermeticum*, Frances A. Yates, *Giordano Bruno and the Hermetic Tradition* (London: Routledge & Kegan Paul, 1964), pp. 6–9.

39 Lactantius, *The Divine Institutes*, translated by Mary Francis McDonald, volume 49 of *The Fathers of the Church* (Washington: Catholic University of America Press, 1964), p. 192. Emphasis added.

40 *Divine Institutes*, p. 61.

41 Augustine, *The City of God*, translated by Demetrius B. Zema and Gerald G. Walsh, volume 8 of *The Fathers of the Church* (New York: Cima Publishers, 1950), p. 270.

42 Demons are featured by Augustine, *The City of God*, translated by Gerald G. Walsh, volume 24 of *The Fathers of the Church* (New York: Cima Publishers, 1954), pp. 90–1, 95, 99–100, 353–4. Occasionally, men are mistaken for gods, pp. 94, 102.

43 Jeremy Bentham, *Auto–Icon; or, farther uses of the dead to the living* (not published [1832]), p. 7. I used the copy in the Library of Congress Rare Book Room. Bentham's statement might be compared with the traditional Platonic–Christian view that only atheists are criminals which is discussed in Chapter 14.

44 *Auto-Icon*, p. 7.

45 *Auto-icon*, p. 3.

46 John F. Muth, 'Rational Expectations and the Theory of Price Movements', *Rational Expectations and Econometric Practice*, edited by Robert E. Lucas, Jr., and Thomas J.

Sargent (Minneapolis: University of Minnesota Press, 1981).

47 Adam Smith, *The Theory of Moral Sentiments*, edited by D. D. Raphael and A. L. Macfie (Indianapolis: Liberty Classics, 1982), pp. 250–1: 'Great success in the world, great authority over the sentiments and opinions of mankind, have very seldom been acquired without some degree of this excess self-admiration. . . . This presumption was, perhaps, necessary, not only to prompt them to undertakings which a more sober mind would never have thought of, but to command the submission and obedience of their followers to support them in such undertakings. When crowned with success, accordingly, this presumption has often betrayed them into a vanity that approached almost to insanity and folly. Alexander the Great appears, not only to have wished that other people should think him a God, but to have been at least very well disposed to fancy himself such. Upon his death-bed, the most ungodlike of all situations, he requested of his friends that, to the respectable list of Deities, into which himself had long before been inserted, his old mother Olympia might likewise have the honour of being added. Amidst the respectful admiration of his followers and disciples, amidst the universal applause of the public, after the oracle, which probably had followed the voice of that applause, had pronounced him the wisest of men, the great wisdom of Socrates, though it did not suffer him to fancy himself a God, yet was not great enough to hinder him from fancying that he had secret and frequent intimations from some invisible and divine Being. The sound head of Caesar was not so perfectly sound as to hinder him from being much pleased with his divine genealogy . . .'.

48 Adam Smith, *The Wealth of Nations*, edited by W. B. Todd (Oxford: Clarendon Press, 1976), p. 123.

49 *Wealth of Nations*, pp. 126–7.

50 Frank H. Knight, *The Ethics of Competition* (New York: Harper & Row, 1935).

51 David Levy, 'Diamonds, Water and Z Goods', *History of Political Economy* 14 (1982): 313–22.

52 I have been discussing these matters with Jennifer Roback for years now. I thank her for remaining amused even though progress has been slow.

53 Kenneth J. Arrow, 'The Theory of Discrimination', *Discrimination in the Labor Market*, edited by Orley Ashenfelter and Albert Rees (Princeton: Princeton University Press, 1973), and Edmund S. Phelps, 'The Statistical Theory of Racism and Sexism', *American Economic Review* 62 (1972): 659–61.

54 I. J. Good, *Good Thinking* (Minneapolis: University of Minnesota Press, 1983), p. 153: '*The principle of rationality* of Type I is the recommendation to maximize expected utility. The principle of rationality of Type II is the same except that the costs of theorizing and calculations are allowed for.'

55 E. L. Lehmann, *Testing Statistical Hypotheses* (New York: John Wiley, second edition, 1986).

56 This immediately suggests that the gross stereotypes one hears so often on AM radio are probably not the stereotypes that employers use to make hiring decisions. They would surely be too costly. However, crude stereotypes might matter if voting behavior is expressive. Susan Feigenbaum, Lynn Karoly and David Levy, 'When Votes are Words not Deeds: Evidence from the Nuclear Freeze Referendum', *Public Choice* 58 (September 1988): 201–16.

57 Computing the current mean by updating the past mean is feasible, but much more costly in terms of division operations.

58 The problem of computing medians is severe enough to merit attention at the highest level, cf. Niklaus Wirth, *Algorithms + Data Structures = Programs* (Englewood Cliffs, N.J.: Prentice-Hall, 1976), pp. 82–4. The statement in the text, as well as the algorithm Wirth gives, assumes that the number of observations is odd.

59 Part of the simplification is that we assume that all K observations will be used. As the loss function is formulated, the sample size is endogenous and might well be connected

with a choice of estimator. The following might very well be equally cheap estimators: a median with sixty observations, a mean with 250 observations, or a midrange with 10,000 observations.

60 Least square regression is a linear estimator; least absolute deviations is nonlinear. For those who are not persuaded of the inexorability of the normal distribution, the great charm of least squares has been tractability. Least absolute deviations did not become a viable technique until the work by Abraham Charnes and W. W. Cooper in the 1950s. Few students of my generation actually worked with least absolute deviations regressions until a decade after graduate school. Now, with the vanishing of computational cost, my undergraduates perform monte carlo studies comparing these two techniques in the first half of a one-semester course! *Tempus fugit*.

61 Maurice Kendall and Alan Stuart, *The Advanced Theory of Statistics* (New York: Macmillan Publishing, fourth edition, 1977), 1:366, establish that the midrange is an unbiased estimator when the underlying distribution follows a symmetrical, exponential-type population. At pp. 349–50 Kendall and Stuart give the standard error of the midrange for small samples when the underlying parent distribution is normal.

62 Kendall and Stuart, *The Advanced Theory of Statistics*, 1:41.

63 On influence curves, see Frederick Mosteller and John W. Tukey, *Data Analysis and Regression* (Reading, Mass.: Addison-Wesley, 1977).

PART V A COMPETITIVE EPISODE: THE MALTHUSIAN CONTROVERSY

1 Christine Holden and David M. Levy, 'Birth Control and the Amelioration Controversy', Public Choice Working Paper, 1990.

2 Charles Bradlaugh, *Jesus, Shelley, and Malthus* (London, 1861), p. 3.

3 No secret was made of his importance or his courage by those who would live long enough to become reputable, [Margaret Sanger], *One Hundred Years of Birth Control* (New York: Birth Control Review, 1921).

4 Samuel Hollander, *The Economics of David Ricardo* (Toronto: University of Toronto Press, 1979); Samuel Hollander, 'On Malthus's Population Principle and Social Reform', *History of Political Economy* 18 (1986): 187–236.

Chapter 11 Ricardo and the iron law

1 David Ricardo, *On the Principles of Political Economy and Taxation*, edited by Piero Sraffa, volume 1, *The Works and Correspondence of David Ricardo* (Cambridge: Cambridge University Press, 1962), p. 93.

2 George Stigler, 'Does Economics Have a Useful Past?' *History of Political Economy* 1 (1969): 220, suggests that someone who understands the first five chapters of Ricardo's *Principles* should be able to write his history of taxation. One interesting difficulty is how to distinguish between 'slips' of the economist being studied and the 'misreading' of the commentator. If there is a real slip, then perhaps controversy following publication will bring this out. If the economist is still alive, he presumably would make a correction. This, I shall argue, in fact happened to one aspect of the first two editions of the *Principles*. There is, I believe, a 'slip' which Ricardo 'corrected' in the third edition.

3 George Stigler, *Essays in the History of Economics* (Chicago: University of Chicago Press, 1965), pp. 171–2. Paul A. Samuelson, *The Collected Scientific Papers*, edited by Joseph E. Stiglitz (Cambridge, Mass.: M.I.T. Press, 1966), p. 414: 'Ricardo followed Torrens in tending to neglect the long time period it would take for population to bring the

real wage back to the conventional subsistence level. This is in accordance with his tendency to treat long-run relations as if they held in the shorter run'. Mark Blaug, *Ricardian Economics* (New Haven: Yale University Press, 1958), p. 28: 'The same ambiguous resort to different clock periods vitiates Ricardo's dismissal of the possibility of serious influences arising from improvements in agricultural technique.'

4 Stigler, *Essays*, pp. 163–6, and Blaug, *Ricardian Economics*, pp. 105–6, read Malthus in such a way that if delay of marriage is introduced into the theory it becomes empty of content. A theory which posits a fixed age of marriage is at best uncomfortable with considerations which might speed or delay marriage. The fact that Malthus discusses such considerations at great length can then be produced as 'evidence' of Malthus's inability to understand the simple consequence of his own theory.

5 Stigler, *Essays*, p. 171: 'Ricardo accepted the simple version of the first edition of the *Essay*, in which wages were always equal to some fixed ("subsistence") level in the long run.' Joseph A. Schumpeter, *A History of Economic Analysis* (New York: Oxford University Press, 1954), p. 569: 'it occurred to Ricardo, wages are not really a variable either, at least not within that equation. He thought he knew, from external considerations, what they will be in the long run: here the old Quesnay theory comes in, reinforced by Malthus' law of population'.

6 W. Stanley Jevons, *The Theory of Political Economy* (New York: Augustus M. Kelley [1957], 1965), 268–9; Leon Walras, *Elements of Pure Economics*, translated by William Jaffe (Homewood, Ill.: Irwin, 1954), pp. 424–5; Frank H. Knight, *On the History and Method of Economics* (Chicago: University of Chicago Press, 1956), p. 71: 'the fallacy of plural residuals does occur in the classical theory of profits and wages, which reduces to the absurdity that each claimant gets what is left after the other is paid.' Schumpeter, *History*, p. 569: 'That theory of rent having fulfilled its only purpose, which is to get rid of another variable in our equation, we are left, on the margin of production, with one equation and two variables – still a hopeless business'.

7 W. Stanley Jevons, *The Principles of Economics* (New York: Augustus M. Kelley, [1905] 1965), pp. 233–4, commented on Ricardo's opinion with respect to the possibility of taxing workers. Knight, *History and Method*, pp. 82–4.

8 James Mill, *Selected Economic Writings*, edited by Donald Winch (Chicago: University of Chicago Press, 1966), p. 343. This assertion was not in the first edition; hence, we do not have Ricardo's comments.

9 Mountifort Longfield, *Political Economy*, in *The Economic Writings* (New York: Augustus M. Kelley, [1834] 1971), p. 265: 'Mr. Ricardo's opinion is, that a tax upon wages falls entirely upon profits.' J. E. Cairnes in Herbert Spencer *et al.*, *John Stuart Mill: His Life and Work* (Boston: J. R. Osgood, 1873), pp. 68–9: 'So completely had this belief become a fixed idea in Ricardo's mind that he confidently drew from it the consequence, that in no case could taxation fall on the laborer'. F. Y. Edgeworth, *Papers Relating to Political Economy* (New York: Burt Franklin [1925]), 2:67: 'An instance of infinite elasticity of supply is afforded by the labour market upon the Ricardian hypothesis'. Edgeworth's citation with respect to the incidence of taxation on workers comes from J. S. Mill and W. J. Ashley, 'The Rehabilitation of Ricardo'. *Economic Journal* 1 (1891): 485: 'Taxes on wages will raise wages.' His citation that the workers will pay no taxes comes from James Mill's reading of Ricardo, Ashley, 'Rehabilitation', pp. 485–6. Edwin Cannan, *A History of the Theories of Production and Distribution in English Political Economy from 1776 to 1848* (London: Rivington Percival & Co., 1894), p. 250: 'when wages are taxed directly, money wages will rise sufficiently to prevent the labourer's real wage from being affected'. Wesley C. Mitchell, *Types of Economic Theory*, edited by Joseph Dorfman (New York: Augustus M. Kelley, 1967), 1:321: 'Perhaps the most remarkable of all the dicta is his claim that "A tax on wages is wholly a tax on profits".' Lionel Robbins, *The Theory of Economic Policy in English Classical Political Economy* (London: Macmillan, 1953), p. 83: 'In common

with the other Classical Economists, Ricardo believed that *in the absence of deliberate restraint*, the number of labourers would increase so as eventually to bring wages to subsistence level, and in his analysis of the effects of different kinds of taxes and bounties he tended to assume that this actually happened'. Mark Blaug, *Economic Theory in Retrospect* (Homewood, Ill.: Irwin, 1968), p. 138: 'Since the supply curve of labor is perfectly elastic, real wages net of taxes remain the same, and if landlords do not themselves consume grain, the whole burden of the tax falls on profits'. D. P. O'Brien, *J. R. McCulloch* (New York: Barnes & Noble, 1970), p. 240: 'Ricardo was very much inclined to argue that the principle of population would ensure that such taxes were passed on to employers in the form of increased wages, applying much of the time, as was his wont, long-run considerations to short-run problems'.

10 T. R. Malthus in the later editions systematically reported the influences on the age of marriage in different societies. E.g., *An Essay on the Principle of Population* (London: J. M. Dent, Everyman's Library, 1973) on Formosa (1:55), Scandinavia, ancient and modern (1:71), Siberia (1:108), Persia (1:114), India (1:119), Greece (1:145), Norway (1:156), Sweden (1:174), Switzerland (1:205, 211–12), France (1:217), Scotland (1:269). Gary Becker's reading of Malthus is quite accurate. Gary Becker, 'An Economic Analysis of Fertility', in *Demographic and Economic Change in Developed Countries* (Princeton: National Bureau of Economic Research, 1960), p. 212.

Because Patricia James's splendid new edition arrived too late for me to employ systematically, I shall employ the Everyman edition as the default, cited as *Population*, in this and the next two chapters. The Everyman edition is the least bad of a particularly gruesome lot. The first edition will still be needed and will be cited as *Essay*.

11 Malthus, *Population*, 1:280: 'In the statistical account of Scotland it is said that the average distance between the children of the same family has been calculated to be about two years'.

12 Malthus, *Population*, 1:14: 'Promiscuous intercourse, unnatural passions, violations of the marriage bed, and improper arts to conceal the consequences of irregular connections, are preventive checks that clearly come under the head of vice'. Malthus did not believe that moral restraint – 'the restraint from marriage which is not followed by irregular gratifications' (1:14) – 'prevail[ed] much among the male part of society' (1:315). Since 'it can scarcely be doubted that in modern Europe a much larger proportion of women pass a considerable part of their lives in the exercise of this virtue than in past times and among uncivilised nations' (1:315), it would seem that the bulk of the male population was acquiring its irregular gratification with a smaller share of the female population.

The impact of prostitution on population growth was clearly explained by Bernard Mandeville, *A Modest Defence of Publick Stews* (London, 1725), p. 4: 'And since the Prosperity of any Country is allow'd to depend, in a great measure, on the Number of its Inhabitants, the *Government* ought, if it were possible, to prevent any Whoring at all, as it evidently hinders the Propagation of the Species: How many thousand young Men in this Nation would turn their Thoughts toward Matrimony, if they were not constantly destroying that Passion, which is the only Foundation of it?'

13 Malthus, *Population*, 1:7: 'Whether the law of marriage be instituted, or not, the dictate of nature and virtue seems to be an early attachment to one woman; and where there were no impediments of any kind in the way of an union to which such an attachment would lead, and no causes of depopulation afterwards, the increase of the human species would be evidently much greater than any increase which has been hitherto known'. Malthus concluded his section on modern Europe with the observation that 'the most powerful of the checks' to population was 'principally a delay of the marriage union from prudential considerations, without reference to consequences' (1:315).

14 Adam Smith, *An Inquiry into the Nature and Causes of the Wealth of Nations* edited by W. B. Todd (Oxford: Clarendon Press, 1976), p. 71, reported that children represented 'a hundred pounds clear gain' to the parents. 'The value of children is the greatest of all encouragements to marriage. We cannot, therefore, wonder that the people in North America should generally marry very young'.

15 Malthus, *Population*, 2:14.

16 Karl Marx and Friedrich Engels, *Marx and Engels on the Population Bomb*, edited by Ronald L. Meek, translations by Dorothea L. Meek and Ronald L. Meek (Berkeley: Ramparts Press, second edition, 1972), p. 16: 'The hatred of the English working class against Malthus . . . is therefore entirely justified. The people were right here in sensing instinctively that they were confronted not with a *man of science* but with a *bought advocate*, a pleader on behalf of their enemies, a shameless sycophant of the ruling classes.' In particular, p. 88: 'the "principle of population" . . . proclaimed with drums and trumpets as the infallible antidote to the teachings of Condorcet, etc., was greeted with jubilance by the English oligarchy as the great destroyer of all hankerings after human development'.

17 Malthus, *Population*, 2:48: 'A poor man may marry with little or no prospect of being able to support a family without parish assistance. They may be said, therefore, to create the poor which they maintain'. 1:269: 'In those parishes where manufactures have been introduced, which afford employment to children as soon as they have reached their 6th or 7th year, a habit of marrying early naturally follows'.

18 T. R. Malthus, *A Summary View of the Principle of Population*, is included with *An Essay on the Principles of Population*, edited by Anthony Flew (Harmondsworth, England: Penguin Books, [1798] 1970), p. 263. Later citations to the first edition shall be *Essay* and publication date of 1798.

19 Malthus, *Essay* [1798], p. 264.

20 Malthus, *Population*, 2:45–6: 'The price of labour, when left to find its natural level, is a most important political barometer . . . it further expresses clearly the wants of the society respecting population; that is, whatever may be the number of children to a marriage necessary to maintain exactly the present population, the price of labour will be just sufficient to support this number, or be above it, or below it, according to the state of the real funds for the maintenance of labour, whether stationary, progressive, or retrograde'. This 'able passage' – Ricardo's term – is quoted in Ricardo's discussion of taxes on wages, *Principles*, pp. 218–19.

21 Ricardo, *Principles*, p. 5: 'But in different stages of society, the proportions of the whole produce of the earth which will be allotted to each of these classes, under the names of rent, profit, and wages, will be essentially different . . . To determine the laws which regulate this distribution, is the principal problem in Political Economy.' Smith, *Wealth of Nations*, p. 87: 'It is not the actual greatness of national wealth, but its continual increase, which occasions a rise in the wages of labour. It is not, accordingly, in the richest countries, but in the most thriving, or in those which are growing rich the fastest, that the wages of labour are highest'.

22 Cannan, *Theories of Production and Distribution*, p. 295.

23 Edward West, *Application of Capital to Land* (Baltimore: Johns Hopkins University Press, [1815] 1903), pp. 23–4, argued that an increase in productivity of labor and capital outside of agriculture could offset the decrease inside of agriculture.

24 Ricardo, *Principles*, p. 133: 'Foreign trade . . . has no tendency to raise the profits of stock, unless the commodities imported be of that description on which the wages of labour are expended'.

25 The sentence in the text assumes that before the change none of either input was thrown away. With fixed proportions the right-hand partial derivative of output with respect to an input is not equal to the left-hand partial derivative.

26 Milton Friedman, *Price Theory* (Chicago: Aldine Publishers, 1962), pp. 162–5.

27 Ricardo, *Principles*, p. 35: 'There can be no rise in the value of labour without a fall of profits. If the corn is to be divided between the farmer and the labourer, the larger the proportion that is given to the latter, the less will remain for the former'.

28 Ricardo, *Principles*, p. 46: 'although I fully allow that money made of gold is subject to most of the variations of other things, I shall suppose it to be invariable, and therefore all alterations in price to be occasioned by some alteration in the value of the commodity of which I may be speaking'.

29 Ricardo, *Principles*, p. 72: 'When land of an inferior quality is taken into cultivation, the exchangeable value of raw produce will rise, because more labour is required to produce it'.

30 Ricardo, *Principles*, p. 116. Ricardo is discussing the division of the produce of ten men with a constant amount of capital on a constant quality of land as that piece of land moves from the margin of cultivation (zero rent) to inside the margin (positive rent).

31 Ricardo, *Principles*, p. 99, separates the analysis of countries with an insecurity of property from his general argument.

32 Ricardo, *Principles*, p. 122: 'no one accumulates but with a view to make his accumulation productive . . . The farmer and manufacturer can no more live without profit, than the labourer without wages. Their motive for accumulation will diminish with every diminution of profit, and will cease altogether when their profits are so low as not to afford them an adequate compensation for their trouble, and the risk which they must necessarily encounter'.

33 David Ricardo, *Notes on Malthus's Principles of Political Economy*, edited by Piero Sraffa, volume 2, *The Works and Correspondence of David Ricardo* (Cambridge: Cambridge University Press, 1957), p. 241: 'To say that I have a very abundant capital is to say that I have a great demand for labour'. Complications arise if fixed capital is substituted for circulating capital.

34 Ricardo, *Principles*, p. 98: 'under favourable circumstances population may be doubled in twenty–five years; but under the same favourable circumstances, the whole capital of a country might possibly be doubled in a shorter period. In that case, wages during the whole period would have a tendency to rise'.

35 Ricardo, *Principles*, p. 101: 'In the natural advance of society, the wages of labour will have a tendency to fall, as far as they are regulated by supply and demand; for the supply of labourers will continue to increase at the same rate, whilst the demand for them will increase at a slower rate. If, for instance, wages were regulated by a yearly increase of capital, at the rate of 2 per cent., they would fall when it accumulated only at the rate of 1½ per cent. They would fall still lower when it increased only at the rate of 1, or ½ per cent, and would continue to do so until the capital became stationary, when wages also would become stationary, and be only sufficient to keep up the numbers of the actual population'. Notice that the case which Ricardo has defined as the 'natural wage' occurs only in the stationary state.

36 Ricardo, *Principles*, p. 292: 'no point is better established than that the supply of labourers will always ultimately be in proportion to the means of supporting them.' If $L = cK$ and if c is a constant during equilibrium, then $dL/dt = cdK/dt$. Dividing to find the percentage rate of growth, we arrive at the equilibrium condition in the text.

37 Ricardo, *Principles*, p. 116. Again these are the corn wages for ten men.

38 Ricardo, *Principles*, p. 289: 'no accumulation of capital will permanently lower profits, unless there be some permanent cause for the rise of wages . . . If the necessaries of the workman could be constantly increased with the same facility, there could be no permanent alteration in the rate of profits or wages, to whatever amount capital might be accumulated'.

39 Ricardo, *Principles*, pp. 94–5: 'Notwithstanding the tendency of wages to conform to their natural rate, their market rate may, in an improving society, for an indefinite

period, be constantly above it'. This discussion is cited in Cannan, *Theories of Production and Distribution*, pp. 246–50, Mitchell, *Types of Economic Theory*, p. 320, Stigler, *Essays*, pp. 171–2. Alfred Marshall's 'rehabilitation', *Principles of Economics* (London: Macmillan, 1890), pp. 553–4, mentions only Ricardo's discussion of the possibility of changes in tastes raising money wages. Because of the index–number problem, this would not (unambiguously) raise real wages.

40 Ricardo, *Principles*, p. 125: 'each labourer would receive more money wages; but the conditions of the labourer, as we have already shown, would be worse . . . The only real gainers would be the landlords'.

41 T. R. Malthus, *Principles of Political Economy*, included in Ricardo, *Notes on Malthus*, p. 257.

42 Ricardo, *Notes on Malthus*, p. 258: 'I agree throughout this section with Mr. Malthus in principle, we only differ in our ideas of what constitutes a real measure of value'.

43 Malthus, *Political Economy*, pp. 227–8; Ricardo, *Notes on Malthus*, p. 227, replied: 'By the natural price I do not mean the usual price, but such a price as is necessary to supply constantly a given demand'.

44 Edward West, *Price of Corn and Wages of Labour* (London, 1826), pp. 64–5; Longfield, *Political Economy*, pp. 226–7.

45 Mitchell, *Types*, pp. 319–25.

46 Ricardo, *Principles*, pp. 226–7.

47 Ricardo, *Principles*, p. 222: 'Taxes then, generally, as far as they impair the real capital of the country, diminish the demand for labour, and therefore it is a probable, but not a necessary, nor peculiar consequence of a tax on wages, that though wages would rise, they would not rise by a sum precisely equal to the tax.' Ricardo, *Principles*, p. 166: 'no other inconvenience would be suffered by this class [labourers], than that which they would suffer from any other mode of taxation, namely, the risk that the tax might infringe on the funds destined for the maintenance of labour, and might therefore check or abate the demand for it'.

48 Ricardo, *Principles*, p. 225: 'All the effects which are produced . . . [by] increasing difficulty of production, will equally follow from a rise of wages in consequence of taxation; and, therefore, the enjoyments of the labourer, as well as those of his employers, will be curtailed by the tax; and not by this tax particularly, but by every other which should raise an equal amount, as they would all tend to diminish the fund destined for the maintenance of labour'.

49 *Principles*, pp. 159, 233, 235.

50 *Principles*, pp. 347–8.

51 *Principles*, p. 348.

52 Ricardo, *Principles*, p. 107: 'They have rendered restraint superfluous, and have invited imprudence, by offering it a portion of the wages of prudence and industry'. *Principles*, pp. 105–6: 'The clear and direct tendency of the poor laws . . . [is] to deteriorate the condition of both poor and rich'.

53 G. S. L. Tucker, 'Ricardo and Marx', *Economica*, n.s., 28 (1961): 257–8.

Chapter 12 Some normative aspects of the Malthusian controversy

1 E.g., Kenneth Smith, *The Malthusian Controversy* (London: Routledge & Kegan Paul, 1951), p. 34: 'For minds which had lost their bearings it was gratifying to have their course restored. Man had tried to do too much. He had been too enthusiastic in the cause of progress. His well-meant efforts had disordered the laws of nature which are the laws of God. Malthus offered a scientific pessimism, which, gloomy and fatalistic as it was towards the hopes of the working classes, absolved the ruling classes from the need to make "futile" efforts on their behalf'. Also, [William Hazlitt], *A Reply to the*

Essay on Population (London, 1807), p. 19. The Marxian reading of Malthus common to literary critics presupposes all this, e.g., Raymond Williams, *Culture and Society* (London: Chatto & Windus, 1958), p. 81, and Philip Rosenberg, *The Seventh Hero* (Cambridge, Mass.: Harvard University Press, 1974), pp. 132–4.

2 What does the word 'vice' in Malthus's argument signify? Malthus in the first edition used early marriage as one of the defining characteristics of 'virtue'. *An Essay on the Principles of Population*, edited by Anthony Flew (Harmondsworth, England: Penguin Books, [1798] 1970), p. 73: 'Whether the law of marriage be instituted or not, the dictate of nature and virtue seems to be an early attachment to one woman'. And conversely, Malthus, *Essay* [1798], p. 76: 'These [prudential] considerations are calculated to prevent, and certainly do prevent, a very great number in all civilized nations from pursuing the dictate of nature in an early attachment to one woman. And this restraint almost necessarily, though not absolutely so, produces vice'.

3 Paul A. Samuelson, *Foundations of Economic Analysis* (New York: Atheneum, 1965), p. 223. Milton Friedman, *Essays in Positive Economics* (Chicago: University of Chicago Press, 1959), p. 104, warns: 'The reader should perhaps be warned that the identification of "being on a higher indifference curve" with "is preferable to" is a far less innocent step than may appear on the surface'.

4 The problem is that, if the costs of effecting transactions are introduced into the discussion, an individual might choose a lower indifference curve because the extra costs in obtaining a higher indifference curve exceed the gain in utility. This issue comes up again in Chapter 18.

5 The relevant citations to Malthus' positive theory are collected in Chapter 11.

6 William Godwin, *Enquiry Concerning Political Justice*, edited by K. Codell Carter (Oxford: Clarendon Press, 1971), p. 304. It should be noted that in this model children do not enter the utility function of their parents, at least not at the time of marriage. This is, I think, in keeping with the classical result that if people can expect to destroy their children with minimal cost, early marriages will result. For example, Adam Smith, *An Inquiry into the Nature and Causes of the Wealth of Nations*, edited by W. B. Todd (Oxford: Clarendon Press, 1976), p. 90, on the ghastly habits of the Chinese. Malthus agreed with David Hume's argument that individuals will marry expecting to destroy their children, but will find themselves unable to do so. T. R. Malthus, *An Essay on the Principle of Population* (London: J. M. Dent, Everyman edition, 1973), 1:49. Godwin, in his first reply to Malthus, *Thoughts Occasioned by the Perusal of Dr. Parr's Spital Sermon*, in *Political Justice*, pp. 329–30, thought infanticide a reasonably satisfactory option to misery or vice. As a result of excluding children from the utility function, the classics did not worry much about the problem of whether children shared in their parents' income. I am indebted to Professor Stigler for pointing out this problem to me.

7 George J. Stigler, *Essays in the History of Economics* (Chicago: University of Chicago Press, 1965), pp. 164–6, discusses Godwin's objections to Malthus: 'men of the more enlightened classes already postpone marriage to avoid the poverty resulting from a great family, and in Godwin's society this prudence will be characteristic of the entire population. Surely Godwin was right, judged not only by the historical fact that this was the one objection to his system that the nineteenth century removed but also by contemporary evidence of widespread postponement of marriage, which indicated that this sort of behavior was not beyond mortal man. Malthus capitulated, while still claiming victory, when in the second edition of the *Essay* (1803) he gave special prominence to a new preventive check (in addition to vice) to population – moral restraint. . . . Given the possible – although in Malthus's opinion the improbable – efficacy of the moral restraint, Godwin had carried this issue.' Hence, in Stigler's reading, the issue between Godwin and Malthus hinges upon whether delay of marriage was possible; indeed, Malthus lost when this consideration was introduced

into the second edition of the *Essay* as the moral restraint. Stigler simply confuses moral with prudential restraint. Joseph A. Schumpeter, *A History of Economic Analysis* (New York: Oxford University Press, 1954), pp. 254–5.

8 Malthus, *Population*, 1:14. This definition of moral restraint was added in the 1806 edition, T. R. Malthus, *An Essay on the Principle of Population*, edited by Patricia James (Cambridge: Cambridge University Press, 1989), 1:18. Perhaps this precision was added to address the ambiguity detected by one of Malthus's early supporters. *Remarks on a Late Publication, entitled, 'An Essay on the Principle of Population . . .' by T. R. Malthus* (London, 1803), pp. 32–3: 'I have all along used the term *moral* restraint . . . to signify that principle, from whatever motives it may arise, which restrains men under certain circumstances from forming matrimonial alliances. But there is a singular obscurity and uncertainty in Mr. Malthus's use of the term . . . Sometimes . . . he uses it in this general but definite signification; at other times, and where he is peculiarly disposed to heap blame, and vice, and misery upon mankind, he confines the use of the term to signify merely the virtue of chastity in single life . . . Chastity is too nice a point of calculation to enter into the rough estimate, which is all that we can attain of population'.

9 1 Corinthians 7:1–2, 7–9. This is noted by William D. Grampp, 'Malthus and his Contemporaries', *History of Political Economy* 6 (1974):302.

10 Service of Matrimony: 'Secondly, it was ordained for a remedy against sin, and to avoid fornication; that such persons as have not the gift of continency might marry, and keep themselves undefiled members of Christ's body'.

11 [Josiah Tucker], *A Brief Essay . . . with Regard to Trade* (London: second edition, 1750), pp. 90–1. It might be noted that the Neomalthusians raised the same point in their polemics against the Malthusians. E.g., Francis Place, *Illustrations and Proofs of the Principles of Population* (London, 1822), pp. 175–7; Owen, in Thomas Skidmore, *Moral Physiology Exposed and Refuted* (New York, 1831), pp. 25–32; and Annie Besant, *The Law of Population* (London, 1879), p. 27. In a semi-systematic reading of *The Malthusian*, I have found only one Malthusian who was willing to explicitly defend prostitution *vis-à-vis* birth control.

12 Robert Wallace, *A Dissertation of the Numbers of Mankind* (New York: Augustus M. Kelley, [1809] 1969), p. 19.

13 Malthus, *Population*, 1:14–15: 'the rejection of the term vice would introduce a considerable confusion into our language and ideas . . . The gratification of all our passions in its immediate effect is happiness, not misery; and, in individual instances, even the remote consequences (at least in this life) may possibly come under the same denomination. There may have been some irregular connections with women, which have added to the happiness of both parties, and have injured no one. These individual actions, therefore, cannot come under the head of misery. But they are still evidently vicious, because an action is denominated, which violates an express precept [of the Creator] . . . whatever may be its individual effect'.

14 Frank H. Knight, *Ethics of Competition* (New York: Augustus M. Kelley, 1951), p. 20: 'If human wants are data in the ultimate sense for scientific purposes, it will appear that there is no place for ethical theory in the sense in which ethicists have conceived that subject, but that its place must be taken by economics'.

15 Godwin, *Enquiry*, p. 279: 'Hence it follows, upon the principles of equal and impartial justice, that the good things of the world are a common stock, upon which one man has as valid a title as another to draw for what he wants'.

16 Malthus, *Essay* [1798], p. 136: 'I cannot conceive a form of society so favourable upon the whole to population . . . we are supposing no anxiety about the future support of children to exist. I do not conceive that there would be one woman in a hundred, of twenty-three, without a family'.

17 Under private property and the institution of marriage, the private costs of a family are

the social costs. Malthus argued that this explains why a family structure would re-establish itself after communism had been attempted. Malthus, *Essay* [1798], p. 141: 'The institution of marriage, or at least, of some express or implied obligation on every man to support his own children, seems to be the natural result of these reasonings in a community under the difficulties that we have supposed'.

18 *Thoughts Occasioned by the Perusal of Dr. Parr's Spital Sermon*, in *Political Justice*, p. 332.

19 Malthus, *Essay* [1798], p. 136: 'With these extraordinary encouragements to population, and every cause of depopulation, as we have supposed, removed, the numbers would necessarily increase faster than in any society that has ever yet been known'.

20 Malthus, *Essay* [1798], p. 143: 'We have seen the fatal effects that would result to a society, if every man had a valid claim to an equal share of the produce of the earth.' Also (Malthus, *Essay* [1798], p. 141): 'while every man felt secure that all his children would be well provided for by general benevolence, the powers of the earth would be absolutely inadequate to produce food for the population which would inevitably ensue . . . some check to population therefore was imperiously called for; thar the most natural and obvious check seemed to be to make every man provide for his own children'.

21 A problem passed on by Grampp, 'Malthus', pp. 298–9, is worth noting: is there a link between the theological optimism of L. Euler and G. W. Leibniz, and Malthus' attempt to work out the theological consequences of his position? Malthus here seems to prove that evil is necessary in the world. It is not necessary to assume that Malthus was directly influenced by Euler or Leibniz, since the problem of the origin and stability of evil was so vigorously stated in P. Bayle's *Dictionary*. The English discussion surveyed in John Bird Sumner, *A Treatise on the Records of the Creation and on the Moral Attributes of the Creator* (London, third edition, 1825), 2:224–31, points to the formative influence of Bayle. Malthus, *An Essay on the Principle of Population* (New York: Augustus M. Kelley, seventh edition, [1872] 1971), pp. 525–6, was not satisfied with Sumner's solution.

22 Malthus, *Population*, 1:14: 'I have been accused of not allowing sufficient weight in the prevention of population to moral restraint; but when the confined sense of the term, which I have here explained, is averted to, I am fearful that I shall not be found to have erred much in this respect.' John Weyland, *The Principles of Population and Production* (London, 1816), p. 400: 'a *general system* of [moral] restraint among the lower orders is, from the nature and construction of mankind, extremely difficult and improbable; and supposing the abstinence from marriage *only* to be attained, there would be great danger of encouraging the worst vices among them.' Michael Thomas Sadler, *The Law of Population* (London, 1830), 1:317–18; 'Physically speaking, we may hold that it is possible for mankind to remain chaste, without marriage; morally considered, it is impossible. And it is worse than idle – it is immoral, indecent, and false, to assert otherwise. It contradicts nature, reason, scripture, and common sense, in order to build up a theory contrary to them all. But it is useless to enforce so obvious a truth: even Mr. Malthus himself admits it.' See also George Purves, *Gray versus Malthus* (London, 1818), p. 321, and Owen, in Skidmore, *Moral Physiology*, pp. 24–5.

23 Malthus, *Population* [1872], p. 499. Unfortunately, the appended replies of Malthus to his critics are contained in none of the modern editions I have seen prior to Patricia James's.

24 Malthus, *Population* [1872], p. 499.

25 E.g., T. Jarrold, *Dissertations on Man* (London, 1806), pp. 362–3: 'Very few persons have such an opinion of the Deity as to suppose that he would endow with life without providing the means of its support, yet this is the idea that Mr. Malthus holds out: I need not say such an idea banishes the Deity from the world'. Piercy Ravenstone, *A Few Doubts as to the Correctness of some Opinions Generally Entertained on the Subjects of the*

Population and Political Economy (New York: Augustus M. Kelley, [1821] 1966), p. 20: 'Those who would deprive the Deity of his most endearing attributes, would soon deprive him of all; those who have brought themselves to doubt of his goodness, will soon learn to disbelieve his existence'. See also, Hazlitt, *Reply*, p. 340; Purves, *Gray versus Malthus*, pp. 323–4; William Manning, *The Wrongs of Man Exemplified* (London, 1838), p. 288. This line of criticism was disavowed by George Ensor, *An Inquiry Concerning the Population of Nations* (London, 1818), p. 78.

26 James Grahame, *An Inquiry into the Principle of Population* (Edinburgh, 1816), pp. 240–1. Smith, *Malthusian Controversy*, p. 109, neglects to report that Grahame admitted that the poor would be made poorer. This theme is also argued by Weyland, *Principles*, pp. 400–2, and Purves, *Gray versus Malthus*, p. 296.

27 Grahame, *Principle of Population*, pp. 24–5: 'if, insensible to the wisdom of that policy which would represent poverty as a reason for neglecting the usual securities against vice [Note: See the Form of Matrimony in the Book of Common Prayer] they should refuse to be diverted from the high road of nature, and the track of their forefathers, into a path which their pastors themselves might be unwilling to tread; what is to be done with a poor man and his family in this situation?' Weyland, *Principles*, p. 15: 'it seems utterly impossible to reconcile his practical conclusions either with the nature of man, or the plain dictates of religion upon the subject of marriage'. Sadler, *Law of Population*, 1:326: 'It may be here observed, that true morality, any more than divinity, knows nothing of this balancing of vices, so as to present them as the alternatives of each other'. Ravenstone, *A Few Doubts*, p. 19: 'If this system be true, virtue is not merely a name, it is something worse; it is a morbid sensibility, it is a pernicious indulgence of our feelings, which sacrifices the general good to the gratification of our own individual prejudices: our reason must reject it'. This theme is also argued in Hazlitt, *Reply*, p. 365, and David Booth, *A Letter to the Rev. T. R. Malthus* (London, 1823), p. 67.

28 Malthus, *Population*, 2:179–80.

29 Malthus, *Population*, 2:175.

30 Malthus, *Population*, 2:257.

31 It is this radicalism which explains the contemporary charges that Malthus was a Mandevillian. Hazlitt, *Reply*, pp. 5–6; Owen, in Skidmore, *Moral Physiology*, p. 23; and Ensor, *Enquiry*, p. 87.

32 Malthus, *Population* [1872], pp. 511–12.

33 Place, *Illustrations*, pp. 176–7.

Chapter 13 Libertarian communists, Malthusians and J. S. Mill

1 *A Treatise of Human Nature*, edited by L. A. Selby-Bigge (Oxford: Clarendon Press, 1888), pp. 494–5. See Chapters 2 and 7 above.

2 *Enquiry Concerning Political Justice*, edited by K. Codell Carter (Oxford: Clarendon Press, 1971), pp. 294–5.

3 Basil Willey, *The Eighteenth Century* (New York: Columbia University Press, 1940), pp. 230–1.

4 *Political Justice*, 285.

5 I agree with John M. Robson, *The Improvement of Mankind* (Toronto: University of Toronto Press, 1968), p. x, that Mill's ethical concerns unify his work. The construction below will show why Himmelfarb's charge of massive inconsistency between *On Liberty* and Mill's other work is false. Gertrude Himmelfarb, *On Liberty and Liberalism* (New York: Random House, 1974), p. 139: 'It was not only the socialist mode of organization that was at variance with *On Liberty*; it was also the reform of human nature required by the new social organization'. As I will argue, even in *On Liberty* Mill considers moral development a higher-order good than liberty, and

socialism is simply a means to attain this moral, motivational development.

6 A. Lovejoy, *The Great Chain of Being* (Cambridge, Mass.: Harvard University Press, 1936), p. 3.

7 This argument is considered in detail in Chapter 15 below.

8 This is the subject of an important article by John M. Robson, 'Rational Animals and Others', in *James and John Stuart Mill: Papers of the Centenary Conference*, edited by John M. Robson and Michael Laine (Toronto and Buffalo: University of Toronto Press, 1976), pp. 143–60.

9 A modern exposition of this tradition can be found in George J. Stigler and Gary S. Becker, 'De Gustibus Non Est Disputandum', *American Economic Review* 67 (1977): 76–90.

10 T. R. Malthus, *An Essay on the Principle of Population*, edited by T. H. Hollingsworth (London: Dent, Everyman edition, 1973), 2:48: 'A poor man may marry with little or no prospect of being able to support a family without parish assistance. They may be said, therefore, to create the poor which they maintain . . . .'.

11 *An Essay on the Principles of Population*, edited by Anthony Flew (Harmondsworth, England: Penguin Books, [1798] 1970), p. 102.

12 Nassau W. Senior, *Two Lectures on Population . . . to Which is Added a Correspondence between the Author and the Rev. T. R. Malthus* (London, 1831), pp. 35–49.

13 Senior, *Population*, pp. 78–9: 'Nothing can be more accurate than your statement, "that population is always ready and inclined to increase faster than food, *if the checks which repress it are removed.*" But many, perhaps the majority of your readers, adopt the proposition without qualification'. A letter from Malthus, in Senior's *Population*, p. 65, states: 'In no old country that I have yet heard of, have the wages of labour, so determined, been for any length of time such as to maintain with ease the largest families. Consequently, in all old states there will always be a constant pressure specifically arising from the tendency of food to increase not being so great as the tendency of population to increase.' Archbishop Whately, quoted in Nassau W. Senior, *An Outline of the Science of Political Economy* (London: Allen & Unwin, 1938), p. 47, emphasizes the verbal issues in the use of 'tendency'. Hence, J. S. Mill: 'Others have attached immense importance to a correction which more recent political economists have made in the mere language of the earlier followers of Mr. Malthus'. *Principles of Political Economy*, edited by J. M. Robson, *Collected Works* (Toronto: University of Toronto Press, 1965), 2:353.

14 Senior's Malthusian reputation troubled the *Quarterly Review*. Before the Poor Law Commission report is issued, G. P. Scrope protested Senior's role in the Poor Law inquiry, 'The Poor-Law Question', *Quarterly Review* 50 (1834): 349–50: 'He had declared himself, *ex cathedra*, as a professor of political economy, of the opinion of Mr. Malthus and Mr. Ricardo, that the only effective way of improving the poor-law is to *abolish* it *in toto*'.

15 Nassau W. Senior, *Statement of the Provision for the Poor* (London, 1835), p. 84: 'We have now given a very brief outline of the institutions of those portions of the Continent which appear, from the returns, to have adopted the English principle of acknowledging in every person a right to be supported by the public. It will be observed that in no country, except, perhaps, the Canton de Berne, has compulsory relief produced evils resembling, either in intensity or in extent, those which we have experienced; and that in the majority of the nations which have adopted it, the existing system appears to work'.

16 Senior, *Provision*, p. 88.

17 Mountifort Longfield, *Four Lectures on Poor Laws* in *The Economic Writings of Mountifort Longfield* (New York: Augustus M. Kelley, [1834] 1971), pp. 19–30, 75–9, contrasts the right to a minimum income with the perversity of the English practice. A particularly acute discussion found in William Forster Lloyd, *Lectures on Population,*

Value, Poor-Laws and Rent (New York: Augustus M. Kelley, [1837] 1968), pp. 18–27.

18 'The recent investigations of the poor-law commission . . . seem to us as conclusive in support of the *principle* of a poor-rate, as they are in condemnation of the existing practice', 'Miss Martineau's Summary of Political Economy', in *Essays on Economics and Society*, edited by J. M. Robson, *Collected Works* (Toronto: University of Toronto Press, 1967), 4:227–8.

19 *Political Economy, Collected Works*, 3:1135, has the index of citations to Senior's study in the *Political Economy*.

20 Henry Sidgwick, *The Principles of Political Economy* (London, 1883), p. 522: 'The objections above stated apply with increased force, if we suppose – what experience shews to be most probable – that the increase through equalisation of the incomes of the poorer classes will cause the population to increase at a more rapid rate than at present; so that ultimately the increment of an average worker's share will be partly spent in supporting a larger number of children . . .'.

21 Alfred Marshall, *Principles of Economics*, edited by C. W. Guillebaud (London: Macmillan, ninth (variorum) edition, 1961), p. 177n. In fact, Aristotle presents an early analysis of the public-goods problem, Aristotle, *Politics*, translated by Benjamin Jowett, *The Complete Works of Aristotle*, edited by Jonathan Barnes (Princeton: Princeton University Press, 1984), 1262b14–24: 'Whereas in a state having women and children common, love will be diluted; and the father will certainly not say "my son", or the son "my father". As a little sweet wine mingled with a great deal of water is imperceptible in the mixture, so, in this sort of community, the idea of relationship which is based upon these names will be lost; there is no reason why the so-called father should care about the son, or the son about the father, or brothers about one another. Of the two qualities which chiefly inspire regard and affection – that a thing is your own and that it is precious – neither can exist in such a state as this'.

22 Bernard Mandeville, *Fable of the Bees*, edited by F. B. Kaye (Oxford: Clarendon Press, 1924), 1:39; Hume, *Treatise*, pp. xix–xx; Smith, *Wealth of Nations*, pp. 28–30.

23 Malthus, *Essay* [1798], p. 126.

24 Godwin, *Thoughts*, p. 332.

25 Aristotle, *The Physics*, translated by R. P. Hardie and R. K. Gaye, in *Complete Works of Aristotle*, II, 8, 199a, 199ab. Such a teleology is responsible for charges of methodological inconsistency leveled at Mill by modern philosophers. H. J. McCloskey, *John Stuart Mill* (London: Macmillan, 1971), pp. 138–9, notes that Mill's argument for communism follows rules different from those which are formally laid down in his Humean analysis of cause.

26 Aristotle, *Politics* I, 2.

27 'Coleridge', in *Essays on Ethics, Religion and Society*, edited by J. M. Robson, *Collected Works* (Toronto: University of Toronto Press, 1969), 10:150.

28 *Collected Works*, 10:150. Here Mill parts company with Godwin's anti-establishment opinion in *Political Justice*, p. 236.

29 Robson, *Improvement*, 168.

30 *A System of Logic*, edited by J. M. Robson, *Collected Works* (Toronto: University of Toronto Press, 1973), 8:865–71.

31 *Collected Works*, 8:913: 'It is one of the characters, not absolutely peculiar to the sciences of human nature and society, but belonging to them in a peculiar degree, to be conversant with a subject matter whose properties are changeable. I do not mean changeable from day to day, but from age to age; so that not only the qualities of individuals vary, but those of the majority are not the same in one age as in another'.

32 *An Examination of Sir William Hamilton's Philosophy*, edited by J. M. Robson, *Collected Works* (Toronto: University of Toronto Press, 1979), 9:453: 'The difference between a bad and a good man is not that the latter acts in opposition to his strongest desires; it is that his desire to do right, and his aversion to doing wrong, are strong enough to

overcome, and in the case of perfect virtue, to silence, any other desire or aversion which may conflict with them . . . The object of moral education is to educate the will: but the will can only be educated through the desires and aversions; by eradicating or weakening such of them as are likeliest to lead to evil; exalting to the highest pitch the desire of right conduct and the aversion to wrong . . .'.

33 *Utilitarianism, Collected Works*, 10:211: 'there is no known Epicurean theory of life which does not assign to the pleasures of the intellect, of the feelings and imagination, and of the moral sentiments, a much higher value as pleasures than to those of mere sensation'.

34 Jacob Viner, *The Long View and the Short* (Glencoe, Ill.: Free Press, 1958), pp. 325–6.

35 *Utilitarianism, Collected Works*, 10:211.

36 Mandeville, *Fable*, 1:151: 'how can I believe that a Man's chief Delight is in the Embellishments of the Mind, when I see him ever employ'd about and daily pursue the pleasures that are contrary to them?' Immanuel Kant, *Critique of Practical Reason*, translated by Lewis White Beck (Indianapolis: Library of Liberal Arts, 1956), p. 22: 'As the man who wants money to spend does not care whether the gold in it was mined in the mountains or washed from the sand, provided it is accepted everywhere as having the same value, so also no man asks, when he is concerned only with the agreeableness of life, whether the ideas are from the sense or the understanding; he asks only how much and how great is the pleasure which they will afford him over the longest time'.

37 *Utilitarianism, Collected Works*, 10:212.

38 So charges Robson, *Improvement*, p. 157.

39 *Political Economy, Collected Works*, 2:205.

40 *Collected Works*, 2:206. The critical issue of self-interest and community interest is first raised by Mill in a letter to Harriet Taylor of 19 February 1849, discussing the revisions of the *Political Economy*. He wrote to her (*Political Economy*, Appendix G, *Collected Works*, 3:1028): 'Then again if the sentence "the majority would not exert themselves for anything beyond this & unless they did nobody else would &c" is not tenable, then all the two or three pages of argument which precede & of which this is but a summary, are false, & there is nothing to be said against Communism at all – one would only have to turn round & advocate it – which if done would be better in a separate treatise . . .'.

41 For example, when Mill discusses the effect of communism on incentives to labor, *Political Economy, Collected Works*, 2:205: 'To what extent, therefore, the energy of labour would be diminished by Communism, or whether in the long run it would be diminished at all, must be considered for the present an undecided question.'

42 *Utilitarianism, Collected Works*, 10:232. But Mill admits, in the same paragraph, that use of the religious imperative poses danger: 'I entertain the strongest objections to the system of politics and morals set forth in [Comte's] treatise; but I think it has super-abundantly shown the possibility of giving to the service of humanity, even without the aid of belief in a Providence, both the psychical power and the social efficacy of a religion; . . . the danger is, not that it should be insufficient, but that it should be so excessive as to interfere unduly with human freedom and individuality'.

43 J. S. Mill, *On Liberty*, in *Essays on Politics and Society*, edited by J. M. Robson, *Collected Works* (Toronto: University of Toronto Press, 1977), 18:224. Here Himmelfarb's inconsistency argument has considerable difficulty (*On Liberty and Liberalism*, p. 107): 'The primary goods in *Utilitarianism* were morality and a sense of unity; the primary goods in *On Liberty* were liberty and individuality'. To preempt such an obvious counter-example to her inconsistency thesis, Himmelfarb argues (p. 21) that this passage refers only to the distant past of the human race. The fact that Mill means his restriction to be of contemporary relevance is clear from a longer, parallel discussion in *Representative Government, Collected Works*, 19:377: 'Again, a people must be considered

unfit for more than a limited and qualified freedom, who will not co-operate actively with the law and the public authorities, in the repression of evil-doers. A people who are more disposed to shelter a criminal than to apprehend him; who, like the Hindoos, will perjure themselves to screen the man who has robbed them . . . like some nations of Europe down to a recent date . . . require that the public authorities should be armed with much sterner powers of repression than elsewhere, since the first indispensable requisites of civilized life have nothing else to rest on'.

44 A very strong statement of this is found in the preface to the third edition of Mill's *Political Economy, Collected Works*, 2:xciii.

PART VI OBJECTIONS AND APPLICATIONS

Chapter 14 Must one believe to obey?

1 Plato, *Republic*, translated by Paul Shorey (Cambridge, Mass.: Loeb Classical Library, 1937): 589D–E: 'the things which law and custom deem fair or foul have been accounted so far a like reason – the fair and honourable things being those that subject the brutish part of our nature to that which is human in us, or rather, it may be, to that which is divine, while the foul and base are the things that enslave the gentle to the wild?'

2 Plato, *Laws*, translated by R. G. Bury (Cambridge, Mass.: Loeb Classical Library, 1926), 885B–C. Leo Strauss, *The Argument and the Action of Plato's Laws* (Chicago: University of Chicago Press, 1975), p. 140: 'To believe that gods are and to believe that the gods as the laws declare them to be are, are obviously different things'.

3 The reader should not neglect the collection of learned articles by D. P. Walker, *The Decline of Hell* (Chicago: University of Chicago Press, 1964).

4 Plato, *Laws*, 908E–909A: 'those criminals who suffer from folly [atheism], being devoid of evil disposition and character, shall be placed by the judge according to law in the reformatory for a period of not less than five years, during which time no other of the citizens shall hold intercourse with them, save only those who take part in the nocturnal assembly, and they shall company with them to minister to their souls' salvation by admonition; and when the period of their incarceration has expired, if any of them seems to be reformed, he shall dwell with those who are reformed, but if not, and if he be convicted again on a like charge, he shall be punished by death'.

5 Leo Strauss, *Natural Right and History* (Chicago: University of Chicago Press, 1953), pp. 4–5: 'If our principles have no other support than our blind preferences, everything a man is willing to dare will be permissible. The contemporary rejection of natural right leads to nihilism – nay, it is identical with nihilism'. It would be helpful if contemporary Platonists would build a theory of principled behavior instead of assuming that the eighteenth-century attacks on Platonism did not occur.

6 John Locke, *The Fundamental Constitutions of Carolina, The Works of John Locke*, (London: eighth edition, 1777), 4:534, Article 95. This insufficiently studied work was written 'in association' with the Earl of Shaftesbury. Richard Ashcraft, *Revolutionary Politics and Locke's Two Treatises of Government* (Princeton: Princeton University Press, 1986), p. 122, reports that the literature finds this text to be an unproblematical representation of Locke's beliefs in his *liberal* period. We should all have such protection from the consequences of our transgressions.

7 *Works*, 4:532, Article 80.

8 [Pierre Bayle], *Pensées Diverses*, (Rotterdam: fourth edition, 1704), 2:349: 'On voit à cette heure, combien il est aparent qu'une société d' Athées pratiqueroit les actions civiles & morales, aussi bien que les pratiquent les autres societez . . .'

9 John Locke, *The Reasonableness of Christianity*, edited I. T. Ramsey (Stanford: Stanford University Press, 1958), p. 61: 'Experience shews that the knowledge of morality, by mere natural light (how agreeable soever it be to it), makes but a slow progress, and little advance in the world. And the reason of it is not hard to be found in men's necessities, passions, vices, and mistaken interests, which turn their thoughts another way'.

10 Locke, *Reasonableness*, p. 62: 'I will suppose there was a Stobæus in those times, who had gathered the moral sayings from the sages of the world. What would this amount to, towards being a steady rule, a certain transcript of a law that we are under? Did the saying of Aristippus, of Confucius, give it an authority? Was Zeno a law-giver to mankind? If not, what he or any other philosopher delivered, was but a saying of his. Mankind might hearken to it or reject it, as they pleased, or as it suited their interest, passions, principles or humors: they were under no obligation; the opinion of this or that philosopher, was of no authority . . .'

11 Locke, *Reasonableness*, p. 70. Needless to say, the original text makes it clear that Heaven and Hell are places, not just states of mind.

12 John Locke, *An Essay Concerning Human Understanding*, edited by John W. Yolton (London: J. M. Dent, Everyman's Library, 1965), 1:233: 'But when infinite happiness is put in one scale against infinite misery in the other; if the worst that comes to the pious man, if he mistakes, be the best that the wicked can attain; if he be in the right, who can without madness run the venture? Who in his wits would choose to come within a possibility of infinite misery, which if he miss, there is yet nothing to be got by that hazard? Whereas on the other side, the sober man ventures nothing against infinite happiness to be got, if his expectation comes to pass. . . . I have forborne to mention anything of the certainty or probability of a future state, designed here to show the *wrong judgment* that anyone must allow he makes upon his own principles, laid how he pleases, and who prefers the short pleasures of a vicious life upon any consideration, whilst he knows and cannot but be certain that a future life is at least possible'. The argument depends, of course, upon the supposition that positive time preference is irrational, *Essay*, 1:224–33.

13 John Locke, *A Letter Concerning Toleration*, edited by Mario Montuori (The Hague: Martinus Nijhoff, 1963), p. 93: '*Lastly*, those are not at all to be tolerated who *deny the being of a God*. Promises, covenants, and oaths, which are the bonds of human society, can have no hold upon an atheist. The taking away of God, though but even in thought, dissolves all'.

14 John Locke, *Some Considerations of the Consequence of the Lowering of Interest, and Raising the Value of Money* in *Several Papers Relating to Money, Interest and Trade, &c.* (London, 1696), p. 4: 'Faith and Truth, especially in all Occasions of attesting it upon the solemn Appeal to Heaven by an Oath, is the great Bond of Society: This it becomes the Wisdom of Magistrates carefully to support, and render as sacred and awful in the Minds of the People as they can. But if ever Frequency of Oaths shall make them be looked on as Formalities of Law . . . [and the incentive to perjury] has once dipt Men in Perjury, and the Guilt with the Temptation has spread it self very wide, and made it almost fashionable in some Cases, it will be impossible for the Society (these Bonds being dissolved) to subsist: All must break in Pieces, and run to Confusion'.

15 I glance at some of the issues in the debate in 'Rational Choice and Morality', *History of Political Economy* 14 (1982): 1–36.

16 Bernard Mandeville, *Free Thoughts on Religion, the Church, and National Happiness* (London, 1720), p. 8.

17 *Free Thoughts*, p. 21.

18 Bernard Mandeville, *A Letter to Dion* (Los Angeles: Augustan Reprint Society, [1732] 1953), p. 31.

19 Bernard Mandeville, *An Enquiry into the Origin of Honour and the Usefulness of Christianity*

in War, introduced by M. M. Goldsmith (London: Frank Cass & Co., [1732] 1971), pp. 42–3.

20 Levy, 'Rational Choice'.

Chapter 15 S. T. Coleridge replies to Adam Smith's 'pernicious opinion'

1 Basil Willey, *More Nineteenth Century Studies* (New York: Columbia University Press, 1956), p. 62: 'Here it must suffice to remark that wherever Coleridge's influence was felt, it acted as a seminal force, not conveying systematic doctrine, but quickening and warming both heart and head, revealing the shallowness of the unenlivened understanding, and calling men back to an awareness of spiritual realities.'

2 John Stuart Mill, *Essays on Ethics, Religion and Society*, edited by J. M. Robson, volume 10, *The Collected Works* (Toronto: University of Toronto Press, 1969), p. 150. Mill's reliance on Coleridge for the linkage between moral reform and social institutions is discussed in Raymond Williams, *Culture and Society* (New York: Harper Torchbooks, 1966), p. 62. How Mill's concern for moral reform unifies his work is stressed in J. M. Robson, *The Improvement of Mankind* (Toronto: University of Toronto Press, 1968).

3 Adam Smith, *An Inquiry into the Nature and Causes of the Wealth of Nations*, edited by W. B. Todd (Oxford: Clarendon Press, 1976), pp. 772–3: 'In general, the richest and best endowed universities have been the slowest in adopting those improvements in philosophy's branches, and the most averse to permit any considerable change in the established plan of education. Those improvements were more easily introduced into some of the poorer universities, in which the teachers, depending upon their reputation for the greater part of their subsistence, were obliged to pay more attention to the current opinions of the world'. Technically, there is the possibility that the wealth-enhancing aspect of an endowment, combined with a positive wealth elasticity of intellectual output, could dominate the substitution effect. This possibility is not part of the nineteenth century discussion so it will not be further considered.

4 Samuel Johnson, as reported in James Boswell, *The Life of Samuel Johnson, LL.D.* (New York: Modern Library, n.d.), p. 116. This is, of course, only one of many paeans to the free market reported by Boswell. I have the impression that such tributes are somewhat harder to find in Johnson's own works. Could it be that Boswell has been taught to think this way – and so report the thoughts of his mentor – by his great teacher, Adam Smith? John Rae, *Life of Adam Smith* (New York: Augustus M. Kelley, [1895] 1956), p. 58.

5 S. T. Coleridge, *The Notebooks of Samuel Taylor Coleridge*, edited by Kathleen Coburn (New York: Pantheon Books, 1957), volume 1, No. 661.

6 The decay of the endowed Oxford and Cambridge relative to their poorer, unendowed rivals in Scotland is stressed by Garry Wills, *Inventing America* (Garden City: Doubleday, 1978), pp. 175–6, in his explanation of the importance of the Scottish thinkers in eighteenth-century America. News of this corruption would, of course, have come as no surprise to Coleridge, who praises Robert Southey for stepping around the muck, *Biographia Literaria*, edited by J. Shawcross (Oxford: Clarendon Press, 1907), 1:47: 'To those who remember the state of our public schools and universities some twenty years past, it will appear no ordinary praise in any man to have passed from innocence to virtue, . . .'.

7 There is some interest remaining in the critics of the classical British economists. A recent look at Robert Southey and Thomas Carlyle by a historian of economics is provided by George J. Stigler, *The Economist as Preacher and Other Essays* (Chicago: University of Chicago Press, 1982). Albert O. Hirschman, 'Rival Interpretations of Market Society: Civilizing, Destructive, or Feeble?' *Journal of Economic Literature* 20 (1982): 1463–84, glances at Coleridge. The older historians of economics paid a good

deal more attention to these critics, for example, Joseph Schumpeter, *History of Economic Analysis* (New York: Oxford University Press, 1954), pp. 409–11, discusses Carlyle in some detail.

8 In spite of Mill's explicit statement that there is a debate between Smith and Coleridge, and Coleridge's explicit *Notebook* statement corroborating this interpretation, Coleridge's proposal for an endowed cultural class is not discussed in relation to Smith's or Johnson's claims by David P. Calleo, *Coleridge and the Idea of the Modern State* (New Haven: Yale University Press, 1966), pp. 97–9, nor by John Colmer in his edition of *Church and State* in *Collected Works*, nor by R. J. White in *The Political Thought of Samuel Taylor Coleridge* (London: J. Cape, [1938] 1970), nor by Charles Richard Sanders, *Coleridge and the Broad Church Movement* (New York: Octagon Books [1942]). The tradition is continued by Peter Allen, 'S. T. Coleridge's *Church and State* and the Idea of an Intellectual Establishment', *Journal of the History of Ideas* 46 (1985): 89–106.

9 Willey, *More Studies*, p. 62; Williams, *Culture and Society*, p. 62.

10 Samuel Taylor Coleridge, *The Collected Letters of Samuel Taylor Coleridge*, edited by Earl Leslie Griggs (Oxford: Clarendon Press, 1956), 1:137: 'I go farther than Hartley and believe the corporeality of *thought* . . . .'.

11 Coleridge himself seems to have coined the term 'neo-platonist', *Marginalia*, edited by George Whalley, volume 12, *The Collected Works of Samuel Taylor Coleridge* (Princeton: Princeton University Press, 1980), p. 296.

12 It is not accidental, I think, that those studies which emphasize Coleridge's debt to the post-Kantian idealistic developments in Germany have very little to say about political economy or social policy, e.g., G. N. G. Orsini, *Coleridge and German Idealism* (Carbondale and Edwardsville: Southern Illinois University Press, 1969). Also, Norman Fruman, *Coleridge, The Damaged Archangel* (New York: G. Braziller, 1971), who has nothing to say about political economy, says this, p. 476: 'The extreme overemphasis on the importance of the Neoplatonists on Coleridge's intellectual development would be utterly inexplicable were it not for the necessity of justifying Coleridge's assertions of independence from the Germans'. On the other hand, studies which emphasize Coleridge's use of both the German tradition and the Neoplatonic tradition often have a good deal to say about his proposals for social reform, e.g., Owen Barfield, *What Coleridge Thought* (Middletown, Ct.: Wesleyan University Press, 1971).

13 The critical nature of this assumption for a series of debates is discussed in Chapter 13.

14 Calleo, *Idea of State*, p. 89: 'Many of Coleridge's critics have treated the whole notion of the Idea as incomprehensible philosophical moonshine. But there is nothing necessarily occult in such a theory of the Constitution'. E.g., Harold Beeley, 'The Political Thought of Coleridge', *Coleridge: Studies by Several Hands on the Hundredth Anniversary of his Death*, edited by Edmund Blunden and Earl Leslie Griggs (London: Constable & Co., 1934), p. 169: 'Coleridge insisted on the supreme importance of education because he believed in what may be termed, by contrast with the Marxian formula, the metaphysical theory of history . . . Existing evils he traced back through a chain of consequences to the atomism of Locke, and posterity, he hoped, would similarly attribute its blessings to his own philosophical system. Now the lever by which abstract philosophy operates on political and economic circumstances is the "predominant state of public opinion", and that can only be controlled by an educational system in the hands of the State'.

15 Calleo, *Idea of State*, pp. 21–2: 'Coleridge believed that public opinion is dominated in the long run by what he called "Ideas", notions that are often dimly comprehended by the average man, but that nevertheless mold his thoughts and perceptions. These dominating Ideas are ultimately derived from the speculations of those few in society who concern themselves with philosophic truth.'

16 John Maynard Keynes, *The General Theory of Employment, Interest and Money*, volume 7, *Collected Works* (London: Macmillan, 1973), p. 383: 'the ideas of economists and political philosophers both when they are right and when they are wrong, are more powerful than is commonly understood. Indeed the world is ruled by little else . . . Madmen in authority, who hear voices in the air, are distilling their frenzy from some academic scribbler of a few years back'.

17 The temptation to read Coleridge as if he wrote in modern traditions is a well-known problem. Kathleen Coburn, 'Introduction', Samuel Taylor Coleridge, *The Philosophical Lectures* (London: Routledge & Kegan Paul, 1949), p. 40: 'I do not wish to try to do for Coleridge what Ritter did for Plato, i.e. de-Platonize him. Nor do I mean to commit the ironical error of making Coleridge out to be one of the naturalistic philosophers he spent his life combating'.

18 *Corpus Hermeticum*, edited by A. D. Nock and translated by A.-J. Festugière (Paris: Société d'éditions Les Belles Lettres, 1978), 1:10–11: 'Or, lorsqu'il eut remarqué la création que le démiurge avait façonnée dans le feu, l'Homme voulut lui aussi produire une oeuvre, et permission lui en fut donnée par le Père. Etant donc entré dans la sphère démiurgique, où il devait avoir plein pouvoir, il perçut les oeuvres de son frère . . .'.

19 Lynn Thorndike, *A History of Magic and Experimental Science* (New York: Columbia University Press, 1923), 1:290: 'Only the chosen few who possess *gnosis* or are capable of receiving *nous* can escape the decrees of fate as administered by the stars and ultimately return to the spiritual world'. John G. Burke, 'Hermetism as a Renaissance World View', *The Darker Vision of the Renaissance*, edited by Robert S. Kinsman (Berkeley: University of California Press, 1974), p. 101: 'the Hermetic texts declare that man was created as a divine being with divine creative power, and man is characterized as being a "brother" of the creating demiurge . . . man takes on a mortal body of his own volition, and in so doing he voluntarily submits to the domination of the stars and other celestial bodies . . . man can recover his divinity through a regenerative experience, by casting away material preoccupations'.

20 *Asclepius*, translated by James Brashler, Peter A. Dirkse and Douglas M. Parrott, *The Nag Hammadi Library in English*, edited by James M. Robinson (New York: Harper & Row, 1977), p. 301. The modern edition of the received text is *Corpus Hermeticum, Asclépius*, 22–3.

21 The texts are cited below.

22 The subtitle of David Hume's *Treatise of Human Nature* is 'An attempt to introduce the experimental method of reasoning into moral subjects'. Without stability of human nature, the evidence from experiments in time t have no bearing on experiments in time $t + 1$.

23 *Collected Letters*, 1:214.

24 *Collected Letters*, 1:114.

25 *Collected Letters*, 1:163.

26 *Collected Letters*, 1:119.

27 *Collected Letters*, 1:119–20.

28 *Collected Letters*, 1:260.

29 Samuel Taylor Coleridge, *Aids to Reflection*, edited by Henry Nelson Coleridge (Port Washington, N.Y.: Kennikat Press, [1840] 1971), p. 108: 'Whatever is comprised in the chain and mechanism of cause and effect, of course necessitated, . . . is said to be natural; . . . It is, therefore, a contradiction in terms to include in this the free-will, of which the verbal definition is – that which originates an act or state of being. In this sense, therefore, which is the sense of St. Paul, and indeed of the New Testament throughout, spiritual and supernatural are synonymous'.

30 Frances A. Yates, *Giordano Bruno and the Hermetic Tradition* (Chicago: University of Chicago Press, 1964); *The Art of Memory* (Chicago: University of Chicago Press, 1966); *The Rosicrucian Enlightenment* (London: Routledge & Kegan Paul, 1972).

31 Yates, *Memory*, p. 176: '[Lull] believed that if he could persuade Jews and Muslims to do the Art with him, they would become converted to Christianity . . . Starting from premisses common to all, the Art would demonstrate the necessity of the Trinity'.

32 Yates, *Memory*, pp. 147–8: 'It is because he believes in the divinity of man that the divine Camillo makes his stupendous claim of being able to remember the universe by looking down upon it from above, from first causes, as though he were God . . . The microcosm [man] can fully understand and fully remember the macrocosm, can hold it within his divine *mens* or memory'.

33 Thomas Carlyle, *Life of John Sterling*, p. 53, quoted in Thomas McFarland, *Coleridge and the Pantheist Tradition* (Oxford: Clarendon Press, 1969), p. 333: 'he had, especially among young inquiring men, a higher than literary, a kind of prophetic or magician character. He was thought to hold, he alone in England, the key of German and other Transcendentalisms . . . to the rising spirits of the young generation he had this dusky sublime character; and sat there as a kind of *Magus*, girt in mystery and enigma'.

34 John Livingston Lowes, *The Road to Xanadu* (Boston and New York: Houghton Mifflin, 1927), pp. 229–36.

35 McFarland, *Pantheist Tradition*.

35 Kathleen Coburn, *Experience into Thought* (Toronto: University of Toronto Press, 1979), pp. 29–54.

37 The occult is, however, rather hardy, cf. Mircea Eliade, 'The Occult and the Modern World', *Occultism, Witchcraft, and Cultural Fashions* (Chicago: University of Chicago Press, 1976).

38 Coleridge attributes some of the Old Testament to the Chaldean Sages [? Oracles], Notebook F, Huntington Library, HM 17299, p. 24: 'It is highly probable that the origin of this Chronometry is to be sought for in the astronomical or astrological Sciences, in which Daniel as a Pupil of the Chaldean Sages had been initiated'. There is an interesting marginale on Jeremiah 52, Coleridge, *Marginalia*, p. 440: 'The 52nd Chapter was probably written by the Author of the Book of Kings, who resided in Chaldea – & was appended to the Oracles, as a *Note*, as we now should say'. Similarly, he is willing to assert the great antiquity of the Kabbala, in the Manuscript Commonplace Book of Samuel Taylor Coleridge, Huntington Library, HM 8195, p. 157: 'With still less hesitation may the statement of the Jewish Cabbala in the purest state, with the grounds for its existence before the Christian era . . .'. I have not found his opinion of the *Corpus Hermeticum* itself. Below, we see that he knew that a 'false Dionyius' was responsible for the angel lore and he thought very poorly of Agrippa.

39 There is another strategy which I shall not consider. Could Coleridge's rather impressive consumption of opiates have given credence to the reality of the supernatural? Karen Vaughn made this suggestion. Mircea Eliade, *Zalmoxis: The Vanishing God*, translated by Willard R. Trask (Chicago: University of Chicago Press, 1972), p. 42 notes that the translation of one of the traditional names of shamans is 'those who walk in smoke'. He glosses this as 'an ecstasy induced by smoke of hemp'.

40 Coleridge's opinion of the Bible as revelation is discussed in Sanders, *Broad Church*, pp. 82–3. J. Robert Barth, *Coleridge and Christian Doctrine* (Cambridge, Mass.: Harvard University Press, 1969), p. 71, makes the important point about 'Coleridge's profound respect for the literal sense of the Bible'.

41 Kathleen Raine, 'Thomas Taylor in England', *Thomas Taylor the Platonist*, edited by Kathleen Raine and George Mills Harper (Princeton: Princeton University Press, 1969), pp. 45–6: 'It will be obvious that the historicity or otherwise of Orpheus would not, from the standpoint of metaphysics, either establish or diminish the "authenticity" of the Hymns that bear his name. In this charge against Taylor's unhistorical point of view we hear an echo of Isaac Casaubon's "discrediting" of the *Hermetica* a century and a half earlier, . . . [both] embody a tradition, and it is not upon their date but upon

their content that their authenticity rests'.

42 Here I am timidly disagreeing with Yates, *Bruno*, pp. 423–31, and Wayne Shumaker, *The Occult Sciences in the Renaissance* (Berkeley: University of California Press, 1972), p. 210, about the extent of the salvage. The continuity between the Florentine Academy and the Cambridge Platonists is stressed in Ernst Cassirer, *The Platonic Renaissance in England*, translated by James P. Pettegrove (New York: Gordian Press, [1953] 1970), p. 9: 'For Cudworth and More, as for Ficino and Pico della Mirandola, Plato formed but one link in that golden chain of divine revelation, which besides him includes Moses and Zoroaster, Socrates and Christ, Hermes Trismegistus and Plotinus.'

43 Jean Bodin, *De la Demonomanie des Sorciers* (Paris, 1580), pp. 14–14r: 'Nous auons assez d'exemples, que le Diable s'efforce de cotrefaire les oeuures de Dieu, comme nous lisons des sorciers de Pharaon'.

44 This is, of course, not the only such appeal to occult authority in the Bible. The reader will doubtless think of Matthew 2:1–11 where the 'Wise Men' in the King James Version or 'Magi' in the Greek, *Novum Testamentum Graece*, cum apparatu critico; D. Eberhard Nestle and D. Erwin Nestle (Stuttgart: Württembergische Bibelanstalt, 1952), are such able astrologers that they can read the hidden hand of God in the sky. Modern pictures of the passage strip the Wise Men of all need for wisdom – the guiding star is a super-nova – and make absolutely no sense. If the star were obvious enough to show up on a Hallmark card, it would be plain enough for Herod's associates to follow.

The translation in the King James Version is worthy of note because when used to describe Simon (Acts 8:9) the cognate is translated as 'sorcery'. The complicated philology of the Persian 'Magus' is discussed by Arthur Darby Nock, *Essays on Religion and the Ancient World*, edited by Zeph Stewart (Cambridge, Mass.: Harvard University Press, 1972), 1:308–30.

A classic study of the magical presuppositions of the Bible and Apocrypha is, of course, Thorndike, *History*, 1:385–479. Here is what Thorndike writes about the Matthew verses, 1:471: 'When the writer of the Gospel according to Matthew included the story of the wise men from the east who had seen the star, there can be little or no doubt that he inserted it and that it had been formulated in the first place, . . . to secure the appearance of support for the kingship of Jesus from that art or science of astrology which so many persons then held in high esteem'.

A. D. Nock, *Conversion* (London: Oxford University Press, 1961), p. 210, stresses the importance of Christianity's various superhuman claims for its early acceptance. Also, Nock, *Essays*, 2:517: 'though Egypt afforded no such *point de départ* as the story of the visit of the Magi to Bethlehem, thrice-greatest Hermes and Zoroaster were alike pressed into the service of Christianity'.

45 Exodus 7:10–12.

46 Exodus 7:19–22.

47 Exodus 8:5–7.

48 Exodus 8:12–15.

49 Exodus 8:16–19. Thorndike, *History*, 1:437, quotes Celsus (via Origen, of course) as characterizing both Moses and Jesus as wizards and at 1:438 quotes Origen as pointing out that the 'Egyptians charge Moses and the Hebrews with the practice of sorcery during their stay in Egypt'.

50 Exodus 9:11: 'And the magicians could not stand before Moses because of the boils; for the boil was upon the magicians, and upon all the Egyptians'.

51 Coleridge, *Marginalia* (Exodus 7.15 to 8.11) p. 419: 'Hieroglyphicè historical. Predictiones Astrologicae – *Baculus* Astronomicus – Enchantments = Constellated Talismans – Metallic Almanachs.' Whalley provides no gloss for 'Constellated Talismans' but cannot we read in this phrase Coleridge's respect for the powers of Zodiac, the Hermetic Governors? Plotinus, *Ennead* 4.44 (cited in note 60 below),

might be read in conjunction with this. Also, John Henry Cardinal Newman, *Apologia Pro Vita Sua* (London: Oxford University Press, 1964), pp. 29–30: 'Also, besides the hosts of evil spirits, I considered there was a middle race, δαιμόνια, neither in heaven, nor in hell; partially fallen, capricious, wayward; noble or crafty, benevolent or malicious, as the case might be. These beings gave a sort of inspiration or intelligence to races, nations, and classes of men . . . I thought it countenanced by the mention of "the Prince of Persia" in the Prophet Daniel; and I think I considered that it was of such intermediate beings that the Apocalypse spoke, in its notice of "the Angels of the Seven Churches".'

52 Paul Oskar Kristeller, *The Philosophy of Marsilio Ficino*, translated by Virginia Conant (New York: Columbia University Press, 1943), p. 163: 'According to the Neoplatonic doctrine it [Idea] is nothing but a concept of the divine mind. But in so far as the difference between knowing and known is canceled in the perfect thought, all Ideas are identical with the essence of divine thought and therefore with each other'.

53 Giovanni Pico Della Mirandola, 'Oration on the Dignity of Man', translated by Elizabeth Livermore Forbes, *The Renaissance Philosophy of Man*, edited by Ernst Cassirer, Paul Oskar Kristeller and John Herman Randall, Jr. (Chicago: University of Chicago Press, 1948), p. 235: 'Then the saying γνωθι σεαυτόν, that is "Know thyself", urges and encourages us to the investigation of all nature, of which the nature of man is both the connecting link and, so to speak, the "mixed bowl". For he who knows himself in himself knows all things, as Zoroaster first wrote, and then Plato in his *Alcibiades*. When we are finally lighted in this knowledge by natural philosophy, and nearest to God are uttering the theological greeting, εἶ, that is, "Thou art", we shall likewise in bliss be addressing the true Apollo on intimate terms'.

54 Marsilio Ficino, 'Five Questions Concerning the Mind,' translated by Josephine L. Burroughs, *The Renaissance Philosophy of Man*, pp. 209–10: 'the Magi, followers of Zoroaster and Hostanes, assert something similar. They say that, because of a certain old disease of the human mind, everything that is very unhealthy and difficult befalls us; but, if anyone should restore the soul to its previous condition, then immediately all will be set in order . . . [Pythagoreans and Platonists] . . . say that the soul is manifestly afflicted in the sensible world by so many ills because, seduced by an excessive desire for sensible goods, it has imprudently lost the goods of the intelligible world'.

Pico, Oration, p. 235: 'But after we have, through the agency of moral philosophy, both voided the lax desires of our too abundant pleasures and pared away like nail-cuttings the sharp corners of anger and the stings of wrath, only then may we begin to take part in the holy rites . . . and to be free for our contemplation'.

Kristeller, *Ficino*, p. 225: 'The mind can therefore achieve the highest act of contemplation under certain conditions, but it is hindered from remaining in that state by the needs of the body and of external life'.

55 Taylor, *Taylor*, p. 443: 'I believe that the rational part of man, in which his essence consists, is of a self-motive nature, and that it subsists between intellect, which is immoveable both in essence and energy, and nature, which both moves and is moved'.

56 Pico, *Oration*, p. 238: 'it has come to the point where none is now deemed wise, alas, save those who make the study of wisdom a mercenary profession . . .

'I speak all these accusations . . . against the philosophers, who both believe and openly declare that there should be no study of philosophy for the reason that no fee and no compensation have been fixed for philosophers, . . . that since their whole life is set either on profit or on ambition they do not embrace the very discovery of truth for its own sake'.

57 Thomas Hobbes, *Leviathan*, edited by C. B. MacPherson (Harmondsworth, England: Penguin Books, 1972), p. 160: 'For there is no such *Finis ultimus*, (utmost ayme,) nor *Summun Bonum*, (greatest Good), as is spoken of in the Books of the old Morall

Philosophers. Nor can a man any more live, whose Desires are at any end, then he, whose Senses and Imagination are at a stand. Felicity is a continuall progresse of the desire, from one object to another; . . .'.

58 *Taylor*, p. 444.

59 Albrecht Dihle, *The Theory of Will in Classical Antiquity* (Berkeley: University of California Press, 1982), pp. 2–3. A. J. Festugière, *Epicurus and his Gods*, translated by C. W. Chilton (Cambridge: Cambridge University Press, 1956), pp. 73–6.

60 Plotinus, *The Six Enneads*, translated by Stephen MacKenna and B. S. Page (Chicago: University of Chicago Press, 1952), 4.40: 'But magic spells; how can their efficacy be explained? By the reigning sympathy and by the fact in Nature that there is an agreement of like forces and an opposition of unlike, and by the diversity of those multitudinous powers which converge in the one living universe. There is much drawing and spell-binding dependent on no interfering machination; the true magic is internal to the All, its attractions and, not less, its repulsions. Here is the primal mage and sorcerer – discovered by men who thenceforth turn those same ensorcellations and magic arts upon one another'.

61 Plotinus, *Enneads* 4.43. Cf. Cassirer, *Platonic Renaissance*, p. 50.

62 *Enneads* 4.44.

63 Porphyry, *Life of Plotinus*, quoted in J. M. Rist, *Plotinus: The Road to Reality* (Cambridge: Cambridge University Press, 1967), pp. 16–17.

64 E. R. Dodds, *The Greeks and the Irrational* (Berkeley: University of California Press, 1951), p. 286: 'And as to the Plotinian *unio mystica*, it must surely be clear to any careful reader of passages like *Enn.* 1.6.9 or 6.7.34, that it is attained, not by any ritual of evocation or performance of prescribed acts, but by an inward discipline of the mind which involves no compulsive element and has nothing whatever to do with magic'.

65 Shumaker, *Occult Sciences*, p. 206.

66 *Occult Sciences*, p. 206. Shumaker regards the 'idol making' passage (*Asclépius*, xiii, 37) as an outlier, and accordingly gives it little weight in his interpretation.

67 *Corpus Hermeticum*, 2:325–6 (*Asclépius*, viii, 23–4). The Nag Hammadi *Asclepius* reads this way, p. 302: 'Just as God has willed that the inner man be created according to his image, in the very same way man on earth creates gods according to his likeness'. Shumaker has no trouble discarding a passage which suggests that working idols are created by tricking demons. The fatal problem that I see with his interpretation is the passages where we create gods by the power within ourselves. The Hermetic treatises after all describe our divine origin, e.g., *Corpus Hermeticum*, Traite, I, 13.

68 D. P. Walker, *Spiritual and Demonic Magic* (South Bend, Ind.: Notre Dame University Press, [1958] 1975), p. 75. Coleridge, *Marginalia*, p. 296, writes of 'gross impieties in Paracelsus'.

69 Newman, *Apologia*, p. 100: 'while he indulged a liberty of speculation, which no Christian can tolerate, and advocated conclusions which were often heathen rather than Christian, yet after all installed a higher philosophy into inquiring minds. . .'.

70 One critical piece of evidence is Plotinus' opinion of the Gnostic philosophy, Plotinus, *Enneads* 2.9. This conflict is stressed by E. R. Dodds, *Pagan and Christian in an Age of Anxiety* (Cambridge: Cambridge University Press, 1968), pp. 12–13: 'Marcus Aurelius, Plotinus and Palladas were men brought up in the Greek tradition, who thought and felt within the limits set by that tradition. They could recognise with Plato that this sublunar world "is of necessity haunted by evil", . . . But no Stoic or Aristotelian, and no orthodox Platonist, could condemn the cosmos as a whole . . . Where we find the visible cosmos set in opposition to God, the opposing principle may be described in any or all of three ways: . . . (2) as Fate, whose agents are the planetary demons, the Keepers of the Seven Gates which cut off the world from God . . .'. It is not clear whether this distinction could be made in the nineteenth century because

there was a tradition, now discredited, that Plotinus himself engaged in theurgy, Dodds, *Irrational*, pp. 283–311. Dodds's interpretation is supported by Rist, *Plotinus*, p. 250. John Dillon, *The Middle Platonists* (Ithaca: Cornell University Press, 1977), pp. 384–96 describes the Gnostic and Hermetic groups as part of the 'Platonic Underground'.

71 Reference should be made, again, to Dodds's separation of Plotinus from the Hermetists, cited in note 64.

72 The importance of study for its own sake is apparent in the Notebook passages cited in Kathleen Coburn, *The Self Conscious Imagination* (London: Oxford University Press, 1974), p. 49: 'The noblest feature in the character of Germany I find in the so general tendency of the young men in all but the lowest ranks (N.b. and highest) to select for themselves some favorite study or object of pursuit, besides . . . their Bread-earner – and where circumstances allowed, to choose the latter with reference to the former. But this, I am told, is becoming less and less the fashion even in Germany; . . .'.

This ideal is contrasted with the actual experience in England, where the only study undertaken is for the sake of material reward: 'but in England it is the misery of our all-sucking all-whirling Money-Eddy – that in our universities those, who are not idle or mistaking Verses for Poetry . . . appreciate all knowledge as means to some finite and temporal end, the main value of which consists in its being itself a means to . . . another finite & common end – Knowledge – Profession – Income – and consequently selecting their particular Profession in exclusive reference to the probability of their acquiring a good income & perhaps ultimately a Fortune thereby, then set about getting in the easiest way exactly that sort and that quantity of knowledge, which will pass them in their examinations for the Profession, and which is requisite to . . . making money . . . by his Profession'.

73 Coburn, *Imagination*, p. 49.

74 Ms. number HM 8195.

75 The important passages are those where Coleridge acknowledges that the 'Plotian school' could tap the same occult power as Christians. Samuel Taylor Coleridge, *The Philosophical Lectures*, edited by Kathleen Coburn (London: Routledge & Kegan Paul, 1949), p. 243: 'the great object of Eclectic philosophy was to persuade men Heaven was already practicable on earth; not to raise men up to God, but by pernicious practices and contrivances of rites to bring God down to man'. *Philosophical Lectures*, p. 244: 'Yet let me not say this without acknowledging that truths are to be found in those writers, and in my mind, awful truths'.

Coleridge summarizes the differences and similarities between Eclectics and Christians as a controversy not over whether Christ was God (freely admitted) but whether Pythagoras and Plotinus were too, *Philosophical Lectures*, p. 295. Coleridge notes the *engineering* difference: 'This constituted them enemies of Christianity, if they were so; which should teach us to look not only at what a man disbelieves, but at what he believes beyond or besides it, for on that the nature of his belief and disbelief must depend. This was, however, very fascinating, especially as the Eclectic philosophy was connected with the boldest purposes for the extension of the human powers'.

Coleridge's emphasis on Pythagoras is consistent with Dodds's discussion of the importance of Pythagorean themes in the wider literature, Dodds, *Pagan and Christian*, p. 23–4. Perhaps, Neopythagorean is a fairer characterization of the tradition.

76 *Divine Ideas*, pp. 3–5.

77 *Divine Ideas*, p. 31. Coleridge's marginal comments on Marcus Aurelius's 'the God within us' point out its resemblance to St John's Gospel, *Marginalia*, p. 178: 'the Spirit, (or principle of the Will, the Conscience, and the Reason) he is fond of considering <as God> & callings it <the> God within us – /Something very like this is noticeable in many Texts of St John's Gospel'. The Neoplatonic philosophers obviously would have little to quarrel with John 1:1 – 'In the beginning was the

Word, and the Word was with God, and the Word was God.' Dodds, *Pagan and Christian*, p. 104: 'His Logos-doctrine appealed to the philosophers: Amelius, the pupil of Plotinus, cited it with approval . . . and a Platonist quoted by Augustine thought that the opening words of St John's Gospel "should be written in letters of gold and set up to be read in the highest places of all churches".'

78 The interest in the interrelations of truth within us and outside is brought out in Coburn's summary of her findings from the notebooks, Coburn, *Imagination*, p. 28: 'Thus we see that Coleridge's poetry and prose, like his notebook memoranda, took root in his minute inspection not only of the inner self, but of external relations; and the two were never severed from each other but seen always in some dynamic tension of opposition or reconciliation'. She quotes one especially illuminating example of the word becoming real, p. 64: 'I have always an obscure feeling as if that new phaenomenon were the dim Awaking of a forgotten or hidden Truth of my inner Nature/It is still interesting as a Word, a Symbol! It is Λόγος the Creator! <and the Evolver!>'.

79 See the passage cited above in note 72. The Neoplatonic concern over the cost of the attention given to experimental matters is not unique to Coleridge, e.g., Taylor, *Platonist*, pp. 138–9: 'Where, says Mr. Harris, is the microscope which can discern what is smallest in nature? Where the telescope, which can see at what point in the universe wisdom first began? Since then there is no portion of matter which may not be the subject of experiments without end, let us betake ourselves to the regions of mind, where all things are bounded in intellectual measure; where every thing is permanent and beautiful, eternal and divine'.

80 *Wealth of Nations*, p. 772.

81 *Wealth of Nations*, p. 771.

82 *Aids to Reflection*, p. 69.

83 *Aids to Reflection*, pp. 69–70.

84 This qualification made to reputation could, in the eyes of an untender critic, provide evidence of a rather careless handling of the tools of the mechanical school. Hobbes, *Leviathan*, p. 162: 'Desire of Praise, disposeth to laudable actions, . . . Desire of Fame after death does the same . . . yet is not such Fame vain; because men have a present delight therein, from the foresight of it, . . .'.

85 *Biographia Literaria*, 1:152–3. Is this hypothesis – 'three hours of leisure is as productive as weeks of compulsion' – the basis for Coleridge's systematic underreporting of his compositional difficulties, the facts of which are brought out by Fruman, *Coleridge*, pp. 3–12? Perhaps, Coleridge simply confused what ought to be with what is.

86 Smith, *Wealth of Nations*, p. 759, argues that all difficult choice requires strong motivation. Boswell, *Life*, p. 182: 'In 1756 Johnson found the great fame of his Dictionary had not set him above the necessity of "making provision for the day that was passing over him". No royal or noble patron extended a munificent hand to give independence to the man who had conferred stability on the language of his country. We may feel indignant that there should have been such unworthy neglect; but we must, at the same time, congratulate ourselves when we consider, that to this very neglect, operating to rouse the natural indolence of his constitution, we owe many valuable productions, which otherwise, perhaps, might never have appeared'.

87 *Biographia Literaria*, 1:154.

88 *Biographia Literaria*, 1:155.

89 Samuel Taylor Coleridge, *On the Constitution of the Church and State*, edited by John Colmer, volume 10, *The Collected Works* (Princeton: Princeton University Press 1976), p. 44. Colmer notes 'a close connection between C's poetic explorations of the supernatural and his psychological and religious speculations'.

90 *Church and State*, pp. 46–7.

91 *Church and State*, p. 47.

92 *Church and State*, pp. 48–9.

93 *Church and State*, pp. 52–3.

94 *Church and State*, pp. 52–3.

95 *Church and State*, p. 64.

96 *Church and State*, p. 66.

97 *Church and State*, p. 68.

98 *Church and State*, p. 68.

99 *Church and State*, p. 68.

100 *Church and State*, pp. 64–5.

101 For details on Ficino's academy and its influence, Frances A. Yates, *The French Academies of the Sixteenth Century* (Nendeln, Liechtenstein: Kraus Reprint, [1947] 1968), pp. 1–13, 36–76.

102 Stephen Orgel and Roy Strong, *Inigo Jones* (London: Sotheby Parke Bernet and University of California Press, 1973), 1:49–75, have an extensive discussion of the 'Platonic Politics' involved in the Stuart court masques. Here is some of their discussion of Inigo Jones's contributions: '[he,] realising the royal ideas by creating what were essentially models of the universe, was a living demonstration of the power of the mind to comprehend and control the workings of nature, both human and elemental, through intellect and art. And thus in *Love's Triumph*, once the anatomy of neo-Platonic politics has been completed, the universe is at the King's command'. Orgel and Strong provide a history of the considerable expenses of this activity.

103 Frances A. Yates, *The Occult Philosophy in the Elizabethan Age* (London: Routledge & Kegan Paul, 1979).

104 Yates, *Occult*, pp. 79–93.

105 *Philosophical Lectures*, p. 312.

106 *Philosophical Lectures*, p. 312.

107 *Philosophical Lectures*, p. 333.

108 *Philosophical Lectures*, p. 332.

109 *Philosophical Lectures*, p. 193

110 Immanuel Kant, *Critique of Pure Reason*, translated by Norman Kemp Smith (New York: Macmillan, 1937), A536=B565: 'if appearances are things in themselves, freedom cannot be upheld. Nature will then be the complete and sufficient determining cause of every event'.

111 Coleridge, *Biographia Literaria*, 1:100: 'In spite therefore of his own declarations, I could never believe, that it was possible for him to have meant no more by his *Noumenon*, or THING IN ITSELF, than his mere words express; or that in his own conception he confined the whole *plastic* power to the forms of the intellect, leaving for the external cause, for the *materiale* of our sensations, a matter without form, which is doubtless inconceivable'.

In his discussion of Swedenborg, Kant made an unsurprising claim, Immanuel Kant, *Dreams of a Spirit Seer*, translated by John Manolesco (New York: Vantage Press, 1969), p. 70: 'the spiritual nature can never be known but only assumed and can never be thought of in a positive sense because no data are available to us in our total experience'. His attitude toward the occult is expressed in terms that might surprise those who know only the grand seriousness of Kant's great critiques, p. 66: 'Perhaps the clever *Hudibras* alone could have solved the riddle for us; according to his opinion, when a hypochondriac wind rattles through the intestines, it all depends on the direction it takes: if down, it becomes a f——, if up, it turns into an apparition or a holy inspiration'.

112 Dodds, *Irrational*, pp. 283–4.

113 1 Henry IV, III.i. Coburn glosses a passage in *Philosophical Lectures*, p. 316, 'call forth spirits FROM THE VASTY DEEP', as recalling only Milton's *Paradise Lost*, I.177, 'vast and

boundless deep'. Coleridge's reference occurs in an illuminating context where he discusses magical operations.

Chapter 16 The impossibility of a complete methodological individualist

1 F. A. Hayek, *Individualism and Economic Order* (Chicago: University of Chicago Press, 1948).

2 F. A. Hayek, *Prices and Production* (London: Routledge & Kegan Paul, second edition, 1935), p. 4: '[we ought not to] try to establish *direct* causal connections between the *total* quantity of money, the *general level* of all prices and, perhaps, also the *total* amount of production. For none of these magnitudes *as such* ever exerts an influence on the decisions of individuals; yet it is on the assumption of a knowledge of decisions of individuals that the main propositions of non-monetary economic theory are based. It is to this "individualistic" method that we owe whatever understanding of economic phenomena we possess.' Hayek's quotation marks acknowledge an older literature; indeed, Viktor Vanberg, *Die zwei Soziologien* (Tübingen: JCB Mohr (Paul Siebeck), 1975) finds that Joseph Schumpeter coined the phrase and used it as the title of a 1908 article.

3 F. A. Hayek, *The Counter-revolution of Science* (Indianapolis: Liberty Classics, 1979), p. 64. Also, at p. 95.

4 W. H. Dray, 'Holism and Individualism in History and Social Science', *The Encyclopedia of Philosophy*, edited by Paul Edwards (New York: Macmillan, 1967), 4:53–8, considers the claim that only individuals really exist, an ontological claim which he finds denied by no one.

5 My point is related to a very old consideration which Vanberg recalled to my attention. Even if we (as scientists) have very little warrant to assert that the Devil exists, we cannot *a priori* deny the reality of belief about the Devil. If beliefs and knowledge are important to explain choice, it is probably a good idea to take them as they are, not as they would be if we were allowed to replace the strange terms with those with which we are more familiar. While the Devil may not exist, 'the Devil' certainly does.

Rowley points out that more recently Hayek has criticized such terms as 'social justice' on the grounds that no one knows what they mean in some contexts. This will be discussed a little later.

6 Hayek, *Prices and Production*, pp. 4–5: 'In fact, neither aggregates nor averages do act upon one another, and it will never be possible to establish necessary connections of cause and effect between them as we can between individual phenomena, individual prices, etc. I would even go so far as to assert that, from the very nature of economic theory, averages can never form a link in its reasoning . . .'. Hayek repeats his views on economic aggregates in *Counter-revolution*, pp. 109–10: 'Most of the economic statistics which we ordinarily meet, such as trade statistics, figures about price changes, and most "time series", or statistics of the "national income", are not data to which the technique appropriate to the investigation of mass phenomena can be applied'. Such a position that the indices and aggregates have no role to play in the explanation of individual choice is consistent with the modern Austrian school's disparagement of all macroeconometric research activity.

7 If I read Dray, 'Holism', correctly, this 'reductionist' thesis is the weakest of the theses of methodological individualism in controversy; that is, methodological collectivists deny that establishing this 'reductionist' thesis will establish the harder assertions which some methodological individualists make. Obviously, if the least restrictive thesis can be refuted, considerable doubt will be cast upon the more restrictive claims.

8 The machinery is developed in W. V. O. Quine, *From a Logical Point of View*

(Cambridge, Mass.: Harvard University Press, second edition, 1961), pp. 21, 150–1, and in *Word and Object*, (Cambridge, Mass.: Harvard University Press, 1960), pp. 141–51, in terms of 'referential opacity'. Roderick M. Chisholm, *Perceiving* (Ithaca: Cornell University Press, 1957), p. 171, describes the 'third mark' of intentionality this way: 'We can now say of certain cognitive sentences – sentences using "know", "see", "perceive", and the like in one of the ways which have interested us here – that they, too, are intentional. Most of us knew in 1944 that Eisenhower was the one in command; but although he was the man who was to succeed Truman, it is not true that we knew in 1944 that the man who was to succeed Truman was the one in command'. (I have removed Chisholm's parenthentical notational marks.)

9 (1) James Buchanan, (2) Charles Rowley and Viktor Vanberg.

10 Aristotle, *Politics*, translated by H. Rackham (Cambridge, Mass.: Loeb Classical Library edition, 1946), I.i.11–12: 'Thus also the city-state is prior in nature to the household and to each of us individually. For the whole must necessarily be prior to the part . . . if each individual when separate is not self-sufficient, he must be related to the whole state as other parts are to their whole'.

Chapter 17 Spinoza and the cost of thinking

1 I. J. Good, *Good Thinking* (Minneapolis: University of Minnesota Press, 1983), p. 153: '*The principle of rationality* of Type I is the recommendation to maximize expected utility. The principle of rationality of Type II is the same except that the costs of theorizing and calculation are allowed for'.

2 Lewis Carroll, *Through the Looking-Glass and What Alice Found There*, edited by Selwyn H. Goodacre (Berkeley: University of California Press, 1983), p. 54: '"I ca'n't believe *that*!" said Alice.

"Ca'n't you?" the Queen said in a pitying tone. "Try again: draw a long breath, and shut your eyes".

Alice laughed. "There's no use trying", she said: "one *ca'n't* believe impossible things".

"I daresay you haven't had much practice", said the Queen. "When I was your age, I always did it for a half-an-hour a day. Why, sometimes I've believed as many as six impossible things before breakfast"'.

3 Douglas J. Den Uyl, 'Passion, State and Progress', *Journal of the History of Philosophy* 25 (1987): 369–98, has drawn attention to the remarkable similarity between the social analysis in Spinoza and Mandeville. It goes without saying that F. B. Kaye has important and interesting things to say about Mandeville's debt to Spinoza. I would disagree with one aspect of this interpretation. Kaye's reading, 'Introduction', Bernard Mandeville, *The Fable of the Bees*, edited by F. B. Kaye (Oxford: Clarendon Press, 1924), 1:cxi: 'Except one very general unfavourable reference to Spinoza (*Fable*, ii. 312) Mandeville did not explicitly cite him' is far from compelling. It is not Mandeville who disparages Spinoza but 'Cleomenes' and at the moment 'Cleomenes' is giving 'Horatio' a sermon about the natural ignorance of the divine essence and will shortly worry about the growth of deism. Deism is a problem for 'Cleomenes' because of *Fable*, 2:213, 'for without the Belief of another World, a Man is under no Obligation for his Sincerity in this: His very Oath is no Tye upon him'. 'Cleomenes' here states the Platonic position of John Locke and George Berkeley that those who do not believe the right things will not obey the law. It is difficult to believe that Mandeville accepts *this* position. Fortunately, Mandeville wrote some straightforward exposition, so we can check the readings from dialogues to avoid the tangles of the dialogue form to which Strauss has drawn attention. Leo Strauss, *Persecution and the Art of Writing* (Glencoe, Ill.: Free Press, 1952), p. 30.

4 I hope I make myself clear that I do not claim that the Straussian technique is true. Rather, I should be read as making the extremely modest claim that without the Straussian device it is very hard (impossible?) to obtain a series of interpretations. *This is not to presume these interpretations to be correct* because this would be tantamount to justifying the Straussian device on operational grounds. Rather, I look upon the Straussian link between form and content as a mathematician might regard a counter-intuitive axiom in set theory. It is instructive to determine whether a theorem can be proven both with a certain axiom and without it.

5 *Spinoza's Ethics*, translated by Andrew Boyle (London: J. M. Dent, Everyman's Library, 1970), pp. 83–4. Emphasis mine.

6 Richard von Mises, *Positivism* (New York: G. Braziller, 1956), pp. 348–50, and David M. Levy 'Rational Choice and Morality', *History of Political Economy* 14 (1982): 7.

7 Spinoza does not have the Hermetic outlet that would allow the conclusion of 'Many previous thinkers are gods', since god is both determined and explicable in Spinoza's system, Spinoza, *Ethics*, p. 16: 'from God's supreme power or infinite nature, infinite things in infinite modes, that is, all things, necessarily flow, or always follow from the same necessity'.

8 Benedict de Spinoza, *The Political Works*, translated by A. G. Wernham (Oxford: Clarendon Press, revised edition, 1965), p. 261: 'they have generally written satire instead of ethics, and have never conceived a political system which can be applied in practice; but have produced either obvious fantasies, or schemes that could only have been put into effect in Utopia, or the poets' golden age, where, of course, there was no need of them at all. Thus while theory is supposed to be at variance with practice in all the sciences which admit of application, this is held to be particularly true in the case of politics, ...'.

9 Pierre Bayle, *Historical and Critical Dictionary*, translated by Richard H. Popkin (Indianapolis: Bobbs-Merrill, 1965), pp. 313–14.

10 Of course, I am not the only one who has read something funny in these words, e.g. Leo Strauss, *Spinoza's Critique of Religion*, translated by E. M. Sinclair (New York: Schocken Books, 1965), pp. 225–7, who opposes Spinoza to Machiavelli in point of style. At p. 227: 'Unlike his precursor, he says no word on their perniciousness or their impairment of political practice. Spinoza sees them only under their ridiculous aspect – and he sees in this the disgrace of philosophy'. For a case of unintended irony (I think) consider Stuart Hampshire, 'Spinoza and the Idea of Freedom', *Proceedings of the British Academy 1960* (London: Oxford University Press, 1960), 46:210: 'Spinoza says that the attitude of the severe moralist, which issues in denunciations of the vices and vanities of man, and of the common conditions of human life, is always the mark of a diseased mind'. Hampshire does not even grin when he uses 'diseased mind' to report an argument against philosophers who are rebuked for speaking of *defects* in human nature.

11 To whom does 'his' refer? Other philosophers or mankind in general? The reading in the text presupposes the latter. The ambiguity is lessened by Appuhn's translation, Benedict de Spinoza, *Ethique*, translated by Charles Appuhn (Paris: J. Vrin, 1977), p. 241: 'qui sait le plus éloquemment ou le plus subtilement censurer l'impuissance de l'Ame humaine est tenu pour divin'. Here is Spinoza's Latin: 'et qui humanæ Mentis impotentiam eloquentius vel argutius carpere novit, veluti divinus habetur'.

12 Yes, 'one' in this sentence is strictly redundant.

13 Abraham Wald, *On the Principles of Statistical Inference* (South Bend, Ind.: Notre Dame University Press, 1942), p. 1.

14 Of course, Spinoza's physics are nonatomic.

15 This reading is similar to Thomas Carson Mark, *Spinoza's Theory of Truth* (New York: Columbia University Press, 1972), pp. 66–7.

16 Suppose we can formulate the theory as a unique rational number on the unit interval. Then what is the probability of picking this unique rational number when one selects

at random? Obviously: a positive, nonzero infinitesimal which is only almost equivalent to zero.

17 *Ethics*, p. 30.
18 *Ethics*, p. 31.
19 *Ethics*, p. 32.
20 Harry Austryn Wolfson, *The Philosophy of Spinoza* (New York: Meridian Books, 1958), 1:117: 'The third class of ideas which are true or adequate, says Spinoza, are common notions and ideas which follow by logical reasoning from common notions'.
21 Spinoza, *Political Works*, p. 129.
22 Spinoza, *Ethics*, p. 128.
23 Spinoza, *Ethics*, p. 135.
24 *Fable of the Bees*, 2:210.

Chapter 18 The myth of monopoly

1 The sharpest form of this disagreement that I know comes when Jack Wiseman quotes Frank Hahn as explaining failure to attain efficiency as the result of cost considerations: the costs of obtaining efficiency outweigh the benefits. Jack Wiseman, 'General Equilibrium or Market Process', *Cost, Choice and Political Economy* (Aldershot, England : Edward Elgar, 1989). A detailed discussion of this controversy is found in in Tyler Cowen's collection, *Theory of Market Failure*, edited by Tyler Cowen (Fairfax, Va.: George Mason University Press, 1988).
2 Abba Lerner, 'The Concept of Monopoly and the Measurement of Monopoly Power', *Readings in Microeconomics*, edited by William Breit and Harold M. Hochman (New York: Holt, Rinehart & Winston, second edition, 1971), pp. 207–23.
3 Jennifer Roback taught me to say it this way.
4 It should be noted that Lerner credits V. Edelberg for the suggestion that indifference curves could be applied to this question.
5 The difference does not change the logic of the argument, but the traditional Chicago argument has been not that efficiency is attained by moving to competition, but that efficiency is attained by moving to complicated forms of price discrimination. Here, one ought to refer to the famous price discrimination puzzles propounded in Milton Friedman, *Price Theory* (Chicago: Aldine, 1962), pp. 270–2.
6 Michael D. Intrilligator, *Mathematical Optimization and Economic Theory* (New York: Prentice-Hall, 1971), pp. 144–6.
7 Intrilligator, *Mathematical Optimization and Economic Theory*, p. 406. Unfortunately, Intrilligator does not point out to students that there is any difference. Indeed, in the section where a cardinal function is to be integrated, his endnote blandly assures students, p. 444, 'For a discussion of utility functions see Sec. 7.2' – the very section in which Intrilligator claims that all utility-theoretic results hold under any rank-preserving transform!
8 Richard H. Strotz, 'Myopia and Inconsistency in Dynamic Utility Maximization', *Review of Economic Studies* 23 (1956): 165–80.
9 Donald N. McCloskey, 'The Limits of Expertise', *The American Scholar* (summer 1988): 393–406.
10 Ronald Coase, 'The Problem of Social Cost', *Readings in Microeconomics*, edited by William Breit and Harold M. Hochman (New York: Holt Rinehart & Winston, second edition, 1971), pp. 484–517.
11 James M. Buchanan, 'Positive Economics, Welfare Economics, and Political Economy', *Journal of Law and Economics* 2 (1959): 124–38.
12 Buchanan's political economist gives advice to fellow citizens, not to the benevolent

despot; hence, in Buchanan's world view, there is no outside vantage from which an economist can cast judgment.

13 Jacob Viner, *The Long View and the Short* (Glencoe, Ill.: Free Press, 1958), p. 107.

14 Jean Seznec, *The Survival of the Pagan Gods*, translated by Barbara F. Sessions (Princeton: Princeton University Press, 1972).

15 Richmond Lattimore, 'Hercules at the Crossroads', in *Poems* (Ann Arbor: University of Michigan Press, 1957), pp. 56–7.

Index

Gosling, J.C.B. 266
Grafton, A. 286
Grahame, J. 194, 310,
Grampp, W. D. 309–10
Greene, D. 282
Gregg, J. R. 269
Greig, J.Y.T. 272
Griffen, J. 133, 286, 290–1, 293
Griggs, E. L. 317
Griswold, C. 292–3
Grote, G. 294
Guillebaud, C.W. 313
Gunn, J.A. 277

Habermas, J. 258
Hadas, M. 287
Hades 114, 120, 122, 124, 138
Hahn, F. 330
Hammond, N.G.L. 294
Hampel, F.R. 295
Hampshire, S. 329
Hard problem xviii, 17, 260–1.
Hardie, R.P. 313
Harman, G. 262, 268
Harman, M. 175, 176
Harper, G. M. 320
Havelock, E. A. 132, 282, 292, 298
Hayek, F.A. 207, 233–4, 236–7, 262, 270, 292, 326
Hazlitt, W. 307, 310
Headlam, J. W. 294
Heiner, R. 48, 262, 268
Hektor 130–1, 285, 291
Helen of Troy 283–5
Henry VIII 274
Hephaestos 118, 286
Hera 113–15, 117, 130, 283, 286.
Heraclitus 40, 158, 298–9
Herakles 114, 293
Hercules 163, 255, 287
Hermes 113, 283
Hermetism xviii, 219–32, 320
Herod 320
Herodotus 290
Hesiod 39–40, 86, 125, 127, 266, 282, 289–90
Hicks, R.D. 298
Hillis, A. E. 263
Hillis, W.B. 299
Himmelfarb, G. 311, 314
Hintikka, J. 269
Hirsch, A. 270
Hirschman, A. O. 317

Hirshleifer, J. 268
Hobbes, T. xiv, xxi, 63, 65–8, 73–4, 158, 164, 211, 221, 271–3, 299, 322, 325; 'words without swords' 66–7
Hobbes's problem xix, 65–9; Smith on 72–3, 75–91
Hobbs, E. C. 276, 280
Hochman, H. M. 330
Holden, C. 302
Hollander, S. 302
Hollingsworth, T.H. 311
Home, H. (Lord Kames) 99–100, 280
Homer xix, 13, 35, 40, 43, 109–34, 155–6, 159–61, 265, 283–5, 290–1, 295, 299
Horatio 328
Hostanes 322
Huber, P. J. 277, 296
Hume's theory of property xix, 23–5, 95–101, 197
Hume, D. vi xvii xxi, 15, 23–5, 32, 51–2, 61, 63, 65, 68–70, 72, 74–5, 79–80, 88, 92, 95–100, 105, 109, 197, 201, 210, 213, 262, 264, 270–5, 277, 279, 308, 319; 'ridiculous theory of' 51
Hutcheson, F. 98–100, 280

Ina, 279
Infinitesimal xix, 37, 126; optimal sacrifice 125–7
Influence curve xix, 154, 174
Interpretation xix
Intrilligator, M. 250, 330
Ireland, T. 262
Isaac, R. M. 280
Isoquant xix, 36–7, 140–1, 170

Jaffe, W. 303
Jaki, S. L. 270
James, P. 304, 308
James, W. xxi
Jarrold, T. 310
Jensen, M. S. 286
Jevons, S. 178, 303
Johnson, D. 264
Johnson, S. 109, 214–17, 227, 231–2, 317, 325
Jones, A.H.M. 293, 296
Jordon, B. 295
Jowett, B. 296, 313
Judgment 3, 203–4; as constraint 43–5, 47–8, 59, 63; of 'right'/'wrong' xiv, xxii, 267; of 'true'/'false' xviii, xxiii,